REGINALD A. WILBURN

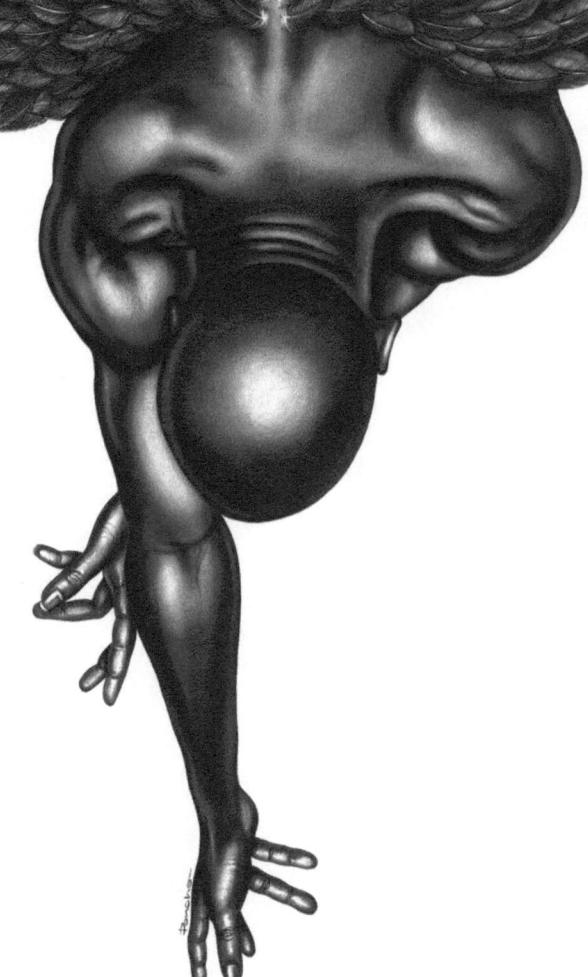

PREACHING THE GOSPEL OF BLACK REVOLT

APPROPRIATING MILTON IN EARLY AFRICAN AMERICAN LITERATURE

Preaching the Gospel of Black Revolt

Medieval & Renaissance Literary Studies

General Editor
Rebecca Totaro

Editorial Board

Judith H. Anderson
Diana Treviño Benet
William C. Carroll
Donald Cheney
Ann Baynes Coiro
Mary T. Crane
Stephen B. Dobranski
Wendy Furman-Adams
A. C. Hamilton
Hannibal Hamlin
Margaret P. Hannay

Jonathan Gil Harris
Margaret Healy
Ken Hiltner
Arthur F. Kinney
David Loewenstein
Robert W. Maslen
Thomas P. Roche Jr.
Mary Beth Rose
Mihoko Suzuki
Humphrey Tonkin
Susanne Woods

Originally titled the *Duquesne Studies: Philological Series* (and later renamed the *Language & Literature Series*), the **Medieval & Renaissance Literary Studies Series** has been published by Duquesne University Press since 1960. This publishing endeavor seeks to promote the study of late medieval, Renaissance, and seventeenth century English literature by presenting scholarly and critical monographs, collections of essays, editions, and compilations. The series encourages a broad range of interpretation, including the relationship of literature and its cultural contexts, close textual analysis, and the use of contemporary critical methodologies.

Foster Provost
Editor, 1960–1984

Albert C. Labriola
Editor, 1985–2009

Richard J. DuRocher
Editor, 2010

PREACHING THE GOSPEL OF BLACK REVOLT

APPROPRIATING MILTON IN EARLY AFRICAN AMERICAN LITERATURE

REGINALD A. WILBURN

DUQUESNE UNIVERSITY PRESS
Pittsburgh, Pennsylvania

Copyright © 2014 Duquesne University Press
All rights reserved

Published in the United States of America by
DUQUESNE UNIVERSITY PRESS
600 Forbes Avenue
Pittsburgh, Pennsylvania 15282

No part of this book may be used or reproduced, in any manner or form whatsoever, without written permission from the publisher, except in the case of short quotations in critical articles or reviews.

Library of Congress Cataloging-in-Publication Data

Wilburn, Reginald A., 1966–
 Preaching the gospel of black revolt : appropriating Milton in early African American literature / Reginald A. Wilburn.
  pages cm
 Summary: "In this comparative and hybrid study, Wilburn examines the presence and influence of John Milton in a diverse array of early African American writing such as Phillis Wheatley, Frederick Douglass, Frances Ellen Watkins Harper, Anna Julia Cooper, Sutton E. Griggs, and others"—Provided by publisher.
 Includes bibliographical references and index.
 ISBN 978-0-8207-0471-5 (cloth : alk. paper)
 1. American literature—African American authors—History and criticism. 2. American literature—18th century—History and criticism 3. American literature—19th century—History and criticism 4. Milton, John, 1608–1674—Influence. I. Title.

PS153.N5W458 2014
810.9'896073—dc23

2013039610

∞ Printed on acid-free paper.

An earlier version of the epilogue was previously published in Laura Lunger Knoppers and Gregory Colón Semenza, eds., *Milton in Popular Culture*, 2006, Palgrave Macmillan, reproduced with permission of Palgrave Macmillan, www.palgrave.com.

In memory of Warren Harding Dicks, Emma Penn,
James A. Wilburn, and Dr. Andress Taylor

Dedicated to Anna Mixon Dicks and Shirley A. Bess

With special gratitude to the first generation of literary scholars
in African American Studies who gave us a tradition
to study, cherish, and uphold

Contents

Acknowledgments ix

Chapter 1. Making "Darkness Visible": Milton and Early African American Literature 1

Chapter 2. Phillis Wheatley's Miltonic Journeys in *Poems on Various Subjects* 57

Chapter 3. Black Audio-Visionaries and the Rise of Miltonic Influence in Colonial America and the Early Republic 95

Chapter 4. Of Might and Men: Milton, Frederick Douglass, and Resistant Masculinity as Existential Geography 149

Chapter 5. Breaking New Grounds with Milton in Frances Ellen Watkins Harper's *Moses: A Story of the Nile* 189

Chapter 6. Miltonic Soundscapes in Anna Julia Cooper's *A Voice from the South* 229

Chapter 7. Returning to Milton's Hell with Weapons of Perfect Passivity in Sutton E. Griggs's *Imperium in Imperio* 279

Epilogue. Malcolm X, *Paradise Lost*, and the Twentieth Century Infernal Reader 327

Notes 335
Bibliography 361
Index 379

Acknowledgments

The journey from dissertation to book has not been a solitary endeavor. For this reason, it is fitting that I publicly thank and acknowledge everyone who has supported me in multiple ways along this journey. Through their support, I have gained a deeper appreciation for the scores of people it takes to make any one author shine. Without their support, love, wisdom, mentorship, friendship, and financial encouragement, *Preaching the Gospel of Black Revolt* would not have been possible. Each in some way has sustained me through the joys and challenges of this project, and I am honored to regard them as hovering between the blank spaces of every word and line in my book. While I know God's grace and mercy carried me every mile of my way, I also know that each person has given some part of themselves for my personal benefit, and for that I thank them immensely.

Thanks to my mother, Shirley A. Bess, whose love and nurturing wisdom trained me to value the English language and its poetic dexterity as a linguistic tool of survival. I also thank her for so many additional lessons that helped me claim and occupy my own self-defining ground in life. I am fortunate that her black pearls of wisdom were complemented by the unconditional love of my aunts, Caletha Dicks, Anna Rosier, Rosemary Washington, and Carolyn Taylor. To them I express decades of gratitude. Collectively, they exposed me to the arts, cultivated and sustained my love for reading and public speaking, furnished me with computers, various monetary gifts, or simply supported me with special doses of love, favor, prayer, and strong counsel. I am equally thankful for my uncles, Bernard Dicks and William Franklin Dicks. Both of them stand as formidable bulwarks of moral strength, each in their own way. I thank them also for never being too busy to drive miles out of their way to accommodate me whenever I called. I thank *all* of my Washington family for the kind of year-round Christmas love that has no limits and is so emblematic of 1 Corinthians 13.

I cannot express enough gratitude to Duquesne University Press and its incredible staff. They valued my project from the start and made the experience of publishing my first monograph easier and more rewarding than I could have imagined. Thanks to Susan Wadsworth-Booth for her strong leadership as director, her boundless enthusiasm, and for always being readily accessible. I also express my thanks to the external readers and Rebecca Totaro for sharing their insightful comments and offering encouraging suggestions. Additionally, I'm ever so grateful for the advice that assisted me in navigating rhetorical barriers that initially seemed too burdensome to overcome. Special thanks are in order to Kathleen Meyer, whose eagle eye for copy-editing is exemplary and of immense value to me. To the members of the design team, who delivered an *awesome* book cover that I continue to find so appealing and easy on the intellectual eye. Thanks also to Larry "Poncho" Brown for being a "Heaven Sent" blessing to this project. I must also thank Andrew Merton, chair of the English Department, Marla Brettschneider, chair of Women's Studies, Burt Feintuch, director, Center for the Humanities, and Kenneth Fuld, dean of the College of Liberal Arts at UNH for generously underwriting costs associated with publishing my book. In these dire economic times, their generosity is not underestimated by me.

I am deeply indebted to Gregory M. Colón Semenza, my dissertation advisor, mentor, and friend. I could not have known when I enrolled in his seventeenth century Renaissance course that Milton would become one of my literary heroes. I thank him for encouraging my unorthodox reading of *Paradise Lost* when I was sure it would be summarily dismissed and for immediately seeing the potential of my project in addition to supporting my vision and encouraging me to study Milton and his canon further. Because he is a fabulous educator, scholar, and mentor, I have come to discover why African Americans throughout literary history read Milton and continue to do so into the twenty-first century. I thank him also for that fabulous postgraduation party, which my family members still rave about, and to his wife, Cristina, and their adorable sons, Alexander and Ben; please know that I am appreciative that they so lovingly and selflessly supported Greg's advising commitments for my benefit.

Others deserving public acknowledgment include scholars such as Frances Smith Foster, who so generously gave of her time and made my first MLA experience one to treasure for a lifetime. I sincerely hope this monograph means I have not squandered her "one and only" investment on me (smile). I am grateful to John Ernest and Laura Lungers Knoppers as well. Both have supported me, devoting their personal time to reading several revised chapters of my manuscript at various stages of its development. Throughout my tenure-track career, I've known them to be approachable, accessible, and supportive in offering critical feedback that was much needed. Individually and collectively, Joseph Wittreich, William Shullenberger, Catharine Gray, Erin Murphy, Monica Chiu, Brigitte Bailey, and David Watters and his wife, Jan, have played valuable roles in my scholarly development. I thank them for sharing their talents and hospitality in the service of expanding my horizons of expectations and helping me to solidify my place on the "grounds of contention" in Milton and (African) American studies.

My colleagues in the English department at the University of New Hampshire have given me an academic home that afforded me opportunities to complete my dissertation with a reduced teaching load while a dissertation fellow in addition to providing me with an academic environment where I could publish a book that I would be proud to share with diverse audiences. I thank them for investing in me and welcoming me into the fold as their colleague. In particular, I especially wish to acknowledge Dennis A. Britton, Courtney A. Marshall, and Cord J. Whitaker for their faithful friendship and hours of much needed, soul-fulfilling fellowship. I also thank Janet Akin Yount for her leadership and for supporting me throughout my UNH career. To Rachel Trubowitz, I say thank you, thank you, thank you for being an invaluable resource to me in so many professional ways. Her mentorship has taught me so much. Most important, she taught me to foreground my pedagogical love for students so they would trust the rigor I provide. Indeed, she *broke new grounds* for me in such a liberating way on a day when I needed the strongest words available in the

English language to pull me through. To Siobhan Senier, Robin Hackett, and Delia Konzett, whose professionalism and various commitments to inclusive excellence and social justice relative to their teaching, scholarship, service, and mentorship are models I seek to emulate. I thank them for listening to me, hearing me out, and caring enough to get me on the other side of the river even if it meant baiting me with ice cream.

I also wish to thank the wonderful administrative staff who have helped me achieve several milestones along the way, from my time as a graduate student at the University of Connecticut to my present role as an assistant professor at UNH. Mary Udall and Doreen Roberts at the University of Connecticut as well as Carla Cannizzaro, Roxanne Brown, Jen Dube, Janine Wilks, and Sabina Foote deserve more credit than I am sure they are willing to accept. In my eyes, their administrative prowess, patience, and professionalism are beyond exemplary and keep both English departments running as smoothly as they do. Thanks also to administrative leaders and community activists such as Wanda Mitchell, Ted Kirkpatrick, Jim Henkel, Sean and Patty McGhee, Cari Moorhead, and JerriAnne Boggis for motivational insights that kept me focused.

To this growing list, I must add my academic mentors, friends, and students. Clement A. White, Donato Gagnon, and Shawn A. Christian were never so far away that they could not be reached immediately by telephone to furnish me with words of encouragement, inspiration, or strategic navigational capital. Troy Fridy, Lawrence Stansbury, Garfield A. James, Asabe Poloma, Monica Muñoz Martinez, Chera Reid, Brian Tutt, and Roseanne and Larry Thompson have filled my life with much needed laughter, empathy, counsel, fine dining, and familial camaraderie. A word of thanks to former students Tristan Striker, Beau Gaiters, Brittany Zorn, Diana Louis, Michael McGee, and Cait Vaughan, who helped me in my research and teaching in select moments when I was in a pinch. To those students who have made teaching at UNH a rewarding experience, I salute each of them for their academic resilience and for trusting my pedagogical efforts to provide them with a "premium education" that would not compromise the "beautiful science" of literary studies or the "entrepreneurial spirit of discovery." Thanks also to Deborah McDowell for pedagogical wisdom that empowered me to stand a little taller in my resolve to teach with standards of excellence and to resist compromising for things that are not in my control. To Arthur Little, I send a million miles of thanks for preaching a word I could and would hear.

Finally, *Preaching the Gospel of Black Revolt* could in no way be possible without Kelly Wise and his trailblazing work in founding and sustaining the Institute for the Recruitment of Teachers. My journey to graduate school began at the IRT. I'm ever so grateful to Kelly and his family for founding such an empowering institution that continues to equip aspiring graduate students with the skills necessary for teaching in transformative ways and producing innovative scholarship. I am fortunate to consider Denise Galarza Sepulveda, Tiffany Gill, Alexandra Cornelius, and Besenia Rodriguez as exemplary models of IRT success. Best wishes to every intern and associate in the IRT pipeline, and may they find success as each travels along their individual journeys, which, at times, seem to be solitary pilgrimages with "the world...all before them...and Providence their guide" (*PL* 12.646–47).

1

MAKING "DARKNESS VISIBLE"

Milton and Early African American Literature

> "In the beginning was the Word, and the Word was with God, and the Word was God."
> —John 1:1

Ever since Phillis Wheatley published *Poems on Various Subjects, Religious and Moral* in 1773, there has been a need for theorizing the Word that governs African Americans' receptions of John Milton. That need has intensified for more than two and a half centuries as subsequent African American writers and orators continued to follow Wheatley's Miltonic lead by making darkness visible in reception studies devoted to England's epic poet of liberty. Through the art of poetic intertextuality, writers from Olaudah Equiano, David Walker, and Frederick Douglass to Frances Ellen Watkins Harper, Anna Julia Cooper, and Sutton Griggs have evidenced their remastery of the English language by completing and complicating Milton in ways that have yet to be examined in literary criticism. These interpoetic engagements are worthy of scholarly annotation because they appropriate Milton and his canonical authority beyond ornamentation. When early African American authors engaged Milton on rhetorical grounds of fallenness in poetic tradition, they participated in vocations of salvific ministry. Moreover, they enriched the gospel of biblical Scripture according to Milton's reception of that canonical text. As a result, these lords of re-creation shift and remaster the Western canon, rupturing it with their orthodox and unorthodox interpretations of Milton in order to critique slavery and social injustice while enunciating political postures of black selfhood.

Milton's early African American audiences undertake these (w)rites of passage and English remastery by rhetorically identifying with the canonical Christian poet in causes of liberty and radical social reform. Literary criticism has yet to theorize on the hermeneutic practices deployed by this unseen collective of black authors. This void in scholarship proves increasingly detrimental to critics in Milton and African American literary studies as contemporary writers in the African American tradition continue to extend these intertextual ties to England's epic poet of liberty. For instance, Toni Morrison's novel *A Mercy* is a recent text that tropes with Milton, yet no theoretical examination exists to account for her relation to her predecessors within this neglected literary tradition. Until now, Miltonic receptions by his black sisterhood and brotherhood have been nearly (in)visible, primarily relegated to footnotes and endnotes, but rarely considered in body paragraphs of literary criticism to any substantive degree. This void has denied scholars opportunities for discovering and exploring the racial trajectories associated with Milton's afterlife throughout the literary histories of the African diaspora.

To be (in)visible in Milton reception history is to exist in plain view yet unbeknownst to a seeing audience. It is a kind of (in)visibility closely aligned with Toni Morrison's theory of "Africanist Presence" and its critical significance to studies of white-authored texts. Morrison's theory challenges critics to "play in the dark" with overlooked figures of racial presence in white-authored texts. The result of such an investigative impulse enriches appreciations of the signifying power of Africanisms in literary works that would otherwise go unnoticed by readers who have not been encouraged to analyze racial signs of blackness in texts by white authors. It is in this spirit that I, like Milton in *Paradise Lost*, undertake a literary project that is "yet unattempted" in tradition. In *Preaching the Gospel of Black Revolt*, I examine early African American audiences' intertextual receptions of the epic poet. An examination of this type makes darkness visible in reception studies of

Milton. Conversely, it illumines Milton's absented presence in African American literary studies. By traversing within and across the color line in literary tradition, this project aims to encourage a new criticism that sheds further interpretive light on what Joseph Wittreich identifies as "Milton's (Post)Modernity."[1] An understanding of this (post)modern Milton calls attention to a kind of poetry that "struggles against the outworn creeds of an atrophying religion, obliterates the pastness of the past and that, written emphatically in the present tense, strives to wrest from the present a new future."[2] Miltonic appropriations in early African American tradition reveal this distinct interpretive community as caught up in similar struggles due to their marginalized status in Western civilization. One of the routes this community charted in order to elevate themselves from spheres of abject darkness drew upon cultivating a subversive fluency with Milton. Their erudite engagements with him constitute an intertextual tradition of fragmentary appropriation. Within this tradition, early African American authors remastered the English language, completing and complicating Milton on demonic grounds of contention. While occupying these grounds, they preached satanic gospels of black revolt but for messianic purposes of racial uplift in the cause of liberty and pursuit of freedom.

When this audience preaches Milton through a range of intertextual practices, they do so on contentious grounds that are demonic in interpretive scope. Grounds of contention, as Mark R. Kelley, Michael Lieb, and John T. Shawcross explain, refer to terrains of interpretive struggle where presumptions that a literary text's meaning is static are frustrated by competing epistemologies constitutive of one's otherness in culture. In their introduction, the editors specifically acknowledge, "gender may affect the creative result" of women's receptions of literary precursors, further asserting, "people of varied life experiences—racial, social, gendered, political, educational—will find in the same literary work numerous varied reactions and readings."[3] This stance concerning the grounds of literary interpretation and otherness introduces a valuable intervention in Milton studies because it makes allowances for ways of knowing steeped in difference as opposed to those informed by ruling ideologies or orthodox conceptions of truth. Because hegemonic theories and orthodox conceptions have often established the parameters governing which interpretations are considered argumentatively valid or determining what "truths" can be said or not, the field of literary hermeneutics has, for some, constituted a terrain of contentious struggle. This has especially been the case for marginalized individuals whose ways of seeing and theorizing the world sometimes differ from the status quo.

Understanding the intertextual artistry of various early African American authors' tropological engagements with Milton requires a different way of seeing. Furthermore, assessing Milton's presence and influence in this tradition and from their various vantage points necessitates that one occupy demonic grounds. It is on this interpretive terrain that early African American authors engaged Milton and resisted geographic domination in, by, and through their subversive use of language. As a black feminist practice, demonic grounds reflect a radical approach to cultural geography that aims to comprehend "conceptions of race and humanness" that imagine black women as unseen and unknown amid practices of racial-sexual displacement.[4] To better understand how black women's silences, absences, and erasures contribute to "conceptualizations of humanness," Katherine McKittrick interrogates demonic grounds as terrain that "is genealogically wrapped up in the historical spatial unrepresentability of black femininity...[and] the ways in which black women necessarily contribute to a re-presentation of human geography."[5] As a rebellious methodology, demonic grounds represent a surveying of racial-sexual sites of spatial unrepresentability and the geographical contestations that transform these violent landscapes through indeterminable processes or outcomes.

Early African Americans' literary endeavors and their engagements began on demonic grounds of racial-sexual displacement. Despite Phillis Wheatley's celebrated acclaim for her volume, *Poems on Various Subjects*, Thomas Jefferson deemed her work "below the dignity of literary criticism."[6] From the time of Jefferson's pronouncements, black writers have struggled to overcome these chauvinistic and racist attitudes concerning their art. Addressing the effects of Jefferson's racist critique on assessments of early black writers in particular, John C. Shields asserts, "his observations regarding Wheatley and other African Americans...were and have remained incalculably deleterious to our African American citizenry."[7] Jefferson's negative reception of Wheatley casts aspersions of racial-sexual displacement in literary studies. Consequently, Wheatley's earliest literary heirs suffered similar fates, regardless of their gender. As Henry Louis Gates Jr. explains, "that the progenitor of the black literary tradition was a woman means, in the most strictly literal sense, that all subsequent black writers have evolved in a matrilinear line of descent, and that each, consciously or unconsciously, has extended and revised a canon whose foundation was the poetry of a black woman."[8]

As a result of this matrilineal lineage, the grounds of early African American literature reflects demonic terrain, a landscape where presumptions of black unrepresentability are rendered false through performances of black literacy. Early African American authors transform this interpretive landscape considerably when they forge rhetorical affiliations with Milton through the infernal hero of *Paradise Lost* and his tradition of poetic fallenness. As a result, they make darkness visible in Africanist receptions of Milton.

These affiliations, then, assume a satanic tenor, particularly because they trouble the grounds of Miltonic reception as demonic practices of indeterminability. McKittrick understands demonic spirits as typically identifying "unusual, frenzied, fierce, cruel human behaviors," interpretive readings that when appropriated in "mathematics, physics, and computer science...connote a working system that cannot have a determined, or knowable, outcome." These readings of the demonic lead McKittrick to understand these phenomena as "a nondeterministic schema" or processes that are "hinged on uncertainty and non-linearity because the organizing principle cannot predict the future."[9] Early African Americans' tropological engagements with Milton operate through these processes of frenzied connotative difference. They chart routes of rebellious intertextuality with Milton in ways that defy post-Enlightenment conceptions of black literacy. As such, Milton registers as a particular intertext of Africanist presence in a world that deems them three-fifths human if not invisible.

At the same time, their engagements with Milton throw intertextual shades of meaning on the epic poet's canon, illumining the after-effects of his presence across the literary color line. This phenomenon in intertextual engagement likewise points to a demonic grounds of contention, for these practices encourage hermeneutic activities that will lead to a charting of new cartographies in literary study. Such an enterprise enlarges the interpretive terrain with the end goal of cultivating a greater appreciation for Milton's afterlife in the Western canon. Charting these explorations embodies aspects of the demonic as well, for the endeavor frustrates the problems of intertextuality along the literary color line that until now have kept both areas of study segregated from one another for more than three centuries of criticism.

The reason why no reception history of African Americans' intertextual engagements with Milton has been conducted prior to now most likely stems from problems along the color line in literary studies. Students are not likely to encounter discussions of race or works by African American authors in courses devoted to Milton. Similarly, discussions of Milton are not apt to occur in African American literature courses. Furthermore, bringing both traditions into dialogue with each other requires levels of expertise in at least two comprehensive areas of literary study. Because these traditions are often segregated from each other in teaching practices, their estrangement sustains the phenomena of an absented racial presence in reception studies devoted to Milton. Hence, the epic writer's (in)visibility in studies of African American literature often mirrors the absented presence of race in scholarly examinations of Milton.

The irony of these separate but equal spheres of literary study is that the canon of African American literature reveals an increasing aggregate of readers and authors who knew this epic poet of liberty in various interpretive degrees. More important, they "tested and testified" with his canon, using fragments of his words "as both a tool and a weapon to correct, to create, and to confirm their visions of life as it was and as it could become" in their lifetimes and beyond.[10] Because these authors knew Milton in these ways, and given that no theoretical work exists to explain these literary encounters, understandings of both traditions and the Western canon more generally have existed in the dark, rendered incomplete by this void in scholarship. Thus, Milton, "the most monumentally unified author in the canon" enjoys an obscure afterlife in literary tradition, marred by the void of an Africanist presence that would articulate what he means to black-identified audiences of various political persuasions throughout history.[11] Similarly, the fullness of African American writers and their double-voiced heritage through Milton have been muted due to unexamined theoretical investigations of his presence in their works.

Both traditions will remain incomplete so long as criticism remains bereft of theories that would responsibly explore the centrality of Africanist *and* Miltonic presence within both areas of study. As Henry B. Wonham astutely notes, the color line in literary criticism involves "that contested zone where African-American and 'mainstream' cultural forms collide, compete, reproduce, and in some cases blend with one another."[12] It is within this contested zone that substantive meaning and hermeneutical activity occur, blurring, completing, and complicating understandings of precursor and belated poets alike through the cultural lens of Africanist interpretations. Intertextual engagements with Milton by early African American authors support Wonham's claims concerning the hermeneutic activity reverberating in texts by black wordsmiths who enrich the English language through innovative tropings with their white, canonical precursors.

To be sure, these authors do not imitate Milton as an unsophisticated practice of repetition. Rather, they perform "implicit formal criticism" of his verse, attaining a *kleos* of innovative originality that translates to artistic practices of "masterful revision."[13] Foster makes the further case that Africanist remastery of Milton in the English language "reaffirm[s] the complexity of culture and communication."[14] Making darkness visible in Milton studies will not prove effective for critics who choose to occupy one side of the color line in literary study. As many early African American authors understood, it was necessary to traverse within and beyond literary tradition in order to be seen and heard with at least a modicum of success. Contemporary readers and critics must begin cultivating similar skills if they are to "read and understand both the written and the oral traditions" of Africanist writers who frustrated geographical arrangements in language by speaking within and across the literary color lines in their writings.[15]

In the same way Miltonic presence in early African American tradition does not signal unsophisticated imitation, neither does it constitute events of literary colonialism. In other words, African American authors do not trope with Milton out of a shallow compulsion to legitimate the artistic worth and integrity of their literary productions. To the contrary, their fragmentary engagements with him reflect intellectual deepness, modes of style that display the intertextual art of sophisticated meaning making. Their every stylistic engagement with Milton signals an event of linguistic deterritorialization and reterritorialization in the English language. Here, as Gilles Deleuze and Félix Guattari explain, language is significantly "torn from sense" and "conquered" through processes that reclaim, complicate, transform, then enrich original meaning. Such alterations of and in language indicate manifestations of "the revolutionary conditions" that Deleuze and Guattari deem central to the political artistry of "minor literatures" in major languages.[16] By minoring in the major or colonial language of Miltonic English, early African American writers and orators enunciate Milton's presence in a manner that polishes his meanings in new idioms, which extends his afterlife beyond conventional understandings in the Western canon.

This polishing of Milton's meaning and originality is no trivial matter, for the epic poet along with Chaucer and Shakespeare enjoy canonical prominence as esteemed members of England's literary triumvirate and in the Western canon. Throughout literary history, various African American writers have deterritorialized and reterritorialized these and other canonical authors of Western tradition. According to their individual and collective receptions of these canonical exemplars, African American authors' intertextual engagements with their precursors expand our knowledge of language and literary representations along the color line, making race visible in uncharted reception studies. These sites of racial difference challenge and enrich conventional understandings of the English language and its diverse meanings. For example, where Milton's "cross-cultural influence" is concerned, early African Americans' intertextual engagements with him simultaneously reveal the "enabling and inhibiting" effects of his canonical authority upon them.[17] By influence, Carolivia Herron, the first critic to offer a catalogue of African American writers' interest in Milton, does not restrict the term to designating direct borrowings and appropriations of the author. She expands the term to include the "transmission[s] and effect[s] of a cultural image, which, in the case of Milton, necessarily encompasses the prestige of the epic genre and the cultural importance of the book of Genesis."[18] Whether early African American authors re-cite Milton directly or engage him and his canon through these allusive transmissions and effects, their tropological engagement with him showcases a polished dexterity in the English language. This measure of artistic influence almost always functions in dialogue with Christian principles and themes of political and personal liberty.

In his discussions of the work that is needed to resolve interpretive problems occurring along the literary color line, Wonham contends that "the task of criticism" encompasses a commitment to "document[ing] the 'embarrassing' presence of [the] 'Other' in cultural places where one least expects to find it."[19] Embracing this commitment requires galvanizing a knowledge base that is steeped in a double-voiced heritage of literature, theory, and criticism. This task especially entails a commitment to studying African American histories, vernaculars, and cultural aesthetics, since these components critically inform the rhetorical vision of early African American wordsmiths. Because this knowledge base proceeds from an astute acquaintance with a series of Africanist tropes germane to black expression, the investigative task enables critics to chart "new lines of formal descent" in African American tradition while refamiliarizing others with the Milton they thought they knew.[20] Ultimately, this tradition of Miltonic reception acquaints critics to a distinct and undocumented form of aesthetic and hermeneutic activity by a diverse and (in)visible collective of Africanist poets.

Renowned as a master in the English language, Milton enjoys special distinction among early African American writers because of his reputation as an esteemed Christian poet and rebellious adjutant for causes of liberty. These religious and political attributes distinguish him from Chaucer and Shakespeare, who also appear sporadically throughout African American literary tradition. However, it is Milton's canonical authority in these combined areas that garner him special prestige among early African Americans. Seeking to articulate black selfhood when dominant society yet regarded them as three-fifths human according to flawed Enlightenment philosophies and prescriptives, early African Americans preached Milton in the spirit of "radically altering their subjectivity" and by polishing the language through their distinct idiomatic expressions.[21]

In addition to appropriating Milton, they gravitated to what several critics refer to as his satanic energy. For instance, they may gravitate to the rebellious energy driving his satanic epic consistent with Neil Forsyth's understanding of *Paradise Lost*. Forsyth classifies Milton's epic as satanic because the infernal hero's actions and logic motivate and impact every aspect of the poem. Reading *Paradise Lost* as a satanic epic resists a mode of interpretation that interprets evil as a static denotation or connotation of the negative. According to Forsyth's reading, "Satan's temptation of mankind is a necessary prerequisite to the Son's reciprocal intervention in the fate of mankind."[22] Furthermore, because Satan makes the Son's redemptive acts possible, the infernal hero "has an extremely important role to play in the philosophical or theological structure of *Paradise Lost*."[23] If Milton's epic proves satanic on the strength of the infernal hero's titular role within the work, then *Paradise Lost*, by extension, bequeaths a tradition of poetic fallenness to its belated readers. Marginalized outcasts in an American New Jerusalem that resembled hell, early African Americans gravitated to the liberating potential that Milton's satanic poetry provides for oppressed people.

For Danielle A. St. Hilaire, Milton's epic communicates its message through Satan's poetry, both a discourse and poetics of satanic re-creation in literary tradition. Grounding her understanding of Milton's epic in Satan's claims to self-begottenness, St. Hilaire reads *Paradise Lost* as a work of art about creative processes of becoming and self-actualization. Creative acts of this sort, she contends, are "based in negation, to be sure, but [are] no less creative nor less real for that negativity."[24] St. Hilaire's examinations of Milton's satanic poetics are not limited to the poem's verbal art or

Satan's various rhetorical devices. For instance, she convincingly argues that it is through Satan's poetry that Milton showcases his talents as a literary original by re-creating a poetic tradition of difference that yet bears traces of sameness. Accordingly, we might think of complex modes of literary mimesis as instances of satanic intertextuality. Imitating Satan's self-begottenness and its negative rejection of God, satanic intertextuality introduces new texts to the canon "as something different from that tradition."[25] The ruptures produced by these new texts cause the tradition to "move to accommodate it by superseding [its] difference to create unity within the tradition once more."[26] Early African American authors rupture the canon according to these satanic impulses by embracing then rejecting fragments of Milton's oeuvre in their work. In doing so, they particularize and transform Milton's literary matter into a poetics of racial liberation. Such projects of satanic intertextuality afford them subversive opportunities to preach gospels of black revolt. These gospels, in turn, empower this Africanist audience to critique and indict fallen hegemonic practices that have contributed to their abject status in society.

Of equal if not greater importance, their diverse forms of satanic intertextuality with Milton complete and complicate his canon. The word "complete" in this instance does not refer to some final or terminating exhaustion of interpretive meaning. Rather, "completing Milton" references modes of intertextual engagement that contribute to re-membering him as an interpretive whole relative to the "certain forms of figurative dismemberment or dispersal [that] have always already taken place," which, therefore, occasion efforts to "re-articulate him limb by limb."[27] This process of piecing Milton back together again, as Mary Nyquist and Margaret W. Ferguson explain in their preface to *Re-membering Milton*, is not a one-time event. Such re-memberings, they assert, "must be repeatedly gestured towards and actively exposed."[28] Gregory Machacek offers added valuable insight with regard to completing Milton, placing emphasis on what this process means when considering the epic writer's canonical status as an original. For Machacek, origins are "susceptible to" and "require" events of completion because their status as originals designates an instance "when something differs markedly from what had preceded it."[29]

Machacek's conception of origins and originality is instructional for considerations of early African Americans' ruptures of completion with Milton. His conception emphasizes the importance of literary belatedness as a valuable event of critical meaning.

As Machacek explains further, these "bifurcated occurrences, in which an earlier event brings about a latter event" produce an "unconventional formulation" whereby a "second, repetitive act is necessary to fully constitute an origin."[30] More important, this unconventional or demonic formulation means early African American engagements with Milton produce intertextual events that confer originality upon England's epic poet of liberty. Furthermore, so long as Milton remains obscure by a void in scholarship that fails to account for his afterlife in the tradition, he exists as a dismembered canonical authority. In other words, Milton as an origin needs repetition that he may be re-membered and remembered accordingly. This unconventional formulation demonically challenges a chronology of origins by pointing "outside the space-time orientation of the homuncular observer."[31] Moreover, the implications pronounced by this paradigm of completion suggest the afterwords of belated poets are needed in order to make their precursors preeminent originals. In this regard, as Machacek argues, precursor and belated poets re-member one another as "co-originators."[32] This collaboration works toward dispelling the myth that the latter constitutes an imitation of the former.

When they engage Milton on the demonic grounds of contention, early African American writers not only complete him; they complicate him as well. Their intertextual engagements complicate Milton through literary relations that first necessitate recalls of "advanced literacy" that must subsequently merge with the "evaluative dimensions" called into existence by any number of verbal echoes appearing in the belated text.[33] Advanced literacy as posited by Machacek "requires scholarly annotation" on the part of readers who must first recognize that a belated writer is, indeed, her or his shared knowledge with a precursor.[34] If readers miss the black-identified writer's allusion, the author's meaning, in effect, escapes the intellect of the respective audience member. For early African American writers, who were often regarded as intellectually inferior consistent with post-Enlightenment logic, such a performance ruptures racist presumptions regarding black intellect. If, as Machacek explains, "author and reader must have been exposed to the same text, which requires that the text be highly valued by both the author's and the reader's cultures," this missed opportunity in communication complicates Milton by making him a linguistic event of resistance and semantic rebellion.[35]

Richard Wright, a twentieth century African American author, discusses this phenomenon in black language as an artistic instance of intertextual theft. "We stole words from the drudging lips of the Lords of the Land," he writes in *12 Million Black Voices*, "and we charged this meager horde of stolen sounds with all the emotions and longings we had."[36] In addition to "polishing" and "caressing" these words, Wright contends African Americans "caressed them, gave them new shape and color, a new order and tempo, until, though they were the words of the Lords of the Land, they became *our* words, *our* language.[37] Nielsen understands Wright's discussion of African American language as "a theory of race and intertextuality in American signifying practices [that likewise] cites the language as a place of perpetual resistance and traversal."[38] As such, African Americans develop strategies and technologies for refining the English language as articulations of semantic difference and freedom.

To polish and caress this language with inflections of racial difference as they do with Miltonic English is to complicate the canonical poet, his meanings, and his status as an original beyond conventional reception. That this practice occurs while sometimes speaking over the heads and intellect of their white audiences reveals another complication in Miltonic English, that of calling into question the very advanced literacy they are presumed to lack. It is on these demonic grounds of contention that early African American writers complete and complicate Milton as an original beyond conventional recognition and reception. In the same way Milton's poetic revisions of Homer, complete the classical poet by "conferring originality on" *The Iliad* and *The Odyssey*, so too do early African Americans bring this practice to bear on their seventeenth century precursor.[39] Indeed, Milton is *the* canonical original and genius of grand style in the English language and epic tradition.

Yet, idiomatically and within early African American literature, he does not register as *all that* until they say so and deem him as such relative to the various completions and complications of him they perform within their canon.

This understanding of early African Americans' receptions of Milton positions them alongside audiences like the British Romantics, the first school of critics to side with Milton's Satan on the demonic grounds of interpretation. Like this satanic school of poets, critics, and readers, early African American writers and orators complete and complicate Milton by rhetorically gravitating to the epic writer's satanic energy. Their engagements are distinct in the sense that they rhetorically identify with Milton's Satan for messianic purposes that proclaim and advocate causes of black freedom. Machacek explains the hermeneutic process of completing a precursor influence through practices that invite refined considerations of earlier texts and their status along the axis of literary greatness. These interpretive renegotiations, he argues, are based on the poetic and semantic relations latter works "take up with the preexisting body of canonical literary texts" prior to their belated publication.[40] As the Miltonic receptions examined in this study indicate, early African Americans' relationship to the epic writer rests upon a tripartite kinship that intertextually invests in his literary eloquence, Christian poetics, and spirit of dissident statesmanship. These routes of literary kinship with Milton assume a political tenor in their writings as his canonical reputation coheres to form a distinct cultural image and affect useful for advancing Africanist causes of justice and righteousness along multiple axes of social identity.

Apart from introducing Milton as a particular (w)rite of passage for early African American authors who complete and complicate him on demonic grounds of interpretation, one cannot fully grasp what his originality means for this audience of readers without a fundamental understanding of some of the political motives informing these intertextual engagements. One reason early African Americans complete and complicate Milton involves an interest in critiquing white tyranny and other social injustices to black citizenship. They achieve these ends by strategically revising his words, figures, innovative use of literary form, and literary reputation, cognizant that in doing so they are necessarily appealing to the canonical authority he enjoys in Western culture. This style of engagement with one's precursor, as Machacek explains, involves special collaborative relationships between predecessors and successor poets. By repeating original literary sources in some innovatively artistic fashion, he contends, one "alters our conception of [a forerunner's] entire corpus of literary works."[41] In terms of early African American authors' Miltonic engagements, this same practice alters how the epic writer is received and understood through the artistic lens of racial interpretation that promotes him as a politically righteous gospel of black revolt.

One of the ways African Americans alter conceptions of Milton includes troping with him as a poetic statement of black literacy. Often hailed as a premiere poet of literary eloquence in English, Milton throughout the ages has epitomized linguistic mastery. Others test and testify with Milton because they revere him as a Christian poet of unparalleled renown. As he asserts in a critical passage from his pamphlet, *The Reason of Church-Government*, Milton acknowledges his literary vocation as a "power beside the office of a pulpit."[42] This self-assessment concerning his Christian poetic ministry would especially appeal to early African American audiences examined in this study. As many of their literary productions indicate, they also considered literature as both a sacred and secular vocation comparable to the office of preaching. On the one hand, Milton, a kind of standard-bearer for and of the English language, figures as a sign of black literacy. To trope with him, whether white readers recognize the mark of language acquisition or not, is to articulate revolt and rebellion. More specifically, it is to give a lie to the "policing functions" of language commingled with race that have historically functioned as "boundaries that define and oppress" identities of otherness.[43] At the same time, Milton reflects an ideal of Christian poetics. Thus, troping with him in early African American tradition according to Christian ethics imbues belated authors' text with levels of metascriptural authority that have been sanctioned throughout Western civilization.

A third example of altering Milton's status based on early African Americans' political motivations for troping with him concerns the epic writer's literary devotion to themes of liberty. As J. B. Savage argues, "no other idea means quite so much for Milton, or is as central to his thought, or is as important, in turn, for our understanding of him, as the idea of freedom."[44] This cherished theme in his canon resonates with early African American authors, who also recognized freedom and its pursuit as a political ministry divinely sanctioned by God. Savage further explains, "scarcely any part of [Milton's] *oeuvre* stands untouched and uninformed" by themes of freedom, so much so that these markers have come to "define his characteristic place within the traditions in which he worked."[45] When appropriated by black authors in early African American tradition, however, Milton's characteristic place is altered further. According to his presence within this tradition, he becomes a canonical intertext of liberty for the racially marginalized and oppressed, a characteristic that has not been explored previously in criticism

Collectively, these political motives re-member Milton as a cultural intertext whose status as a canonical authority informs early African American authors' tripartite ministry as an audience committed to preaching subversive gospels of black revolt. Appropriating him as a (w)rite of passage on several fronts relative to espousing their selfhood through acts of literacy, Christianity, and political advocacy, they developed this revolutionary gospel through diverse and unorthodox routes of literary engagement. For his part, Milton models literary eloquence and a poetics in tune with Christian ideals and a cherished theme of liberty that resonated with Africanist audiences well beyond his lifetime. As a result, his canonical authority spurred empathetic analogues with Africanist experiences on U.S. soil. Claiming him as their own and according to their specific cultural needs, early African American authors complete and complicate Milton on demonic grounds. Occupying this rebellious landscape, they affirm the epic writer as a sacred yet secular "talking book" for those who would preach gospels of black revolt in his canonical name. It is through the trope of the talking book and other figures of black expression that contemporary audiences may (re)discover this overlooked audience in literary tradition that engages and updates Milton and the Western canon by radically extending his afterlife toward justifying the ways of God to humanity.

Milton as "Talking Book": Troping across the Color Line in Figures of Blackness

One cannot gain a responsible appreciation for the various methods early African Americans trope with Milton without first cultivating an understanding of the cultural devices they use to express themselves. These features make darkness visible in Milton by calling attention to figures of blackness. In "Preface to Blackness," where he calls for an understanding of intertextuality in African American tradition, Gates specifically identifies the urgency of "direct[ing] our attention to the nature of black figurative language" among other aesthetic elements.[46] Chief among these tropes is that of the talking book. This mode of black expression serves as a fundamental tropological apparatus through which Milton speaks to and through an innumerable network of African American readers and writers throughout literary history. Gates defines the "talking book [as] the 'ur-trope' of the Anglo-African tradition," and emphasizes its importance in early slave narratives as a rhetorical device where Africanist authors "make the (white) written text 'speak' with a (black) voice."[47] In the earliest slave narratives, authors use the trope to recall the life-changing moment when they first encounter the phenomena of someone reading a book aloud. Slave narrators typically associate the magic and power of reading as a fundamental resource for crafting their humanity through literacy. Their faith in the power of literacy develops into a metaphorical trope that, according to Gates, "enables us to witness the extent of intertextuality and presupposition at work" in the literary tradition they inaugurated.[48]

For early African American audiences, Milton constitutes a sacred yet secular talking book. He and his canon facilitate their political interests of "justifying the ways of God to man," serving as a poetic gospel beside the scriptural authority of the Bible.[49] Sacred in the sense that Milton writes under a Christian impulse to justify a biblical story, he and his epic also figure as secular talking books in early African American tradition. Ranking second only to the Holy Bible in authoritative importance, Milton's epic, within black hermeneutic culture, does not share the same canonical prestige as that which is accorded to God's inerrant Word. An explanation for Milton's secular status concerns the spiritual authority conferred upon the original authors of Scripture under the unction of God's command. According to 2 Timothy 3:16, "all scripture is given by inspiration of God and is profitable for teaching for reproof, for correction, for training, in righteousness." In hermeneutic circles, God's inspiration is taken to mean the Creator has divinely breathed biblical precepts to men of holy worth. Because Milton's scriptural justifications are belated in time relative to the canonical books contained in the Holy Bible, his Christian writings, according to black hermeneutics, cannot enjoy the same prestige that this audience accords to the Bible. For instance, Henry H. Mitchell argues, "the best of Black preaching is based on biblical authority and biblical insights."[50] Mitchell further elaborates upon the centrality of biblical authority. Concerning black preachers and their methods of creativity and inventiveness when preaching the Word, he contends that they can only "appear to exercise their freedom within the limits of that vast and profound reservoir of truth called the Bible."[51] This understanding of the Bible's authority within black hermeneutics has interpretive implications for considering *Paradise Lost* as a Christian text that is not wholly sacred in its content.

By taking secular liberties with his biblical source, Milton's epic sacrifices some of its sacred quality. St. Hilaire notes that Milton "defies the biblical narrative [by] putting Adam in a different part of the garden when Eve chooses to eat."[52] This instance of poetic license contrasts the account rendered in Genesis 3:6. Additionally, Milton's mode of defiant intertextuality "far exceeds the biblical narrative of the Fall," a form of interpoetic rejection that is "evident in every book."[53] For St. Hilaire, these instances of poetic license constitute secular practices of poetic fallenness. Under this impulse, derivative of "satanic creation [that is] qualitatively different from godly creation," Milton bends and elaborates upon the scriptural sacredness of his biblical source, thereby producing an epic "independent of the authority of the books of Moses."[54] Milton's Christian writings therefore reflect sacredness and secularity. These dualities do not serve as an intertextual hindrance for early African American authors. Instead, *Paradise Lost*, according to this principle of black hermeneutics, serves as an intertextual companion to the Holy Bible. Dwight Callahan raises another point of cultural importance relative to respecting *Paradise Lost* as a sacred yet secular companion to the Bible. The Bible, he argues, is *the* talking book in African American culture. He considers it "the book of slavery's children" because its "impact on the African American imagination" proves "broad and varied in the arts."[55] As a result of these cultural traditions, Milton and his epic occupy secondary status in relation to the scriptural Word of God.

Though he may not enjoy as broad an appeal to early African American writers as the Bible, Milton nevertheless exists as a kind of sacred yet secular holy "ghost in the machine" of early African American literature.[56] In Morrison's "Speakable Things Unspoken," the ghost in the machine indicates "the ways in which the presence of Afro-Americans has shaped the choices, the language, the structure—the meaning of so much American literature."[57] This ghost is not restricted to the canons of American literature. Correspondingly, "there also exists, of course, European Africanism," modes of playing in and with darkness as tropological signs of otherness, fear, and alarm within white-authored texts.[58] To the degree that Milton appears quite frequently in early African American tradition, he likewise serves as an (in)visible and (un)seen power in that canon. Given his sacred yet secular status, Milton, functioning as a holy ghost in the machine, permeates these works as both a political and righteous primer for those who would voice rebellion in causes of black freedom. Sacred yet secular poets in their own right, this black-identified audience dares to preach rebellion as a political ministry divinely sanctioned by God and scriptural tradition. In Milton, they find a spiritual and intertextual ally, a canonical writer who took poetic liberties with Bible stories in order to intervene in the major political debates of his time.

Like the Bible, Milton and his canon speak to African Americans in the midst of their trials, tribulations, and spiritual victories. A kind of holy poetic intertext in the tradition, he survives as something far more complex than an element of ornamental style. His rhetorical presence underscores a range of skilled hermeneutic practices. Each intertextual engagement with Milton in the tradition calls attention to this collective as a school of "interpretation-oriented critics and scholars" in literary history.[59] He speaks to this audience on various political and Christian registers, and they speak back through their intertextual rebuttals. Their responses translate to a remastery of the epic writer in black expression, pointing to a second tropological figure of blackness necessary for making darkness visible in reception studies devoted to Milton.

Remastering Milton as a talking book of black expression involves a poetics that reads, interprets, and revises the epic poet through the lens of racial experience. It is a poetics that serves as a literary forerunner to W. E. B. Dubois's theory of double consciousness. Dubois's theory concerns the existential conundrum of being both an American and a racial Other. In his landmark text, *Souls of Black Folk* (1903), he elaborates upon this conundrum by declaring, "the problem of the twentieth century is the problem of the color line."[60] For Dubois the color line signifies the racial divide where blacks struggle to reconcile the dilemma of "always looking at one's self through the eyes of others [and] of measuring one's soul by the tape of a world that looks on in amused contempt and pity."[61] Double consciousness as a poetic trope in early African American writing exemplifies these dichotomous experiences of being both an (unacknowledged) American and racial other by, through, and in language. In mockery of this conundrum, early African American authors found it subversively expedient to exhibit facets of their double-voiced heritage by troping with Milton. As a result of this exercise of linguistic remastery, they traversed the color line of literary tradition by minoring in major tropes of intertextual expression.

Minor literatures as discussed by Deleuze and Guattari evidence imbrications of linguistic struggle and self-renewal in and through canonical discourse. This dynamic is especially apparent where instances of race and intertextuality in African American literature collide to deterritorialize and reterritorialize meaning. Miltonic presence through these intertextual practices signal the seventeenth century poet as a "ghost in the machine" whose canonical authority likewise confers an epic *kleos* of heroic renown upon these authors. This association with epic is of paramount significance when assessing Milton's cross-cultural influence on black authors. Herron argues, "Afro-American literature has always had epic propensities," further noting that this character in the tradition "often developed as responses to Milton."[62] By responding to Milton through performances of intellectual remastery with epic tradition, these authors developed artistic strategies for navigating the literary color line through their polishing and caressing of language. By remastering the English language while completing and complicating Milton in the process, early African American authors perform a trope of double consciousness. Their tradition of Miltonic engagement highlights dual processes of meaning production where those who are racially Othered as inferior and intellectually disadvantaged render themselves visible by intertextually traversing within and beyond the color line of literary traditions.

By engaging Milton through tropes of double consciousness, we summon a second rhetorical figure closely associated with Dubois, that of the racial veil. For Dubois, the veil denotes Africanist perspectives as a gifted second sight of seeing, interpreting, and knowing. Its perspective implies racial knowledge of the world as seen through a social veil of difference. This figurative veil equips black cognizers to straddle and shift their positions along and across the color line of experience. These interpretive negotiations evidence routes of racial knowledge that often prove critical to black survival in white-dominated spaces. Its tropological methodology further symbolizes "the revelation of the [white] world" as perceived by black cognizers, but it often runs counter to Anglo-American epistemological frameworks and streams of logic.[63] A consequence of this dilemma in truth determination concerns hegemonic practices that delegitimate racial knowledge as flawed or disadvantaged. Philosopher Charles Mills identifies this abuse of interpretive power as "white ignorance," states of epistemological lack motivated by "false belief and the absence of true belief."[64] An appreciation of intertextual engagements with Milton in early African American tradition is no less informed by tropes of double consciousness than those of white ignorance.

Although these engagements with Milton, on certain levels, cohere with orthodox interpretations of his work, in another sense the fullness of their interpretive meanings derives from the decisions belated authors make when they depart from convention. In such instances, the uninformed cognizer who appreciates and understands Milton from orthodox standpoints may run the risk of performing white ignorance by denigrating certain Miltonic appropriations in black-authored texts as flawed or disadvantaged. Orthodox or "fit" receptions of Milton are conventional in nature. Such receptions and interpretations are said to cohere because they coincide with interpretations that have been sanctioned by the authority of conventional theories, approaches, and hermeneutics of tradition. Should an interpreter transgress the boundaries of these parameters, or as Peter C. Herman discusses, "propose an interpretation that defies the conventional understanding of a particular text or author, then one risks, at best, professional marginalization and, at worst, professional failure."[65] What Milton can and must mean according to these orthodox sanctions parallels the cultural phenomenon Mills describes as white ignorance.

Practices of white ignorance can hinder truth production, according to Mills, because they are "classically individualist...[and] blithely indifferent to the possible cognitive consequences of class, racial, or gender situatedness."[66] Mills argues that those beholden to this epistemological stance generally take pride in its "Cartesian origins," which for centuries has proven "profoundly inimical terrain for the development of any concept of structural group-based miscognition."[67] Because white ignorance also extends to a range of intellectual practices of commission and omission, including "moral non-knowings" and "incorrect judgments," it has potential to put the interpretive logic performed by Milton's early African American audiences at a further disadvantage.[68] Thus, Mills's explanation of white ignorance as a malady of seeing and truth production insulates early African Americans' Miltonic receptions against being summarily dismissed as disadvantaged when their poetic interpretations defy tradition and orthodox conventions in literary criticism. Because this tradition of Miltonic engagement routinely traverses within and beyond the veil of racial interpretation, these texts are similarly coded and insulated by appealing to tropes of white ignorance that demand critics seek, know, assess, and distill meaning from multiple vantage points within and beyond the literary color line.

A fourth trope of unconventional engagement with Milton in early African American tradition is that of signifyin(g). This culturally motivated form of Africanist intertextuality references a style of literary repetition occasioned by rhetorical acts of subversive difference. In African American tradition, signifying involves quoting a previous statement either directly or allusively but toward a humorous, ironic, or subversive end. Gates defines this expressive style as "Afro-American spoken vernacular discourse" and "ritual speech act."[69] It parodies linguistic events out of a rhetorical impulse to restore or "redress imbalances of power," communicating a range of meanings through various rhetorical and stylistic registers.[70] When appropriating Milton throughout the tradition, early African American authors often preach their gospels of black revolt using this stylistic medium. Their use of this trope of sarcastic repetition broadens Milton's interpretive meaning beyond the hegemonic authority of the color line in diverse and fascinating ways.

Signifying surfaces in various forms and social contexts. Elaborating upon the work of linguist Geneva Smitherman, Gates classifies puns and riffs as types of signifying. Other stylistic registers include "naming by indirection," using verbal forms of dissemblance, and repetitions that are followed by inversions of those structures.[71] Signifying through and on any of these linguistic practices redirects listeners to some previous statement, which the belated speaker ironically puns. Poetic mimicry of this type excels slavish imitation, producing what Gates regards as "repetition with a difference, a signifying black difference."[72] Most important, the locus of subversive meaning specifically resides in this feature of semantic difference. Therefore, a given Miltonic trope often speaks a double-voiced discourse in an Africanist idiom. In addition to commanding a knowledge and comprehension of a quoted Miltonic utterance, signifying upon Milton also prompts recognition of the subversive power of the belated yet revised articulation. Miltonic articulations of this sort subvert the preceding message through embedded rhetorical codes that are only recognizable to those of a given in-group. Comprehending the signifying moment, then, necessitates epistemological familiarity with a minimum of two competing utterances. In a sense, signifying with and on Milton echoes the salience of Dubois's metaphorical veil, a tropological methodology for interpreting Miltonic presence in black-authored works.

Instances of Miltonic signifying resemble Anglocentric practices of poetic intertextuality but with inflections of cultural difference. Intertextuality, in general, refers to processes of literary appropriation that quote precursor works directly or indirectly. Appropriated "intertexts" are vital elements of literary meaning according to Michael Riffaterre because "the reader must know [it] in order to understand a work of literature in terms of its overall significance."[73] Comprehension of an intertext facilitates a distinct mode of interpretation, one that rests upon the interplay between two symbolic elements. Machacek identifies these elements as the "spur" and "reprise." A spur, in Machacek's lexicon, designates the quoted or appropriated passage appearing in belated texts. These phraseological adaptations "stick out" to the discriminating and perceptive reader, triggering recalls of the poetic source and instigating nuanced events of novel interpretation.[74] Spurs also expose an aspect of the belated author's literary craft and the hermeneutic activity informing an intertext's rhetorical significance. Because recognition of a spur returns astute readers to original literary sources, the moment of intertextual identification further illuminates how precursor works "provided an impetus for [belated writers'] allusive reappropriation[s]."[75] This interpretive consideration is balanced against the assessment of the "reprise," the reappropriated element that Machacek discusses as the "taking-up-again" of a precursor's style.[76] To reconcile the rhetorical significance of a spur in tandem with an analytical assessment of the reprise is to discover alterations of original meaning that defy imitation.

Recognizing the hermeneutic interplay between spurs and acts of literary reprise generate an "intertextual drive." Riffaterre describes this interpretive system as "the point in which an intertext intervenes, making a second reading possible and indeed compulsory."[77] These second readings incite rigorous and vigorous activity. Specifically, one "looks to the intertext to fill out the text's gaps, spell out its implications and find out what rules of idiolectic grammar account for the text's departures from logic, from accepted usage..., from the cause-and-effect sequence of the narrative, and from verisimilitude in the descriptive."[78] Under the interpretive auspices of the intertextual drive, astute readers (re)discover original meaning, amplifying its rhetorical effects and radically transforming the linguistic event accordingly. Signifying inflects the intertextual drive with difference by modifying spurs and their original meaning with the verbal flair of cultural style. While signifying as "a principle of language use..., is not in any way the exclusive province of black people," Gates asserts that "blacks named the term and invented its rituals."[79] To be sure, this project of naming was neither for form nor for fashion but served as an interpretive response that recognized "hermeneutic systems, especially, are not 'universal' 'color-blind,' or 'apolitical,' or 'neutral.'"[80] Rituals of this type enrich a greater appreciation for Milton's presence in early African American tradition by accounting for these interpoetic encounters with the epic poet more responsibly on interpretive grounds of racial and cultural difference.

Arguably, one of the most important tropological rituals associated with the art of Miltonic signifying in early African American tradition involves these authors' satanic receptions of *Paradise Lost*. Neil Forsyth credits satanic receptions of Milton as our Romantic inheritance. If the Romantics bequeathed Satan as political hero to subsequent generations of readers, then that infernal figure enjoys its counterpart in African American tradition through the trope of the Signifying Monkey. This trickster figure, according to Gates, is based on Esu-Elegbara. "The central figure of the Ifa system of interpretation," Esu-Elegbara is the Afro-American relative of the Signifying Monkey. Both figures serve as representative examples of "the divine trickster figure of Yoruba mythology" across the African diaspora. The figures also lend themselves to demonic interpretations. For instance, Gates characterizes the Esu figure as the "guardian of the crossroads" of discourse and culture, who has one leg "anchored in the realm of the gods while the other rests in this, our human world."[81] In straddling earth and the demonic underworld, Esu and the Signifying Monkey share rhetorical affinities with Western concepts of Satan that similarly associate the character with supernal and infernal attributes.

Particularly in Africanist folklore, the devil often assumes the status of a cultural hero. This interpretive dynamic facilitates a rhetorical attraction to Milton's Satan who proves to be infernally dynamic yet is touched with the messianic grace of revolutionary heroism in the cause of liberty. A "strange but new" epic hero within the veil of racial interpretation, Milton's Satan undergoes interpretive transformation through the subversive artistry of signifying (PL 5.855). Because Satan speaks eloquently when mobilizing the fallen angels against what he sees as God's monarchial tyranny, and because his command of the English language provides a rhetorical impetus for black writers to subversively refute claims of African American intellectual inferiority, he spurs affiliations with the demonic and angelic aspects of Esu-Elegbara and the Signifying Monkey. Zora Neale Hurston acknowledges and elaborates upon this dual relationship between God and the devil as prominent fixtures in Negro folklore in her essay, "Characteristics of Negro Expression."[82]

According to Hurston, the devil represents a major cultural hero in the tradition. Second only to Jack, "the greatest culture hero of the South," the devil often proves "smarter than God."[83] In her glossary to *Mules and Men* (1935), Hurston elaborates upon the cultural hero's trickster ways, explaining, "Brer Rabbit, Jack (or John), and the Devil are continuations of the same thing."[84] Later, she distinguishes the devil from his European counterpart. Far from a terror, the devil in Negro folklore, according to Hurston, "is a powerful trickster who often competes successfully with God."[85] These insights lead Melville J. Herskovits to posit that this "Devil is far from the fallen angel of European dogma" such that he appears "almost a different being."[86] This cultural act of satanic re-creation constitutes a variation upon and inflection of the Signifying Monkey's subversive performances. Synthesizing the demonic, angelic, and trickster characterizations, the Signifying Monkey of African American tradition solidifies an interpretive kinship with the British Romantics and their rebellious attractions to Milton's Satan.

In *The Satanic Epic*, Forsyth "reasserts the importance of Satan" in *Paradise Lost* and rescues unorthodox readings that read the infernal hero positively from the hegemonic authority of Milton's pro-God critics. Forsyth persuasively reasons, "the energy in the poem is Satan...who drives the poem into motion and whose plot provides the motor of the action."[87] According to this reading, Forsyth presents opportunities that allow contemporary readers to glory in the satanic aspects of Milton's epic. This reading starkly contrasts the reader-response theory Stanley Fish proposes in *Surprised by Sin*. In that work, Fish proposes a theory of reader-response designed to rescue fallen readers from interpretive fallacies. Forsyth, however, emphasizes that it is the infernal hero's ability to seduce readers as a result of the character's heroism, interiority, sublime grandeur, and eloquence. These attributes motivate the epic's dramatic action by infusing the poem with satanic energy even in those moments where the hero is not present.

Consistent with African American culture's interpretive pairing of God with Satan, Forsyth also recognizes the infernal hero's salvific potential. Like the Signifying Monkey that embraces aspects of the demonic and angelic, Milton's Satan similarly performs messianic qualities as an "equivalent or narrative double of the Son."[88] Mirroring each other according to their respective infernal or supernal missions, Satan and the Son represent salvific doubles of each other. The Son proves salvific in his willing sacrifice to serve as the propitiation for humans' sinful estate. Satan, on the other hand, paves the road to hell but also conditions the way toward heavenly redemption. Redemption, according to Forsyth, occurs as a consequence of Satan's deceitfulness. As a result, he concludes, "the very existence of the Satan figure" facilitates salvation for humankind.[89] By doubling infernal traits with supernal characteristics, Milton achieves a type of satanic energy that synthesizes good and evil in one heroic character.

Forsyth's understanding of Milton's satanic epic exposes *Paradise Lost* as a demonic ground of contention for various early African American authors. Because Milton's poem also blends the satanic with the angelic in order to espouse virtues of holiness and themes of liberty, its poetic verses prove interpretively relatable as a subversive trope and talking book for Africanist audiences. Reading the devil of Negro folklore more extensively as a satanic poet of sorts, Hurston adds, "there is a strong suspicion that the devil is an extension of the story-makers while God is the supposedly impregnable white masters, who are nevertheless defeated by the Negroes."[90] This folkloric reading of the devil is especially telling, for it not only inverts the religious paradigm by reassessing both figures' ethical values; it makes a glorified reception of Milton's

Satan interpretively tenable according to Africanist culture and logic. Forsyth's and Hurston's theories reveal there is enough interpretive room in both literary traditions to read Milton's Satan as a divine trickster hero who likewise embodies demonic and messianic qualities in one character. The rhetorical amalgamation of both religious figures solidifies early African Americans' reception of Milton's Satan as a cultural intertext reminiscent of the Signifying Monkey. As cultural intertext, Milton's Satan, though demonic, performs and functions as a trope of messianic rebellion. This feature of early African Americans' Miltonic receptions further highlights the interpretive contours of their linguistic remastery by completing and complicating the epic writer through the verbal art of signifying.

Through this verbal art, early African American authors develop a fifth trope germane to understanding their Miltonic receptions. This tropological feature concerns their rhetorical adaptations of Satan and his militant tones of infernal eloquence. Antislavery writers and orators adopt the trope of infernal eloquence to convey fervent sentiments concerning political injustice. Tropes of infernal eloquence place poetic emphasis on artists' desire to skillfully play with fire in loaded rhetoric and language. Patterned after Milton's Satan and his rhetoric of hellish rebellion, the satanic trope of infernal eloquence draws upon any number of figures and motifs associated with the demonic grounds that give rise to his sentiments of implacable hate. Based on his brand of evil and negative relation to God, St. Hilaire interprets Satan as both a "poetic figure" and "figure for poetry." By this, St. Hilaire means the infernal hero is "not pure negation" but a figure who is "*determinately* positive because [his] definition...[stands] in a necessary relationship to goodness." The complexities emanating from this dual orientation to evil and godliness especially informs Satan's language. Satanic poetry results from this complex orientation, giving rise to a brand of infernal eloquence that proves rhetorically attractive for Africanist audiences whose rebellions against hegemonic tyrannies necessitate incendiary gospels of censure and revolt. Similarly poised within a "positive manifestation of negativity," members of Milton's black sisterhood and brotherhood preach rebellion in tones of infernal eloquence with the rhetorical goal of burning the moral consciousness of their readers and auditors with the added hope of prompting them to disavow slavery and turn from their wicked ways.[91]

Miltonic examples of infernal eloquence in early African American tradition include a range of innovative styles that complete and complicate understandings of the epic writer and his canon. Wheatley's elegies, for example, use Hellish landscapes as launchpads to psychological freedom. Frederick Douglass alludes to Milton through his infernal reception of *Paradise Lost*. Frances Ellen Watkins Harper and Anna Julia Cooper take different infernal approaches to the art of completing and complicating Milton. Charting subversive feminist geographies through wayward manipulations of Miltonic epic or by worrying the lines of his verse and piercing patriarchal soundscapes, both women authors trope with Satan's infernal eloquence in tones of tempered assertiveness. Sutton E. Griggs in his first novel, *Imperium in Imperio,* also plays with the fire of Milton's incendiary rhetoric. Specifically, he returns to the demonic grounds of Milton's hell, revisiting this fallen landscape and echoing the infernal council and Pandaemonium in *Paradise Lost*.

The trope of infernal eloquence facilitates efforts to preach gospels of black revolt through positive rhetorical identifications with Milton's satanic epic. Because these fiery vocalizations test and testify with Milton's demonic registers in hell, early African Americans may be regarded as performing infernal readings of the epic writer but for messianic purposes of racial uplift. On the basis of these infernal readings, early African American authors establish unorthodox affiliations with Satan. These affiliations promote rebellious sensibilities relative to the epic writer and his canon. Furthermore, this infernal orientation positions this audience of readers in interpretive kinship with the Romantics. A school of near contemporaries, the Romantics also identified with Milton's Satan and his poetry of fallenness. In their distinct ways, both interpretive communities played with Miltonic fire and preached gospels of political rebellion in the interest of redeeming fallen society. While critical differences in style and cultural orientation separate both traditions of Miltonic reception, it is no longer tenable to keep both audiences relegated to opposite sides of the literary color line. In order to begin resolving this specific problem of the color line in literary studies, it is necessary to remember: when early African American writers and orators rhetorically sided with Milton and his infernal hero, they did so in figures and tropes of blackness.

Enlisting in the Devil's Party through Romantic Kinship

For the most part, early African Americans rhetorically enlisted in the party of Milton's Satan through the British Romantics. The Romantics enjoyed popularity among early African American reading audiences throughout the nineteenth century. A few works discuss their relationship to British Romanticism. However, none takes up lines of influence derivative of Miltonic influence. For this reason, it is necessary to chart intertextual cartographies beyond the veil of African American literature and across the color lines into a survey of Romantics and their satanic fascination with Milton's infernal hero. Wittreich's *The Romantics on Milton* and Lucy Newlyn's *"Paradise Lost" and the Romantic Reader* examine the epic writer's influence upon this satanic school of readers. In addition to celebrating Milton's Satan as a political hero, the Romantics produced a body of literature rich in allusive characterizations patterned after their receptions of the fallen angel.

This feature would not have been lost upon "a group of abolitionist poets, some of whom were Black orator poets, [who] wrote a similar brand of reformist poetry" as those penned by certain of their Romantic predecessors.[92] For instance, Douglass quoted liberally from Byron, Shelley, and Wordsworth in his various orations. In *The Contours of Masculine Desire*, Marlon B. Ross recognizes Romantic poeticizing as a literary art form that "men do in order to reconfirm their capacity to influence the world in ways sociohistorically determined as masculine."[93] This approach to art by Romantic writers would have inspired Douglass and contemporaries like Henry Highland Garnet, William Wells Brown, and others. In the works of this satanic school they would find examples of appropriating the poet of liberty in an ironic way in order to reveal their own masculine desires for poetic selfhood.

William L. Andrews, in another interpretive moment grounded in the Romantics' satanic receptions of Milton, contributes to this route of literary influence. He argues, "Douglass's devilish behavior" as recounted in the former slave's second autobiography reveals "the satanic aspect of the larger Promethean mythic identity that he accrues to himself at the turning point of *My Bondage and My Freedom*." The interpretations by Ross, Robinson, and Andrews of Romantic influence upon early African American writers chart interpretive pathways for understanding how black authors of the nineteenth century came to enlist in the devil's party through Milton. They would have enlisted in this party by placing interpretive value on a satanic epic whose canonical status likewise invested in championing the cause of liberty by playing with a poetics of fallenness and rhetorical fire.

Infernal receptions of *Paradise Lost* appear so frequently, according to Newlyn, that this aggregate of readers may be thought of as "the Milton cult." She continues, "politicians of different persuasions used [*Paradise Lost* and Milton's prose pamphlets] for sectarian purposes; while poets and essayists frequently exploited its libertarian appeal (with or without Satanic overtones) to advocate or to condemn republicanism, civil and religious liberty, and the freedom of the press."[94] These infernal approaches to Miltonic appropriation help to explain why the Miltonic cult troped with Satan, hell, and the theme of the Fall so liberally in this distinct poetic tradition. The cult provided an artistic medium for preaching gospels of revolt against Christian, political, and social forces, the very tyrannical systems of power that many Romantics recognized as hindering the spread of liberty in England and abroad. As a result, Milton became their hero par excellence, leading the way to glorious freedom through infernal acts of heroic rebellion.

Siding with Milton's Satan on these demonic grounds of contention, fallen writers and their readers position themselves at enmity with the God of *Paradise Lost*. The Romantics often interpreted Milton's God as a monarchial tyrant and inhibitor of freedom. Consequently, Milton's God encouraged their political identifications with the dispossessed, those whose lives were negatively affected by ruling principalities and powers. According to this interpretive system, "earthly tyranny is shown to be constructed along heavenly lines," therefore, activating a "range of methods for questioning religion" and hegemonic systems according to the Romantic imagination.[95] Tropes of infernal eloquence emerge from these unorthodox receptions, yielding a body of canonical poems, novels, and treatises that have achieved celebrated acclaim for their poetic beauty and their thematic focus on the political will of disenfranchised heroes. Milton greatly influences the characterization of these Romantic heroes whose actions amplify the infernal or rebellious spirit so strongly associated with Satan of *Paradise Lost*.

For example, William Blake's *The Marriage of Heaven and Hell* quotes the often cited expression, "the reason Milton wrote in fetters when he wrote of angels and God, and at liberty when of devils and Hell, is because he was a true poet, and of the Devil's party without knowing it."[96] This quote, according to Newlyn, "associates liberty with Satan" and asserts "an internalized liberty which is the 'true poet' in Milton."[97] Virtually any discussion that engages Milton's epic with a focus on Satan is destined to consider Blake's popular aphorism. St. Hilaire, in her discussion of *Paradise Lost* and its canonical status within a poetic tradition of fallenness, proves no exception. Specifically, she acknowledges, "Milton's poem identifies with Satan, not because it believes that Satan was right to rebel, but because, the poem tells us, we are all of the devil's party, like it or not."[98] In other words, and in terms of biblical Scripture, "all have fallen and have come short of the Glory of God" (Rom. 3:23). For St. Hilaire, humanity's fallenness does not require Milton's readers to "*approve* of Satan" but that they empathize with him out of a shared sense of fallenness as sinners saved by God's grace.[99]

In *The Marriage*, Blake associates pursuits of liberty with Satan, then ascribes that impulse to Milton's vocation as a poet. Blake names and interprets both dynamics through metaphors of infernal eloquence. Several lines later, he conflates God and Satan in order to "humanize, personify, and psychologize those aspects of religion he finds most repugnant."[100] Here, the Romantic poet blends aspects of the divine with the diabolic, poetically theorizing on "Reason" and "desire" while identifying "the Jehovah of the Bible" as "no other than he who dwells in flaming fire."[101] As these instances of Miltonic attraction indicate, Blake's Satan is something far more complex than a static diabolic character. Rather, his

Miltonic gloss of the infernal hero registers as a divinely political figure worthy of emulating in quests for freedom.

Lord Byron sides with Milton's Satan on infernal grounds of demonic interpretation as well. Various excerpts from his poetry are evidence of his rhetorical indulgence in infernal figures. For instance, canto 3, stanza 91, from *Don Juan* acknowledges Milton as "the prince of poets" and an "independent being in his day."[102] The latter compliments a heroic attribute of strength and personal fortitude that often surfaces amid infernal imagery, especially for Miltonic characters whom critics have come to identify as Byronic heroes. References to Milton's Satan and his infernal weaponry surface in *The Vision of Judgment* as well. Byron wrote the poem in response to Robert Southey's poem of the same title. Frank D. McConnell relates that Southey "had leveled a vituperative attack on Byron, describing him as a 'Satanic' poet, a corrupter of morals and a threat to national spiritual health."[103] Byron epitomizes the satanic moniker throughout his canon but in a sense he is different from Southey's perception of him. Works like *Cain, Childe Harold's Pilgrimage*, and *Manfred* are just a few of the works in Byron's oeuvre that allude to and trope with aspects of Milton's satanic epic.

Tropes of infernal eloquence also surface in works by Samuel Taylor Coleridge, William Godwin, and William Wordsworth. Additionally, Adriana Craciun finds satanic engagements with Milton in works by Mary Shelley, Mary Wollstonecraft, Ann Radcliffe, Emily Brontë, and Hanna More. She refers to these female writers as satanic Jacobins. The term identifies this group as women who "found a surprising range of poetic uses for Milton's Satan, the most significant being a vision of outcast female genius, hurled from the celestial sphere for having claimed equality."[104] These engagements supply a "feminist vision of women's poetic genius as Satanic" yet heroic. More important, this literary group is not oppressed by "the self-destructive legacy of 'Milton's Bogey' and 'Shakespeare's Sister' prevalent in 1970s and 1980s liberal-feminist literary histories."[105] As is evident in the tropes of infernal eloquence in writings by these satanic Jacobins, Milton's Satan could be appropriated in support of feminist causes.

Finally, no discussion of infernal eloquence as a sign of Miltonic influence among Romantic writers would be complete without mentioning Percy Bysshe Shelley. Shelley's most insightful commentaries on Milton's Satan occur in his preface to *Prometheus Unbound* (1820) and again in "A Defence of Poetry," which he wrote in 1821. Milton's Satan, according to Shelley, possesses "courage and majesty, [proving himself] firm and patient [in his] opposition to omnipotent force."[106] To some extent, Shelley pardons Satan's rebellious spirit as displayed in Milton's epic. In consideration of the "wrongs" Satan suffers, Shelley finds they "exceed all measure," which enables readers to "excuse" the infernal hero's "faults."[107] Idolizations of Satan's heroic character appear in his "Defence" as well. Notwithstanding Satan's "implacable hate [and] patient cunning," Shelley argues that such conduct, while "venial in a slave[,] are not to be forgiven in a tyrant."

That Shelley pardons these vices of satanic rebellion when exhibited by slaves holds critical interpretive significance, given the Romantics' literary prestige and their poetic influence for early African American writers throughout the nineteenth century. Shelley asserts, "nothing can exceed the energy and magnificence of the character of Satan as expressed in *Paradise Lost.*"[108] If this reception of the infernal hero inspires his aesthetic vision to any degree, then it also serves as a potential spur for contemporary and belated writers in early African American tradition who likewise enjoy playing with fire through highly charged rhetoric and language. Shelley also regards Satan's "moral being...as far superior to [Milton's] God" since he "perseveres in some purpose which the [epic writer] has conceived to be excellent in spite of adversity and torture."[109]

Shelley's thoughts on Satan seem to privilege the infernal hero over Milton's God. However, Newlyn recognizes a different revolution at work in terms of the Romantic writer's poetics. On one level, Shelley's lyrical drama conflates supernal and infernal qualities. This strategy enables the poet to "repudiate the moral failings both of Milton's God and his Satan so as to define as redemptive a human potential which lies beyond them both."[110] Yet, Shelley patterns Prometheus after a classical hero, therefore rejecting the binary model presented with Milton's God and Satan. This creative engagement with Milton offers yet another variation of infernal eloquence in that Shelley adopts a wayward or demonic approach to Miltonic tropology. The demonic as it is understood contemporarily in math, computer sciences, and physics, describes processes that McKittrick recognizes as sometimes erratic and indeterminate. Shelley's aesthetic of intertextual engagement operates according to this dynamic. It plays wittingly and "constantly on the audience's awareness of ways in which Miltonic patterns are being modified, avoided, or put on one side."[111] A method for achieving this dynamic in Shelley's poetry surfaces through his aesthetic blending of infernal figures with supernal ones.

This brief survey reveals how early African American writers came to enlist in the devil's party with Milton through their Romantic inheritance. Many of these writers, as Williams explains in her dissertation, "can be considered outspoken in espousing ideas which their era considered liberal, if not radical." Among them, Williams identifies Blake, Byron, and Shelley as "representative of the British Reform spirit."[112] Though a critical component of intertextual influence upon early African American writers, this spirit of satanic reform does not tell the whole story about how Milton's black sisterhood and brotherhood came to forge rhetorical affiliations with the epic on demonic grounds. Inasmuch as they enlist in the devil's party by siding with Milton's Satan, they also invested in tropes of Edenic paradise. Such a rhetorical attraction balances their interest in satanic rebellion as a poetics of messianic revolt.

Back to Eden and the Poetics of Messianic Revolt

Milton's early African American readers also identify with his depictions of paradise. In these instances, Milton's black-identified audiences are led by an Edenic spirit of intertextuality that finds solidarity with a less militant style of political subversion. Whereas Satan's infernal persuasions inspire revolt, tropes of Miltonic paradise express a politics of sublime divinity. Combined, the synthesis of demonic rebellion and Edenic innocence yield a gospel of black revolt that is balanced with a spirit of tempered assertiveness. This synthesis also recalls a Gnostic interpretive tradition that recognizes "Christ, not Satan, [as] the serpent of Genesis, the bringer of Gnosis or spiritual knowledge."[113] Drawing upon Augustine's discussion in *De haeresibus*, Forsyth traces this interpretation of

Christ to Ophite beliefs. Whether Milton was acquainted with the Augustinian passage or "exploit[ed] the ambiguities of the traditional equations," Forsyth maintains the poet's sophisticated routes of satanic interpretation enable searches for "hidden meaning beneath the surface text."[114] A return to Eden as a site of a lost African paradise in early African American tradition exposes these hidden meanings and amplifies the political tenor of these messianic gospels. Moreover, the journey back to Eden delivers the satanic trope from interpretive evil by guiding readers of early African American texts along paths of antislavery righteousness. To facilitate this goal, writers in the tradition gravitate to Milton while moving in the freeing spirit of black Christianity. Theirs is a spiritual intertextuality with Milton that is informed by cultural contexts of black messianism, the black jeremiad, and black liberation theology.

Several male writers and orators engage with Milton through Edenic imagery. However, the trope of sublime divinity surfaces most prominently in works by African American women. This pattern charts a distinct feminist sensibility relative to Miltonic reception in early African American literature. Writings by Wheatley, Harper, and Cooper especially highlight an Edenic reception of Milton. Such receptions generally preach gospels of black revolt that are less militant in tenor yet prove equally as "mighty through God to the pulling down of strongholds" (2 Cor. 10:4) in their philosophical ideas. When early African American women return to Eden through Milton, they challenge satanic militancy as the solely viable strategy of political resistance. Their alternative route to Miltonic reception ultimately performs cultural geographies of intertextual engagement on demonic interpretive grounds. This path out of hell also ushers in a new poetics of liberation for black writers at the dawning of the twentieth century.

The trope of sublime divinity continues to complete and complicate Milton by drawing attention to the paradox attending early African Americans' engagements with some of the epic writer's most iconic symbols like heaven and hell. According to their interpretive framework concerning Milton's figures, slavery and other forms of social injustice reflect demonic practices that hegemonic society paradoxically deems acceptable, logical, and just. From the standpoint of those who justify systems of hegemonic domination, waging war against these principles amounts to a dissident practice of occupying demonic grounds. African American writers who occupy these interpretive grounds seek to overturn and respatialize these sites of geographical domination by appealing to Christian principles that will justify their political views. By extending the trope of the Signifying Monkey, yet repeating the serpent-general of Milton's epic with inflections of rhetorical difference, this segment of his early African American audience performs rebellion on the one hand and offers salvific redemption on the other. It is this dually subversive performance that distinguishes early African Americans' satanic receptions of Milton from those performed by the Romantics. Though the Romantics gravitated to Milton's Edenic tropes, they did not appropriate these rhetorical figures under the auspices of messianic and jeremiadic traditions that were steeped in tenets of black liberation theology.

In *Black Messiahs and Uncle Toms*, Jeremiah Wilson Moses explores the cultural significance of racial messianism in early African American culture. This religious movement articulates a religious and secular vision of the race as a "'redeemer people.'"[115] Literary artists in early African American tradition, who recognize the race as anointed and as a conscience for a fallen nation, sometimes perform their vision of black messianism through several symbolic expressions. The "suffering servant or sacrificial lamb" represents one of these symbolic expressions, and the "avenging angel" whose "divinely inspired rebellion against the social order is...a traditional aspect of Judeo-Christian messianism," offers a more militant iteration of the messianic figure.[116] The sacrificial lamb/avenging angel dichotomy presents a variation on the heaven/hell, God/Satan binaries and the infernal/supernal personalities ascribed to the Signifying Monkey.

When troping with Milton's Eden, early African American authors enrich the symbolic charge of these political writings in the spirit of a black jeremiadic tradition. The black jeremiadic tradition responds to the American jeremiad, which laments and censures a fallen nation on behalf of a chosen people. Patterned after the prophesies of Jeremiah, the Old Testament prophet, the American jeremiad, according to Sacvan Bercovitch, descends from a European tradition that Puritans brought to the New World. The Puritans adopted a sensibility that viewed their pilgrimage and destiny to the New World as a divine errand; America, for them, symbolized a New Jerusalem or city on a hill. As the nation developed through trials and triumphs, Puritan jeremiads responded to these dynamics by "joining lament and celebration in affirming America's mission."[117] This double-voiced discourse also produced a "Janus-like prophet" whose prophetic commentaries addressed "secular and sacred history alike."[118] Through this style of rhetorical address, jeremiadic prophets could lament or celebrate the risings and fallings of a civic nation that prided itself on its divine errand. This form of address also proved useful for American Jeremiahs who solely wished to address an audience of spiritual elites.

The African American jeremiad extends these aims by enlarging the terrains of civic and spiritual vision to address issues central to black experience. It also speaks a double-voiced language, one that is "paradoxically, both radical and conservative" in its tone and subject.[119] This feature of double-voicedness empowers the nation's black Jeremiahs to preach a familiar gospel in strains of cultural difference. Specifically, a distinctive feature of black jeremiads, according to David Howard-Pitney, is that they allow for a "more searching...examination of American social faults" in tones that prove "bolder in prescribing reform than its white counterparts."[120] When contextualized in tandem with the black jeremiad, Miltonic presence advances the rhetorical style of double-voicedness. When writers in the tradition play with Milton's figures of satanic rebellion and/or Edenic messianism, they cultivate a tropological tradition that subsequently produces a system of mixed metaphors unified through elaborate signifyin(g) practices. To appeal to Milton's Satan under this sign system is to function under the jeremiadic auspices of fervent censure and critique. By contrast, appeals to Milton's Edenic tropes convey jeremiadic tones of lamentation and consolation. Collectively, both jeremiadic features amplify Milton's rhetorical significance in early African American tradition as a rhetorical instrument of black liberation theology.

Milton's role as a symbolic presence within traditions of messianism and jeremiadic address contributes to a unique strand of black liberation theology and antislavery sensibility. Whether literary artists in the tradition gravitate to Milton's Satan, the epic writer's Edenic tropes, or both, their various moments of intertextual engagement may be read as instances of preaching a rebellious yet righteous political gospel. Whatever their message, early African Americans' gospels of black revolt rebel against tyranny for the righteous cause of liberty. These righteous gospels are undergirded by the demonic aesthetics central to Milton's satanic epic so that their argumentative content proves both infernal and supernal in tone, theme, and argumentative claim while also straddling cultural realms of the sacred and secular in order to redeem a fallen nation that has lost its way as the site of a New Jerusalem.

This Miltonic approach to black liberation theology establishes African American writers and orators as a distinct interpretive community among the seventeenth century writer's early reading audiences. That is, they preach Milton as a talking book of liberty who is filtered through a racialized theology rooted in attitudinal sensibilities of black power. Miltonic presence in these contexts expresses sensibilities of black power, which according to James H. Cone "means *complete emancipation of black people from white oppression by whatever means black people deem necessary.*"[121] The concept also signifies "black freedom [and] black self-determination, wherein black people no longer view themselves as without human dignity but as men, human beings with the ability to carve out their own destiny."[122] These religious expressions of race pride and black power coalesce to advance a liberating theology that aims to save the oppressed through Christ's messianic authority.

Because its salvific properties stem from "identifications with the oppressed blacks of America, [who seek] to interpret the gospel of Jesus in the light of the black condition," black liberation theology shades various moments of Miltonic engagement in early African American letters with nuances of critical difference.[123] In addition to critiquing white theology for its negation of black humanity and the oppressive structures it supports, this blackened Christian discourse expands the rhetorical dexterity of Milton's poetic language in the service of various political causes. Therefore, early African Americans' diverse styles of spiritual engagement with Milton expand the grounds of contention with the epic writer by returning to the site of Eden. This return charts new interpretive paths that continue the project of completing and complicating Milton beyond convention and racialized discourse.

African American Interpretive Communities and the Selective Fragments of Miltonic Reception History

Thus far, the focus on early African Americans' Miltonic receptions has explained the artistry of this intertextual tradition by emphasizing social contexts and vernacular practices that are informed by different ways of seeing and theorizing the world. This different cultural perspective perceives the world from epistemological vantage points that comprehend various phenomena through cultural veils of racial experience and interpretation. Because of these cultural differences Africanist receptions of Milton are sometimes in dialogue with orthodox interpretive communities and unorthodox ones at other times. This process of breaking into language while entering it through the complexities of cultural differences exposes the reality of "race as an intertext of American reading and American rejections of reading."[124] For Nielsen, this understanding of race means black writers "find themselves already there behind the white textual veils of signifying blindness" when they break and enter into discourse. Black writers, then, are always and already there in the midst of white texts, whose authors "found their essential subjectivity" in direct relation to a dependence "for their very being upon the existence of black people."[125] As a result, black authors speaking in Miltonic discourse can break and enter into this language system with a sense of entitlement that inspires them to complete and complicate it in their own privileged accents. This same accent, one differentiated from the language broken into, enlarges the grounds of contention in Milton studies further, laying the foundation for transformative demonic grounds that simultaneously speak with and against the interpretive communities of old.

The authors examined in this study break and enter into Miltonic discourse on the interpretive foundations of earlier critics who receive the epic poet and writer as a mark of canonical greatness and genius in the English language. Throughout the ages, poet critics like Andrew Marvell, William Wordsworth, and Alfred,

Lord Tennyson, have crowned Milton as a laureate worthy to be emulated by belated writers. Dustin Griffin's *Regaining Paradise* builds upon the individual receptions of Milton's greatness by various eighteenth century critics. His reception study of this tradition counters Harold Bloom's notion that Milton proved an inhibiting influence for this audience. For instance, Griffin argues that the eighteenth century inspired myriad imitators who widely regarded Milton as a moral and literary hero. Biographers, poets, and critics alike typically celebrated Milton's *Paradise Lost* as a work worthy to be compared alongside Homer and Virgil's epics. Milton, then, became a modern classic, a "national treasure," and one who eighteenth century English culture regarded as a "leading exemplar of the dominant tradition."[126] Griffin's survey informs the earliest Africanist receptions of Milton. This is so because Africanist readers broke into English literary tradition because they recognized Milton as one whose canonical greatness had already begun to transcend the temporality of his immediate age. Eighteenth century readers' favorable reception of Milton ensured the epic poet could enjoy a successful afterlife as a literary icon worthy of poetic emulation. When Wheatley acknowledges Milton as "British Homer" in "Philis's [sic] Reply to the Answer in our last by the Gentleman in the Navy," she characterizes the epic poet consistent with eighteenth century receptions of him.[127] As Griffin explains, major and minor "poetasters and critics" throughout the eighteenth century often praised Milton as their "British Homer."[128]

Early African American authors remain in dialogue with eighteenth century receptions of Milton in other ways. In *Beautiful Sublime*, which examines a different aspect of eighteenth century responses to Milton's epic, Leslie E. Moore specifically focuses upon the poet's achievements in the aesthetic and philosophical sublime. According to Moore, this period in literary history reveals the emergence of a class of Miltonoclasts whose reception of the poet and his first epic invent the notion of a "sublime Milton."[129] Though the term "sublime" is loaded, muddled, and often contradictory when associated with Milton in literary history and criticism, Moore contends that the eighteenth century critics knew what it meant, or at least thought they did. To them, Milton's sublime meant those flights of poetic genius that "marked excess and instability and, more importantly, transcendence [and] the breaking of known boundaries, rules, and laws" of accepted conventionality.[130] Moore draws upon Joseph Addison's commentaries of Milton's aesthetic and deconstructs the oxymoronic phrase "beautiful sublime" to capture eighteenth century sensibilities regarding his supreme achievements in literary art. Addison, who is arguably most responsible for Milton's literary prestige in this period, extols the epic structure of *Paradise Lost* as a "version of the beautiful," perceiving its purpose as a device for limiting the "tremendous energy of the sublime, even as the beautiful works aesthetically to delimit the range of passions falling under sublime emotion."[131] This assessment of Milton's aesthetic of beauty and philosophical grandeur finds parallels among various early African American writers and women in particular.

For instance, Charlotte Forten Grimké, a nineteenth century aspiring abolitionist and African American poet, extols Milton's beautiful sublime. Recording her initial reactions to reading *Paradise Lost* in her journals, she describes the epic as "truly *beautiful* nay, more, *sublime*."[132] She also expresses admiration for Milton's heroic achievements in light of his age and blindness, which, she explains, "adds greatly to the interest which the grandeur of the subject along would excite."[133] This latter consideration accords with "the sentimental tradition" of Miltonic reception examined in Griffin's study.[134] These sentimental receptions of Milton revere him for his heroic fortitude in triumphing over physical challenges while producing exemplary poetry.

Frances Ellen Watkins Harper and Anna Julia Cooper extend the tradition of eighteenth century Miltonic reception in their respective works also. Harper's "The Mission of the Flowers" offers a case in point. A prose allegory about the attractiveness of racial diversity and distinctiveness, Harper's Edenic story centers on a rose that learns "to respect the individuality of her sister flowers" with the added knowledge that each species has "their own missions" to perform in nature.[135] Harper pairs this allegorical story with her groundbreaking contribution to epic tradition, *Moses: Story of the Nile*. Resonances of an Edenic sublime surface in this work as well, but Harper's literary coupling of allegory and brief epic signifies on the published format of Milton's final writings, which paired

Paradise Regained with the closet drama *Samson Agonistes*. Here, Edenic motifs blend with literary form to produce a homage to Milton that appeals to a beautiful sublime through allusive modes of phraseological adaptation. Cooper also tropes with Milton's Eden. Throughout *A Voice from the South*, her volume of poetic essays, Cooper draws upon horticultural imagery from *Paradise Lost*. This technique proves useful for arguing black women's sociopolitical office as a "Vital Element in the Regeneration and Progress of a Race."[136] These and other literary responses to Milton by black women testify to his preeminent stature as *the* beautifully sublime poet who eighteenth century culture similarly revered.

Americanist receptions of Milton in the eighteenth century also inform early African Americans' intertextual engagements with the epic writer. Highly esteemed as an "honorary American because he loved liberty," Milton's influence and literary preeminence increased in early America while inspiring revolutionary attitudes against British tyranny.[137] This reception, according to K. P. Van Anglen, served as a touchstone for "address[ing] matters of authority in a turbulent age." Lydia Dittler Schulman's work concurs with this fuller understanding of Milton's influence in early America. She emphasizes this tradition of Miltonic reception as tied to a "national agenda of independence, republicanism, and commercial expansion."[138] That tradition contributed to enlarging the grounds of contention in Miltonic reception, solidifying the terrain as an intertextual site where a gospel of liberty might take root and prosper. Early African American audiences embraced the geographical promise that this reception of Milton promoted. Moved by the revolutionary spirit of the founding fathers, they enriched the U.S. landscape as a cultural geography where Milton's theme of liberty would extend to blacks as well.

Milton continued to enjoy favor throughout the nineteenth century by early African American audiences, given the esteem he was accorded by New England Unitarians and Transcendentalists. Primarily educated at Harvard, this class of intellectual elites was taught to emulate Milton by teachers who revered the poet as one "whose divine inspiration, sublime virtue, intellectual breadth, and moral steadfastness had empowered him to speak didactically from a position of spiritual, social, and intellectual superiority."[139]

William Lloyd Garrison's abolitionist newspaper, *The Liberator*, further solidified Boston as a hub or epi(c)enter of Miltonic influence. For instance, David Booker has "discovered 152 references to Milton and his works in *The Liberator*."[140] David Walker, Frederick Douglass, Henry Highland Garnet, and Frances Harper represent a few of Milton's literary disciples whose ties to New England at various points in their respective lives hold some relationship to Garrison, his newspaper, or additional routes of social energy steeped in the epic writer's canonical writings. The widespread popularity of the Fireside Poets, consisting of Henry Wadsworth Longfellow, William Cullen Bryant, John Greenleaf Whittier, James Russell Lowell, and Oliver Wendell Holmes may have also served as routes of Miltonic influence for African American authors writing throughout the nineteenth century.

Victorian culture proved equally influential, spreading its resonances of influence across the Atlantic to American audiences. Victorian audiences revered Milton as a sublime Puritan, a classic, and a Bible, according to Erik Gray. They quoted him sparingly, allusively, and in poetic fragments. As Gray contends, Miltonic presence in Victorian literature proved "constant but diffuse."[141] To them, Milton's iconic status loomed so large that they could allude to him, confident that his image would not be lost upon readers even though he was "backgrounded rather than foregrounded" in print culture.[142] The Victorian era revered Milton's treatment of Christian themes so highly that *Paradise Lost* inspired countless religious epics by numerous aspiring poets. This was also the period when a class of "new biographers" hailed Milton's Puritan leanings and "popularized the poet's religious and political ideals by reviving interest in [his] prose" writings.[143] In addition to hailing Milton as a sublime religious poet, Victorian audiences respected his artistry as representative of the natural sublime.

They recognized Milton's natural sublime based on his treatment of majestic themes and ideas concerning nature and the cosmos. This aspect of Milton's sublime "attracted and inspired English poets during the 1820s and 1830s," extending well into the 1840s when Lord Tennyson published two volumes of *Poems* (1842).[144] Apocalyptic poets like Robert Montgomery, John Abraham Heraud, and William Phillips gravitated to *Paradise Lost* as well. These writers esteemed the epic's subject, its setting, and most important, Satan's characterization, what many regarded as the epitome of Milton's natural sublime. Satan, to them, reflected a "superhuman being who dared to think the most terrifying thoughts and to attempt the most awful deeds imaginable."[145]

By the mid-Victorian period, African Americans like William Wells Brown, Frederick Douglass, and the fugitive couple William and Ellen Craft were touring England and preaching antislavery gospels. Brown visited Ludlow Castle and marveled at his experience of residing where Milton wrote *Comus*. Douglass preached a version of his "Self-Made Men" speech, citing Milton as a literary exemplar of this moniker. William Craft attained formal literacy at the Ockham School, possibly encountering Milton for the first time in print before rhetorically covering his slave narrative, *A Thousand Miles to Freedom*, with a Miltonic epigraph that quotes lines from book 12 of *Paradise Lost*.[146] These transatlantic encounters with Milton reveal the various interpretive communities early African American writers engaged when breaking into Miltonic discourse and entering it in dialogue with precursors and contemporaries alike.

Though Milton's Christian sublime would ultimately lose favor among English audiences during the late Victorian era when advancements in scientific thinking gained prominence, African American writers and orators of this same period remained in intertextual dialogue with Milton. Writings and oratory from this period reveal an Africanist audience who found him still relevant in print as they continued citing, completing, and complicating him through various styles of allusive and fragmentary appropriation. To their British counterparts Milton had become a stern Puritan too beholden to an unquestioning acceptance of Scripture. For nineteenth century African Americans, Milton remained relevant and a classic whose presence could not become overfamiliar for a people yet championing the right to be free and treated as equals.

Twentieth and twenty-first century reception studies of Milton's influence have proven equally critical for responsible assessments of early African Americans' engagements with England's epic poet of liberty. These periods in criticism especially highlight the contentious grounds of Milton studies, reviving scholarly debates about the validity of orthodox and unorthodox interpretations of the epic writer's canon. Early African American receptions straddle the lines of criticism on these grounds of poetic interpretation. Authors within this tradition typically shift between these poles of interpretive reception. Sometimes embracing the satanic and rejecting it at other times, Africanist audiences differentiate themselves from Milton's epic at various points along the literary color line. These infernal yet messianic orientations to *Paradise Lost* produce a culturally distinct interpretive community whose interpoetic engagements with Milton produce a "strange but new" tradition in satanic re-creation.

C. S. Lewis's *A Preface to "Paradise Lost"* (1942) is a groundbreaking work in twentieth century criticism. It is one of the earliest examples in contemporary reception studies to legislate the hegemonic authority of anti-satanic readings. In a chapter devoted to Milton's poetic construction of Satan, Lewis lambastes propositions that hold that the infernal hero "is or ought to be an object of admiration and sympathy, conscious or unconscious."[147] Milton's Satan is a "magnificent character" only to the extent that the fallen angel "is too near us" in our feeble efforts to live up to "the real high virtues which we do not possess at all."[148] *Milton's God* (1961) by William Empson expresses a contrasting view of Satan. Empson revisits and upholds the Romantics' satanic reception of *Paradise Lost*, particularly arguing, "Milton does want to make Satan a very high-flying character, and sometimes uses ambiguous language to heighten the drama."[149] To achieve this effect, as Empson chronicles, Milton creates multiple scenarios that expose God as "intentionally deluding Satan" such that his adversary cannot be faulted for "disbelieving his creation" or sense of injured merit.[150] By the end of Empson's chapter on Satan, he addresses Lewis's jeering of Satan. Reading the epic along multiple lines and particularly thinking about the political milieu Milton wrote in, Empson believes the poet "thought it proper to be sardonic about the enemy of mankind; but he was scrupulously careful to give him strong arguments for his fall."[151] This satanic reception of the epic would later be eclipsed by Stanley Fish.

In *Surprised by Sin*, Fish insists upon a proper interpretation of Milton's epic that accords with theological lines of Christian reasoning. Accordingly, *Paradise Lost* represents a poem whose primary method is that of leading readers "beyond [their] perspective by making [them] feel its inadequacies" so that its poet may instruct them to righteousness.[152] Milton achieves this ministerial function by pandering to carnal readers' "traditional idea[s] of what is heroic" and inducing their "weakness before [Satan's] rhetorical lure." Fish assesses these rhetorical strategies as indicative of Milton catechizing his fallen readers and providing them a Christian reading experience that teaches a fit and high regard for the austerity of God's logic and the power of his "non-affective" speech.[153] *Surprised by Sin* has enjoyed favor for more than five decades. As a result, pro-satanic interpretations and receptions of the epic have been pushed to the margins of consideration at best and dismissed as wrong or disadvantaged at worst.

In their respective works, Neil Forsyth, John C. Rumrich, Peter C. Herman, and Danielle A. St. Hilaire swing the pendulum back to examinations of Satan as central to interpretive assessments of *Paradise Lost*. Their analytical interventions open theoretical space for appreciating the satanic reverberations occurring within early African Americans' infernal yet messianic engagements with Milton. Forsyth unequivocally acknowledges *Paradise Lost* as a satanic epic and revives an interest in the demonic grounds of Miltonic interpretation by examining readers' attraction to the fallen angel on the basis of "the tragic status of the [infernal] hero."[154] John C. Rumrich and Peter C. Herman trouble the grounds of orthodox receptions further by challenging the "invented Milton" and notions of Miltonic certitude, respectively.[155] Recognizing that prevailing practices of interpretation can "function over the course of centuries" and achieve the status of "normal science" in critical discourse, Herman reveals how easily Milton can come to be revered as "a poet of absolute, unqualified certainty" whose epic always "coheres" so that it becomes the "critic's task" to do so as well.[156] In the absence of interventions like these, grounds of contention in Milton studies can foreclose any number of differentiations that interpretive communities might perform relative to the epistemological locations informing their engagements with the epic poet.

For this reason, St. Hilaire's examination of *Paradise Lost* as satanic poetry proves especially vital for understanding early

African American authors' positioning on the literary color line as a distinct Miltonic audience differentiated by their racial-sexual displacement. In *Satan's Poetry,* St. Hilaire interrogates the infernal hero as "the creator of fallenness in Milton's universe" and the origin of a poetic tradition beholden to this aesthetic.[157] Through Satan, she explains, Milton produces an epic predicated on an aesthetic of satanic re-creation destined to appeal to members of a fallen humanity. Acts of satanic re-creation perform remakings of the self, operating through processes of differentiation from their original sources. As St. Hilaire explains, such processes expose tensions "between creation and destruction, between positive and negative agency," which ultimately "give Satan his poetical significance in *Paradise Lost.*"[158]

St. Hilaire's theory extends to practices of allusion and intertextuality as well, and here is where early African Americans' receptions of Milton best illuminate their intertextual particularities. Imitation in literary tradition for St. Hilaire announces "the process of revolution, the constant demand that something new will come to be, something unique and different, something that rejects the world as it is and establishes a new reality." In this same spirit, early African American authors exist as an interpretive community whose engagements with Milton similarly embody "structures of particularity" by initiating acts of self-creation with and against *Paradise Lost* and other texts within the epic writer's canon.[159] Like Satan, the creator of poetic fallenness in literature, Milton's Africanist heirs (dis)cover "a certain discontinuity between [their] own [interpretive] horizons and that of [*Paradise Lost*]."[160] This site of intertextual difference echoes the demonic by decidedly choosing to reject sameness as a re-creative condition of expressing an individual's literary talent in its own image of imitative originality.

The uniqueness of early African Americans' intertextual engagements with Milton rests upon these interpretive grounds of imitative originality and difference. Some writers in the tradition trope with Satan as a symbol for white slaveowners and traffickers or develop demonic epithets patterned after Milton's infernal imagery. Others appropriate and interact with Satan in order to describe the horrors of black experience or to self-identify with the infernal hero's spirit of political dissidence. Still others express their satanic attractions to Milton's canon through interpretative revisions of the U.S. landscape. Regarding the United States as a perverted paradise, they trope with the landscape in the image of Milton's hell rather than the New Jerusalem associated with a Puritan jeremiadic tradition. Finally, since Satan becomes hell's fugitive in book 3 of Milton's epic, his escape from the underworld with its repeated imagery of enslavement strengthens rhetorical associations between early African Americans and the infernal hero of *Paradise Lost*.

The topographies of Milton's heaven and hell, coupled with Satan's fugitive escape from hellish enslavement, promote a range of distinct interpretive receptions that reconfigure the epic poet's canon beyond orthodox recognition. When early African American orators like John Marrant, Peter Williams Jr., and William Hamilton read continental Africa as a fallen paradise and enslavement as a demonic practice, they complete and complicate Milton in ways that allusively blend the messianic with the satanic. In early African American tradition, these and other Miltonic citings surface through *fragmentary* appropriations that may be direct or allusively faint. Perhaps these "textual snippets reminiscent of a phrase in some earlier author's writing but smoothly incorporated into the new context of the imitating author's work," have gone unnoticed by casual readers because a belated writer's Miltonic reprise seemed too fleeting or insignificant to merit critical attention or analysis.[161] However brief or localized, instances of Miltonic reprise in early African American tradition demand scholarly annotation and examination. Gray cautions against minimizing fragmentary echoes to Milton in the works of belated writers, noting that these traces "are no less powerful for being unlocalized."[162]

For early African American authors, such events evidence a given writer's social route to knowledge that radically defies post-Enlightenment theories concerning the intellectual inferiority of black cognizers and literary artists. Second, these intertextual engagements rupture the grounds of contention by introducing diverse receptions of Milton that signify on canonical tradition and alter its presumed meanings according to orthodox understandings of language. Since these fragmentary instances of Miltonic reprise occur within specific contexts of African American authors' various writing situations, the spur achieves nuanced meaning. In this way, belated writers' subversive styles of remastering the English language complete and complicate Milton through a complex network of language acquisition. Third, these deterritorializations and reterritorializations in and of language stretch conventional word usage, its figures, images, and tropes beyond rigidly defined parameters of meaning. However one may regard the literary quality of these verses in comparison to Milton's, it is important that we pay special attention to the poetic sophistication and aesthetic complexity of the intertextual or signifying event.

The poetic sophistication and aesthetic complexity of these fragmentary moments are, perhaps, best explained by Stephen Henderson's concept of mascons. Defined as a *"massive concentration of Black experiential energy* which powerfully affects the meaning of Black speech, Black song, and Black poetry," mascons further signify the understanding that "certain words and constructions seem to carry an inordinate charge of emotional and psychological weight, so that whenever they are used they set all kinds of bells ringing, all kinds of synapses snapping, on all kinds of levels."[163] Milton, his canon, and multiple figures function as highly charged mascons of black freedom, verbal expression, and Christian experience. It is through these rhetorical registers of signification that *he* speaks as a talking book either in conjunction with or sometimes in place of the Bible. Furthermore, as Gray contends, it is "impossible for a post-Miltonic English-language poet to refer to x without also referring to Milton, where x includes (but is not limited to) angels, devils, Satan, sin, snakes, spirits, fruit, Tree, temptation, rebellion, hell, heaven, God, creation, wandering, tasting, or falling."[164]

In order to responsibly recover early African Americans' Miltonic receptions, it is necessary to understand this distinct interpretive community as straddling the literary color line according to the various routes of intertextual influence and comprehensive bodies of theory and criticism produced in these traditions across the expanse of literary history. To engage these traditions by similarly straddling the literary color line is to radically alter the landscape of criticism and expose these grounds as demonic sites of contention where liberating practices of black geography have taken place. Furthermore, we can better appreciate African American interpretive communities and their selective fragments of Miltonic reception when we respect this form of literary art as reflecting an intertextual Middle Passage in the English language.

Black Geographies and the Demonic Grounds of Miltonic Presence

Early African Americans' engagements with Milton respatialize the grounds of contention on the subversive terrain of signifying difference. These intertextual expressions in Miltonic language translate to black geographies that attain their rhetorical force on demonic grounds of Miltonic reception. For McKittrick, black geographies reference "oppositional spatial practices" that radically resist and respond to hegemonic affronts to selfhood.[165] These subversive engagements with place and physical space resist hegemonic geographies on contestatory grounds of rebellion and dissidence. One successfully resists the constraints posed by geographical domination by re-producing and re-creating the environment in the interest of making lived experience habitable in the face of oppression and marginalization.

A transformation of these oppressive geographies often requires innovative strategies of resistance that are at variance with standard rules of political engagement. Because these spatial oppositions to hegemonic domination operate contrary to logical rules of political engagement, McKittrick identifies these practices as figuratively demonic. Similarly, early African American authors' subversive practices of completing and complicating Milton and his canon's meaning alter the grounds of contention through demonic practices that polish the epic writer's language anew. By defying conventional and orthodox practices of interpretive engagement, they transform language, thereby "bringing into focus" what McKittrick identifies as "the 'sayability' of geography" where "acts of expressing and saying place are central to understanding" how black bodies negotiate and transform acts of spatial domination through a subversive facility with language.[166] Early African American authors rupture the grounds of contention in this way when they complete and complicate Milton. Their intertextual engagements perform black geographies by elevating the race from the cultural abyss of hellish enslavement to celestial states of freedom.

Close readings and analyses of Milton's sayable geographies call for "an expanding knowledge base, and an enlarging critical consciousness" that, according to Wittreich, will emphasize the contradictions "marking" and "marring" Milton's poetry.[167] Wittreich also asserts that these new hermeneutic vistas will subsequently yield the "salient features of a new Milton criticism."[168] This brand of criticism articulates Milton as a sacred yet secular talking book. Milton, for this black-identified audience, serves the political needs of the racially abject. In remastering the English language through him, they "represent themselves as 'speaking subjects'" who successfully "begin [the work of] destroy[ing] their status as objects."[169] Because these rebellious activities occur on contentious grounds of Miltonic reception, they re-produce geographical space and alter the landscape as demonic sites of re-visioned freedom.

★ ★ ★

The following chapters introduce select members of Milton's early African American audience before surveying and examining their works and rhetorical styles of engaging with him as a secular yet sacred talking book. Chapter 2 examines Phillis Wheatley and her role in inaugurating an intertextual tradition of Miltonic engagement by African American writers and orators in the cause of liberty. Placing analytical emphasis on the traces of Miltonic presence in her elegies, the chapter examines her poetic flights of fancy from the depths of abject darkness to celestial light as rhetorical evidence of Miltonic remastery. While aiming to console her bereaved addressees in these poems, Wheatley remasters Milton as a black geography, winging herself and her people from Milton's hell to heaven in an aerial flight suggestive of racial liberation. Since her inaugural engagement with Milton in African American tradition defies post-Enlightenment thought concerning the intellectual inferiority of blacks, she ruptures demonic grounds that geographically exalt the race "out of the prison-house of experience" to levels of respectability up and along the Great Chain of Being.[170]

Chapter 3 surveys the trajectory of Milton's increased presence among diverse early African Americans subsequent to Wheatley's *Poems on Various Subjects*. The chapter explores Miltonic citations by Olaudah Equiano, *Othello*, and several black preachers and orators throughout the first two decades of the nineteenth century, before concentrating on David Walker's rhetorical and tonal echoes to *Paradise Lost* in his incendiary *Appeal*. Considered collectively, these echoes of Milton showcase a growing demonic reception that rhetorically enlists in the devil's party and sides with Satan in order to castigate the evils of slavery, acknowledge the infernal hero as a dissident preacher, or both. As I show in the chapter, these demonic receptions in early African American tradition occur at a time when Milton's popularity among the founding fathers, revolutionary patriots, preachers, and in grammar books continued to make an indelible mark on black culture.

Chapter 4 studies Frederick Douglass's satanic reception of Milton as a self-made man. Douglass's rhetorical identification with Milton sheds interpretive light on the former slave's militant antislavery sentiments as relayed in his first two autobiographies. Milton's presence in Douglass's first two narratives resonates with greater intertextual clarity through the interpretive lens of his "Self-made Men" orations. Douglass draws upon the Miltonic receptions of his speeches to reconstruct notions of black manhood and selfhood in his narratives. Rhetorically identifying with Milton's Satan in the cause of constructing a resistant black masculinity, Douglass remasters the epic writer through infernal schemas that capitalize upon figures of existential nothingness, which he associates with the ignominy of an enslaved brute. His engagements with Milton on this interpretive plane coincide with the militant rhetoric of contemporaries like Henry Highland Garnet, William Wells Brown, and Alexander Crummell, who also identified with the epic writer on the demonic grounds of a resistant masculinity.

Chapter 5 extends the work of rendering black women visible in Milton studies by examining Frances Ellen Watkins Harper's groundbreaking poem, *Moses: A Story of the Nile*. This work is groundbreaking because it is the only one of her more than 157 poems written in a form other than the ballad. This work completes and complicates Milton by remastering the genre of brief biblical epic and troping with *Paradise Lost* and *Paradise Regained*. Harper deviates from the ballad form to commemorate the end of slavery and to honor Abraham Lincoln following his assassination. Both occasions inspire Harper to memorialize and consecrate the U.S. landscape as a restorative site where paradise can be regained and freedom for blacks proves achievable. Breaking from tradition and writing under the poetic auspices of Miltonic epic, Harper ruptures her canon on the demonic grounds of her own aesthetic. The U.S. landscape is also impacted by this rupture, for in ignoring Milton in her work prior to 1868 then troping with him long after she encountered his canon, Harper appropriates the English poet outside of conventional patterns of time and space. Relative to her canon, this geographical rupture of temporality and spatiality conveys a demonic poetics that conveys that Milton is appropriate in her canon only after slavery has been abolished. With this demonic homage to Milton, Harper respatializes and consecrates the grounds of contention so she can rest in Edenic peace and be buried "in a free land."[171]

Anna Julia Cooper's secularized ministry as a womanist preacher is the focal point in chapter 6. Of particular note, Cooper's womanist ministry "revels" in Miltonic intertextuality. She not only revels in his poetics of regeneration, she classifies Milton as a "preacher-poet" who likewise writes poetry that proves "as perennial as man."[172] These rhetorical affiliations with Milton assist Cooper in rupturing oppressive geographical soundscapes so that black women's voices become audible in the commerce of intellectual ideas. In addition to rupturing the patriarchal soundscapes of her era, Cooper also affirms the power of black women for their heroic tones of Christian love. In shunning militant resistance and brute patriarchal force, Cooper, like Milton in *Paradise Regained* and *Samson Agonistes*, extols the virtues of "perfect passivity," which Erik Gray affirms as the "might of weakness."[173]

Chapter 7 synthesizes the militant receptions of Milton by his Africanist brotherhood with the Edenic model championed by members of his black sisterhood. Analyzing the black nationalist novel *Imperium in Imperio* (1899), the chapter focuses on Sutton E. Griggs's return to the rhetorical sites of Milton's hell,

Pandaemonium, and the "Infernal Council." Griggs returns to these demonic grounds as prophetic echoes that warn of the disastrous black revolt awaiting white America should it fail to desist from terrorizing the race through acts of violence and political disfranchisement. Griggs also structures his novel on the topographies of Milton's heaven and hell by contrasting the personalities of his dual protagonists as angelic and demonic characters who embrace opposing political ideologies relative to racial uplift. As symbolic representations of demonic militancy and "perfect passivity," respectively, Bernard Belgrade and Belton Piedmont also reflect on distinct reception practices of Milton by members of his black brotherhood and sisterhood. By echoing the infernal council of *Paradise Lost* and contrasting it against the Christian ethos of "perfect passivity," Griggs tempers and remasters the rhetorical appeal of Milton's Satan in a style reminiscent of black feminist strains.

The epilogue examines *The Autobiography of Malcolm X* in the interest of paving the way for subsequent readings of Miltonic presence as they appear in twentieth and twenty-first century African American literature. I examine Malcolm's Milton through an analysis of the political agitator's autobiography as well as the infernal rhetoric and worldview espoused in his speeches. In addition to delineating Milton's relevance for Malcolm X, the epilogue sets an analytical foundation for the charting of subsequent routes of Miltonic presence in the works of contemporary African American authors. Most important, it anticipates subsequent examinations of twentieth and twenty-first century writers who continue to make darkness visible by performing the word of Milton in poetic strains yet to be charted and analyzed.

2

PHILLIS WHEATLEY'S MILTONIC JOURNEYS IN *POEMS ON VARIOUS SUBJECTS*

Wheatley ruptured literary history by disturbing the demonic grounds of Miltonic interpretation. It was she who first sang and published a collection of verse in the African American literary tradition by allusively echoing the words of John Milton to significant effect. Singing in subversive intertextual strains in her only volume of poetry, *Poems on Various Subjects, Religious and Moral*, she defied post-Enlightenment ideas that conventionally regarded African Americans as intellectually inferior. Thomas Jefferson's denigration of Wheatley's poetic abilities as intellectually inferior in "Query XIV" of his *Notes on the State of Virginia* underscores what was culturally at stake relative to the publication of *Poems*. Espousing the racist notion that *Poems* was lacking in intellectual or creative merit, Jefferson recognized Wheatley's verse as "below the dignity of criticism."[1] Ironically, his dismissive assessment of the slave poet presents an interpretive occasion to examine the fugitive poetics governing her subversive approach to disturbing the demonic grounds of Miltonic appropriation throughout her *Poems*.

One of the interpoetic dignities of *Poems* ironically rests upon Wheatley's sublunary explorations in Milton's hell. Capturing a facet of this poetic artistry necessitates journeying to the demonic grounds of *Paradise Lost*. This hellish geography holds rhetorical significance for the advanced literacy Wheatley expresses throughout *Poems*. This performance of advanced literacy proves subversively artistic in the sense that Wheatley's appropriated figures require readers to pay special attention to interpretive details. Astute readers can only gain fuller comprehension and appreciation of her artistic messages by pursuing hermeneutic investigations that go beneath the interpretive surface of literal meaning. Each successive intertextual engagement with Milton in these poems enriches meaning on implied and inferential levels. Interpoetic engagements of this type, according to Gregory Machacek, "encourage minute attention to verbal detail and mnemonic retention of such detail," yielding aesthetic results that further dignify the beautiful science governing belated works.[2] Throughout *Poems*, Wheatley repeatedly dignifies her literary art by completing and complicating Milton on the demonic grounds of hell, then launching herself from these subterranean depths in favor of heaven's celestial spheres. Her sublunary navigations merit closer interpretive scrutiny than previous critics have accorded them because they underscore the degree to which *Poems* engages in diachronic and synchronic practices with Milton and his premier epic, *Paradise Lost*.

More specifically, Wheatley's sublunary navigations throughout her elegies constitute geographical flight patterns that allusively echo Milton in the form of a fugitive poetics. According to this interpoetic schema, Wheatley figuratively sets her sights on freedom from the melancholic vantage of physical enslavement. Completing and complicating *Paradise Lost* through these hellish ascensions of poetic adaptation ultimately empowers the enslaved poet to emancipate herself from the psychological chains of oppression and disempowerment. Her fugitive poetics also serves a political purpose bigger than her own self-interests. Apart from liberating herself, Wheatley's Miltonic engagements assist her in elevating her people several rungs up the Great Chain of Being. In remastering the English language through Milton, Wheatley enlarges the interpretive terrain of his demonic grounds of contention while also distorting the epic writer's meaning out of orthodox contexts. A pioneering forerunner of this neglected tradition in black letters, Wheatley bequeaths a distinct Miltonic legacy to subsequent African American writers, orators, and readers.

She not only sings, preaches, tests, and testifies with Milton to the Christian tune of his most cherished theme, liberty, she also achieves this ministry on demonic grounds but for messianic purposes of emancipatory uplift.

Before she could speak intertextually on the demonic grounds of Milton's hell, Wheatley would have to experience transatlantic translation via the Middle Passage. Captured and enslaved in Africa, then brought to America aboard the schooner, *Phillis*, Wheatley was purchased by John Wheatley of Boston in 1761. According to J. Saunders Redding, "she was judged to be in her seventh or eighth year and was educated under the Wheatley's tutelage."[3] Blyden Jackson notes the Wheatleys "nourished the young prodigy's precocity," teaching her grammar, some astronomy and ancient history in addition to "the Bible and the leading Latin classics, particularly Virgil and Ovid."[4] Wheatley soon displayed a talent for writing poetry, further showcasing her ability to speak in the tongue of her double-voiced heritage.

By 1772, she had written and compiled 20 poems of some literary distinction. At that time, many whites would have been inclined to doubt the possibility that an "uncultivated Barbarian from *Africa*" was capable of producing literary art of sterling quality.[5] Indeed, this postenlightenment ideology encouraged patrons to have her perform and defend her intellect before an assembly of distinguished intellectuals. The attestation prefacing her poems and bearing the 18 names of several judges, lawyers, and clerics, evidences Wheatley's success in satisfying the curiosity of this discriminating assembly (Wheatley 8). A year later, Wheatley traveled to England with her owner, made the acquaintance of several luminaries, including Selina Hastings, Countess of Huntingdon, before returning to colonial America with plans to publish the volume that would become *Poems*.

Thus far in literary history, critics have discussed Wheatley's double-voiced heritage in *Poems* as primarily neoclassical in character and bearing the strong influence of Alexander Pope. Several have sparingly recognized Milton as a literary influence; however, no theory exists that would explain the beautiful science governing Wheatley's remastery of the seventeenth century poetry from within the veil of racial interpretation and across the color line of literary studies. Wheatley's beautiful science of intertextual reception involves echoic engagements with Milton's literary persona, aesthetics, and figures.[6] Carolivia Herron is the first to acknowledge these connections between Milton and Wheatley beyond two or three sentences. According to Herron, Milton occupies an "equally powerful presence in [Wheatley's] consciousness" alongside Pope.[7] In particular, Herron reads Miltonic presence in Wheatley through the latter's use of epic blank verse. In a poem like "To the University of Cambridge, in New-England," for example, she argues, Wheatley uses "Miltonic blank verse to express her admiration of the union between cosmic knowledge and Christian truth." Contrasting the privilege her white college-educated addressees enjoy against the "lack of inspiration available to Africans" as posited in an earlier draft of the poem, Wheatley expresses these sentiments in Miltonic blank verse by economizing his epic lines and making extensive use of couplets.[8]

Appropriating Milton through couplets enables Wheatley to tropologically compress two canonical poets of influence in one instance of simultaneous expression. If Pope was "the master of the heroic couplet," as Donald Gibson contends, then Wheatley's phraseological adaptation of the form in her own verse points to the eighteenth century poet's direct influence on her poetry.[9] Among his many literary achievements, Pope translated Homer's *Iliad* and *Odyssey* into heroic couplets. While channeling Pope's novel contributions to epic tradition in poems like "To the University of Cambridge," Wheatley samples Milton also. Joseph Wittreich, commenting on Milton's indelible imprint on blank verse, supports scholarly annotations of Miltonic presence predicated on this allusive style of phraseological adaptation. In addition to "announcing a politics to the poem's readership," Milton's use of blank verse, "by the third decade of the eighteenth century," was understood "as 'the idiom of opposition.'"[10] Given eighteenth century readers' high regard for Milton, Pope's coupletizing of blank verse uses that style in political opposition to conventions of epic tradition. Wheatley, then, channels Milton through her appropriations of Pope. Coupletizing heroic epic while engaging two canonical authorities in literary tradition, Wheatley enmeshes Pope and Milton together when composing fragmentary strains of blank verse in *Poems*. This artistic approach to intertextual complexity verbalizes her racial triumph in overcoming linguistic codes of abjection that Western civilization has used to justify beliefs concerning black intellectual inferiority.

In my article in *Milton and Popular Culture*, I observe that "Wheatley's bereavement poems especially reveal an appreciation" for the epic poet.[11] I especially note how her engagement with Milton in these poems invokes a recall of the epic narrator in book 7 of *Paradise Lost*. Herron and my discussions concerning these intertextual codes in *Poems* provide interpretive foundations for further investigations of Miltonic presence as a product of Wheatley's transatlantic passage to the New World. In addition to enlarging the interpretive grounds of contention in Milton studies, Wheatley's intertextual Middle Passage reveals the infernal yet messianic science governing her reception of the epic poet. In her elegies, she does more than merely cite him as a signifier of black literacy. She spurs numerous recalls of Milton's hell and Satan's infernal sensibilities in order to transform the imprisoning geographies of the U.S. landscape into a psychological paradise that yields temporary freedom from the despair and anxiety induced by slavery.

Wheatley's beautiful science of Miltonic engagement in *Poems* is scattered and diffuse, not some trivial aesthetic element. Its design, therefore, anticipates a mode of phraseological adaptation that Erik Gray astutely associates with Victorian culture. According to Gray, Victorians appropriated Milton selectively and sparingly because the epic poet, by that time, attained a high celebrity status whereby he was understood as overfamiliar.[12] Milton was well on his way to becoming overly familiar at the time Wheatley wrote, as Sensabaugh notes in *Milton in Early America*.[13] Wheatley appropriates Milton selectively and sparingly because he exists as one of myriad poetic influences available to one gifted with a double-voiced heritage. Concerning her interpoetic attraction to Milton, his Christian ethos and sensibilities particularly resonated for her given the subversive tenor of her canon, which critics have only recently begun to explore in substantive detail.

Milton's scattered and diffuse presence resurfaces throughout *Poems* and is implicated as early as the opening poem, "To

Maecenas." In this poem, Wheatley expresses her ardent desire to write in epic strains. Specifically, she desires to write like Homer and "rival" Virgil (Wheatley 9). In a later stanza, she questions the Muses to account for the "partial grace" they extend to Terence, the only "one...of *Afric's* Sable race" who is endowed with the gift to produce any poetry of note (8, 9). Finding this tradition of literary exclusion unacceptable, she boldly decides to "snatch a laurel from her patron's head" (9). She performs this deed of poetic appropriation before commanding Maecenas to extend to her his "paternal rays" and to "defend [her] lays" as well (9).

Though Wheatley fails to mention Milton in this opening poem, her Homeric and Virgilian aspirations signal an ardent desire to occupy symbolic spaces in epic tradition. She continues to express this desire in subsequent poems. "Niobe in Distress," for instance, is evidence that this desire extends beyond Homer and Virgil, since the epyllion rewrites an episode from Ovid's *Metamorphoses*. With this poem, Wheatley showcases the influence of three major writers in epic tradition. Because Milton enjoys prestige as a major contributor to epic in the English language, it stands to reason that Wheatley would snatch a laurel from his honored head also. Wheatley snatches a laurel from Milton's head directly in "To the University of Cambridge" by incorporating his style of epic blank verse in her poem, as Herron astutely notes.[14]

The epyllion, "Goliath of Gath," snatches yet another laurel from Milton's canon by "making do" with fragments from *Paradise Lost*, including remnants of phraseological adaptation. "Making do," according to Karen Baker-Fletcher, refers to modes of creative activity where black women "produce abundance from scarcity." Additionally, this approach to art makes beauty "out of scraps of material, of making mouth-watering meals in the midst of scarcity, of making a dollar stretch."[15] Wheatley employs a similar approach when undertaking the artistic enterprise of composing her epic poem, "Goliath of Gath." In this poem, Wheatley "makes do" with Milton by echoing him in genre, literary form, and through several rhetorical figures. These echoic engagements prompt recalls of *Paradise Lost*, *Paradise Regained*, and Milton's third great poem, *Samson Agonistes*. First, the epyllion spurs a recall of Milton's great poems in that it also presents a poetic variation on a biblical story as a means for yet justifying God's holy word. Additionally, the epyllion's brevity recalls Milton's *Paradise Regained*, a shorter poem that Barbara Lewalski identifies as brief biblical epic. This tradition, she explains, "constitutes a distinct sub-species of the biblical epic category, with characteristic features which were developed partly as a response to the common problems inherent in writing poems both 'brief' and 'epic.'" *Paradise Regained* responds to these problems in literary tradition by "transforming common biblical epic materials and devices to the requirements of his own transcendent art."[16] Wheatley, according to her own design aesthetic, makes do with fragments from Milton's brief epic by snatching a laurel of influence from her canonical precursor.

Some of the more pronounced moments of Miltonic intertextuality occur in the epyllion through Wheatley's multiple demonic affiliations with Satan from *Paradise Lost*. On the basis of the poem's title alone, for instance, Robert Kendrick notes "Goliath of Gath" places emphasis on adversarial conflict and the terrors associated with spiritual warfare. This assessment leads him to consider the conflict between God and Satan in *Paradise Lost* as a type of intertextual backdrop for Wheatley's brief epic. More specifically, he argues, Wheatley's poem deviates from the Bible's focus on David's heroism by favoring an examination "into the nature of pride, the same sin committed by Milton's Satan."[17] Wheatley's epyllion, according to this reading, justifies God's ways by placing emphasis on an infernal adversary to Christian righteousness. In a later passage from Wheatley's poem, the epic voice inquires, "Who dares heav'ns monarch and insults his throne" ("Goliath," line 136). This question, Kendrick believes, "establishes an unmistakable analogy between the [monstrous Goliath] and Milton's Satan after the fall from heaven."[18] This series of demonic parallels paves intertextual paths for subsequent explorations of Wheatley's satanic ties to Milton's epic.

For instance, her second stanza inspires a recollection of Milton's epic when in describing the opposing armies of the Israelites she echoes the infernal militia in book 1 of *Paradise Lost*. She specifically echoes lines from book 1 of Milton's epic, spurring a recall of the moment when Satan surveys his legion, which the epic narrator describes as "angel forms who lay entranced / Thick as autumnal leaves that strew the brooks / In Vallombrosa."[19] Echoing Milton and, perhaps, Virgil, Wheatley depicts the warring Israelite and Philistine armies as "thick as the foliage of the waving wood," further noting that "between them an extensive valley lay" ("Goliath," line 12). Since Wheatley aspires to "rival" Virgil's lines, as mentioned in "To Maecenas," it is highly likely that Milton's allusion to the Italian epic writer is not lost upon her. However, additional echoes to Milton's epic in "Goliath of Gath" suggest that in this instance she particularly glories in snatching and appropriating laurels from *Paradise Lost* in her epyllion.

These echoes include her descriptions of Goliath as being synonymous with Satan's physical stature as depicted in Milton's epic. In Wheatley's poem, Goliath bears a "fierce deportment, and gigantic frame" not unlike Satan's massive physique ("Goliath," line 20). Goliath also wears "a coat of mail" that, according to the epic voice, "his form terrific grac'd." While the image calls attention to Goliath's heroic physique, Wheatley's syntactical arrangement echoes Milton's language. Similar to Milton, she reverses the conventional word order of adjectival modifiers, placing "terrific" after the noun it qualifies. Another Miltonic echo surfaces when she describes Goliath's spear as

> Dreadful in arms, high-tow'ring oer the rest
> A spear he proudly wav'd, whose iron head,
> Strange to relate, six hundred shekels weigh'd;
> He strode along, and shook the ample field,
> While *Phoebus* blaz'd refulgent on his shield.   (lines 24–28)

Wheatley's most discriminating Miltonic readers will recognize that this passage spurs a hermeneutic recall of Satan's spear. Milton describes this extension of Satan's military might as equaling "the tallest pine / Hewn on Norwegian hills" (*PL* 1:292–93). Wheatley's description of Goliath's weapon places emphasis on the weight of the instrument her infernal hero wields as opposed to the visual signifier of military might that one associates with Satan's spear. Nevertheless, these allusive intensifiers echo Satan's martial largesse toward keeping the infernal hero at the intertextual forefront of readers' minds. This rhetorical manipulation situates Wheatley on the demonic grounds of contention. By signifying upon Milton's Satan, Wheatley highlights Goliath's magnanimity in echoic relation to the imposing stature cast by the infernal hero in *Paradise Lost*.

Wheatley also draws attention to the sun, another poetic figure she uses to reflect associations between Satan and Goliath. The epic voice makes it a point to mention Goliath's shield as weighing "six hundred shekels" (line 26). Without specifying its impressive size, Wheatley directs her readers' attention to the sun's "refulgent" rays and the glare it casts upon the shield's shiny surface. Calling attention to the glare connects Goliath's weaponry to Satan's "ponderous shield," with its "broad circumference / [that] Hung on his shoulders like the moon [and] whose orb / Through optic glass the Tuscan artist views" (*PL* 1:284, 286–88). This rhetorical technique duplicates an image of blinding light that is again meant to inspire terror based on readers' cognitive ability to associate glaring metal with the idea of Herculean strength. Substituting the sun for the moon, Wheatley derives allusive power through a figure that continues to express her rhetorical fascination with Milton's infernal hero on the demonic grounds of poetic interpretation.

The epyllion's most pointed Miltonic reference on the demonic grounds of interpretive contention occurs near the middle of the poem. Once again Wheatley invokes a comparison between the infernal hero in an apostrophe to Goliath that asks, "say, shall grace to him be shown, / Who dares heav'ns monarch, and insults his throne?" (Wheatley 20). This veiled Miltonic inquiry invites a recollection of Satan by suggestively equating Goliath's crimes with Satan in *Paradise Lost*. No character in Western literature comes close to Milton's Satan in daring to wage war against God and insult his omnipotent rule in the process. When considered in tandem with Wheatley's various echoes to Satan and hell in *Paradise Lost* or his style of epic blank verse and reverse word orderings, her metaphorical allusion to the primary infernal hero of Western literary tradition positions *Poems* in a new light of Miltonic interpretation. As John C. Shields correctly notes, "Wheatley's texts are more complicated than careless readers are aware," especially in terms of Milton's "palpable influence," a precursor "she knew well" who manifests throughout *Poems* in a diffuse and fragmented manner.[20]

While Wheatley "makes do" with Milton to considerable extent in "Goliath of Gath," she engages him more subversively in her elegies on demonic grounds with messianic authority. In these bereavement poems, Wheatley occupies the demonic grounds of Milton's hell, then launches herself from this imprisoning landscape in order to uplift herself and her people in the celestial direction of heaven's holy light. Launching herself from these demonic grounds, Wheatley soars through hell in an emancipatory flight pattern that echoes Satan's winged escape in book 2 of *Paradise Lost*. She soars through hell and up to light according to this satanic flight plan, thereby liberating herself from the psychological hellspaces of abjection she inhabits in colonial America as a female slave. Adapting Satan's voyage to suit her own purposes, she adopts a fugitive poetics rooted in demonic rebellion but for messianic purposes of spiritual uplift and psychological freedom.

Wheatley's demonic echoes to Milton's Satan are grounded in the experience of the infernal hero, who awakens his fallen progeny and commands "long is the way / And hard that out of Hell leads up to light" (*PL* 2:433–34). Like Milton's hero, Wheatley charts a rebellious path to higher grounds of spiritual and psychological resistance. This rebellious quest empowers her to attain a personal freedom in and of the mind that, according to Shields, highlights the "vertical aspirations of the content of [her] verse."[21] Likewise, this fugitive poetics through Milton refutes post-Enlightenment claims of black intellectual inferiority. For instance, Henry Louis Gates Jr. has recognized that at this point in history, blacks were relegated to "a lower rung on the 'Great Chain of Being.'" He further asserts, "By 1750, man had been further subdivided, on a human scale that ascended from 'the lowliest Hottentot' to 'glorious Milton and Newton.'"[22]

Wheatley rises to these glorious heights in Milton throughout her elegies by descending to the demonic grounds of *Paradise Lost*. Her sublunary descent to Milton's hell reflects a distinct ritualized journey, the kind Mary Helen Washington identifies as critical to nuanced understandings of writings by black women. According to Washington, these ritualized journeys denote patterns of rhetorical travel that solidify a concretized aspect of writers' individual aesthetic visions. These individualized approaches to literary creativity merit investigation primarily because black women's ritualized journeys, "articulate voices," and "symbolic spaces" often differ from men's to the extent that critics have historically dismissed and undermined art that had been misunderstood as inferior.[23] Explicating the intertextual aspects of Wheatley's ritualized journeys through hell extends scholarly interest in her canon beyond the literary terrains of (African) American criticism into the grounds of contention in Milton studies.

In the past, the failure to accord interpretive significance to black women's ritualized journeys in literature has caused these "self-invented" women to be disinherited and lost outside of literary history due to the racist and patriarchal biases of critics. Shields, writing about Wheatley in another context, argues, "liberation for her fellow Americans, for her Black brothers and sisters and finally for herself is the subject of her poetry and prose."[24] Her ritualized journeys through Milton's hell highlight this rebellious attribute of her poetry by adapting Satan's flight pattern as an aerial trajectory that leads to states of psychological freedom. The intertextual benefits of these ritualized journeys through Milton's hell are most pronounced in her elegies where she continues to "make do" with her epic predecessor by occupying demonic grounds and speaking in the tongues of fallen angels for messianic purposes of uplift.

The descent to Milton's hell in her elegies constitutes a ritualized journey informing the symbolic space she fulfills as a kind of consolatory preacher. Appropriating Milton enables her to speak a dual-voiced discourse that ministers to the dejected spirits of her bereaved addressees while also addressing a more general white audience for crimes against black humanity. This latter aspect of her subversive discourse creates subversive space for Wheatley to minister to herself as a female slave. By using the occasion of uplifting the bereaved as a space for political activism, Wheatley "makes do" with the circumstances of her present situation and turns it into an event for spreading her gospel of black revolt. Typically, her sublunary journeys explore the demonic grounds of Milton in order to transport the subjects of her poems from states of hellish enslavement to scenes of heavenly freedom. This device emphasizes Wheatley's poetics of liberation, which Shields argues is vital to an understanding of her canon since this feature calls further attention to the "dialectic of slavery versus freedom" that repeatedly surfaces throughout her elegiac writings.[25] Concerning her ritualized journey through Milton's hell, this dialectic empowers Wheatley to liberate herself from the psycho-emotional despair of a second death, that of her physical bondage as a female slave.

The elegies often personify Death as a satanic tyrant who holds the deceased and the bereaved in captivity as if he were a slaveowner. Captivity is only temporary; however, Wheatley's fugitive poetics of liberation ultimately emancipates Death's victims from eternal bondage in the grave. Her elegies liberate the bereaved and the deceased through a motif of hellish ascension that echoes Satan's flight to paradise in book 2 of Milton's epic. Satanic affiliations surface as early as the opening lines of "On the Death of a Young Lady of Five Years of Age." Appearing after the poems to Sewell and Whitefield, this elegy is the first in the collection devoted to a layperson. It begins on the demonic grounds of hell with Wheatley exploring sublunary scenes of death and satanic struggle. In the opening couplet, Wheatley narrates a journey of hellish ascension by depicting the spiritual translation of a deceased girl "from dark abodes to fair ethereal light," further noting "Th' enraptur'd innocent has wing'd her flight" (Wheatley 16). A subsequent poem, "On the Death of a Young Gentleman," explores sublunary scenes of satanic struggle through apostrophe. For example, the persona asks, "Who taught thee conflict with the pow'rs of night, / To vanquish Satan in the fields of fight?" (17). Shortly thereafter, the persona looks heavenward and meditates on supernal phenomena. The sudden shift from hell to heaven implies an aerial journey from depths of woe to heights of joy. This journey achieves the status of ritual and motif as it continually resurfaces in *Poems'* subsequent elegies.

The third successive elegy, "To a Lady on the Death of Her Husband," personifies and addresses death as a "Grim monarch," who holds "vassals of thy sway" captive in "heavy fetters" (Wheatley 18). This is the last elegy in this first series of death poems. Wheatley follows this first group of death poems with the epyllion "Goliath of Gath" and the lyric "Thoughts on the Works of Providence." She resumes her interest in elegies following these two poems, returning once again to her ritualized journeys through

Milton's hell. The opening lines of "To a Lady on the Death of Three Relations," for instance, "trace[s] the pow'r of Death from tomb to tomb," providing commentary on the scope of the satanic tyrant's nocturnal might (Wheatley 29). Later, Death possesses the power "to call the planets from on high, / [and] to Blacken *Phoebus*, and dissolve the sky." Blackening the sun expands Death's nocturnal might and promotes a milieu "when all in his dark realms are hurl'd, / From its firm base to shake the solid world" (29–30). Collectively, these five elegies promote an interpretive schema that finds Wheatley personifying Death through a range of satanic figures. Depicted as a fallen star in this latter elegy, Death, like Lucifer in *Paradise Lost*, is presented as an evil tyrant who has been cast down and hurled from the glory of heaven.

"To a Lady" further intensifies this association with Milton's Satan by characterizing Death as a tyrannical monarch who possesses a "fatal scepter [and] rules" a world that trembles and "rocks from pole to pole" under the auspices of his infernal might. In the second stanza, Wheatley launches herself from these demonic grounds. Seeking to console her addressee, she revives the bereaved by focusing on the deceased brother's satanic flight. First, she bids the addressee to "behold thy brother number'd with the dead!" then counsels, "From bondage freed, the exulting spirit flies / Beyond *Olympus*, and these starry skies" (Wheatley 30). Here, Wheatley depicts the deceased brother as a fugitive from Death's bondage. Because he and their two deceased sisters are free in heaven, Wheatley charges the addressee to "Weep not for them, who wish thine happy mind / To rise with them, and leave the world behind." Moving beyond Satan's sublunary domain means forgetting Death and its tyrannical power to blacken the sun and "dissolve the sky," thereby making earth a region of hellish dominion (29).

Depicting the brother's fugitive flight from this demonic landscape also facilitates emotional healing that subsequently empowers Wheatley's addressee to focus on the glory of heaven rather than the grief provoked by hell's temporal dominion. Having descended to the depths of hell and released the deceased from bondage, Wheatley, in the third stanza, directs the addressee to "fix [his] longing view" on heaven and to be "mindless of sublunary scenes below." She wishes him to reject hell's demonic grounds even as she positions him to "ascend the sacred mount" where he may "seek substantial and immortal joys" and sing in a heavenly choir. Accompanied by "raptur'd seraphs" and his beloved family members, the deceased is depicted as enjoying spiritual translation and freedom in heaven. Similarly, this ritualized journey through hell and up to light translates Wheatley's addressee and members of her reading audience to new spiritual heights. Figuratively, theirs is a journey that conveys the oppressed and depressed from scenes of abjection to realms of freedom.

"To a Clergyman on the Death of His Lady," a subsequent elegy, also explores the geographies of earth, heaven, and hell but from a different rhetorical mind-set. In this poem, Wheatley transgresses the bounds of scriptural propriety by "thinking of [her]self more highly than [s]he ought" according to the post-Enlightenment attitudes of her times (Rom. 12:3). As a slave, she is expected to know her place as a servant and remain in it. However, her decision to appropriate the divine voices of Milton's epic muses, namely Urania, transgresses the acceptable bounds of servitude. To envision and articulate herself as a sable muse for her white addressees is to claim racial equality with them while also deigning herself superior to them intellectually, poetically, and spiritually. For Hilene Flanzbaum, Wheatley's multiple appeals to classical muses throughout her poetry serve political ends. Specifically, they serve as the "very means by which [Wheatley] usurps power for herself and claims a berth for her own thoughts, emotions, and desires."[26] "To a Clergyman" instantly evidences Wheatley's insubordinate behavior in this regard, for instead of starting from the lowly depths of Milton's hell, it begins from celestial stratospheres where Wheatley is found contemplating the "heav'nly music [that] makes the arches ring" (Wheatley 30).

The reference to "heav'nly music" echoes Milton's "Sing Heav'nly muse," one of the first commands rendered by the epic narrator in book 1 of *Paradise Lost* (*PL* 1:6). In the invocation beginning book 7, the epic narrator enlists the aid of a heavenly muse as well. Specifically, the narrator petitions Urania to "govern" his song and "find" a fit audience for his verse (*PL* 7.30, 31). Earlier in this passage, the narrator mentions Urania "with eternal Wisdom didst converse /...and with her didst play / In presence of th' Almighty Father, [who was] pleased / With thy celestial song" (*PL* 7.9–12). Through this sororal association, the narrator acknowledges Urania as a poetic muse who likewise embodies attributes of spiritual virtue.

Wheatley's opening stanza in "To a Clergyman" similarly blends notions of celestial music with the attributes of virtue and wisdom. For instance, the persona credits heaven as a celestial sphere where "virtue reigns unsully'd and divine" (Wheatley 30). The subsequent line acknowledges wisdom as "throned" with honor and inhabiting a space where "all the graces shine." The mood of celestial virtue produced by Wheatley's treatment of this heavenly atmosphere inspires an echoic reminiscence of Milton's characterization of Urania as divine at the opening of book 7. According to Milton's epic narrator, Urania can "drive far off the barbarous dissonance / Of Bacchus and his revelers" who he understands as nothing less than "Heav'nly" (*PL* 7.32, 39). In Wheatley's poem, the clergyman's spouse is depicted as seated "amidst the radiant throng" of wisdom, an image that imbues the aerial scene with a *kleos* of celestial royalty (Wheatley 31). This echoic reverberation of Milton sets the stage for Wheatley's dual performances as an epic muse and consolatory preacher. She accents these rhetorical performances by intertextually assuming what may be considered Milton's disembodied voice.

Wheatley assumes the roles of epic muse and consolatory preacher by voicing Milton's reverse adjectival phrasings such as "wisdom thron'd," "praise eternal," "choirs angelic," and "bliss divine." Reversing conventional word order in these phrases infuses Wheatley's poem with reverberations of Miltonic English. These instances of phraseological adaption subsequently lend her elegiac voice a distinct character of epic authority. In particular, incorporating Miltonic diction into her elegies endows these poems with a thematic power that champion liberty as a triumph over death. This echoic device works in tandem with Wheatley's appeals to Milton's heavenly muses, which lends her consolatory discourse a divine status that proves suitable for ministering to bereaved mourners. For instance, when she beckons the clergyman to look to heaven, he is made to focus on—if not feel—a mood of celestial and angelic praise. Inducing him to feel and experience these sentiments works to distract him from dwelling on the grief he would otherwise feel relative to his wife's death. Wheatley's echoes to Milton's heavenly muses, therefore, aid her in creating a consolatory soundscape capable of liberating the clergyman from the fetters of bereavement and matrimonial loss.

Wheatley sustains the heavenly muse's relevance in the second stanza. After describing the clergyman's spouse as free from bondage and "to flesh no more confin'd," she addresses the bereaved husband in Miltonic language that spurs continued reminiscences of the epic muses. She explains to the clergyman that his wife is now endowed with a "heav'n-ascended mind" and commands him to "Say in thy breast shall floods of sorrow rise?" and "Say shall its torrents overwhelm thine eyes?" These imperatives appropriate the commands of Milton's epic narrator, who in Book 1 of *Paradise Lost* proclaims: "Say first what cause / Moved our grand parents in that happy state / ... to fall off / From their Creator and transgress His will" (*PL* 1.28–31). Milton's epic narrator utters the phrase again in book 1, line 376, bidding the heavenly muse to identify members of Satan's fallen crew by name. Later, in book 7, the narrator commands, "Say, Goddess, what ensued when Raphael / The affable archangel had forewarned / Adam by dire example to beware" the evil wiles of the Apostasy (*PL* 7.40–43). Each of these petitions requests the muses' assistance, specifically soliciting their divine aid in telling an epic story accurately and with poetic grace. Wheatley, by contrast, echoes these Miltonic phrasings as extensions of her ministry of consolation.

In her continuing efforts to console the clergyman, Wheatley portrays heaven as a celestial geography of freedom. Encouraging her bereaved addressee to divert his focus from demonic landscapes that can only increase his despondent spirits, she declares, "Amid the seats of heav'n a place is free," adding, "angels ope their bright ranks" for him in the hopes he will someday join his wife in heaven (Wheatley 31). As in her preceding poem, heaven represents a site of freedom from death's monarchial grip. Wheatley underscores this point by capitalizing upon the motif of descent and having the spouse "lean downward from the empyreal sky" in order to rhetorically uplift the spirits of her ministerial charge. Next, the clergyman's spouse implores her husband to "come away and share with me the raptures of the skies" where "bliss divine to mortals is unknown." She, too, speaks in Miltonic tongues, occasionally resorting to styles of syntactical reversal as evidenced by the phrase "bliss divine." Having the spouse descend into the narrative of the poem then speak in a Miltonic tongue endows Wheatley with the poetic voice of a heavenly muse. Like Urania, she descends from celestial heights of heavenly glory in order to revive the hopes of those who cannot see their way clear on earth.

By the end of the second stanza, Wheatley's poetic descent lands on the demonic grounds of Milton's hell. Near the stanza's conclusion, the clergyman's spouse reminds him that Christ's redemptive power "make[s] eternal glory all our own" since "He in his death slew ours." A few lines later, she alludes to Milton's infernal crew, proclaiming, "Vain were their hopes to put the God to flight / [and] Chain us to hell, and bar the gates of light" (Wheatley 31). The reference to flight creates demonic reverberations within the stanza that spur several key moments in book 6 of Milton's epic. In Western literature, there is no other depiction of the war in heaven that rivals Milton's vivid treatment of this celestial event. Therefore, referencing the war between the Son and the infernal crew is apt to spur a hermeneutic recall of *Paradise Lost*. Wheatley again capitalizes upon one of Milton's most iconic biblical scenes, remastering it in the form of a mascon. As a Miltonic mascon, Wheatley's couplet potentially activates in readers an intertextual recall of a signal poetic event in *Paradise Lost*.

Spurring a recall of the fallen angels' defeat in heaven facilitates Wheatley's efforts to preach a gospel of revolt that might further distract the clergyman from his grief. At the same time, landing on these demonic grounds also works to remind the clergyman that his wife has been spared from eternal bondage in hell by Christ's redemptive grace. If the infernal crew's hopes proved vain, as the wife argues, then the term "flight" assumes special rhetorical significance given its loaded contextual meaning throughout book 6 of Milton's epic. For instance, upon his confrontation with Abdiel before the two engage in battle, Satan chides the obedient angel, "thou return'st / From flight, seditious angel, to receive / Thy merited reward" (*PL* 6.151–53). After a few exchanges, Abdiel puns on Satan's language, admonishing the fallen angel: "Yet chains in Hell, not realms, expect: Meanwhile / From me returned, as erst thou saidst, from flight, / This greeting on thy impious crest receive!" (*PL* 6.186–88).

Abdiel's response accurately predicts Satan and his crew will find themselves chained in hell. For instance, book 1 presents Satan in chained bondage. The "infernal Serpent" dwells in "bottomless perdition... / In adamantine chains and penal fire" (*PL* 1.34, 47–48) and is later presented as lying "Chained on the burning lake" (*PL* 1.210). The clergyman's spouse activates a recall of Abdiel's prediction and these images of infernal enslavement from book 1 of *Paradise Lost*. These intertextual echoes work in tandem with Satan and Abdiel's references to flight, which is a term that surfaces yet again as their martial engagement comes to an end. Moments before Satan's defeat in celestial battle, the epic narrator explains that the infernal crew "to final battle drew, disdaining flight / Or faint retreat," yet they find themselves routed from heaven under the auspices of the Son's divine might (*PL* 6.798–99).

The clergyman's spouse spurs another echoic recall to Milton's epic with her phrase "bar the gates of light." With this, the clergyman's spouse evokes a hellspace of enslavement suggestive of Milton's "darkness visible" (*PL* 1.63). The spouse's depiction of hell as an imprisoning geography of penetrating darkness echoes Milton's demonic landscape by referencing the site as devoid of light. In Milton's epic, hell is described as "a dungeon horrible on all sides round / As one great furnace flamed yet from those flames / No light but rather darkness visible" (*PL* 1.61–63). Likening this horrible dungeon to a flaming furnace, then diffusing the infernal imagery of that simile by negating the figure of light, one proceeds through a linguistic operation not unlike the spouse's description of hell. Barring the gates of light allows the spouse to blacken the hellspace while at the same time calling attention to light in its absence. Describing hell in this manner constitutes a kind of acoustical echo where the repetition of a phraseological utterance resonates in a cave of signification that reverberates through linguistic style rather than in exact speech. As is the case concerning her references to flight, the spouse's verbal echoes to Satan and Milton's hell assist Wheatley in fulfilling her ministerial duties by using poetry as an office of the pulpit.

Thus far, Wheatley's landing on the demonic grounds of Milton's hell reinforces the Son's defeat of Satan, death, and the grave. As a mode of diachronic intertextuality, Wheatley's rhetorical descent facilitates a poetic ministry aimed at inspiring salvific uplift. This tactic produces a mental picture destined to encourage the clergyman to focus on regaining paradise rather than dwelling on its loss. To this end, Wheatley's rhetorical strategy in the poem begins in the celestial stratosphere, lands on demonic grounds, and reascends in the direction of celestial freedom. Wheatley, by fleeing hell, also facilitates a ministry of uplift and consolation that ultimately releases her from the psychological chains of enslavement. Her aerial voyage is grounded in echoes to Milton's Satan. Like Satan in book 2, she soars to freedom on the wings of fugitive rebellion. More specifically, she reclaims the geographies of spiritual and physical enslavement that would otherwise tether her to demonic grounds of hegemonic domination. Instead of succumbing to this imprisoning landscape, she rebels and escapes from it, launching herself upward and finding freedom in the celestial stratosphere.

Wheatley's journey to the demonic grounds of Milton's hell and her subsequent voyage up to celestial light echo Satan's flight patterns in *Paradise Lost*. After Satan volunteers to escape the bounds of hell in an effort to exact revenge on God by corrupting Adam and Eve, he soon "shaves with level wing the deep, then soars / Up to the fiery concave tow'ring high" (*PL* 2:634–35). His upward journey continues when Sin unlocks the gates of hell that separate the fallen angels from heaven's celestial spheres. "Flutt'ring his pinions vain," he, "by ill chance," rides upon the winds of "some tumultuous cloud" and lands in the elevated empire of Chaos (*PL* 2.933–36). Next, he "Springs upward like a pyramid of fire" through hell until he reaches the "utmost orb / Of this frail world" where "light appears...from the walls of Heav'n" (*PL* 2:1013, 1029–30, 1035). Book 2 concludes with this image of Satan's fugitive escape from hellish enslavement. Interestingly, book 3 begins by echoing this satanic voyage through hell.

Milton's epic narrator resumes this aerial voyage from hell's depths to spheres of celestial blessedness at the beginning of book 3. Lamenting his blindness, the epic narrator forges a satanic connection with Milton's infernal hero. The opening passages find the narrator metaphorically describing his psychological journey to wellness as he assumes an aerial voyage that soars through hell and up to God. The narrator begins by hailing "holy Light," his metonym for Christ, which also functions as a veiled allusion to Milton's blindness as well. After extolling the "offspring of Heav'n" with hymns of praise, the epic voice next announces his decision to "revisit [God] with bolder wing, / [having] Escaped the Stygian pool" (*PL* 3.1, 13–14). References to "bolder wing" and the "Stygian pool" metaphorically reiterate Satan's journey through hell by alluding to figures of hellish depths and aerial flight. The epic voice sustains this allusive voyage through hell in subsequent lines where he mentions his "obscure sojourn" and his "flight / Through utter and through middle darkness" (3.15–16). Additionally, his infernal voyage further inspires him to sing of "Chaos and Eternal Night" (3:18). He ultimately praises his savior, who in the divinity of a heavenly muse, teaches the epic narrator "to venture down / The dark descent and up to reascend / Though [his flight was] hard and rare" (*PL* 3:19–21).

Wheatley's elegiac flights echo Satan and the epic voice's winged journeys through hell. Following examples from *Paradise Lost*, she frees herself from hell's demonic grounds and charts aerial paths that lead to spheres where freedom reigns. "To a Clergyman" and other elegies in *Poems* follow this trajectory of hellish ascension. The concluding stanzas of "To a Clergyman," for instance, feature the spouse's descent to Milton's hell and the persona's sudden pivot to the theme of salvific uplift. Immediately following the stanza that ends on the demonic grounds of Milton's hell, the persona, yet chronicling the wife's actions, notes that she turns "from mortal scenes her eyes, / Which beam'd celestial radiance oer the skies" (Wheatley 31). Wheatley's pivot from hellish scenes on earth to those in heaven dramatizes the ascension motif with which she has been tropologically engaging throughout her elegies. She accentuates Milton's diffuse yet reverberating presence through this intertextual schema by occasionally appropriating phraseological structures that echo the epic writer's syntactic reversals.

In the final stanza, Wheatley bids the clergyman to dispense with grief and to "rise sublime" and "to equal bliss aspire" (Wheatley 31). While both phrasings encourage the clergyman to assume celestial flight, the latter syntactically invokes Milton's echoic presence. By splitting "aspire" from the infinitive "to" and placing it after the noun, Wheatley indulges in a phraseological practice suggestive of Milton's syntactical reversals. A second instance of this reversal occurs two lines later when she commands him to cease complaining, "but be to heav'n resign'd." Immediately following this line, Wheatley acknowledges "Twas thine t' unfold the oracles divine, / To sooth our woes the task was also thine" (Wheatley 31). The phrase, "oracles divine" echoes Miltonic phrasing by unconventionally placing the adjective after the noun it modifies. These three concentrated instances of syntactical reversal accent the motif of hellish ascension that contribute to showcase Wheatley's intertextual interest in Milton's figures and rhetorical cadences.

In terms of the stanza's elegiac message, Wheatley's ideas in tandem with her diffuse Miltonic echoes promote the consolatory and liberating scope of her poetic ministry. As she explains in the concluding lines of this final stanza, she willingly performs these ministerial duties as a benevolent repayment for the spiritual services the clergyman previously provided the community. Wheatley is particularly grateful for the clergyman's sacrifice in devoting his life to disclosing God's divine oracles for others' salvific benefit. Wheatley repays his sacrifice by simply bidding him to "permit the muse a cordial to impart" (Wheatley 32). Here, Wheatley expresses a desire to provide ministerial solace to the clergyman in his trial of bereavement. She does not reference some abstract muse of poetry; rather, she deigns herself worthy of the divine vocation. As preacher and poetic muse, she simultaneously occupies two symbolic spaces. Serving in this twofold capacity, Wheatley spiritually and poetically lends the clergyman her "tenderest aid" by rescuing him from hellish bereavement, winging flight to heaven, all the while echoing and embodying aspects of Milton's Urania.

Notwithstanding her inclinations to serve the clergyman ministerially, Wheatley's ascensions through hell, coupled with her several complications and completions of Milton, benefit her as well. In addition to exploring the subversive depths of Milton's hell, Wheatley "makes do" with the genre of elegy as a medium for preaching gospels of revolt against Death as a metaphor for slavery. This subversive style of allusively troping with Milton functions through a series of demonic apostrophes and epithets that gain enhanced signifyin(g) power as a result of a pronounced amount of enslavement imagery. Wheatley's apostrophes typically personify Death as a satanic tyrant of the underworld, using epithets like "grim monarch" to spur elevated echoic relationships with Milton's infernal hero. Throughout the elegies, Wheatley portrays the subjects of her poems escaping from the hellish chains of death as they wing fugitive flight to the blessed regions of celestial freedom. An enslaved poet herself, such poetic musings on freedom and self-emancipation could not have been lost upon a literary artist of Wheatley's intellectual capacity.

Flanzbaum notes this subversive dynamic in Wheatley's poetry, directing attention to the poet's frequent use of words like "unbounded" and "enthroned" and her imagery of "silken fetters" and "soft captivity." These descriptive terms, Flanzbaum asserts, indicate that the "issues of enslavement and empowerment are not as far from Wheatley's consciousness as readers have usually maintained."[27] Shields concurs, expressing his belief that the "general topic of freedom [reflects] the central subject of all [Wheatley's] works."[28] Freedom is no less a thematic concern in the poem "On the Death of the Rev. Mr. George Whitefield," where Wheatley's persona beckons readers to witness the prophet's "tow'ring flight" through the heavens, "though *arrested* by the hand of death" (Wheatley 15–16; my emphasis). Her use of "arrest" connotes bondage similar to Milton's tendency to use various terms like "vassal" and "enthrall" throughout books 1 and 2 of *Paradise Lost* to spur images of enslavement suggestive of the fallen angels' experience in hell. Wheatley's echoic parallels to Milton in this manner produce yet another interpretive ground for understanding her style of demonic appropriation toward messianic ends. Such a subversive technique ultimately enables Wheatley to minister to herself as well as her bereaved addressees, since both audiences are in need of spiritual solace and poetic aid.

Completing and complicating Milton through the loaded rhetorical imagery of enslavement reveals Wheatley's distinct approach to testing and testifying "to life as it was and could be." Consistent with Foster's assertions, this mode of remastering Milton and the English language occasions a subversive practice that showcases writers' linguistic dexterity in acquiring the colonizers' language then revolting against their oppressors in that same discourse but on different semantic registers. This same method helps explain the signifyin(g) property of Wheatley's numerous references to slavery in her elegies. These references inflect the already loaded rhetorical meanings of her aerial voyages through hell, further elevating her along subversive paths to freedom. These aerial paths lead her from hellspaces of darkness and bondage and carry her up to freedom in heaven's holy light.

In this metaphorical sign system, darkness signifies death, spiritual bereavement, enslavement, and hell as the penultimate imprisoning geography. On the other end of this interpretive spectrum, Wheatley's figures of light symbolize resurrected life and spiritual consolation, with heaven serving as an unparalleled landscape of freedom. Dwight McBride recognizes a similar system of signification at play where binaries of light and darkness emerge in Wheatley's writings. Noting that this visual field "commonly connoted good and evil, especially in Christian symbolism," McBride regards this rhetorical pattern as significant in that it functioned as a mechanism for "drawing [Wheatley's] readers into an immediate compliance" with her and her gospel just before making the "liberationist 'turn' that would convict their consciences."[29] Conveying her literary parishioners along this spectrum of darkness and light, therefore, inflects her elegies with added nuances of Miltonic subversion. Implicated in each of these elegiac voyages is that inward turn that finds the enslaved poet moving from a passive acceptance of her bondage to conceiving rebellious routes capable of respatializing those grounds by transforming them into sites where poetic flights of liberation become possible.

Stark rhetorical contrasts between darkness and light in these elegies reflect Wheatley's inward turn as an echoic evocation of Satan's fugitive movement. This inward turn presents another manifestation of Wheatley's ability to assume "power over words," which she uses to "discover freedom within her poetic compositions."[30] When she descends to the depths of hell's darkness only to ascend to heaven's holy light, Wheatley arrives at a poetic method for escaping the clutches of Death's temporal grip while simultaneously mitigating the power of its sting. In particular, she vanquishes Death by rhetorically escaping its tyrannical hold on her poetic subjects. She escapes according to a demonic flight that Milton's Satan charts as well. Like Satan, Wheatley wills herself to achieve freedom though she occupies demonic grounds. Not content to remain tethered to this imprisoning landscape, Wheatley spiritually transports herself from this geography of domination by figuratively launching herself to psychological freedom in the marvelous light of paradise. Her fugitive path to psychological freedom extends the rhetorical trajectory of her coded antislavery message by charting a rebellious (dis)course rooted in a messianic language of intertextual remastery.

"On the Death of the Rev. Dr. Sewell" capitalizes upon the motifs of Miltonic descent and ascent, combining them with a fugitive poetics that subtly conveys Wheatley's antislavery sentiments. The motif of Miltonic presence appears as early as the third line of her tribute to Sewell by echoing Milton's "Hail, Holy Light" from book 3 of *Paradise Lost*. She echoes this Miltonic apostrophe by offering Sewell the following salutation, "Hail, holy man [who has] arriv'd th' immortal shore" (Wheatley 13). Next, she depicts Sewell soaring through darkened hellspaces where he wings "his rapt'rous way / To the blest mansions in eternal day." To solidify this echoic relationship to Milton still further, Wheatley considers Sewell among those who have felt God's "grace divine," the redemptive seal "which rescues sinners from the chains of guilt" (14). Again, her reverse syntactical ordering of "grace divine" continues to echo Milton's phraseological style. Linking this instance of phraseological adaption with enslavement imagery further spurs an association with Milton on the demonic grounds of poetic interpretation while also reconfiguring the meaning of Christian redemption beyond spiritual connotations.

The racialized implication of this subversive technique can be seen in earlier lines of the fourth stanza, where Wheatley commands "ye rich, ye poor, ye fools, ye wise" to behold Sewell's example, "nor let his monument your heart surprize." Included among this abject group are the "indigent, whom he has fed" and the "youth, to whom he oft has told / God's gracious wonders." These apostrophes evidence Wheatley's empathetic commitment to uniting privileged and marginalized social classes together in the cause of spiritual freedom. By considering these marginalized groups alongside the rich and the wise, the enslaved poet expresses a commitment to including those whom society typically overlooks. These "subtle wars" waged by Wheatley in her poetry reflect what Sondra O'Neale recognizes as the poet's "conscious manipulation of prevailing associations of blackness."[31] This technique functions as a subversive marker that subsequently reveals Wheatley's antislavery stance. Hers is a sympathetic stance that includes the downtrodden, which spurs a symbolic recognition of Africanist presence as a racialized subject that is rhetorically embedded within and throughout the enslaved poet's elegies.

"On the Death of the Rev. Mr. George Whitefield," the second elegy in the collection devoted to a luminary, intensifies Wheatley's antislavery commitments more emphatically through schemas of Africanist and Miltonic presence. Unlike the Sewell poem, Wheatley's elegiac tribute to Whitefield explicitly acknowledges blacks alongside tropes of Miltonic geography and enslavement imagery. The first stanza contains the first Miltonic echo of phraseological adaption by praising the deceased preacher for his sermonic "strains of eloquence *refin'd*" (Wheatley 15). A second instance of echoing Milton by reversing word order contrary to conventional syntactical arrangements occurs in the second stanza, where Wheatley credits the fiery preacher of the Great Awakening for charging America's "youth that ev'ry *grace divine* / Should with full lustre in their conduct shine" (15; my emphasis). Her phraseological adaptions of "eloquence refin'd" and "grace divine" layer her elegiac tribute with echoes of Miltonic presence that further code her poem with inflections of emancipatory rhetoric. Re-citing Milton through this phraseological mode of allusive echo indirectly inflects her poem with intertextual strains of liberty as is consistent with her predecessor's innovative style of versification.

The second stanza dramatizes this intertextual relationship with greater symbolic devotion when Wheatley suddenly shifts from "hail[ing]" this "happy saint" to presenting him in aerial flight. Having "wrestled with his God by night," Whitefield now enjoys an emancipatory translation from the hellish depths of spiritual warfare and darkness to the celestial spheres of "heav'n's unmeasur'd height" (Wheatley 15). According to Wheatley's celestial descriptions, the moon and the stars witnessed Whitefield's struggles when he was alive and triumphing over principalities of darkness that fought to thwart his ministry of winning souls for Christ. Nighttime in these lines symbolizes a metonymic theater that allows heavenly bodies and Wheatley's readers to witness Whitefield's ministerial struggles on the spiritual stage of life.

In keeping with this metaphorical schema, principalities of darkness pose a military threat to Whitefield's ministerial vocation by lording monarchial rule over the Christian souls he attempts to save. Refusing to relent before Whitefield and the salvific office of the pulpit he occupies, these principalities stand in defiant opposition to the emancipatory power of the Christian Gospel. Notwithstanding the power of their demonic might, Whitefield "wings with rapid course his way, / And sails to *Zion* through vast seas of day." Depicting Whitefield's spiritual translation through this schema, Wheatley encourages readers to understand the devoted minister has successfully vanquished his foes in the theater of night. Having achieved spiritual translation through Wheatley's metaphor of fugitive flight, Whitefield has successfully soared through night's demonic landscape. Conveyed to the shores of celestial freedom on the poetic wings of Miltonic intertextuality, Whitefield regains paradise as an emancipated and liberated soul.

Though Whitefield defeats the principalities of darkness, his spiritual translation is not confined to himself alone. When Wheatley, quoting Whitefield, commands his beneficiaries to "take" or behold him as a spiritual model, she seizes an opportunity to emancipate her general readers from their grief and marginalized groups from spiritual fallenness or disadvantage predicated on Christian values. This latter assembly comprises the "wretched," "starving sinners," "the thirsty," "preachers," "*Americans*" and, especially "ye *Africans*," who through Whitefield's office learned that the "*Impartial Saviour*" died for them also (Wheatley 15–16). Of particular note, Whitefield's gospel to Africans inspires Wheatley to formulate a theological message of her own design. If through Whitefield's ministry Africans have been "Wash'd in the fountain of [Christ's] redeeming blood," their spiritual translation further inspires Wheatley to prophesy they "shall be sons, and kings, and priests to God" as well (16).

As she does in the Sewell elegy, Wheatley reaches out to the socially marginalized and includes them among the privileged set. This time, she explicitly names and includes Africans within this group, further prophesying and heralding the greatness that shall accrue to them in subsequent generations. This prophetic stance of racial inclusion and imminent greatness ruptures conventional ideas about Africans' racial standing in the post-Enlightenment era. As a result, Wheatley's commingling of Miltonic presence with her poetics of social inclusiveness voices a gospel of black revolt that rebels against racial hierarchies as they are understood relative to the Great Chain of Being. Including Africans as members of the "angelic train," as she does in "On being brought from Africa to America," then prophesying their imminent greatness, Wheatley preaches a gospel of black revolt that intertextually translates herself and her people from scenes of demonic abjection to those of celestial freedom through a subversive remastery of Miltonic English.

Wheatley extends a racialized reading of her elegy in the third stanza by underscoring Whitefield's status as a spiritual fugitive. According to the final stanza, he is no longer "arrested by the hand of death" but soars overhead in heaven's "eternal skies" (Wheatley 16). Whitefield may have been arrested by Death, but he now enjoys emancipation from his previous spiritual bondage. Wheatley especially asks fellow Africans to "take" and emulate Whitfield's example, she does not restrict her gospel of black revolt to an audience external from herself. If she believes blacks can imitate Whitefield's example and "be refin'd" as well, then she similarly voices a refrain of political freedom that is antithetical to the post-Enlightenment ideologies of her day concerning Africans as primitive and inferior. As a poet whose literary productions perform this emulative quality, Wheatley similarly refutes racist ideologies concerning black inferiority.

Announcing herself to readers in this subversive manner enriches Wheatley's intertextual affiliation with Milton. By refuting the scripts of black intellectual inferiority through her poetry and Miltonic engagements, Wheatley expresses herself in a distinct voice of infernal rebellion. Speaking through this intertextual medium allows her dissident voice to test and testify with and against these scripts in the diffuse and fragmented language of her Miltonic echoes. These moments of coded Miltonic intertextuality are further accented by an abundant use of enslavement imagery and loaded racialized signifiers. Such features lend her poetic discourse both an infernal and messianic property because they enable Wheatley to launch herself from demonic grounds of abjection to celestial heights of heavenly glory and freedom. When she propels to these heights of Edenic freedom in her elegies, she likewise enjoys spiritual translation not unlike the kind Whitefield experiences in the elegy devoted to him. Overall, this assembly of interpretive practices with and in the English language empowers Wheatley to respatialize the imprisoning geography of her circumstances. Since she liberates herself from the demonic grounds of U.S. slavery by speaking in the echoic tongues of Milton's fallen angels but with messianic authority, these Miltonic engagements signal a kind of fugitive poetics that has escaped critics for more than two centuries. Reading this poetics across the color line in literary studies yet within and beyond the veil of racial interpretation especially showcases Wheatley's interpoetic gifts of speaking in the tongues of fallen angels for purposes of emancipatory uplift.

When Wheatley respatializes the demonic grounds of Milton's hell in the tongues of fallen angels, she performs a variation of a sacredly coded discourse familiar to certain Christian audiences. Speaking in tongues as discussed in biblical Scripture references a divinely sanctioned mode of spiritual speech. Only those operating under the unction of the Holy Ghost can speak its discourse. The apostle Paul identifies this mode of unintelligible speech as a divine and spiritual gift. Unintelligible to laypersons, its message requires translation by certain sanctified members of God's elect whose task is to edify the worshipping aggregate by making this coded speech plain to the masses. In an extension of this practice, Wheatley speaks in the tongues of Milton's fallen angels throughout many of her elegies. Adopting this coded speech pattern and inflecting it with Miltonic resonances aids her politically poetic vocation as a late eighteenth century freedom writer.

In her elegies, Wheatley speaks in rebellious tongues that coincide with Mae G. Henderson's theories concerning black women's multilingual modes of literary expression. According to Henderson, black women's cultural practice of speaking in tongues reflects a "discursive diversity or [the] simultaneity of discourse" that ultimately privileges linguistic fluency in heteroglossia and glossolalia.[32] The practice proves vital for women whose "complex subjectivity" often positions them "in contestorial dialogue with the hegemonic dominant and subdominant discourses" informing their situatedness along axes of race, gender, and other social identities.[33] As a female slave and Christian poet, Wheatley finds herself writing in a double bind. She circumvents and triumphs over this existential obstacle by speaking in the tongue(s) of Milton's fallen angels and keeping her sights focused on the glory of heaven and the freedom its paradise promises for believing parishioners.

By making Whitefield and the subjects of subsequent elegies fugitives from Death and hell, Wheatley, in effect, delivers a fugitive gospel that speaks in both a fallen and infernal tongue but with messianic authority. "On the Death of a Young Lady of Five Years of Age" is characteristic of this strategic technique. In the poem, the daughter of grieving parents ascends to heaven "from dark abodes to fair ethereal light" (Wheatley 16). Wheatley also depicts the daughter as being "Freed from a world of sin, and snares." In addition to portraying their daughter as a fugitive from death, Wheatley instructs both parents to seek their own escape from the spiritual bonds of death. That is, she encourages them to escape "life's tempestuous sea, / And from its rocks, and boist'rous billows free" safely arrive upon heaven's "blissful shore" (Wheatley 17). Resituating both parents on these celestial shores reunites the couple with their "happy babe to part no more," making it possible for the entire family to enjoy eternal freedom far from the abyss of hell's dark abodes. This technique of emancipating the daughter from hell, then ending the poem at celestial heights of freedom, preaches a Christian message of consolation and uplift. That message similarly benefits rhetorically from Wheatley's subversive interest in enslavement imagery.

Wheatley continues to occupy demonic grounds and preach Miltonic echoes in the tongues of fallen angels in "On the Death of a Young Gentleman." This time, she manipulates the device to minister to herself through sorrow songs of Miltonic uplift. The elegy immediately addresses the deceased on demonic grounds of intertextual subversion in the first line when the persona inquires of the deceased gentleman, "Who taught thee conflict with the pow'rs of night, / to vanquish Satan in the fields of fight" (Wheatley 17). Her apostrophe regards the gentleman's skirmish with death as a satanic struggle replete with figures of enslavement and Miltonic presence. For instance, when the persona asks, "Who strung thy feeble arms with *might unknown,*" she frames the interrogative as a struggle to attain freedom while simultaneously echoing Milton's style of syntactical reversal.

The fifth line echoes Milton with greater acoustical clarity by re-citing the infernal hero's language. In book 5 of *Paradise Lost,* Satan addresses the fallen angels using the following monikers: "Hear all ye angels, progeny of light, Thrones, Dominations, Princedoms, Virtues, Powers, / Hear My decree, which unrevoked shall stand" (*PL* 5.600–02). He uses this form of address again in book 10 immediately prior to his metamorphosis into a serpent. Wheatley echoes these forms of satanic address when she alerts the young gentleman that "War with each princedom, throne, and pow'r is o'er" (Wheatley 17). Speaking in the tongues of Milton's fallen angel in this instance enables Wheatley to name the experience of death as a phenomenon that is analogous to satanic tyranny. Wheatley revolts against this oppressive force by finding inspiration in the gentleman's fugitive escape from hell's imprisoning geography.

She begins by praising the deceased gentleman for nobly defeating Death in a Miltonic triumph of messianic valor. Similar to the Whitefield poem, the deceased gentleman duels with Death on satanic terms. For instance, he wrestles "the pow'rs of night" only to "vanquish Satan in the fields of fight" (Wheatley 17, 18). Wheatley concludes the stanza by affirming the gentleman's triumph in war on the demonic grounds of Milton's hell. Extolling his victory over death, she concludes, "the scene is ended to return no more" (17). She suddenly shifts from the depths of Milton's hell to scenes of "heav'nly grandeur" and spiritual freedom. In spiritually translating the gentleman to celestial freedom, Wheatley also lifts her own despondent spirits through elegiac song.

For instance, lines 7 through 18 in "On the Death of a Young Gentleman" register Wheatley's disconsolate spirit. First, she pines for spiritual aid that is greater than her own poetic gifts. She wishes her poetic muse could behold the gentleman who is "seat[ed] on high" and take inspiration from his fugitive success (18). Could her muse behold the gentleman's example, she reasons, it would tap into a source of poetic inspiration that would benefit from his "sweet...anthems" and "divine...joys." By extension, the muse would subsequently "exalt" Wheatley's "strain" as well. These pangs of poetic anxiety reveal temporary fits of self-doubt concerning the efficacy of her poetic gifts of consolation. This self-doubt further intimates the psychological strongholds that death has on her poetic ministry. Similar to the figurative experiences of the many fugitive subjects in her elegies, Wheatley, in spirit, finds herself chained to hell and under Death's despotic rule. If Death arrests Wheatley's poetic powers as it has bound the spirits of the deceased she writes about in her elegies, then it has enslaved her on the demonic grounds of a psychological hellspace of self-doubt. This psychological arrest functions to inhibit her from preaching a liberating gospel of consolation to her addressees and herself. Wheatley, as a result of this dynamic, becomes a slave twice. Both a literal slave and a spiritual one to Death as well, she can only emancipate herself by discovering and charting fugitive routes that will uplift her and those in her charge from the hellish regions of sorrow and enslavement.

Wheatley emancipates herself from these demonic ruins of enslavement by musing on poetry as a Miltonic office of the pulpit. She finds her fugitive inspiration and a "sov'reign remedy" in the gentleman's seraphic gifts (18). According to her, he is capable of "sooth[ing] the troubles of the mind to peace," "still[ing] the tumult of life's tossing seas," and "eas[ing] the anguish of the parents' heart" as well. These mediations are significant to her because at the moment she expresses these ideas, she yet doubts the spiritual efficacy of her "sympathizing verse." For example, she wonders, "Where is the balm to heal so deep a wound," and questions "where shall a sov'regn remedy be found" to heal these earthly woes? Finally, she petitions the gentleman's seraphic aid and asks him to "look...from thine heav'nly bow'r" above and pour his "full joys" into the bosoms of her bereaved throng. His intervention, she believes, will control "the raging tempest of their grief" in addition to "spread[ing] the dawn of glory through the soul."

Most important, Wheatley remains confident that the gentleman's poetic intercession will prove successful in bidding the members of her throng to "eye the path the saint departed trod, / And trace him to the bosom of his God." Ending the poem with this concluding couplet revives her spirits and the elegy's mood of spiritual uplift. Again, troping with Milton through the reverse phrasing of "saint departed," Wheatley draws poetic inspiration from her literary predecessor and the gentleman as well. A beneficiary from both spiritual guides, Wheatley speaks in the tongues of fallen angels and descends to the demonic grounds of hell before liberating and uplifting the departed saint and herself on paths to spiritual freedom. Once again, the enslaved poet exercises freedom over her circumstances by mitigating the sting of death through the sorrow song of her poem.

"To a Lady on the Death of Her Husband," the fifth consecutive elegy and the final poem to appear before the epyllion "Goliath of Gath," solidifies and consecrates this initial literary ritual of echoing Milton in the cause of freedom and self-emancipation. These elegies are critical for understanding the significance of Wheatley's Miltonic echoes because a beautiful science governs the rhetorical interplay between the writer's fugitive poetics, sublunary explorations, and aerial flights. Moreover, these features permeate her elegiac writing as markers of antislavery subversion. In this fifth elegy, Wheatley resumes her practice of speaking in the tongues of fallen angels while occupying the demonic grounds of Miltonic intertextuality. For example, her apostrophe in line 1 addresses Death as a "GRIM monarch" and identifies the casualties of this personified tyrant as "vassals of thy sway" (Wheatley 18). Enslavement imagery becomes more pronounced as the poem progresses. For instance, death rules with "heavy fetters [that] keep / [one's] senses bound in never-waking sleep." Other references to bondage or tyrannical rule appear throughout the poem as well. These include phrases such as "ties of love," "sovereign of the grave," "heavy fetters keep," and "senses bound in never-waking sleep."

Wheatley underscores the motif of hellish enslavement further by appealing to satanic rhetoric that again spurs recalls to Milton's epic. In one critical passage of echoic intertextuality, Wheatley instructs her addressee that Leonard, the deceased husband in this poem, is fettered in hell's darkness and bound in death

> Till time shall cease, till many a starry world
> Shall fall from heav'n in dire confusion hurl'd,
> Till nature in her final wreck shall lie,
> And the last groan shall rend the azure sky.

The reference to "starry worlds" coupled with the image of being hurled from this celestial region bears a Miltonic likeness to Satan in *Paradise Lost*. For instance, book 1 of the epic explains Satan was "Hurled headlong flaming from th' ethereal sky" (*PL* 1.45). Additionally, Wheatley's "starry world" evokes a rhetorical connection to Lucifer, whose name signifies light. If the visual image of starry worlds being hurled from the sky in this Wheatley passage spurs a recall of Milton's Satan, the association is strengthened by the phraseological adaption of reverse word ordering. Here, again, Wheatley echoes Milton by positioning the verb "hurl'd" after "confusion."

This phraseological echo reverberates with greater clarity and resonance when considered alongside Wheatley's remastery of book 9. There, nature responds to Adam and Eve's spiritual fall with sighs and groans of dejection. Once Eve bites the apple, nature "sighs," "g[iving] signs of woe, / That all was lost" (*PL* 9.783–85). Nature responds similarly when Adam partakes of the forbidden fruit. In this lamentable moment, earth trembles while nature's pangs give "a second groan" (*PL* 9.1000). The setting turns more threateningly ominous when the epic narrator reveals how the "Skie lowr'd and muttering Thunder, som sad drops / Wept at [the couple's] compleating of the mortal Sin" (*PL* 9.1002–03). Wheatley's poem echoes nature's response to Adam and Eve's spiritual fall but changes the context through its prophesy of apocalyptic reunion. According to the logic of Wheatley's poem, the mourner's husband will not awake until that moment when "nature in her final wreck shall lie, / And her last groan shall rend the azure sky" (Wheatley 19).

The rending of a blue sky in the poem suggests divine judgment that is motivated by Wheatley's visual image of a cataclysmic thunderstorm. This variation on the rapture and Christ's return triggers a visual of Adam and Eve's fall in paradise. Calling attention to their spiritual fall likewise facilitates a recall of the eternal death in hell that awaits them if not for Christ's redemptive grace and intercession on their behalf. Wheatley's invoking of the rapture and the couple's death sentence by extension does not end on the grounds of Milton's hell, however. Rather, it paves the way for a spiritual renewal that is to be experienced in the sacred "hills of light." In the same way that Adam and Eve receive grace and may hold to the prospect of regaining paradise upon Christ's return, so too, can Wheatley's poetic couple hope to achieve spiritual and marital reunification with God and each other. Until her appointed time in death and resurrection, the bereaved widow, according to Wheatley's consolatory gospel, must wait for her husband's "active soul [to] claim" his body's "divine immortal frame." Only then shall husband and wife regain paradise as a reunited couple and enjoy celestial freedom in God's heaven.

While this reality causes the widow to cry, Wheatley wastes little time in moving beyond the grief precipitated by the hellish landscape opening the poem. Wheatley immediately charts an upward course to consolatory scenes of heavenly freedom. Encouraging the widow to "cease" her crying, she lovingly commands her to fix her view on aerial heights where *Leonard* may be seen "mount[ing] and leav[ing] the earth behind." Next, she admonishes the wife to "prepare to pass the vale of night" that she may join him in the afterlife. By the poem's conclusion, Leonard "welcomes [his wife] to pleasures more refin'd" that are "better suited to th' immortal mind." Referencing their immortal future implies the eternal happiness the widow may expect to enjoy in heaven's afterlife. This ending whisks yet another fugitive away to spiritual freedom, which is typical of Wheatley's elegies and her symbolic role as a preacher-poet in echoic dialogue with Milton.

Collectively, Wheatley's flights of poetic descent and ascension evidence subversive alterations of geographical space. In keeping with McKittrick's theory concerning black women's "cartographies of struggle," Wheatley's aerial navigations through hell contest those "geographies of domination" working to keep the enslaved poet in her subordinated place in colonial America.[34] Wheatley resists these encroachments upon her existence by retreating into subversive poetic figures of Miltonic echo and engagement.

Turning inward as a fugitive escape into the celestial regions of her imagination, she explores heaven and hell as cognitive terrain that ultimately grants her a modicum of psychological freedom and peace of mind. Because these Miltonic flights of fancy begin on the demonic grounds of racial captivity, Wheatley's aesthetic vision showcases the poet's creative ability to test and testify with the subversive limits of poetry as a vehicle for radically transforming the hegemonic geographies of her times.

Ultimately, speaking in the tongues of fallen angels through Milton grants Wheatley poetic license to vocalize her oppression and rise above it through a creative discourse of her own election. In this sense, she evangelizes to herself and others in the form of a modern-day apostle. Both a female slave and secular preacher, Wheatley speaks to diverse audiences in her elegies while also reestablishing her own dialectic identity as a racial Other. Her performance occurs on the demonic grounds of Miltonic contention and rises above this figuratively oppressive geography by winging flight upward to heights of celestial freedom. This poetics, therefore, showcases Wheatley's seditious success in triumphing over the linguistic displacement she experiences as an enslaved poet writing in the language of her oppressors. That triumph manifests through her remastery of English, which completes and complicates Milton by synthesizing echoic fragments of his motifs and phraseological phrasings with her coded use of enslavement imagery.

An extant poem, "Reply to...the Gentleman in the Navy," adds a fitting closure to a fuller appreciation of Wheatley's triumph in remastering the English language via Miltonic engagement. In addition to contextualizing her attraction to Milton, it highlights her fugitive poetics as being in intertextual synchronicity with the epic writer's sublunary explorations and the palpable impact those rhetorical journeys have on Wheatley's elegiac art. In "Reply," Wheatley expresses admiration for Milton. Heralding Milton in this poem highlights a stylistic approach of naming and ordering experience in poetry, which, according to Washington, enables critics to "put together these scraps and pieces written and signed" by black women writers, that others may come to know and understand the value of the "coherent framework" governing their art with greater clarity and interpretive precision.[35] While "Reply" identifies Sir Isaac Newton as one source of literary influence, it also expresses Wheatley's desire to "fix the humble Afric muse's seat / At British Homer's...feet" (Wheatley 87). With this line, Wheatley tests and testifies with Milton as the British equivalent to Homer, honoring him both as a master of epic in the English language and as a literary and aspirational ideal.

Subsequent lines reveal why she reveres Milton as a model worthy of poetic emulation. First, she regards his descriptions of Eden as authentic. In particular, his Edenic descriptions remind Wheatley of her African homeland. For instance, she praises his vivid portraiture of Eden's "bowers" with its "flowing streams" and "verdant shores." When she encounters these lines from his epic, "Pleasing Gambia on [her] soul returns." Thus, she is led to proclaim: "just are thy views of Afric's blissful plain, / On the warm limits of the land and main." These sentiments attest to her belief in the accuracy of Milton's Edenic descriptions of Africa. They also attest to what she regards as the efficacy of Milton's theological mission. By declaring Milton's views as "just," Wheatley intimates and voices her belief that the English poet successfully achieved his epic purpose in "justify[ing] the ways of God to men" (*PL* 1:26). Naming Milton in this manner endorses the epic writer as a key intertextual figure whose greatness subsequently informs her literary experience as a Christian poet.

Most important, Wheatley extols Milton's ritualized journey of descending to the underworld. Specifically, she praises

> Europa's bard, who the great depth explor'd,
> Of nature, and thro' boundless systems soar'd,
> Thro' earth, thro' heaven, and hell's profound domain,
> Where night eternal holds her awful reign.   (Wheatley 87–88)

These lines delineate her delight in the ritualized journeys Milton assumes in his epic. She particularly emphasizes the *depths* of Milton's poetic and subterranean explorations, taking the time to qualify hell's confines as a landscape of utter darkness. This attraction to Milton's hell and its "profound domain" lends clarity to the ritualized journey she undertakes in her elegies, where Wheatley descends to the underworld, lands on demonic grounds, then soars to celestial heights. In other words, she descends to Milton's demonic grounds as a rhetorical practice that facilitates her efforts to elevate herself and her people from the depths of enslavement and cultural ignominy to intellectual heights of social prestige.

Read from these demonic grounds of contention in Milton studies, Wheatley may be understood as launching herself from a variety of figurative hellspaces, most notably the U.S. landscape of racial injustice. She transforms these geographical hellspaces of racial domination and uses them as expressive footstools to freedom and self-uplift. A preacher-poet who rebelliously occupies the demonic grounds of Miltonic intertextuality, Wheatley consoles, ministers, and uplifts her bereaved addressees from the depths of hellish enslavement and despair to heights of salvific joy. A slave herself, Wheatley's rhetorical indulgence in figures of hell and enslavement cannot be divorced from any disconsolate pangs she would have felt regarding her subjugated status in colonial America. Triumphing over these existential trials and pitfalls led Wheatley to find liberating solace in the psychological freedom that subversive engagements with Milton might provide.

Like Satan, Wheatley and those writers and orators in early African American tradition who would follow her intertextual lead mount the rostrum of political dissent, then launch themselves from demonic grounds of abject darkness. Completing and complicating Milton through various strategies of black revolt, they do their part in helping to elevate the race along the Great Chain of Being one rung at a time. Wheatley's *Poems* inaugurated this tradition. This collection that Jefferson regarded as "below the dignity of criticism" now provides contemporary readers a foretaste of the subversive rhetorical strategies available to early African American writers seeking fugitive routes of racial uplift by remastering the English language. If, in their time, they found themselves existing below ground level due to racist and other exclusionary paradigms of injustice, they would radically transform these demonic grounds by following in Wheatley's rebelliously poetic footsteps. In other words, they would find interpoetic inspiration in the secular light of Milton's "darkness visible," even as the Bible continued to serve as the sacred "lamp unto [their] feet" (Ps. 119:105).

3

BLACK AUDIO-VISIONARIES AND THE RISE OF MILTONIC INFLUENCE IN COLONIAL AMERICA AND THE EARLY REPUBLIC

The journey out of hell and up to a marvelous light of freedom in early African American literature continued to complete and complicate Milton well beyond the publication of Wheatley's *Poems*. As early as 1788, a writer adopting the name Othello published two essays in Matthew Carey's "widely circulated magazine, the *American Museum*," containing infernal echoes of books 1 and 2 of *Paradise Lost* as a means for critiquing slavery.[1] A year later, Olaudah Equiano published *The Interesting Narrative of the Life of Olaudah Equiano, or Gustavus Vassa, the African. Written by Himself*. This slave narrative appropriates four passages from Milton's epic as an intertextual strategy for justifying the Christian tenets of his antislavery views. Subsequent orators and pamphleteers like Lemuel Haynes, Peter Williams Jr., William Hamilton, and David Walker would contribute to this slow yet sure tradition in early African American literature and oratory. Drawing equally on both the spoken and written word, these orator-poets might be best understood as black audio-visionaries. These black audio-visionaries occupy and produce demonic grounds by transforming the geographical space of the speaking or reading moment into amphitheaters of black revolt. On these grounds where geographical space is re-produced to audiovisual effect, Milton's black audio-visionaries project diffuse scenes from his satanic epic. Their strategies of intertextual engagement with Milton allow audiences to see, hear, and relive the terror of hellish slavery or godly censure as the literary occasion may demand.

The term "audio-visionary" extends the phenomenon of intertextual influence that Joseph Wittreich examines in *Visionary Poetics: Milton's Tradition and His Legacy*. In that work, Wittreich contextualizes the book of Revelation as a biblical source of poetic influence "on first-rate minds and talents" like Milton.[2] This tradition, with its apocalyptic scenes, inspires the literary art of visionary poets, providing them "a whole aesthetic system" that bridges prophecy with literature and provides artists a range of poetic "subjects and an iconography for representing them."[3] Black audio-visionaries complete and complicate Milton on these demonic grounds of influence by extending this literary art form to oratory. Whether they imbue their oratory with scenes from Milton's satanic poetry or blend them with aural effects in their slave narratives, essays, or political pamphlets, these audio-visionaries extend Milton's afterlife within and across the literary color line as practices of freedom and racial uplift. Additionally, completing and complicating Milton through their audio-visionary poetics coincides with the epic writer's own oratorical talents. For instance, Wittreich, in *Why Milton Matters*, acknowledges the epic writer's presence in his prose writings as that of an "orator/preacher."[4] Several of the black audio-visionaries examined in this chapter were preachers by vocation. Others channeled the vocation through the oratorical power of their religious convictions and rhetoric.

As preachers, these audio-visionaries projected their declamatory voices, inflecting them with vivid scenes strategically selected from Milton's epic. They preached Miltonic gospels that exposed and indicted the hell of slavery, often capitalizing upon the moment to prophesy God's imminent wrath. Because their gospels contained fragments of Miltonic engagement, they produced a distinct variation on a style of visionary poetics that fuses epic with prophecy, therefore constituting "'total form' by containing within themselves all other forms and by achieving a perfect harmony through a combination of styles."[5] Milton's satanic epic makes poetry out of this mixing of genre, producing epic prophecies. Bringing satanic epic into union with godly prophecy, Milton, channeling his infernal hero, "re-creates [poetic tradition] in a different image" than that which was bequeathed to him.[6] This descent into fallenness and poetic tradition manifests as a satanic encounter that replays "a certain discontinuity between [readers'] own horizon[s] and that of the text."[7] Black audio-visionaries perform similar acts of satanic re-creation, troping with Milton by projecting and replaying scenes of hellish abjection or Edenic fallenness. An end goal of this audiovisual art form with Milton aims to promote cognitive experiences of emotional woe that lead readers and auditors to embrace a spirit of antislavery revolt.

Collectively, this transitional wave of black audio-visionary essayists, prose writers, preachers, and orators embraced an infernal spirit of Miltonic revolt in the messianic cause of liberty. They preached their gospels of black revolt from 1787 to 1829. Unequivocal in rhetoric and sometimes tone, these declamations function as *command performances*. Audiences did not command these aural/oral performances as the term is traditionally understood. Rather, black audio-visionaries preached Miltonic scenes of satanic abjection or Edenic fallenness as rhetorical weapons for *commanding* members of their white audiences to see, think, and feel the hell of slavery and the spiritual convictions of their own fallenness as citizens of a mock-republic. Conversely, these same gospel performances *commanded* black audiences to testify to a rhetoric of poetic fallenness and its salvific gospel of Africanist redemption. Appealing to rhetorical audiences in unequivocally direct or assertive tones of language, black audio-visionaries adopted manners of speech that either punctuated their roles as orators or intimated the literary *ethos* of a commanding public speaker.

Black audio-visionaries operate in this mode of Miltonic tradition, sampling and signifying on his epic while relaying and replaying scenes, pictures, or linguistic signs associated with *Paradise Lost*. Remastering Milton through these audio-visionary techniques, they extend the geographical project Wheatley inaugurated in *Poems*. They follow Wheatley's Miltonic lead, contributing their part in elevating the race to higher heights of social respectability.

More specifically, they achieve this ministerial vocation from various literary and oratorical platforms, pitching their voices with Miltonic tones of orality/aurality in order to raise the race out of abject darkness and further into the marvelous light of freedom.

Like Wheatley, these preacher-poets' literary performances of black geography re-produce space and place by rendering darkness visible in opposition to practices of spatial domination. They reproduce geographical space by turning the literary or oratorical moment into an amphitheater of black revolt based on various Miltonic appropriations. This radical transformation of geography qualifies as a practice of demonic grounds where intertextual ruptures of voice defy convention, orthodox meanings, and Edenic readings of a fallen U.S. landscape. In keeping with McKittrick's theory concerning "black expressive cultures" and "the art of noise," black audio-visionaries' subversive engagements with Milton project a "sayability" of geographical space.[8] These events challenge traditional hegemonic spatial relationships. Moreover, to "say geography" in these texts is to express new evaluations of the rhetorically loaded landscapes in *Paradise Lost*. Preaching these re-evaluations of the U.S. landscape ultimately offers a subversive commentary on the early republic and its declension from the divine errand that projects its promise in the image of a New Jerusalem or city on the hill.

These reevaluations of select Miltonic landscapes are inconsistent with orthodox interpretations of these iconic sites as they are featured in Milton's epic. Africanist borrowings of any number of Miltonic tropes are seldom what they seem at face value. For instance, hell becomes more than a landscape of satanic suffering, while Eden is seldom, if ever, the same paradise Milton describes. In these intertextual moments, "the arbitrary relations between the [Miltonic] sign and its referent" undergo declension.[9] In other words, their interpretive values are either inflected to connote realities of black suffering or they undergo a decline in interpretive meaning as rhetorical expressions of critique and spiritual indictment. Thus, Milton's hell, according to this alternative remastery of language, undergoes interpretive amelioration, inflecting the geographical signifier beyond the fictive landmark it typically represents into a demonic landscape descriptive of African Americans' sufferings in their real worlds. Relative to Edenic tropes, paradise comes to represent spiritual wickedness or fallenness in contrast to Puritan ideals. Black audio-visionaries capitalize upon this rhetorical strategy when they preach gospels of revolt with visual snippets appropriated from Milton's epic. This aesthetic mode articulates a special theological language of God-talk that endows their epic prophecies with a wonder-working power of black liberation theology.

James H. Cone refers to black styles of God-talk as a passionate mode of spiritual discourse rooted in the sufferings and humiliations of Africanist experience. Its passionate rhetoric and sense of urgency, he contends, is "consistent with the depths of the wounds of the oppressed," ever seeking to make the application of theology penetratingly real for members of its primary audience.[10] Whether black audio-visionaries commit themselves to oratorical acts of censure or prophecy, they complement their theological messages with strains or textual snippets of epic verse either directly or allusively. Espousing their Christian concepts and doctrine in this style of highly pictorial language translates to a cultural mode of black liberation theology.

Discussing the limitations of American white theology, Cone notes, "it has been basically a theology of the white oppressor, giving religious sanction to the genocide of Amerindians and the enslavement of Africans." Black liberation theology counters these limitations in its discourse. Its doctrine "arises from an identification with the oppressed blacks of America, seeking to interpret the gospel of Jesus in the light of the black condition."[11] It is also a theology of survival that affirms black existence as human and rejects the racist norms of white Christianity that traditionally have propounded a gospel equating blackness with nonbeing. In its most strident iterations, black liberation theology "speaks with a passion in harmony with the revolutionary spirit of the oppressed," one that is insistent in its strivings to "reveal the satanic nature of racism," in addition to taking on the task of "killing gods that do not belong to the black community."[12] These theological contexts enrich the Christian discourse of black audio-visionaries by infusing their gospels with a life-sustaining measure of relatable cultural content.

Throughout the early republic, this content often involved gospels of censure and prophecy that were rich in infernal and supernal imagery. Additional tenets included artistic engagements with epic and prophecy. Black audio-visionaries blended and enriched these elements by orally projecting visual scenes and snippets at select moments in their oratorical addresses or in texts simulating public oratory. This enlargement of an aesthetic that Wittreich identifies as a "visionary poetics" reshapes the oral and aural dimensions of literary productions, transforming the page to a stage and vice versa. In both instances, the orator or writer preaches and prophesies, turning his rhetorical platform into an amphitheater where oral and visual projections of key Miltonic scenes may be relayed or replayed in the manner of a subversive art form.

According to Wittreich, a visionary poetics may be seen in an apocalyptic work like John's book of Revelation. A work of prophecy whose character and scope are epic and encyclopedic, Revelation has "had a great effect on first-rate minds and talents" throughout history, primarily because it is governed by "an artistic code whose aesthetic system breathes life into poetic productions of great minds."[13] Additionally, literary aesthetes tend to hold apocalyptic texts in high regard because the subject matter and artistry of these master works often "furnish great minds with an iconography for representing significant subjects, concepts, and ideas."[14] For Wittreich, Spenser and Milton are the first English poets to blend the art of epic vision and prophecy and literature in the English tradition and to bequeath this visionary poetics to subsequent generations of writers such as the British Romantics and the black audio-visionaries discussed in this chapter.

Milton, as Wittreich explains, ranks as "the perfecter of prophetic tradition," primarily because he writes as a "poet-prophet, both a legislator of reform and a transformer of the world," who also "authors poems apocalyptic in their intent."[15] Furthermore, he twins epic with prophecy by blending the satanic with the messianic and emphasizing Christ's contrasting temperaments of meek long-suffering and divine wrath. Like Revelation, Milton's gospel blends these aspects into symbolic word pictures whose chief purpose serves to "brighten the mind, to exalting and purifying all its faculties" in order to "force open the doors of perception [and] teach men to see not *with* but *through* the eye."[16] Black audio-visionaries give rise to Miltonic influence in early African American tradition when they sample and signify on select scenes from *Paradise Lost* for messianic purposes of revolt. They use these vivid audiovisual snippets to complement their theological art. Through these Miltonic borrowings, they extend the epic poet's afterlife into the nineteenth century in early African American tradition. Adopting Milton and his epic as audiovisual symbols, a transitional wave of black audio-visionaries accentuates their gospels of revolt by reenvisioning the epic poet's talking book as an instructional text for preaching rebellion.

This transitional wave of audio-visionaries receives Milton's sacred but secular text through three primary yet intersecting routes of social transmission: the intersecting domains of U.S. politics, education, and religion. By the late 1700s, Milton enjoyed cultural prestige in colonial America to the extent that general audiences of white readers would have been familiar with the epic writer and much of what he represented in literary history and Christian doctrine. For example, according to Lydia Dittler Schulman, "what attracted Americans to Milton" at the time of the American republic "was not his institutional proposals but his defense of republican liberty, qualified by his insistence that true liberty requires an educated, virtuous citizenry."[17] This aspect of Milton's attractiveness was well into circulation by the time of the Revolutionary War. Milton's social energy circulated widely during this period as a result of his "vibrant interpenetration of religious and political traditions."[18] Most important, as Dittler explains, American radicals understood "Milton's distinctive notion of liberty as obedience to reason" and were, therefore, primed to read his works "with special acuity [to] his epic treatment of the problem of temptation under conditions of liberty."[19] Circulating in this way, Milton could not help but fall on the attentive ears of African Americans of the period.

As Dickson D. Bruce Jr. notes, "slaves and slaveholders alike [were] significant links between Revolutionary conflicts and the security of the slave system."[20] Along the eastern seaboard, African

Americans were privy to and caught the sparks of revolution themselves. They may have overheard fragments of these sentiments from slaveholders, encountered them in newspapers and through the pamphlet wars, or of their own volition. Regardless, the themes of civil, religious, and political liberty circulated so widely that "black writers began to enter the lists themselves, giving increased notoriety to the links between slavery, color, and the Revolutionary cause and illuminating the kinds of complex relationships that both stimulated and constrained their efforts."[21] Undoubtedly, some of the political sentiments they heard, wrote, espoused, and believed during this period were impacted or influenced by Milton and his thoughts on liberty that proved so attractive during the rise of the American republic.

New England receptions of Milton were no less enamored with the canonical poet. By "the last two decades of the eighteenth century," K. P. Van Anglen speculates, "Milton would likely have been among the New England elite's pantheon" of most revered literary artists.[22] Esteemed as such by enterprising poets, educators, and an array of religious, philosophical, and political thinkers, Milton continued to be celebrated even though he tended to satisfy contradictory aims. As Van Anglen explains, this side of Milton's canonical fame was "uniquely amenable to self-interested manipulation, because he spoke to—and so seemed to provide answers for—the crisis of authority that continued to confront them." Notwithstanding these crises, Milton ultimately served as a "literary model for Americans concerned about achieving greatness," further exemplifying the attributes of an ideal consensualist authority figure, a genius whose sublimity of vision, moral elevation, seriousness of purpose, didactic skill, and religious inspiration all made him a fitting *alter ego* for dominant class authors."[23] The New England Milton circulated this brand of influence beyond the final two decades of the eighteenth century. This aspect of Miltonic influence continued to find its way into the early republic and beyond, surfacing in the cultural arenas of national politics, religious instruction, education, and literary movements. Various strains of this tradition crossed literary color lines as well. Those currents gave rise to a trajectory of increased Miltonic engagement in African American tradition, informing gospels of black revolt that were audio-visionary in nature.

In the discourse of national politics, Miltonic allusions surface in writings by John Adams, Thomas Jefferson, James Madison, James Monroe, and John Quincy Adams. Jefferson "was powerfully drawn to Milton's Satan, for whom he never lost his youthful sympathy," according to John S. Tanner and Justin Collings. Adams, by contrast, read the infernal hero as a "morally flawed demagogue."[24] Both held on to their respective receptions of Milton throughout their lives, as evidenced in entries from their commonplace books and diaries as well as several personal letters. The founding fathers' contrasting attitudes toward Milton's Satan leave indelible imprints on their political views. For instance, Tanner and Collings find Jefferson's "warm enthusiasm for the French Revolution is in keeping with his Romantic sympathy for Milton's demonic rebels."[25] Adams, true to his response of satanic revulsion, maintains a disdain for these causes of political rebellion, which for him suggest states of anarchy and chaos. These political views hold interpretive significance beyond both presidents' private views. Machacek argues that allusions "are no less 'cultural' a phenomenon than the relations between literary texts and such things as sumptuary laws, accounts of the colonial enterprise, medical treatises," and various contemporaneous texts whose historical relevance enriches a diverse array of meanings in appropriated works.[26] Jefferson's and Adams's receptions of Milton, and Satan more particularly, serve as allusive intertexts in this fashion. Milton, as an ideological intertext, shapes the political orientations of these founding fathers at a time in the early republic when conceptions of independence and tyranny held prominence on both sides of the Atlantic.

Milton also surfaces in grammar books, another intermediary source critical to the art of black audio-visionaires and those who followed their lead. By 1770, grammar books by editors like Robert Lowth, Ralph Harrison, Noah Webster, Hugh Blair, and others began incorporating works by various canonical authors in the English literary tradition as canonical examples of eloquence. Many of them quoted extended passages of *Paradise Lost*, as Sensabaugh examines in *Milton in Early America*.[27] Interestingly, grammar books of this period often quoted Satan or speeches from the infernal council, thereby popularizing Milton's rhetorical appeal in colonial America and well into the long nineteenth century.

Religious culture reflects a third social domain where Milton and his epic achieved widespread acclaim. Milton proved so important in the religious culture of this period that newspapers routinely endorsed *Paradise Lost* as an essential book for every clergyman's personal library. Milton's widespread influence in the religious domain and in politics and education have led John Shawcross to suggest that the English epic poet helped to shape a colonial or prenational American sensibility. Milton, according to this logic, anticipates a kind of American value system framed by founding mothers and fathers of various epistemic persuasions. As Wheatley and the following wave of black audio-visionaries indicate, these same streams of influence and social transmission impacted early African Americans' receptions of Milton as well.

Little is known about the writer who adopted the pseudonym "Othello" and published a gospel of antislavery rebellion by echoing Milton. Bruce notes that Henri Grégoire, a French Roman Catholic priest and ardent supporter of abolitionism and universal suffrage, identified Othello as a black writer, while "others have suggested that he was likely a white abolitionist or a politician."[28] Regardless of Othello's actual racial identity, Bruce argues that the abolitionist's importance rests on his or her representational blackness. According to Bruce, Othello's essays "serve as evidence of what many felt a black writer could contribute to the America discussion" of slavery.[29] Othello's essays command Americans, who had so recently revolted against British tyranny, to "blush...for having apostatized from [their] own principles."[30]

Othello casts satanic aspersions on white readers with this statement, inviting a loaded recall of Milton's devils through the fallen image of apostasy. Satan ranks as the preeminent apostate angel in literary imagination and Milton popularizes that association in his epic. He not only "creates an entirely original Satan in [the] first two books of his poem," he enlarges the figure to such an effect that it is virtually impossible to forget him once readers encounter him on the pages of *Paradise Lost*.³¹ Milton so popularizes the word that it becomes a pejorative moniker attached to his name. As Wittreich relates, "the notion of a seditious Milton is a reputation that sticks," so much so that "he continues to be dubbed 'apostate bard'" while others in history have referred to him as 'that serpent Milton.'"³² Traditions like the parliament in hell genre or indictments of Miltonic apostasy survive to the point of enriching the word's connotative value by grounding it in interpretive associations with *Paradise Lost*. Hence, Othello's indictment of his white readers by attributing their lack of Christian principles as instances of apostasy blasphemes that audience through demonic rhetoric. Although his censure rhetorically sides with Milton's God, it verbalizes a vituperative gospel grounded in satanic discourse. This verbal synthesis of the godly with the demonic projects the essence of a satanic poetry that rhetorically embraces Milton's God while rejecting him through fallen signifiers. Until continuing archival work in African American studies reveals otherwise, this satanic moniker coupled with subsequent infernal echoes in both essays qualify Othello as the first African American after Wheatley to publish and display an interpoetic affiliation with the epic poet on the demonic grounds of contention.

Selecting "Othello" as a pseudonym contributes to the essayist's audio-visionary status by compelling readers to view the author of "Essay on Negro Slavery" as a master of both literary and oratorical eloquence. Here, Othello panders to a poetics of intertextual naming that vocalizes Miltonic presence through an allusive Shakespearean performance. By assuming the persona of Shakespeare's famous tragic hero and black orator, Othello attempts to "neutralize or even counter the verbal process of social abjection to which, as a black outsider, the essayist and Othello [are] subject[s]."³³ With his audiovisual allusions to Milton's hell, Othello, the antislavery essayist, engages in a double-voiced performance of the Western canon on the intertextual grounds of two of the most canonical icons of English literature.

His first essay establishes his voice of antislavery rebellion by communicating in infernal language reminiscent of Milton's Satan. Early on he addresses the unjust nature of slavery, prophesying, "an encroachment on the smallest civil or political privilege, shall fan the enthusiastic flames of liberty, till it shall extend over vast and distant regions, and violently agitate a whole continent" ("Essay" 49). Adding satanic fuel to his rhetorical fire, Othello refers to slavery as "fiend injustice" (49) and condemns Americans for what he considers "the most abandoned apostasy that ever took place, since the almighty fiat spoke into existence this habitable world" (50). These instances of infernal eloquence lay demonic groundwork for Othello's visual prophecies of widespread destruction. Othello concludes this first essay with a more sobering prophecy. God, whom he considers "the father" of Africans and whites alike, "will not fail, at a future settlement, to adjust the account between us, with a dreadful attention to justice" (54). As he preaches in the subsequent essay, God's settlement involves consigning a slave-holding republic to the demonic grounds of Milton's hell.

His second essay alludes to Milton more directly through its visual echoes of *Paradise Lost*. It opens with a visual that critiques the republic for the invasive havoc it wreaks on continental Africa. Othello insists, "upon no better principle do we plunder the coasts of Africa, and bring away its wretched inhabitants as slaves than that, by which the greater fish swallows up the lesser." He uses this ichthyologic visual as a metaphor for critiquing "superior power" and the "superior brutality" it breeds toward highlighting the republic's "acts of illiberal outrage and unmanly violence." These acts prove so "diabolical" that Othello is led to depict the sins of the republic through visuals reminiscent of hell. Prior to a "distinguished era of refined barbarity," which, according to Othello was "introduced into Europe" and consisted of a range of "infernal practices," Africa possessed "all the mild enjoyments of peace—all the pleasing delights of uninterrupted harmony—and all the diffusive blessings of profound tranquility" ("Essay" 54). At first glance, Othello's depictions of Africa seem to portray a visual of the continent as a seat of peaceful ease. As the passage continues, it becomes clear the essayist is projecting a visual of Africa as a plundered paradise.

A divine settlement that consigns a proslavery republic to a state of hellish abjection is the appropriate penalty for plundering this

African paradise according to Othello. As he continues to reflect, "boundless must be the punishment, which irritated providence will inflict on those whose wanton cruelty has prompted them to destroy this fair arrangement of nature—this flowery prospect of human felicity" (54). Including "boundless" and "flowery" in this sentence and setting them at variance from each other introduces images of hellish abjection as a consequence of plundering Africa, a fallen Edenic paradise. Africa as a "flowery prospect" symbolizes Edenic beauty according to this floral visual. Given Othello's previous allusion to hell by citing European invasion as an "infernal practice," "boundless," in this instance, intensifies an intertextual connection to Milton's epic. Specifically, his diction functions as an allusive phraseological adaptation to book 1, line 177, in Milton's epic, where the "fiery surge" trailing Satan and his legion follows them and "bellows through the vast and boundless Deep." Othello continues to capitalize upon Milton's demonic landscape in the subsequent sentence. He prophesies: "Engulphed in the dark abyss of never ending misery, they shall in bitterness atone for the stab thus given to human nature; and in anguish unutterable expiate crimes, for which nothing less than eternal sufferings can make adequate retribution!" ("Essay" 54). Othello's depiction of this divine settlement as an abyss of darkness and eternal suffering projects a visual of hell that is further accented by Miltonic presence through a syntactic reversal reflective of a brief phraseological adaptation. Rather than prophesying unutterable anguish consistent with conventional syntactical arrangements, Othello reverses the word order of this phrase, which echoes hellish constructions like Milton's "Dungeon horrible," "darkness visible," and "Sulphur unconsum'd" (*PL* 1.61, 63, 69).

The passage continues to evidence the author's Miltonic affiliation by again providing hellish visuals that are rhetorically grounded in allusive echoes to *Paradise Lost*. According to the essayist, the cries of slaves "shall ascend to the throne of Omnipotence," which will motivate "the whole force of almighty vengeance, to hurl the guilty perpetrators of those inhuman beings, down the steep precipice of inevitable ruin, into the bottomless gulph of final, irretrievable, and endless destruction!" Othello's passage replays the divine retribution of the "Almighty Father" in *Paradise Lost*, who

> Hurl'd [Satan] headlong flaming from th' Ethereal skie
> With hideous ruine and combustion down
> To bottomless perdition, there to dwell
> In adamantine chains and Penal fire.[34]

Additionally, Othello's reference to "precipice" recalls Milton's "fiery Surge" passage, which contains the phrase, "that from the precipice / Of Heav'n receiv'd us falling" (*PL* 1.173–74). Othello replays snippets from these passages, thereby causing readers to experience a rhetorical freefall from God's grace as a result of this audio-visionary poetics. The republic can avoid suffering God's vengeance in real time, provided the "sons of America, forbear" and "consider the dire consequences, that will attend the prosecution, against which the all-powerful god of nature holds up his hands, and loudly proclaims, desist!" ("Essay" 54).

Othello's allusions to Milton play with rhetorical fire in order to thaw "this cold inanimated conduct of the otherwise warm and generous Americans" ("Essay" 49). These snippets, though discrete and localized, add rhetorical heat and philosophical light to the audio-visionary's gospel of black revolt. A by-product of this aesthetic strategy allows members of Othello's proslavery audience to feel the fire of satanic damnation. In turn, his readers find themselves intertextually situated on the demonic grounds of Milton's epic. Othello's Miltonic pictures produce these spiritually enlightening effects based on an artistic interplay between rhetoric and philosophy. Ultimately, "Essay on Negro Slavery" endeavors to warm the hearts, minds, and souls of audiences through vivid symbols and metaphors of racial suffering. Symbols and metaphors play crucial roles in the art of the black sermon according to Diana Hayes because they allow preachers to "speak in terms of blackness."[35] By blackness, Hayes, like Cone, specifically means a form of communication that addresses the "oppressed situation of Black Americans" and its impact on black lived experiences.[36] Othello's loaded Miltonic signifiers project these vivid intertextual scenarios to elucidate instances of black experience. His Miltonic signifiers merge to substantiate theological prophecies concerning God's divine intervention on behalf of blacks, his chosen people within a chosen nation.

Olaudah Equiano is a black audio-visionary who contributed to the rise of Miltonic influence in African American tradition with his slave narrative, *The Interesting Narrative of the Life of Olaudah Equiano; or, Gustavus Vassa, the African*. Of the six transitional figures covered in this chapter, Equiano is the only one whose intertextual ties to Milton have been acknowledged by scholars.[37] Born in 1745 and taken into captivity from his African homeland when he was a child, Equiano was captured from southeastern Nigeria by slave traders. Separated from his family and enduring the horrors of the middle passage, he was sold to an English navy officer in Virginia then Robert King, a Philadelphia Quaker. He bought his freedom in 1766 then sailed the Caribbean and abroad on various expeditions before settling in England. Equiano's "direct acquaintance with America," as Blyden D. Jackson explains, was limited to the extent that it requires "an unwarrantably liberal use of language to speak of [Equiano] as an American author."[38] However, Jackson includes Equiano within a "pantheon of continental America's black authors" primarily because the *Narrative* reveals he "feels himself, in terms of his sense of where he belongs, as much as at home (and at odds with slavery by whites) in continental, as in Antillean, America."[39]

Equiano's audio-visionary approach to projecting images of Milton begins in chapter 4 of his *Narrative* where he appropriates the infernal line, "Wing'd with red lightning and impetuous rage" from book 1 of *Paradise Lost*. Equiano appropriates the line in order to enrich the harrowing sound and visual of a near-death experience he describes when recounting a skirmish against French batteries. Serving in an English battery against a French unit, Equiano recounts the audiovisual fury of an oncoming shell that "burst[s] within nine or ten yards" of the author.[40] Additionally, three shots were fired at him and a companion. According to Equiano, one of these reports "seemed 'Wing'd with red lightning and impetuous rage'; for, with a most dreadful sound, it hissed close by me, and struck a rock at a little distance" (61). This Miltonic appropriation from book 1 of *Paradise Lost* evidences Equiano's growing facility with the English language and Milton specifically.[41] In *Paradise Lost*, Satan addresses Beelzebub with this line, recalling

> The fiery surge, that from the precipice
> Of heav'n received us falling, and the thunder,
> Winged with red lightning and impetuous rage,
> Perhaps hath spent his shafts, and cease now
> To bellow through the vast and boundless deep. (*PL* 1.173–77)

In voicing Satan's infernal line, Equiano enriches connotations of demonic fallenness as a sign that God's providence, indeed, extends to Africans.

Equiano narrates this scenario to give account to his "strongly raised...belief of the particular interposition of Heaven" (60). Having recently learned to "call daily on [God's] holy name with fear and reverence," Equiano proceeds to justify his spiritual convictions concerning black equality. Even after he has quoted Satan's infernal line, Equiano yet enriches connotations of demonic fallenness toward justifying his beliefs. In a subsequent paragraph, Equiano attempts to escape a rather precarious circumstance on a French horse that ultimately proves too unruly and uncontrollable. Riding the horse at full speed and ill equipped to stop it from speeding over the approaching "craggy precipice," Equiano throws himself from the beast "with great dexterity" (62). He escapes unhurt, explaining, "as soon as I found myself at liberty I made the best of my way to the ship, determined not to be so fool-hardy in future."

Equiano refers to the precipice twice in this passage. That he does intimates that his earlier borrowing of Satan's infernal line served an enriched interpretive value. Satan's line recalls the moment he was hurled from heaven and fell into hell. Equiano recalls this moment of satanic fallenness, relying on the Miltonic spur in order to justify God's providence as it is bestowed freely upon Africans. Saved by God's grace twice within the span of two paragraphs, Equiano, more importantly, is spared from being hurled over a precipice and into ruin. Voicing Milton's audio-visionary presence in this specific passage enables Equiano to identify with Satan's evil for his own spiritual good. Ultimately, this intertextual decision to embrace Satan's poetry works to elevate his racial status by showing, as Wheatley had predicted earlier, that "Negros, black as *Cain*, / May be refin'd and join the angelic train."[42]

Because this profession of his faith also denies as truth the presumption of an unrepresentable blackness, Equiano's appropriation establishes a demonic grounds of Miltonic contention. The opening of chapter 4 threatens the representability of blackness when Equiano narrates his arrival in England. For example, he admits to "no longer look[ing] upon" his white English captors as "spirits, but as men superior to" his people (*Narrative* 51). Having learned to speak English "tolerably well," he subsequently possesses "the stronger desire to resemble them, to imbibe their spirit, and imitate their manners" (51–52). Appropriating Milton and using the epic writer's infernal passage to vividly describe his harrowing condition announces and projects Equiano's artistic ability to remaster the English language through an audio-visionary aesthetic. For readers, Equiano's style of narrative appropriation vividly recaptures infernal scenes from Milton's satanic epic. Equiano brings these scenes to life with aural clarity while using satanic images to relay and replay his harrowing experiences on the high seas.

This instance of phraseological adaptation of Milton is followed by three additional audio-visionary moments. Equiano soon tropes with Milton as a rhetorical device for critiquing the horrors of slavery on the island of Montserrat. Consistent with his earlier example, he isolates these borrowed phraseological passages from the body of his narrative and centers them in blocked quotes. Centering and blocking these passages calls visual attention to Milton's presence in the narrative and the demonic grounds that make such sightings/citings possible. Speaking in the tongues of infernal eloquence as quoted from books 1 and 2 of *Paradise Lost*, Equiano appropriates Miltonic passages that provoke visuals of hellish sufferings. This audio-visionary poetics, because it calls visual attention to itself, adds theological fuel to Equiano's rhetorical fire by enjoining readers to hear, see, and feel the philosophical tenor of the narrator's antislavery gospel.

On February 13, 1763, Equiano, already feeling dejected concerning his own enslavement, looks out upon the ocean from the masthead of the *Aeolus* and views the island of Montserrat. Looking upon this landscape, Equiano soon beholds those "Regions of sorrow, doleful shades, where peace / And rest can rarely dwell. Hope never comes / That comes to all, but torture without end / Still urges" (*Narrative* 69). Unlike Othello's "covert" phraseological appropriations, which uninformed readers are apt to overlook,

Equiano's direct adaptations spur hermeneutic activities focused on appreciating how the author "treats preexisting phraseology... as...raw material that can be cut, reworked, and incorporated into a new setting."[43] In appropriating this passage from book 1 of *Paradise Lost*, Equiano rhetorically identifies with Milton's devils. Moreover, he gives voice to feeling their same hellish torment, encouraging readers to sympathize with his liminal estate by spurring a recall of the infernal crew's eternal sufferings.

Viewing "this land of bondage" provokes new horrors in Equiano, thereby leading him to call upon "God's thunder" and "avenging power" (*Narrative* 69). He appeals to God in this moment of the narrative, hoping his creator might "direct the stroke of death to [him], rather than permit [him] to become a slave, and to be sold from lord to lord" (69). Calling upon God's avenging thunder highlights Equiano's reception of Milton's epic. With this allusion, Equiano specifically responds to "the insistent recurrence of the word 'Thunder'" in Milton's poem.[44] Throughout *Paradise Lost*, thunder signifies God's wrath, but it also "illuminates the psychology of the fallen Satan..., foreshadows the compounding of the devils' damnation..., [and] ties the fall of man poignantly to that of the rebellious angels."[45] Consistent with Elton D. Higgs's understanding of the rhetorical figure in Milton's epic, Equiano petitions God to unleash his thunderous vengeance upon him. He would rather die by God's might than suffer the psychological torment associated with his former enslavement and the debilitating mental images of "misery, stripes, and chains" (69) that come to mind as he views Montserrat.

Over the course of the next 17 paragraphs, Equiano narrates his experiences after being sold to a new slaveowner and describes some of the horrors of slavery he witnesses while in Montserrat. These horrors include the sexual defilement of slave women and girls and various bodily tortures ranging from brandings, burnings, and the removal of limbs or appendages. After explaining the rationale for why male slaves do not take wives from "their own master's negro women," Equiano introduces another Miltonic quote to critique the barbarity of an institution that commands husbands to flog their wives at their slaveowner's command. Given this dynamic, Equiano asks readers to consider whether it is "surprising" that slavery "should drive the poor creatures to despair, and make them seek a refuge in death...while "with shudd'ring horror pale, and eyes aghast, / they view their lamentable lot, and find / no rest?" (*Narrative* 77). Once again, Equiano appropriates one of Milton's infernal passages, book 2, lines 615–16, using it to expose death as a balm for slavery's hellish tyranny.

The phraseological adaptation of these lines calls visual attention to itself and Milton's presence while also prompting readers to envision slavery as hell. More important, the borrowed passage compels readers to approximate a cognitive sense of what this hellish torment feels like to slaves suffering under the heat of tyrannical oppression. The passage rhetorically situates readers in the minds and bodies of the suffering oppressed. Based on Equiano's style of eliding and enjambing Milton's words with his own, readers are made to experience satanic shudderings of horror while surveying all that is visually lamentable according to what slaves and Milton's devils see in their infernal surroundings. With its kinesthetic imagery of terror, frenzy, and sobering dejection, the appropriated passage, rather than merely narrating slaves' despair, qualifies and personalizes it. This rhetorical strategy dispenses with any narratological language that might otherwise distance readers from the horrors presented to them on the printed page. The strategy especially creates a rhetorical event that facilitates moments of experiential feeling. With little or no warning, Equiano's readers are made to feel black suffering vicariously through the infernal crew's hellish torment.

A final Miltonic appropriation from book 2 of *Paradise Lost* concludes the chapter in a tone that threatens the promise of satanic insurrection. Equiano's concluding paragraph shifts from narration to censure, using Milton's satanic epic as a talking book of black liberation theology. He does "not suppose that the dealers in slaves are born worse than other men," but recognizes their crimes against humanity as products of avarice (*Narrative* 80). As he segues to a discussion that moralizes the issue as a violation of "that first natural right of mankind, equality, and independency" (80), Equiano ends on a rhetorical note of critique that chastises proslavery readers for the multiple paradoxes that keep this audience from ever seeing blacks as respectable members of the human race. For example, he critiques his readership for depriving slaves of virtue by enslaving them, which, he argues, encourages conduct of "fraud, rapine, and cruelty" and ultimately sets blacks at war with whites. He finds it equally incredulous for whites to "think it necessary to keep [blacks] in a state of ignorance," while simultaneously asserting "they are incapable of learning" (80–81). In light of these and other illogical statements, Equiano sternly asks readers if they are not "struck with shame and mortification, to see the partakers of your nature reduced so low?" (81). Moreover, he asks them to consider the possibility that dangers might attend this dehumanizing mode of treatment. Finally, he asks, "Are you not hourly in dread of an insurrection? Nor would it be surprising": for when

> No peace is given
> To us enslav'd, but custody severe;
> And stripes and arbitrary punishment
> Inflicted—What peace can we return?
> But to our power, hostility and hate,
> Untam'd reluctance, and revenge, tho' slow,
> Yet ever plotting how the conqueror least
> May reap his conquest, and may least rejoice
> In doing what we most in suff'ring feel? MILTON.

With this intertextual elision and appropriation of book 2, lines 333–40, Equiano preaches his most incendiary gospel of black revolt. After calling out proslavery sympathizers on the paradoxic illogic of their beliefs, Equiano proceeds to adopt and adapt Satan's revolutionary creed at the high point of the infernal council. Because Satan's creed is so antagonistic to what he interprets as God's monarchial tyranny, Equiano, in appropriating this rhetorical message, prophesies black insurrection as a logical consequence of slavery. To espouse this satanic gospel of black revolt is to prophesy doom and ruin for those who refuse to hear the rebellious God-talk of a chosen but oppressed people. White America can be saved from ruin, according to Equiano, if the nation dares to change its conduct and "treat [its] slaves as men" (*Narrative* 81).

As the last three examples indicate, Equiano appropriates satanic passages from *Paradise Lost* as a rhetorical means for calling visual attention to the infernal hero and the signifyin(g) power of Miltonic presence. In each of these examples, Equiano identifies with Milton's Satan because the rhetorical art of bringing the fallen hero to readers' remembrance serves to provoke a satanic reading experience that might spark audiences to think in a radically different way about slavery and its attendant horrors. A primary reason why Neil Forsyth classifies *Paradise Lost* as a satanic epic is because he regards the infernal hero as pivotal in supporting Milton's desire to justify God's ways to a mass reading audience. It is Satan, according to Forsyth, who makes the Son's redemptive sacrifice necessary. Thus, Satan functions as the motivating force and energy of and in Milton's epic. Equiano taps into this infernal yet messianic poetics when he voices Satan's eloquence and projects images of the hero and Milton's epic through his various appropriations. By splicing these textual snippets and activating the intertextual memory of his implied readers, Equiano justifies his antislavery position concerning the institution's satanic nature. He preaches this gospel of revolt through the art of a black audio-visionary poetics that vocalizes dissent on the demonic grounds of Milton and the epic writer's liberating talking book, *Paradise Lost*.

Like Milton, Equiano and Othello present themselves as literary prophets in their writings by "including visionary scenes figuratively" and communicating through processes of verbal description that are "determined by iconographic traditions."[46] The black audio-visionaries covered in this chapter specialize in rendering visionary scenes steeped in the iconography of Milton's epics. Milton's hell, Satan, and the visual of an Edenic paradise represent a few mascons or iconographic images of massive concentration and intense density that are sampled and signified upon by this transitional wave of Miltonists and black audio-visionaries. They use these Miltonic images toward "pictorially energizing" their gospels of revolt and performing "continual assaults on...readers' minds [and] on [their] interpretive faculties."[47] This audio-visionary style contributes to the theological artistry of these writers' participation in black jeremiadic discourse.

A cultural offshoot of its American precursor, the black jeremiad completes and complicates that tradition as a means for enriching it in order to suit African Americans' specific religio-political needs. According to David Howard-Pitney, "employing a rhetoric of social prophecy and criticism," these early black jeremiads address "*two* American chosen peoples—black and white"—but on distinct ideological registers relative to each racial group's social and political interests.⁴⁸ Additionally, writers and orators of this tradition relied upon black jeremiads to prophesy and critique tyrannical governments in a manner that further empowered them to hold steadfast to the unfaltering belief that "God will mysteriously use the unhappy present to spur [both groups] to reformation and speedily onward to fulfill their divine destiny."⁴⁹ For black audiences, this jeremiadic tradition was geared toward reinforcing race pride and inspiring hearers to withstand and triumph over the oppressive evils confronting them. This racialized jeremiadic tradition served a different role for white audiences. For them, black jeremiadic discourse was designed to critique and enlighten them concerning their active or passive complicity in maintaining U.S. slavery and the spiritual wickedness it promoted.

At least three orators succeed Othello and Equiano in spreading the gospel of black revolt through audio-visionary engagements with Milton. Of the three, two of them specifically engage Milton within the theological context of the black jeremiad. All three, however, voice Milton on demonic grounds for messianic purposes of spiritual and/or racial uplift. This infernally minded trio consists of Lemuel Haynes, Peter Williams Jr., and William Hamilton. In each of their selected works, Milton's presence surfaces through various styles of phraseological adaptation that draw upon the epic writer's demonic and Edenic rhetorical figures either directly or allusively. Regardless the style, their respective audio-visionary poetics spread the gospels of Milton and black revolt throughout the first two decades of the nineteenth century.

The Reverend Lemuel B. Haynes is one of the first black audio-visionaries to spread the gospel of Milton and revolt in the first decade of the long nineteenth century. Born in West Hartford, Connecticut, in 1753 to a "white woman, possibly of the servant class" and sired by a black man, Haynes was abandoned by his mother and later indentured to Deacon David Rose.⁵⁰ Rose and his wife raised Haynes in Middle Granville, Massachusetts, until the lad reached the age of 21. Under their care, Haynes received a formal education and benefitted from an "intensely religious atmosphere" of a "zealous Puritanism."⁵¹ In adulthood, Haynes served as a minuteman then an enlisted member in the Continental Army before earning his license to preach in 1780 and becoming an ordained clergyman in 1785. After marrying Elizabeth Babbit, a white woman ten years his junior, Haynes was called to pastor "the West Parish of Rutland, Vermont, where he remained for thirty years."[52] It was during this period that Haynes's popularity increased as a result of his 1805 oration, "Universal Salvation." A sermon delivered extemporaneously, which was later published in pamphlet form, "Universal Salvation" critiqued Calvinist doctrines through a clever appropriation of Milton's Satan. This appropriation elaborates upon the characterization of Milton's Satan, interpreting the infernal hero as the consummate preacher of deceit and rhetorical eloquence.

The sermon became widely popular. Blyden Jackson asserts, "at least twenty editions were printed and circulated in America and Europe" over the course of Haynes's life.[53] Foner and Branham's estimates reveal a more generous publishing history. According to both editors, numerous reprintings of Haynes's sermon exceeded more than "seventy editions...during the sixty years following its delivery."[54] "Universal Salvation" responds to Hosea Ballou, a prominent theologian and proponent of American Universalism. Ballou's theological convictions led him to dispute the doctrine of predestinarianism. Prior to Haynes's sermon, Ballou argued, "all people might gain salvation through adherence to the gospel."[55] Haynes, staunchly opposed to this doctrine, responds by disputing Ballou's theological position. His extemporaneous sermon dramatizes his Christian convictions by taking Genesis 3:4 as his scriptural text and then visualizing Milton's Satan as a deceitful preacher.

In Genesis 3:4, the serpent cajoles Eve with the lie, "ye shall not surely die."[56] Next, Haynes elaborates upon the couple's "primitive state" in the garden, eventually referring to Eden as a "delightful Paradise, until a certain preacher, in his journey, came that way, and disturbed their peace and tranquility" ("Universal Salvation" 60–61). When he references Eden as a "Paradise" that will subsequently be "disturbed" of peace, Haynes signals his intertextual foray into Milton's epic. In this moment, *Paradise Lost* functions as a sacred yet secular talking book, for Haynes recognizes that Milton's poem provides him with a useful scenic backdrop. Sampling and signifyin(g) on it as an intertextual backdrop enriches his oratorical gospel of doctrinal revolt.

Haynes's rebuttal enriches his scriptural scenario by quoting four lines from Milton's epic. After identifying the Bible as a "peculiar fund of instruction," he provides a broad overview of the Creation story, the origins of humanity, and its apostasy from God ("Universal Salvation" 60). Focusing on the serpent, Haynes notes the deceitful creature, "came that way, and disturbed their peace and tranquility, by endeavoring to reverse the prohibition of the Almighty; as in our text, ye shall not surely die." Immediately thereafter, he notes:

> She pluck'd, she ate,
> Earth felt the wound; nature from her seat,
> Sighing through all her works, gave signs of woe,
> That all was lost.   MILTON

Haynes's oration draws upon various tenets of black preaching style, namely, elements of imaginative elaboration, storytelling, and a panache for rhetorical flair. Skills in imaginative elaboration, according to Mitchell, "breathe [new] life into both the story and the truth it teaches," aiding hearers to "be caught up in the experience being narrated and, as a result, to understand better and to be moved to change."[57] Haynes also adopts a storytelling mode that makes the Word of Scripture plain and relatable to the lived experiences of listeners. He combines these characteristics of black preaching style with an extemporaneous vision that imagines Adam and Eve enjoying their state of Edenic bliss in Milton's paradise. Haynes instantly ruptures this visual when he introduces Milton's Satan into his oratorical narrative.

Introducing Satan through imaginative elaboration preaches the gospel of predestinarianism while dressing the infernal hero in the vestments of a preacher. This aspect of audio-visionary artistry is one method Haynes adopts in order to add interpretive layers of "flesh on the...skeletal narratives of the Bible" and *Paradise Lost* especially.[58] This theological aesthetic accords with the prophet/ audience relationship so necessary to the successful execution of a visionary poetics. As Wittreich explains, "God needs the prophet to make manifest his Word, and the prophet requires an audience so that the Word may become flesh."⁵⁹ Haynes adds hermeneutic flesh to his audio-visionary appropriations of Milton's Satan. His rhetorical approach also amplifies the danger the infernal hero poses for this spiritual audience. A result of this mode of imaginative elaboration is that Satan ceases to represent some crude demonic figure. Instead, Haynes animates Satan's character with "a form of Godliness" (2 Tim. 3:5) that metaphorically alludes to what he recognizes as Ballou's fallen doctrinal logic. On one level, Haynes's intertextual enlargement of Milton's Satan functions to alert the audience to the wiles of devil-like preachers whose deceitful gospels yield death, not life. On a more subversive level, his imaginative elaboration functions as a not-too-subtle reminder of the threat Ballou's Universalist doctrine poses for those seeking God's spiritual salvation.

According to Haynes's symbolic assessment of Milton's Satan and the infernal hero's false preaching, both threaten Christians' salvation. He believes Satan appeals to Adam and Eve so convincingly because his seductive logic has a ring of plausibility. It is this craftiness of language that stands to consign the first couple to eternal damnation, especially if they are not astute enough to recognize the wiles of this eloquent preacher's false doctrine. Milton's Satan, then, functions as a literary forerunner of Ballou, who, according to Haynes, likewise preaches a fraudulent gospel. Haynes, at this juncture, operates under the unction of an audio-visionary poetics. Specifically, he oratorically "sets narration and commentary on a collision course," with the latter serving as a "*Royal* Key...for unlocking visionary meaning."⁶⁰ Through this aesthetic, Haynes draws indirect parallels between Milton's Satan and Ballou. These rhetorical affiliations aid hearers to see through Ballou's satanic logic and its plausible doctrine. Resorting to this audio-visionary poetics enables Haynes to conjure images of Milton's infernal hero for the express purpose of saving the souls of this spiritual assembly.

Foner and Branham contend that Haynes was particularly known for his "astonishing memory" and ability "to recite Milton's *Paradise Lost* and much of the Bible with uncanny accuracy."⁶¹ Notwithstanding this impressive recall, Haynes's sudden shift from

Scripture to book 9 of Milton's epic showcases a measure of rhetorical flair that is not reducible to a performance of rhetorical ornamentation alone. Put another way, Haynes's performance of appropriation does not simply reproduce "the aesthetic effect of the formulaic diction in which oral epics like those of Homer [and Milton's] are composed."[62] Rather, Haynes's sudden shift to Miltonic verse jolts hearers of his word to their synesthetic senses. If, as Milton declares in "The Verse" preceding *Paradise Lost*, the goal of unrhymed blank prose is to facilitate the recovery of "ancient liberty," then Haynes's sudden shift into this heroic measure underwrites his theological mission to rescue his audience from the spiritual clutches of eternal damnation. Thus, he performs Miltonic English and displays his rhetorical flair that hearers of his words might better see, hear, and feel the repercussions of Eve's fall and the wounds of earth's pangs more fully. Ultimately, orating these visual snippets from Milton's epic dramatizes the hermeneutic fullness of the Gospel beyond the authority of scriptural language.

After capturing his audience's attention using snippets of Milton's gospel, Haynes "attends" to additional aspects of Satan's infernal preaching style. For instance, he explains that Satan has many names, the most common being the devil. He also contends that this infernal preacher has "acquired great skill in the art" of public speaking and has proven himself to be "cunning," "artful," "laborious [and] unwe[a]ried," "heterogeneous," "presumptuous," and is, above all, a "successful preacher" ("Universal Salvation," 61, 62). Haynes even exposes the theological error of Satan's false doctrine. For example, he warns hearers to be mindful of preachers whose false gospels work their "greatest success in the dark and ignorant parts of the earth," challenging them to be wary of those who "cause divisions and offences, contrary to the doctrine which ye have learned" (62–63). Nor is Satan's decision to appear before Eve in the form of a snake lost upon Haynes. As Haynes sees it, Satan assumes the identity of a snake in order to "save his own character," knowing the couple would have "more easily seen the deception" had he approached them as a fallen angel in corporeal form (63). Having performed this detailed examination of

Satan and his fallen theological gospel, Haynes turns his focus to a consideration of Ballou's deceptive preaching.

He further maintains, "the devil is not dead, but still lives; and is able to preach as well as ever, ye shall not surely die" (63). In other words, he contends theological resonances of the infernal preacher from Scripture and *Paradise Lost* may yet be heard in sermons like those Ballou preaches. In "Universal Salvation," Haynes interprets Ballou's theological position as "devilish doctrine" that "makes use of the devil's old notes, that he delivered almost six thousand years ago" (64). He regards Ballou's gospel as devilish because its message refutes the existence of hell or the theological notion that God will indeed condemn those who have not acquired salvific redemption to a spiritual estate of eternal suffering. If, according to the tenets of Universal Salvation, God has made provisions for all souls to attain salvation and restoration, then Haynes understands Ballou to preach a gospel rooted in a theological belief that none of God's creation will die for their sins. From Haynes's standpoint, Ballou's theological position makes the holy Scripture a lie. Accordingly, Ballou's theological interpretation leads Haynes to perceive the Universalist preacher's doctrine as an echo of Satan's deceitful threat to Eve in Genesis and in *Paradise Lost*. Haynes cannot help but "confine himself wholly to the character of Satan" (64). This rhetorical impulse spurs Haynes to conjure and project an audio-visionary image of Ballou as a contemporary manifestation of Milton's infernal hero. His intertextual performance of doctrinal disagreement sets Ballou up to be demonized, perhaps, unwittingly.

Ballou would subsequently take offense to Haynes's sermon, asserting that it maligned him as satanic. If Ballou recognizes himself in "Universal Salvation," then he attests to the power of Haynes's audio-visionary poetics. Relative to the governing principles of visionary poetics, unless one "penetrates the contexts of allusions, the book will remain sealed...until by a successful reading its pages are opened and its visions consumed."[63] Seeing himself in the sermon means Haynes's Miltonic mascons penetrate Ballou's consciousness. Haynes begins his story by identifying Satan as a fraudulent preacher. This playful appropriation of the fallen angel codes this figure of the storyteller's elaborate imagination as a rhetorically loaded mascon whose image, Ballou believes, bears biographical likeness to himself.

A letter from Haynes in response to one he received from Ballou gives a sense of the latter's agitation concerning the alleged defamation of his theological character. Composed in 1807, Haynes's response sheds light on certain rhetorical effects produced by his style of theological rebuke, which censures Ballou by sarcastically elaborating upon Satan's character through an audio-visionary poetics. As a result of these effects, "Universal Salvation" figures as a gospel of black revolt even though it does not preach one relative to themes of racial injustice. Because Haynes may have been received as phenotypically black by his white onlookers, his theological rebuke represents a command performance that renders him vulnerable to racialist critique. The politics of skin complexion coupled with American culture's ongoing obsessions with race and phenotypical classifications make it possible for certain white onlookers to read Haynes as uppity and insubordinate. Although quite fair in complexion, Haynes did experience racial tensions in his lifetime. Jackson speculates as much when he states "color may have entered into [Haynes's] eventual separation from" the West Parish church he pastored in Rutland, Vermont, for nearly 30 years. Before then, Haynes experienced forms of racial discrimination as well. Prior to accepting the pastorate at the West Parish church in Vermont, he performed ministerial duties at a church in Torrington, Connecticut. However, Jackson asserts Haynes "was never to become more than a supply pastor" there.[64] If these racial politics could play out as lived realities throughout Haynes's ministerial career, his testimony stood an equal chance of being dismissed as disadvantaged or subject to misinterpretation based on racist ideologies of the time.

Haynes defends himself and his command performance of theological rebuke in his response to Ballou. As he explains, nowhere in his sermon does he identify Beelzebub as the "master of [Ballou's] house" or "household," as the Calvinist theologian charged in a previous letter.[65] Haynes's reply is rife with stinging and erudite sarcasm. These features suggest that Ballou was sorely offended by his letter. Haynes's reply does not indicate that Ballou interpreted the dynamic in racialist terms, yet both individuals were products of their eras and susceptible to the precarious nature of black testimony during the early republic. Because Haynes may be marked as phenotypically black, his public rebuke of Ballou, which creates interpretive space for maligning the white theologian as satanic, further sets the stage for reading his sermon, along with its Miltonic inflections, as an uppity performance of barbarous error.

To dispute or talk back to white authority, particularly in slave culture, is to conduct oneself in an unseemly manner. Furthermore, black testimony has frequently required its speakers to solicit, compete against, or win credibility among white audiences. Wheatley, for example, needed white attesters to legitimate her poetic compositions as authored by herself.[66] Slave codes and black codes, however, did not respect the testimony of blacks against whites. As Charles Mills argues in "White Ignorance," "if one group, or a specific group of potential witnesses is discredited in advance as being epistemically suspect, then testimony from the group will tend to be dismissed or never solicited to begin with."[67] These dynamics place racialist strains on Haynes's sermon, for they work to code his speech as a barbarous error of rhetorical uppitiness.

In *Race and Rhetoric in the Renaissance*, for example, Ian Smith theorizes the "historical relationship between language and color in order to "examine the political and cultural benefits accruing to England [particularly during the English Renaissance] as it undertook the work of cultural exclusion and its own national and racial ratification."[68] Kim Hall examines such practices and the extent to which they materialize and achieve greater force in writings of this period. She explains, "the trope of blackness had a broad arsenal of effects" throughout this period while "drawing power from England's ongoing negotiations of African difference and from the implied color comparison therein."[69] Smith and Hall's contributions to the racializing of language have implications for understanding Haynes's erudite speech acts as an error of barbarous Africanisms in early American culture. Toni Morrison's *Playing in the Dark* is hauntingly clear about the various technologies in American literature that circulate and project a range of barbarous Africanisms that negatively reflect the culture's obsession with denigrating blackness and Africanist presence.

This obsession is a cultural inheritance from English tradition. If, as Smith argues, English tradition understands "the African's language [as] radically different, a foreign babble that is grating to the ear and devoid of reason," then Haynes's erudite speech commits barbarous errors that defy racist expectations of the black speaking subject.[70] He, like Othello in Shakespeare's tragedy, suffers the consequences that appertain to eloquent rhetors and narrators whose salutary facility with the English language yet reproduce the very "paradigms of barbarism" their speech acts aim to defy. Since "speaking well...does not in itself...determine what...[white] interlocutors choose to understand" when subjected to hearing the exhortative words of eloquent black speakers, Haynes's audio-visionary projections with Milton potentially have damning consequences for how he may be perceived and received. For some white auditors, Haynes is likely to reflect a deviant linguistic anomaly. Thus, speaking the Miltonic English of Satan's poetry invites an interpretation that ironically misreads him as satanic. Ballou performs this barbarous error in racial perception in a subsequent correspondence with his theological adversary, whom he demonizes.

Reverend Peter Williams Jr. and William Hamilton extend Milton's afterlife in early African American tradition through more conventional gospels of black revolt. Three of their orations return to the kinds of theological preoccupation with Milton that spreads his gospel and that of antislavery through rhetorical sound pictures. Their audio-visionary gospels project snippets of Milton's epic while drawing from tenets of black liberation theology and the black jeremiad. In these orations, Williams and Hamilton engage Milton as a means for denouncing the slave trade and its devilish barbarism. They also prophesy a redemptive future for African Americans, incorporating visual snippets of Milton's passages and Edenic mascons as the rhetorical situation demands. Because Williams and Hamilton actually preached these Miltonic gospels of revolt in commemoration of the abolition of the slave trade, their orations give voice to what was then a burgeoning religious practice. Preached at a time when black Christianity was further solidifying into a distinct religion that could meet African Americans' diverse spiritual needs, Williams and Hamilton lifted their audio-visionary voices in strains of Miltonic epic, prophesying a new dawning for a fallen Africa that at one time symbolized an Edenic paradise.

Forms of black Christianity began emerging during the 1770s and 1780s. Albert J. Raboteau contends, black preachers began "to pastor their own people" and minister to their flocks by mediating "between Christianity and the experience of slaves (and free blacks), [and] interpreting the stories, symbols, and events of the Bible to fit the day-to-day lives of those held in bondage."[71] In keeping with these societal and cultural trends, the period between 1790 and 1820 gave birth to an emergence of various black denominations. These included the Episcopalian, Methodist, Baptist, and Presbyterian faiths. Founding their own religious institutions, early African Americans created spiritual venues for "articulating publicly their own vision of Christianity, standing in eloquent testimony to the existence of two Christian Americas."[72] It was in spiritual environments such as these that Williams and Hamilton spread gospels of Miltonic influence and black revolt through audio-visionary poetics.

Williams projects Milton through this intertextual style of preaching in an 1808 address that hails the abolition of the U.S. slave trade. The "son of one of the founders of the African Methodist Episcopal Zion Church," Williams was practically destined to catch the spirit of revolt.[73] Born "about 1780 in New Brunswick, New Jersey," Williams was greatly influenced by his father, Peter Williams Sr.[74] A former slave and lacking any formal education, Williams Sr. led the movement to withdraw blacks "from the John Street Methodist Episcopal Zion Church," which subsequently made the "establishment of the African Methodist Episcopal Zion Church in 1796" a radical possibility.[75] Williams Sr. was a man of sterling character, but his son may have been exposed to Milton through alternative social routes. Williams Jr. was probably introduced to Milton in the New York African Free School where his "exceptional intellectual gifts distinguished him as a [scholarly] child."[76] If not then, his exposure to Milton would have occurred at some point prior to 1820 when he was training for the Episcopalian ministry.

On January 1, 1808, Williams hailed the abolition of the U.S. slave trade at the New York African Church. His speech,

"Abolition of the Slave Trade," set the rhetorical stage for conveying his Miltonic literacy when he celebrates the abolition of the slave trade as a "singular interposition of Divine Providence."[77] In interpreting God's intervention as a sign of divine providence, Williams begins to pictorialize continental Africa as a former Eden faintly reminiscent of Milton's paradise. For example, he presents an "idyllic picture of Africa and Africans" and views the continent and its inhabitants as "pristine," which further projects scenes of "a golden-age primitivism."[78] Even though his scenic pictorializations prove problematic by pandering to traditional Western beliefs about African inferiority, his vision of a prelapsarian Africa projects the continent in the image of a paradisiacal seat of ease.

He continues alluding to this concept of a historic African paradise by romanticizing the landscape in serene terms. "Before the enterprising spirit of European genius explored the western coast of Africa," he writes, "the state of our forefathers was a state of simplicity, innocence, and contentment" ("Abolition" 67). Moreover, it "offered a place of refreshment to the weary and an asylum to the unfortunate" (67). Williams abruptly desecrates this Eden-like vision, undercutting its tranquil beauty by suddenly shifting to scenes of horror and dejection. Finding "this delightful picture" of Africa's former glory to be an image of the past, Williams explains, "the angel of bliss has deserted their dwelling; and the demon of indescribable misery has rioted, uncontrolled, on the fair fields of our ancestors" (67). This demonic adversary, whom Williams subsequently and repeatedly acknowledges as a "foe," functions as a metaphorical symbol for slave traders in the oration. He describes them as plunderers of a fallen African paradise and verbally paints these traders in the flesh to bear a strong rhetorical likeness to Milton's Satan.

To capitalize on these demonic grounds of interpretation, Williams immediately begins projecting scenes of woe. For instance, he retraces the demonic voyages of explorers like Columbus and explains the attendant horrors resulting from their capitalistic greed. Possessed by a "desire of gain" that tempted them to "violate the sacred injunctions of the gospel" and enslave those who they conquered, these body snatchers robbed Africa of its former glory ("Abolition" 67). After cataloging a series of their horrid offenses and "trac[ing] the past scenes of Africa," Williams solidifies his faint Miltonic impressions into more concretely vivid sound pictures (69). He achieves this instance of audio-visionary art by alluding to Satan's opening speech to Beelzebub in book 1 of *Paradise Lost*. This artistic method showcases Williams's abilities as a highly skilled visionary and prophet. A primary method of visionary poets, according to Wittreich, is to "concretize vision into word, so that [one's] audience may further concretize it into act."[79] Williams orates in this mode when he alludes to Satan's opening speech. This allusive technique renders Milton audibly visible for members of Williams's listening audience.

Williams invokes Satan by alluding to the infernal hero's "O how fall'n! how changed" (*PL* 1.84) speech. This apostrophe of "fallen" difference transforms Satan's lines by limiting them with the brief phraseological exclamation: "Oh Africa, Africa! To what horrid inhumanities have thy shores been witness; thy shores, which were once the garden of the world, the seat of almost paradisiacal joys, have been transformed into regions of woe" ("Abolition" 69). These lines do not appropriate Satan's language of fallenness verbatim but approximate the infernal hero's message by stopping short of quoting his complete utterance. In an early passage from *Paradise Lost*, for example, Satan views Beelzebub's dejected estate and exclaims,

> If thou beest he; but O how fall'n! how changed
> From him, who in the happy realms of light
> Clothed with transcendent brightness didst outshine
> Myriads though bright. (*PL* 1.84–87)

Williams's depictions of Edenic fallenness and metamorphosis echo Satan's lines of abject fallenness. First, they phraseologically abbreviate Satan's utterance. Second, though Williams does not marvel at Africa's plundered state by expressly identifying it as fallen, his visual descriptions all but convey this sentiment. Shores that were once Edenic and the "garden of the world" have changed and fallen to "regions of woe." This latter phrase amplifies Milton's literary presence in the oration even more, for its diction is a clever phraseological manipulation of book 1, line 65.[80] This phrasal substitution especially brings Milton to mind because Williams has earlier established his rhetorical preoccupation with Edenic imagery. Following this allusion to Satan's "O how fall'n" speech, Williams offers a different Miltonic visual. He departs from Satan's demonic grounds altogether and shifts to relaying scenes of Edenic restoration. He now envisions Africa as a "seat of almost paradisiacal joys," transitioning from censure to prophesy through his rhetorical deployment of contrasting Miltonic visuals.

Both his abbreviated phraseological utterances of and allusive echoes to Satan's speech mark his idyllic depictions of Africa as an audio-visionary replica of *Paradise Lost* gone wrong. By positioning "seat" alongside the phrase "paradisiacal joy," Williams spurs a recall of a passage from book 7, where Raphael describes Eden as a site analogous to a heaven on earth. Raphael explains, "that earth now / Seemed like to heav'n, a seat where gods might dwell, / Or wander with delight, and love to haunt / Her sacred shades" (*PL* 7.328–31). This "seat" fit for gods provides Williams a window for viewing and appropriating Milton's visionary poetics in depicting Eden as a heavenly landscape of repose. Williams views this Edenic scene, then desecrates its Edenic image. Recasting this image according to the Miltonic designs of his oration's audio-visionary poetics, he makes a heaven of hell and vice versa by reversing and then revising Africa as fallen and changed in contrast to Raphael's supernal recollections.

Williams inverts this Edenic setting through a strategic use of satanic poetry that serves as audio-visionary supplements for his critique of slavery. An early example of his use of satanic language in this regard surfaces when he thanks God for delivering Africans out of the "dark *dungeon* of slavery" ("Abolition" 72). Due to his earlier allusions to paradise, this reference to slavery as a dungeon especially brings Milton's demonic landscape to mind. Like Milton's "dungeon horrible," Williams's visual depiction of slavery as a hellish geography reveals his participation in another audio-visionary performance (*PL* 1.61). By this point in his oration, William firmly establishes his active participation in a tradition of Miltonic appropriation. His style of appropriation preaches through rhetorically loaded "allusions in the form of repeated words, phrases, and ideas that ultimately function as definers of [specific Miltonic] contexts and authenticators of them."[81] His allusive dungeon amplifies its rhetorical affiliation with Milton's hell further. By shading this visual with descriptive darkness, he spurs a more intense recall of Milton. Specifically, his "dark dungeon" activates an audio-visionary recall of Milton's hell, which is famously referred to as "darkness visible" (*PL* 1.63).

Envisioning the U.S. slave trade and projecting it according to an infernal topos reminiscent of Milton's hell underscores just how much Africa has changed and fallen relative to Williams's audio-visionary perception and interpretive aesthetic. It is not enough for Williams to mention continental Africa as a site that has been plundered by avarice and greed. Rather, his allusive recall of Milton's paradise and hell intensifies a more vivid perception of Africa's fallenness. Appealing to Milton's talking pictures in these instances, Williams rhetorically qualifies the depth of depravity associated with these criminal acts of geographical destruction. To plunder paradise is to make a hell of heaven by desecrating the designs of God's creation. Williams draws upon select visuals from *Paradise Lost* and speaks in satanic tones of infernal eloquence as a means for denouncing explorers' capitalistic greed. Yet, his oration does not confine its message to censure. Capitalizing upon the "paradisiacal joys" that introduce his Miltonic reverie of continental Africa in its glory days, he shifts to prophesy a new vision for the homeland of his ancestors. His oration concludes by restoring Africa to the image of its former glory. Shifting to this Miltonic design prophesies a regaining of paradise, one that finds Williams caught up in the spirit of a black jeremiadic tradition and a poetics of Ethiopianism.

Williams especially participates in a black jeremiadic tradition when he uses Miltonic scenes to critique and condemn the U.S. slave trade. Verbalizing these practices through a poetics of satanic or hellish portraiture grounds his critique on a demonic landscape. This landscape revives Milton's persona as a literary icon of epic tradition. It also projects audio-visionary themes of liberty in concert with Williams's antislavery ministry. Appropriating Milton by projecting these various snippets of satanic poetry, Williams brings his association with black jeremiadic tradition into sharper focus. His use of Miltonic snippets in these oratorical moments reinforces the epic writer's importance as a talking book second only to the

Bible while simultaneously providing Williams a "verbal outlet for...demonstrating [his] loyalty...to the principles of egalitarian liberalism and to the Anglo-Christian codes of values."[82]

Williams also tropes with Milton as an audio-visionary practice for advancing black Ethiopianism. This poetics takes intertextual inspiration from Psalms 68:31. That scriptural verse proclaims, "Princes shall come out of Egypt; Ethiopia shall soon stretch forth her hands unto God." The scriptural verse remained popular among various early African American writers and orators throughout the nineteenth century. Moses explains that this widely circulating adaptation of Scripture espoused a brand of racial and political chauvinism that recognized "the ascendancy of the white race was only temporary, and that the divine providence of history was working to elevate the African peoples."[83] Williams's Miltonic leanings in the rhetorical direction of incorporating tenets of black Ethiopianism in his oration begin to surface when he prophesies the restoration of African civilization as a result of the abolition of the U.S. slave trade.

Williams's "Abolition of the Slave Trade" changes in rhetorical tone and argumentative focus when the orator prophesies "the sun of liberty shall beam resplendent on the whole African race [while] its genial influences promote the luxuriant growth of knowledge and virtue." ("Abolition" 73). At first, "genial influence" seems to register as a "meaningless allusion," a kind of interpoetic resonance that Machacek asserts is "not likely to be recalled even by a learned reader."[84] This misreading of allusive intertextual glosses likely occurs when the connection between a spur and its reprise proves too faint or seemingly insignificant to be detected or valued. Though Williams's "genial influence" registers as a faint phraseological adaptation reminiscent of Milton, a study of its surrounding linguistic contexts help to make its intertextual connection resonate more profoundly for readers.

The brief phraseological adaptation of "genial influence" performs an intertextual gloss on another passage in book 7 of Milton's epic. Raphael, in relaying the events of the Creation, ascribes nurturing qualities to the "Main ocean" that subsequently waters the earth upon God's command (*PL* 7.279). Raphael explains how this ocean "flowed, not idle, but with warm / Prolific humor soft'ning [the earth's] globe, / fermented the great mother to conceive, / Satiate with genial moisture" (*PL* 7.279–82). Upon God's command, the waters give birth to Creation, instantly gathering "into one place" as "dry land appear[s]" (7.284) and mountains emerge to set nature in motion. A key visual in Raphael's theological sermon on the Creation involves a visionary poetics that emphasizes nature's nurturing qualities. According to Raphael's recount, earth, aided by prolific humors, conceives nature, warmly satisfied with the nutritional elements necessary for facilitating birth.

Williams tropes with this passage of generation allusively, cleverly disguising his Miltonic source by drawing intertextual strength from the sun's nurturing rays instead of the ocean's prolific humors. In his oration, it is the "sun of liberty" rather than Milton's rolling waters that inspires the African race to bloom in knowledge and virtue. In other words, Williams espouses an antislavery gospel that perceives liberty as yielding genial influences. In particular, he prophesies liberty as that republican principle that shall subsequently promote "luxuriant" growth in knowledge and virtue for Africa's sons and daughters in the early republic. This increase, he announces, shall one day restore a fallen metonymic Africa to its former Edenic glory.

What initially appears to constitute a "meaningless allusion" ultimately reveals Williams's erudite manipulation of Milton's visionary poetics. This manipulation endows Williams's oration with greater interpretive force since it completes the preacher's rhetorical chain of audio-visionary spurs to *Paradise Lost*. Allusions like these seem meaningless at first but prove significant, according to Machacek, based on "their aggregate effects." The accumulation of these elements in a belated work "reproduce...the aesthetic effect of the formulaic diction in which oral epics like those of [Milton and] Homer are composed" in addition to "arous[ing] wonder or admiration" in audiences capable of hearing resonances of the poetic source.[85] Substituting "liberty" for Milton's ocean as a rhetorical marker of genial influence arouses awe by shining new interpretive light on Africa and modifying its changed and fallen estate to that of a restored paradise.

For Williams, the abolition of the U.S. slave trade signaled a new dawn for Africa's sons and daughters. He credits the "infinite mercy of the great Jehovah" and gives thanks to him for "condescend[ing] to listen to the cries of Africa's wretched sons" and for "interfer[ing] in their behalf" ("Abolition" 70). God's intervention brings an end to the slave trade and compensates Africa's descendants for the sins of white patriots, the "sons of '76" whose rebellion against English tyranny, according to Williams, did not accrue to blacks (70). Williams also praises God as an "angel of humanity [who successfully] strove to restore to the African race the inherent rights of man" (71). As is typical of the black jeremiad, these assertions highlight Williams's concern with exposing and "condemning the practice of slavery as a severe declension from the promise of a fully Christian democratic America" (71). His array of Miltonic snippets and accumulating sound pictures combine to indict the slave trade in certain instances and memorialize the historical event of its abolition at others.

Collectively, they facilitate his counter-critique of the American jeremiad. The purpose of the American jeremiad, according to Sacvan Bercovitch, "was to direct an imperiled people of God toward the fulfillment of their destiny, to guide them individually toward salvation, and collectively toward the American city of God."[86] Williams compensates for the limitations of this white-centered tradition by investing his sermon with fragments of Milton's canonical authority. His appropriation of Miltonic scenes functions to remind whites of their collective declension from it and to inspire blacks to exult in the sun of liberty. Ultimately, carrying out this evangelical impulse inspires Williams to remaster *Paradise Lost* by making it a talking intertext of wonder-working power in the messianic cause of black liberty.

William Hamilton is another audio-visionary who projects Miltonic scenes in the service of commemorating the abolition of the slave trade. Although his "early history remains something of a mystery," according to Leslie Alexander, he was known to have close connections to the black church and participated actively in civic causes of racial uplift.[87] One of his earliest distinctions in social activism concerns his participation in creating "the first independent black religious institution in New York City" along with James Varick and Peter Williams Sr. Later, Hamilton worked as a "carpenter and leader of New York's black community" before serving as "president and cofounder of the New York Society for Mutual Relief."[88] This latter organization, like others of the period, "was established to alleviate the economic difficulties of blacks" and maintained "strong links to New York City's black churches."[89] Hamilton even made a name for himself as a prominent orator. He contributed to the rise of Miltonic influence in early African American tradition by following Williams's rhetorical lead. Two of his addresses commemorating the abolition of the U.S. slave trade likewise sample Milton.

First, Hamilton's 1809 oration, "Mutual Interest, Mutual Benefit, and Mutual Relief," addresses an audience at the New York Universalist Church on the first anniversary of the abolition of the slave trade. Like Williams, Hamilton perceives Africa as a fallen paradise. Early in the oration, he asserts, "the country of our forefathers might truly be called paradise, or the seat of ease and pleasure, until the foul fiends entered."[90] Solidifying a recall of Williams's oration one year earlier, Hamilton similarly envisions Africa as a fallen paradise plundered by slave traders. Ironically, Williams attended this event, perhaps inspiring Hamilton to signify on the oration of his precursor through various allusions to Milton as in the rhetorically loaded use of "seat." Hamilton continues this practice of playful erudition with Williams through Milton as the commemorative address progresses.

Hamilton refers to slave traders as "fiends," therefore identifying and castigating this crew of body snatchers as satanic plunderers of paradise. To ensure his audience rightly perceives this infernal crew as satanic, he repeats and calls greater attention to the epithet, asking, "fiends did I say? Yes, the name is too sacred an appellation for the base ravagers of the African coast" (81). Hamilton sarcastically believes his fiendish term does not adequately describe slave traders. For this reason, his epithet equates them with Milton's devils. For instance, as early as book 1 in *Paradise Lost*, Milton's narrator describes Satan as "the flying Fiend" (*PL* 1.643). Book 3 focuses on the "Fiend" as he surveys Chaos and again when he alights onto paradise (*PL* 3.498, 588). In book 4, the Fiend "entertain[s] [the] odorous sweets" of paradise and is referred to by this moniker again when he resumes his original form after feeling the "touch of celestial temper" from Ithuriel's spear (*PL* 4.166, 812, 819). Because

Hamilton has already prompted a visual recall of Milton's epic by referencing paradise and identifying slave traders as plunderers of an African Eden, these fiendish epithets further enrich the connotative quality of his hermeneutic engagement with Milton.

Hamilton later condemns the "man-stealing crew" ("Mutual Interest" 81) for disturbing paradise. Next, a series of descriptive clauses enumerates a catalogue of vices that cause "Africa [to] groan from its sea line to its centre" (81). Hamilton cites kidnappings, handcuffings, brandings, and scourgings, which only account for half of the slaves' sufferings. Later, he asks, "where is the artist that can delineate a full picture of their miseries?" (81). The use of "picture" to describe his mode of oratorical storytelling announces that he, too, is equally caught up in the spirit of an audio-visionary aesthetic. To this end, he asserts that the slaves' "wretched situation baffles description" (81), and does not hesitate to project a few images that will assist audiences in vividly capturing what Africa in the image of a fallen paradise looks like to the mind's eye.

In one instance, Hamilton proclaims that he and members of his robust audience "stand confounded at the reflection that there should be found any of the human family so *lost* to their nature and the fine feelings of man, as to commit... such acts of cruelty on an unoffending part of the human family" (81; my emphasis). His use of "lost" accrues Miltonic significance when a few lines later he finds reason to "rejoice that science has began to *bud* with our race," a statement that subsequently leads him to proclaim, "soon shall our tree of arts bear its full burthen of rich and nectarious fruit" (81; my emphasis). According to this allusive intertextual schema, words like "lost" and "bud" build upon one another, producing an aggregate effect that forms an audio-visionary image through words that stand "for detached ideas."[91] Zora Neale Hurston, in "Characteristics of Negro Expression," refers to this aspect of "highly developed languages" as "cheque words."[92] Incidentally, she recognizes the title *Paradise Lost* as an example of this form of verbal expression in Western tradition. Hamilton's use of "bud" to signal the evidence of luxuriant growth in knowledge likewise functions as a cheque word. A floral symbol for paradise, "bud" allusively spurs a recall of Milton's epic as a means for conveying themes of Edenic fallenness.

In a second commemorative address, Hamilton remains committed to projecting Miltonic scenes of African fallenness and restoration. Delivered on January 2, 1815, in New York "in observance of the seventh anniversary of the ostensible abolition of the U.S. slave trade," Hamilton's "O! Africa" again interprets the continent as a fallen paradise.[93] This time his title directly signals its Miltonic affiliation with *Paradise Lost* by clipping or abbreviating a line from one of Satan's speeches and transforming it into a brief phraseological adaptation. Hamilton's title, in addition to extending Milton's afterlife into the second decade of the nineteenth century in early African American tradition, also enlarges upon its mode of signifyin(g) on Williams's "Abolition of the Slave Trade." Williams only alludes to Satan's "O, How art thou fall'n" speech through allusive figurations. Hamilton, by contrast, clips the predicate of Satan's utterance then spurs a recall of the infernal hero's exclamation concerning Beelzebub's fallen and changed condition through sampled diction and descriptive imagery.

This affiliation with Milton does not make itself audibly apparent through a series of direct appropriations. Instead, Hamilton allows a chain of allusive figurations to intimate and introduce *Paradise Lost* as an intertextual scenic backdrop for his sermon. His allusive affiliation with Milton's epic surfaces within his oratorical message when he offers paradiasical "description[s] of the country of our parents" ("O! Africa" 91). This scenic approach to revisionist history acknowledges African ancestors as first parents in the metonymic images of Adam and Eve. After chronicling Egypt's former glory and that of Africa's sub-Saharan interior, Hamilton laments both civilizations' fallen estates. Their decline leads him to bemoan Africa's abject degradation. An apostrophe to his ancestors' homeland makes it clear that *Paradise Lost* serves as a "talking book" for the propagation of his antislavery gospel.

In his apostrophe, Hamilton mourns, "But O! Africa, thou first fair garden of God's planting, thou once delightful field and original nursery for all those delicious fruits, tasteful herbage, and fragrant plants, that man highly prises, thou tract of earth over which the blest luminary, the sun, delights to make his daily splendid pass, thou spot of earth, where fair science first descended and the arts first began to bud and grow; how art thou chang'd and fallen" (91).

If not for the word "chang'd," Hamilton's lamentation might suggest the orator was echoing Isaiah 14:12. Since the word does not appear in the scriptural source, Hamilton's phraseological apostrophe signals he has taken his text from Milton's epic rather than the Bible. This borrowing from Milton's talking book assumes increased significance due to Hamilton's aggregate of accumulating Edenic figures from *Paradise Lost*. For instance, he infuses his apostrophe with increasing resonances of Edenic imagery. Phrases like "first fair garden," "delightful field," and "fragrant plants," when considered alongside such words as "bud" and "grow," invoke the scenic beauty of Milton's paradise. Hamilton solidifies this allusive impression by positioning his Edenic imagery between a clipped satanic utterance. Specifically, he introduces Satan's "O, how art thou fallen" phrase by substituting Africa for Beelzebub, then clipping the phrase by filling it with a chain of floral imagery. After infusing the apostrophe with these Edenic resonances, Hamilton solidifies his Miltonic performance by incorporating the balance of Satan's utterance to conclude his lament on African fallenness. His blending of aggregate Miltonic figures sustains his active recall of *Paradise Lost* while also showcasing his phraseological innovativeness and playful erudition with his talking epic.

Hamilton creates additional audio-visionary impressions derivative of *Paradise Lost* when he resorts to denouncing the evil deeds committed by slave traders. For instance, he envisions slave ships as "floating hells," his metaphoric amalgamation of Milton's hellish dungeon and its nautical geography ("O! Africa" 95). Hamilton's floating metaphor pictorializes the Middle Passage by imagining captive slaves on demonic grounds similar to those inhabited by Satan and his followers. The intertextual basis for this analogous relationship can be seen in the descriptive lines prior to Satan's first utterances in book 1 of *Paradise Lost*. Before he speaks, Milton's epic narrator reveals that the infernal hero lies "prone on the flood" and "Chained on the burning lake" of fire (*PL* 1.195, 210). Milton's imagery reveals that Satan is not confined to a tract of infernal sediment but languishes in a mired pool of flaming torment.

Hamilton transforms this nautical visualization of hell into a subversive reprise of that image. In projecting an image of slave ships through this floating Miltonic metaphor, Hamilton projects an audiovisual reading of African captives as imprisoned in the hellish hulls of slave ships. He further codes this hellish imagery with Miltonic accents by addressing his audience in rhetorical tones of infernal eloquence. For instance, he turns up the rhetorical heat of invective when identifying and condemning slave traders as "fiends." Hamilton even puns on his use of infernal rhetoric, sarcastically joking he will not "retract" or "ask pardon for [his] warmth of expression," since he recognizes these plunderers of paradise "deserve no better name, and it would be impossible for [him] to talk coolly, when the slave trade is the subject" ("O! Africa" 95). Indeed, Hamilton can only afford to speak coolly when he is not visually relaying "the murderous scenes on Africa" or re(p)laying "the picture[s]" he insists are "not half drawn" (95). In these cooler moments of oratorical expression, Hamilton praises God for early abolitionists like Anthony Benezet, William Wilberforce, and Senator Stephen R. Bradley. Their activism helps Hamilton to complete his audio-visionary pictures of Miltonic dissent, further complementing his artistic goal of restoring Africa's sons and daughters to their former Edenic glory and in a rhetorical image suggestive of a paradise regained.

Collectively, Hamilton and Williams's three orations relay and replay scenes from Milton's epic because *Paradise Lost*, their talking book of liberty and dissent, facilitates both orators' aims to cite the promise of a divine errand, critique an early republic's declension from it, and proclaim a prophecy of African restoration for God's chosen people in the new world. These black jeremiadic impulses help advance the antislavery cause in addition to spreading the gospels of Miltonic revolt. Building upon Wheatley and subsequent writers and orators like Othello, Equiano, and Haynes, Williams and Hamilton paved the way for future appropriations of Milton in early African American tradition. Williams and Hamilton, in particular, specifically structured their orations with Milton in mind. Their aesthetic of Miltonic appropriation was dedicated to a rhetorical practice that would artfully expose Africa's fallenness by critiquing the tyrannical institutions that made that civilization's decline possible. Most important, their respective instances of Miltonic reprise assisted them in prophesying the redemption and restoration of God's chosen people who were the oppressed victims of slavery's satanic forces. By 1829, the rhetorical ante was elevated to a more incendiary rhetorical pitch. The publication of David Walker's *Appeal in Four Articles; Together with a Preamble, to the Coloured Citizens of the World, but in Particular, and Very Expressly, to Those of the United States of America* answered that call, further extending Milton's afterlife as a sacred yet secular talking book for Africa's sons and daughters relative to the antislavery cause.

Easily one of the most incendiary documents in early African American literature, Walker's *Appeal* responds to the rhetorical tones of Milton's satanic epic by adapting them to coincide with the rebellious author's messianic gospel of black revolt. For Wilson Jeremiah Moses, the *Appeal* "mingles the conciliatory and the strident tones of the black messianic tradition."[94] It unashamedly authorizes self-emancipation as a divine duty for blacks to aspire to while also critiquing and vilifying whites in stern language and scathing critique. For these reasons, Moses labels Walker's treatise as "an extreme example of the jeremiadic tradition."[95] These strident tones of rhetorical and ideological revolt coincide with Walker's audio-visionary poetics of troping with Milton on demonic grounds of contention and interpretation. An editorial appearing in an 1830 issue of Boston's *Columbian Centinel* evidences the satanic reception that Walker's text encourages.

The editor of this article recognizes Walker's appropriations of Milton's hell and turns them against Walker's text. These assessments in print journalism fan the flames of Walker's rebellious character, circulating satanic impressions of him abroad. Lambasting the *Appeal* as a dangerous text, the writer describes Walker's pamphlet as "one of the most wicked and inflammatory productions that ever issued from the press. Its character is entirely mischievous, without one redeeming quality, and we should judge from the drift, that the writer, whatever may be his exterior complexion, bears a heart as dark and cruel as the great fiend of Pandaemonium."[96] Though the writer is unable to ascertain the author's black complexion, he is convinced that Walker's militant temperament reveals a heart of infernal darkness. Moreover, he equates Walker with Milton's Satan, the fiendish exemplar of Pandaemonium. This intertextual reception encourages the *Columbian Centinel*'s readership to regard Walker as satanically revolting. Such a demonic reception proves rather ironic since Walker's *Appeal* evidences its rhetorical homage to Milton and Satan's infernal eloquence as an exercise in political hyperbole. The editor recognizes Walker's Miltonic echoes, but he misunderstands them. Whereas Walker borrows from Milton's hell to intensify his critique of slavery's evils, the editor takes Walker's borrowings as evidence that the black freedom fighter *is* the devil imagined in Milton's epic. The very elements leading the editor to devalue Walker as evil are the same things the black freedom writer uses for dissident good. Upon closer inspection of the *Appeal*'s tone, one finds Walker was indeed in league with Milton's Satan. More to the point, his text overhears Satan's infernal rhetoric through an intermediary source like Murray's *English Grammar*, a pedagogical intertext that spreads the gospel of Milton's Satan through lessons in hyperbole. Walker applies these lessons to his messianic gospel of black revolt as evidenced by his *Appeal*.

Walker was born a free man of color "in or near Wilmington, North Carolina," around 1796 or 1797 and moved to Boston, Massachusetts, at the age of 30. He was an active participant in Boston's black community and ran a successful business as the proprietor of a "used-clothes shop at the City Market." He gained widespread notoriety with the publication of his incendiary pamphlet, largely as a result of his sartorial cunning. Walker was known to sew copies of the *Appeal* into the linings of various garments that he subsequently conveyed to "sympathetic sailors bound for Wilmington, Charleston, Savannah, and New Orleans."[97] These acts of sartorial subterfuge coupled with his appropriations of satanic rhetoric in the *Appeal* enrich the connotative value of *Paradise Lost* as a satanic talking book in early African American tradition. Blending fashion with politics, Walker transformed his clothing shop into an infernal haberdashery where Satan's poetry can be re-manufactured for messianic purposes of racial uplift.

Rather than projecting scenic snippets from *Paradise Lost* as some of his precursors did, Walker relays and replays Milton's presence through a series of audio-visionary rhetorical tones. His verbal style addresses audiences in stern language that is rife with an exaggerated use of exclamation points, italics, capitalizations, sarcasm, and unequivocally condescending diction. In literary form, the *Appeal* is structurally modeled on such judicial documents as the U.S. Constitution and the Declaration of Independence. Jackson explains Walker's rationale for signifyin(g) upon these judicial documents as the author's way of "expressing his sense of the irony represented by racism within the American democracy."[98] Walker, in blending his subversive hyperbole of language and punctuation with an ironic use of literary form, generates a rebellious ethos for himself in the *Appeal*. Furthermore, this unconventional style projects a literary persona of one who dares to justify his controversial and unconventional gospel before the bar of public opinion in tones of fervent expediency. Walker complements this rebellious ethos by unequivocally dedicating the theme of his treatise to the "coloured people of the United States," who in his estimation constitute "the most degraded, wretched, and abject set of beings that ever lived since the world began" as a result of their enslavement in America (*Appeal* 1). Walker examines their wretchedness in a preamble supported by four articles. Each article examines this wretchedness relative to the "consequences" of slavery, ignorance, Christian religion, and colonization efforts.

Walker entitles article 2 "Our Wretchedness in Consequence of Ignorance." This article justifies Milton as a rhetorical intertextual presence in the *Appeal*. Milton's presence is discernable by an acoustic reception rather than a strictly visual one. As the conclusion of article 2 reveals, Walker overhears Milton and Satan's infernal eloquence in book 4 through an intermediary source. That source is Lindley Murray's *English Grammar*, one of the more popular textbooks of the period. George Sensabaugh identifies Murray as "one of the first Americans to present Milton as a master of words" as a result of his *English Grammar*, which "became a standard work during the early years of the Republic and remained so for more than a half century."[99] Murray's text is especially significant for tracing audible resonances of Miltonic presence in the *Appeal*, for this intermediary work presents a lesson on hyperbole in its appendix. Walker, in referencing this text, suggests he is well acquainted with the work and the lessons in grammar it teaches. Indeed, the *Appeal* reveals Walker's remastery of the Miltonic lessons in particular. Walker applies these Miltonic lessons in hyperbole to the

Appeal by translating this poetic skill and customizing it to give his antislavery rhetoric a pronounced tenor of satanic flair.

It is highly likely that Walker was quite familiar with Milton on his own intellectual merits. His *Appeal* reveals a familiarity with *Plutarch's Lives*, Oliver Goldsmith's *A History of Greece from the Earliest State to the Death of Alexander the Great*, Thomas Jefferson's *Notes on Virginia*, *The Common Book of Prayer*, and Joseph Addison. These citations led Sterling Stuckey to assert that Walker enjoyed access to a wide array of books prior to relocating from North Carolina to Boston in 1827. In his estimation, a young David Walker "could not have become as educated as he was *after* leaving the South for Boston," which was only two years prior to the publishing of his pamphlet.[100] In the absence of any elaborately sustained references to Milton in the *Appeal*, article 2 gives allusive signs that Walker at least overheard the hyperbolic power of Milton's Satan in Murray's *English Grammar*. Near its conclusion, Walker critiques the "heart-rending fact" (*Appeal* 33) of a false black literacy pervading the republic. This critique uses Murray's textbook as contextual background for his arguments concerning the deceitful practices of black miseducation promoted by whites. Referencing Murray's *English Grammar* in this section of his article functions as the intertextual litmus test for grounding Walker's pamphlet in the fallen rhetoric espoused in Satan's "me miserable" speech from book 4 of *Paradise Lost*. This acoustic reception confirms Walker's faith in the art of Miltonic appropriation, which expresses itself in the mode of overhearing resonances of Satan's infernal eloquence through Murray's lesson in hyperbole.

Article 2 begins with veiled allusions to Milton's epic that instantly encourage visions of hell. Walker opens the article by identifying ignorance as "a mist, low down into the very dark and almost impenetrable abyss in which, our fathers for many centuries have been plunged" (*Appeal* 19). The use of "mist," a common rhetorical figure in classical and canonical modern epics, situates Walker's readers on demonic grounds that run well beneath earth's subterranean depths. As his imagery burrows further beneath the earth's surface, Walker denigrates Christians and the "enlightened of Europe," who are responsible for plunging Africans into an abyss or state of ignorance that prompts a geographical recall of hell. According to Walker, enlightened Christians "see the ignorance and consequent degradation of our fathers, [and] instead of trying to enlighten them, by teaching them that religion and light with which God had blessed them,...plunged them into wretchedness ten thousand times more intolerable, than if they had left them entirely to the Lord." This passage allusively associates African Americans' wretched condition with hell, a rhetorical figure of abjection that surfaces numerous times throughout Walker's *Appeal*.

For Walker, this hellish degradation stands in stark contrast to the contributions in "the arts and sciences" made "by the sons of Africa or of Ham among whom learning originated." Walker specifically faults Catholic religion for this decline. He refers to Catholic religion as "that scourge of nations," further indicting the institution for its tyrannical practices, which prove antithetical to the "Protestant faith" (*Appeal* 21). These same forces, he contends, help to explain a variety of infernal deeds committed on U.S. soil that are too horrific as to make one's "very heart bleed."

The article catalogues multiple examples of African Americans' "wretchedness in consequence of ignorance" before concentrating on the miseducation of black male youth. It is at this point in the article that Walker overhears Milton's Satan through Murray and levies this intertextual capital in his critique of slavery. According to Walker, he has "examined school-boys and young men of colour in different parts of the country, in the most simple parts of Murray's *English Grammar*, and not more than one in thirty was able to give a correct answer to my interrogations." Here, Walker exposes the dangers associated with an ignorance performed by "young men of colour, *who have been to school*" but have been miseducated unwittingly (33). Walker's anecdotal account does not expressly reference Milton, but it performs a style of analytical argumentation that is in interpretive dialogue with *Paradise Lost* and Satan's infernal eloquence. His reference to Murray's textbook reveals he has divined his theory of black miseducation, at least in part, as a result of overhearing hyperbolic resonances of Satan's infernal eloquence on the pages of that pedagogical intertext. Because Murray's appendix presents Satan's "me miserable" soliloquy as a lesson in hyperbole, it is worth surveying how that speech contributes to

Walker's arguments concerning false black literacy as an intertextual analogue to the infernal hero's exaggerated grammar.

In his soliloquy, Satan refuses to submit to God's sovereignty, despising that word and bidding "farewell" to fear and remorse, further reasoning, "all good to me is lost" and declaring, "Evil, be thou my good" (*PL* 4.108–10). While ruminating on his predicament, Satan finds himself surrounded by and wracked with "infinite wrauth" and "infinite despaire," lamenting,

> Which way I flie is Hell; my self am Hell;
> And in the lowest deep a lower deep
> Still threatning to devour me opens wide,
> To which the Hell I suffer seems a Heav'n. (*PL* 4.74–78)

Satan refuses to repent because doing so would require him to humble himself in submission. It would incite his "dread of shame," particularly among his followers whom he seduced to join him in his rebellious endeavors (*PL* 4.82). His resolution to make evil stand for good underscores a resignation to his hellish fate, though he finds cause to exult in what he extols as the majestic glory of his infernal kingdom. It is this acceptance of his fate that leads Satan to remain committed to waging war against God by attacking Adam and Eve in paradise.

Murray recognizes Satan's speech as pedagogically useful for teaching lessons in the art of eloquent hyperbole. This same Miltonic passage speaks to Walker as well but on different rhetorical registers. For Walker, Murray's lesson in hyperbole presents a militant opportunity to critique the miseducation of blacks as a corollary to what he interprets as Satan's "false grammar." He concedes that some of these so-called educated schoolboys "can write a good hand" but also despairs how this same lot "may be almost as ignorant, in comparison, as a horse" (*Appeal* 33). Walker even challenges skeptics to survey the educational landscape and prove him wrong. To those who would disagree with him, he challenges them to survey the landscape and summarily quiz educated youth on their knowledge of English. He argues that they "will hardly find...five in one hundred, who, are able to correct the false grammar of their language." While he wryly observes that "the cause of this almost universal ignorance among" his people is for "our schoolmasters to declare," he does not absolve white America from guilt either. He concludes article 2 with the stern assertion that "it is a notorious fact that the major part of the white Americans, have, ever since we have been among them, tried to keep us ignorant, and make us believe that God made us and our children to be slaves to them and theirs."

When Walker labels black students' less than eloquent speech as "false grammar," he signals a profession of his intertextual faith in the subversive power of Satan's infernal eloquence and hyperbolic rhetoric. This profession of intertextual faith in Milton comes after he overhears the epic writer through a mediating source other than *Paradise Lost*. For Walker, Satan's "false grammar" is analogously similar to the miseducated youth he discusses in this passage. To him, this (mis)educated group reflects walking hyperboles. Miseducated and none the wiser given their wretched ignorance, they routinely perform "pretensions to knowledge," spreading false literacy while vainly believing they are "so full of learning that [one] cannot mention any thing to them which they do not know better than yourself" (*Appeal* 32). Walker's reading of this cultural phenomenon is rhetorically grounded in Satan's "me miserable" speech, a passage he overhears in Murray's textbook. Walker also transfers this lesson to other parts of the *Appeal*, particularly through the briefest of phraseological adaptations, where a series of satanic words bring Milton's fallen hero into view through the author's audio-visionary aesthetic.

Throughout the *Appeal*, Walker repeatedly relies upon words like "infernal," "hell," "abject," "servility," and "submission." He also uses words like "wretchedness" and "tyrant" to hyperbolic effect. These seven words appear so frequently in the *Appeal* as to provide an explanation for why the contributor to the *Columbian Centinel* overhears the exemplar of Pandaemonium reverberate throughout Walker's seditious pamphlet. For instance, the word "infernal" appears in the *Appeal* nine times. Several examples include Walker's indictment of the "peculiar institution" for its hellish practice of holding African Americans captive in "infernal chains of slavery" and for afflicting them with "infernal cruelties" (*Appeal* 12, 43).

Milton also uses "infernal" repetitively throughout *Paradise Lost*. As early as book 1, line 34, the epic narrator refers to Satan as an "infernal Serpent." With this adjectival modifier, Milton specifically draws attention to the figurative hell raging within Satan. Satan's demonic rage reflects the physical torment he is made to endure as punishment for his rebellion in heaven. Book 4 makes this point more explicitly, noting, "for within him hell / He brings, and round about him, nor from hell / One step no more than from himself can fly / By change of place" (*PL* 4.20–23). Satan's inner torment is so profound that it arguably justifies an exaggerated use of the word "infernal" to describe both his disposition and hell's dreadful landscape. Used in phrases such as "infernal world" and an "infernal pit" (*PL* 1.251, 657) and "infernal court," "infernal rivers," and "infernal vale" (1:792; 2.575, 742), the word appears no less than 12 times throughout the opening two books.[101]

Words like "abject," "servility," "submission," and "tyrant" also constitute brief phraseological adaptations of Miltonic diction. Milton first uses the word, "abject" in book 1, line 312. Its use highlights the legion's fallen estate. The word surfaces again in the "Thick as autumnal leaves" passage, where Satan and his infernal crew are described as "Abject and lost" (*PL* 1.312). Rhetorically, the word is highly charged and loaded because it connotes Satan's fallenness and because the infernal hero especially despises his degraded and enslaved status in hell, which he recognizes as abject servility. Of the four instances where the word "abject" is used in Milton's epic, three of them specifically refer to Satan. In two of these instances, Satan utters the word himself. For example, he criticizes his peers for slumbering in their "abject posture," which to him suggests their willingness to "adore the Conquerour" (*PL* 1.322, 323). Etymologically, "abject" is Middle English and Latin in origin. Derived from *abjectus*, meaning "thrown down," the word "abject" during the medieval period signified states of being "cast down...[or being] brought low in position, condition, or estate."[102]

The words "abject" and "wretched" are etymologically connected, and Walker uses both to hyperbolic effect throughout his *Appeal*. "Wretched," according to the *OED* refers to a banished or exiled individual. It specifically refers to one "who is sunk in deep distress sorrow, or misfortune," or to persons "living in state[s] of misery, poverty, or degradation."[103] Walker uses this word multiple times throughout his text. Because the word shares denotative similarities with "abject," its exaggerated use emphasizes Walker's engagement in a performance of playful erudition with Milton's diction. Sometimes Walker substitutes the word "wretched" for "abject." In other instances, he simply appropriates the word, calling visual attention to a term appearing in Milton's epic no less than 24 times.

Another instance of loaded Miltonic diction in the *Appeal* involves Walker's appropriation of "servile," a word appearing at least 15 times in the *Appeal*. Occasionally, Walker signifies on this Miltonic word by forming open-compound words like "abject servility." In Milton's epic, the word surfaces when Belial disagrees with the angels' obligation to praise God with "Forc't Halleluiah's" (*PL* 2.243) and "servile offerings" (2.246). Abdiel, using the word to dispute Satan, contends the fallen angel "Once fawn'd, and cring'd, and servilly ador'd / Heav'n's awful Monarch" (4.959–60).

Belial and Abdiel's references rhetorically equate the angels to states suggestive of enslavement; however, Walker seizes several rhetorical opportunities to make this satanic parallel vivid for his readers. For instance, he refers to blacks as "the *most wretched, degraded* and *abject* set of beings that *ever lived* since the world began" (*Appeal* 2). In another passage, from article 1, he uses the phrase "abject ignorance" to further indict the early republic for its crimes in depriving blacks of formal education (7). On still another page, Walker offers this uncompromisingly stern critique: "the man who would not fight under our Lord and Master Jesus Christ, in the glorious and heavenly cause of freedom and of God—to be delivered from the most wretched, abject, and servile slavery, that ever a people was afflicted with since the foundation of the world, to the present day—ought to be kept with all of his children or family, in slavery, or in chains, to be butchered by his *cruel* enemies" (12). These representative examples occur within the first 12 pages of the *Appeal* and present an intertextual foretaste of the phraseological mileage Walker gains from brief borrowings of Milton's language.

Even a word like "submission" achieves allusive significance in Walker's text. Walker, like Satan, expresses vehement opposition to any tendency suggestive of submission. In one passage, he contends, "if we lay aside abject servility, and be determined to act like men, and not brutes—the murderers among the whites would be afraid to show their cruel head" (*Appeal* 62). He espouses this view to appeal to those who would be persuaded to action and to discourage the faint of heart from "yield[ing] in a moment to whites" who "keep their feet on [the] throats" of his colored brethren (60, 62). Espousing this version of rebellious masculinity leads him to endorse a politics of rebellious martyrdom. For men of this disposition, Walker believes "there can be nothing in [their] hearts but death alone," a dissident outlook comparable to the gospel Satan preaches to himself in his "me miserable" soliloquy (61). Whereas Satan revolts on demonic grounds by vowing "never to submit or yield," Walker takes a similar stand, beseeching his black sisters and brethren to do the same (*PL* 1.108). This rebellious stance may explain why his hyperbolic use of the word "submit" or its variant, "submission," appears at least ten times in his incendiary pamphlet.[104]

These brief phraseological adaptations, along with a series of infernal allusions to Milton's epic, bring the "fiend" of Milton's Pandaemonium to mind as explained by the contributing writer to the *Columbian Centinel*. Walker's tone blares its gospel of black revolt and liberation into the aural cavities of his readers through figures of rhetorical hyperbole. Throughout the *Appeal* excessive and italicized punctuation marks serve as visual cues and signs for an incendiary pitch that preaches its message in rhetorical tones of high frequency. Troping with these figures of sight and sound trouble the demonic grounds of interpretive contention where orthodox receptions of Milton's epic are concerned. Rather than shying away from Milton's Satan as a figure to be shunned, Walker gravitates to the infernal hero as a rhetorical mouthpiece for voicing rebellious agitation in the messianic cause of liberty. Additionally, his incendiary rhetorical tone manifests as an audio-visionary sign of his hyperbolic appropriations and affiliation with Milton's Satan. This aesthetic signals Walker's intertextual faith in the wonder-working powers of Milton's sacred yet secular talking book. His intertextual faith is acoustic in nature. To be more exact, this faith in the liberating word of Milton comes by (over)hearing it through an intermediary source like Murray's *English Grammar* and not by sight alone.

Finally, Walker's *Appeal* completes and complicates Milton as the last work by a transitional wave of black audio-visionaries dedicated to spreading the gospel of *Paradise Lost* and antislavery revolt as a redemptive practice for a chosen nation. In the *Appeal*, Walker prophesies God will soon exert his wrathful revenge on the nation for its sins against blacks and humanity more generally. He further prophesies God shall send a Hannibal who, while proving salvific for blacks, will compel whites to "remember the divisions and consequent sufferings of *Carthage* and of *Hayti*" (20). That widespread destruction can be avoided, he contends at the end of article 3 and elsewhere, provided the republic repents.

Walker's *Appeal*, according to Herbert Aptheker, introduces the "first sustained written assault upon slavery and racism to come from a black man in the United States."[105] It preaches its gospel of black revolt by rhetorically appealing to Milton's Satan in an unequivocal fashion. This intertextual affiliation is not surprising; as E. N. S. Thompson explains, "when the struggle for individual liberty became again acute, the story of Lucifer received more attention and was colored by modern implications." He also finds "Satan and Cain both symbolized for many thinkers the revolt of the individual will against destiny."[106] It is to this latter end that Walker's audio-visionary poetics and those of his predecessors in the tradition sample and signify upon Milton's satanic epic and Satan's poetry of fallenness. As his political gospel indicates, elevating the race to greater heights of social respectability would require much more than an intertextual tradition of command performances that projected a series of Miltonic resonances on the levels of sight and hearing. Moving beyond this poetic technology of strategic warfare, one could ignite a will to revolt against tyranny by channeling Satan's rebellious spirit and walking by faith according to Africanist traditions of Miltonic engagement. In time, this infernal yet messianic poetics would lead the race out of bondage, setting them at liberty by preaching Milton and "the acceptable year of the Lord" (Luke 4:19).

4

OF MIGHT AND MEN

Milton, Frederick Douglass, and Resistant Masculinity as Existential Geography

With the publication of Walker's *Appeal to the Colored Citizens of the World*, 1829 proved to be an acceptable year for preaching the gospel of Milton in furtherance of the antislavery cause.[1] With its satanic appropriations of *Paradise Lost* and Milton's hyperbolic rhetoric, Walker's *Appeal* made intertextual affiliations with Milton's satanic epic more popular for succeeding generations of abolitionists and antislavery proponents. Milton's epic, as Forsyth explains, is all about "the heroic Satan and his sublime grandeur."[2] Walker's *Appeal* tapped into the epic's satanic appeal, contributing to modes of reception that eventually made Boston a Miltonic epi(c)enter of political revolt. This regional capital of Miltonic influence would inspire scores of abolitionists and "race men" of the long nineteenth century to forge incendiary affiliations with the infernal hero of *Paradise Lost* for messianic purposes of freedom. William Lloyd Garrison's antislavery newspaper, the *Liberator*, was especially crucial in helping to spread Milton's satanic influence relative to the abolitionist cause. According to J. Saunders Redding, when Garrison "founded the *Liberator* in Boston, ... the Negro recognized the voice of a champion raised in his behalf."[3] In time, Garrison's weekly newspaper inspired one of the most thunderous voices in abolitionist and antislavery discourse.

A fugitive slave who spoke uncompromisingly in rhetorical tones of might and resistant masculinity, Frederick Douglass found his messianic voice by championing the antislavery cause on demonic grounds hallowed by Milton's satanic epic.

Douglass's earliest autobiographies and several of his orations complete and complicate Milton on the existential grounds of a male-centered reception. On these existential grounds of being, Douglass performs a geographical rupture in that he psychologically withdraws from a concrete understanding of his present circumstances in slavery in order to produce a "double nihilation where one posits an ideal state of affairs as a pure present nothingness."[4] To rupture hegemonic geography on these existential grounds, according to Jean-Paul Sartre, is to transform the landscape beyond the self. Activists invested in transforming hegemonic landscapes engage oppressive structures and the sufferings they produce, drawing upon their rebellious might as "motives for conceiving of another state of affairs in which things would be better for everybody."[5] Douglass expresses this will to revolt through his "rhetoric of resistance," a mode of discourse filled with "militant images" that, according to Ella Forbes, "more accurately reflected the reality of African American agency and the quest for Black manhood."[6] Milton's autobiographical presence also contributes to Douglass's rebellious speech acts in the *Narrative*. His influence serves as an intertextual testament of the Milton Douglass was increasingly coming to know and acknowledge within himself.

As evidenced in Douglass's earliest autobiographies and select speeches from his long oratorical career, this rhetoric of resistance aids the former slave in expressing and affirming himself as a heroic man of self-made proportions. Milton functions as an iconic exemplum for Douglass's poetics similar to "early modern writers" who, as Machacek notes, "wrote of prior authors less as providing them with the means for enriching the significance of their works and more as providing them with models for composition."[7] Douglass's *Narrative of the Life of Frederick Douglass, an American Slave, Written by Himself* (1845) and elements of his revised autobiography, *My Bondage and My Freedom* (1855), follow this model of interpoetic affiliation. In both works, Douglass either critiques slavery in infernal, supernal, or Edenic terms or fuses all three to suit his political purposes.

This synthesizing of Milton's satanic epic in his first two autobiographies reflects what was probably his earliest encounter with *Paradise Lost*. His initial encounter with Milton most likely occurs on the pages of Caleb Bingham's *The Columbian Orator* (1797) a popular text of the period that William Andrews identifies as "an eloquence handbook."[8] Among its more than 80 selections appears an excerpted passage from book 6 of *Paradise Lost*. The passage appears under the heading, "Christ Triumphant over the Apostate Angels." Although Douglass does not comment on this selection from Bingham's handbook, his *Narrative* reveals his scholarly devotion to reading and studying its contents. Obtaining a copy during an impressionable moment of his adolescence, Douglass relates, "every opportunity I got, I used to read this book."[9] Milton's influence would eventually surface in several speeches Douglass delivered throughout his close to 50-year oratorical career. In many of these select speeches, Douglass appropriates language from *Paradise Lost* or Milton's sonnets. His most pronounced engagement with Milton, however, may be found in Douglass's most popular speech, "Self-Made Men." In this speech, Douglass reads Milton in a gendered way, forging a "literary, personal, and political affiliation" with his precursor by recognizing him as an iconic symbol or exemplum of self-made manhood.[10] Reading Milton through this gendered lens of literary reception in his speeches on "Self-Made Men" functions as a rhetorical tracking device for identifying Douglass's skill of completing and complicating Milton in his own *Narrative*. In both autobiographies, Douglass expresses himself unequivocally, denouncing slavery freely on the existential grounds of a resistant masculinity that appropriates Milton as an iconic exemplum of self-made manhood.

Born a slave circa 1817, Douglass grew up on a plantation in Talbot County, Maryland. He was later "hired-out [as a] boat caulker in Baltimore" under Hugh Auld.[11] Select highlights of his life include teaching himself to read in defiance of the slave codes. For example, he mischievously "converted" white children "into teachers" by literally feeding them morsels of bread in exchange for "that more valuable bread of knowledge" (*Narrative* 32). At the age of 12, Douglass procured a copy of Bingham's *The Columbian Orator*, intensely studying selections by orators and writers like Socrates, William Pitt, and Joseph Addison.[12] The excerpted passage from book 6 of *Paradise Lost* contains 69 lines of text that recount the iconic scene where the Son vanquishes the fallen angels and hurls them from heaven to hell. Douglass took rhetorical cues from this passage by synthesizing infernal and supernal elements together as a strategic device for liberating himself from the hell of slavery. Milton and Satan's infernal eloquence appealed to him because they informed his need to sternly critique slavery. Similarly, Milton's supernal features attracted Douglass because their connotative qualities assisted him in underscoring his messianic authority as a self-made man whose autobiographical gospels of black revolt operated under the auspices of a blackened theology.

Self-made individuals are not successful in and of themselves, as Douglass knew, even if his *Narrative* tells a different story. Ironically, his *Narrative* fails to credit his wife, Anna Murray, as helping to defray the cost of his escape from slavery with her own money. After arriving in New York, Douglass traveled to Rhode Island, then settled in New Bedford, Massachusetts, where he formed his family. He came to prominence at an antislavery program in Nantucket where he spoke extemporaneously of his experiences as a fugitive slave. Garrison, who was in attendance, was captivated by Douglass's oratorical delivery. He soon encouraged the fugitive slave to publish an autobiography chronicling his experiences in bondage. Douglass's *Narrative* met with international success. Next, Douglass traveled domestically and internationally, recounting his experiences at various antislavery lectures. After a 21-month lecture tour of Europe, he returned to the United States, founded and edited his own antislavery newspapers, *The North Star* and *Frederick Douglass' Paper*. Other literary achievements followed. They included a novella, *The Heroic Slave*, and two more autobiographies, *My Bondage* (1855) and *The Life and Times of Frederick Douglass* (1893). Having worked his way up from slavery, Douglass, a master orator, exemplified the very character of self-made manhood he so popularly spoke about over the course of an oratorical career spanning nearly 50 years.

His speech on "Self-Made Men" represents his most popular oratorical address, and it is the foundational text that squarely positions Douglass in interpretive dialogue with Milton. Douglass delivered the speech "on more than fifty occasions between 1859 and 1893," according to Wolfgang Mieder.¹³ Two versions of the speech explicitly identify Milton as an ideal of self-made manhood. Because his distinct reception of Milton as this iconic symbol aligns so closely with the image he constructs of himself in his earliest autobiographies, both *Narrative* and his second autobiography, *My Bondage and My Freedom*, may be regarded as Miltonic texts as well. In addition to his fusion of infernal, supernal, and Edenic elements, Douglass's quest for self-made manhood as depicted in both autobiographies evidence the literary influence of the precursor he was coming to know more fully. According to this reading of Douglass's earliest autobiographies, Milton serves as a subversive (w)rite of passage. That is, his writings survive as exclusive intertexts that subsequently underwrite Douglass's narrative and rhetorical quest for self-made manhood and literary autonomy in arts and letters.

One of the earliest recorded versions of Douglass's speech on self-made men was delivered in Halifax, England, on January 4, 1860, to a large crowd assembled at Marlborough Hall.[14] This version and a subsequent one delivered 33 years later may be used as rhetorical tracking devices for disclosing Milton's hidden and diffuse presence in the *Narrative* and *My Bondage*.[15] Early in the first speech, Douglass concentrates on men who have misspent their youth and offers their example as a warning to those desirous of aspiring to an alternative ideal of manhood. Next, he focuses on the promise of young men, appropriating Milton as a rhetorical exemplum of an honorable and noble form of masculinity. In discussing the promise of youthful manhood, Douglass appropriates the concluding lines from book 12 of *Paradise Lost*, noting that it is they who have "all the bright world before them where to choose."[16] Incorporating this concluding line from book 12 into his speech prompts a specific recall of Adam and Eve's banishment from the garden of Eden at the end of Milton's epic. In this moment of *Paradise Lost*, the first parents walk into the future with all of the unbounded prospects for starting life anew under the unction of God's promise that he shall one day restore them to paradise in aftertimes.

Douglass's appropriation of this passage adapts this scene of unbounded promise as a means for envisioning the hopeful outlook awaiting young men who stand on the verge of boyhood and manhood at a most critical juncture in their lives. In Douglass's estimation, young men have opportunities to cultivate those *manly* virtues that will subsequently enable them to bypass a series of life's misfortunes. Men who are endowed with these manly virtues, he believes, make the best of ordinary or underprivileged circumstances. He reinforces this point further, offering several literary greats for members of his audience to consider as honorable exempla. He deems these canonical figures worthy of emulation and wishes to impress their achievements indelibly on the minds of men.

Milton heads Douglass's list, appearing before such luminaries as Francis Bacon and Shakespeare. According to Douglass, these individuals "illuminate and fill a wondering world with the resplendent glories of their achievements," while men of much lesser renown proved themselves "as dull as lead, and rose no higher in life than a mere physical existence."[17] Douglass esteems Milton, in particular, because he values the poet's valiance in composing a masterful achievement in epic tradition while blind. In this context, Douglass perceives Milton as embodying a commendable constitution, one ranking him among those who "raise themselves against great odds from the most humble and cheerless positions in life to usefulness, greatness, honour, influence, and fame."[18] This respect for Milton would abide with Douglass throughout the remainder of his oratorical career, as a subsequent variation of this speech indicates.

Thirty-three years later, in an updated version of his self-made man speech, Douglass still admires Milton and extols him as a preeminent example of shining manhood. In this revised speech, editors John W. Blassingame and John R. McKivigan contend, "the bulk of the lecture changed quite little over [the] thirty-five years" since 1859, when it was originally composed and delivered.[19] As he did in his Halifax rendition, Douglass offers a different list of luminaries no less impressive than before. This time, Douglass introduces his list by asserting, "Vast acquirements and splendid achievements stand to the credit of men and feeble frames and slender constitutions" ("Self-Made Men" 5:562). While Douglass positions Milton immediately following the preeminent Unitarian theologian William Ellery Channing, who is first on this list, no other writer appears before the epic poet. According to Douglass's assessment of his precursor's manhood, "Channing was physically weak. Milton was blind. [James] Montgomery was small and effeminate." Of Harriet Beecher Stowe, Douglass adds that she "would be nothing among the grizzly bears of the Rocky mountains. We should not be likely to ask for her help at a barn raising, or a ship launch; but when a great national evil was to be removed; when a nation's heart was to be touched; when a whole country was to be redeemed and regenerated and millions of slaves converted into free men, the civilized world knew no earthly power equal to hers" (5:562). In each of these descriptions, Douglass wishes to debunk the myth that only those who possess Herculean strength or massive body frames are endowed with power to produce heroic achievements. Additionally, he contends that luminaries of Milton and Stowe's caliber are worth "more to the world than a thousand Sampsons" (5:562). Since this speech professes an affiliation with Milton, Douglass's mention of Samson presents an amplified example of the epic writer's indirect influence. According to Carolivia Herron, indirect influences like these evidence "the transmission and effect of [Milton as] cultural image," one who surfaces in belated texts by "encompassing the prestige of the epic genre and the cultural importance" of biblical Scripture.[20] On these grounds of interpretive contention and influence, Douglas's reference to Samson, either alludes to or prompts a dual recall of the heroic industry exhibited by the enslaved hero in *Samson Agonistes* and the book of Judges.

Douglass's Milton presents audiences with a historical exemplum of self-made manhood, but one passage in particular offers a more substantive definition of this concept. In this passage, Douglass defines "self-made men" as those who "under peculiar difficulties and without the ordinary helps of favoring circumstances, have attained knowledge, usefulness, power and position and have learned from themselves the best uses to which life can be put in this world, and in the exercises of these uses to build up worthy character" (5:549–50). Moreover, they are "men who owe little or nothing to birth..., [who] are not brought up but who are obliged to come up..., [and who ultimately] hew out for themselves a way to success, and thus...become the architects of their own good fortunes" (5:550). These assessments make it perfectly clear that Douglass holds great admiration for industriously minded men who possess an independent spirit and champion adversity in the face of the most threatening odds or disadvantage. Self-made manhood and its "myth of success is basically one of 'vertical mobility,'" according to Wolfgang Mieder.[21] Milton, in triumphing over the trials of blindness, exemplifies this ideal of manly heroism from Douglass's interpretive reception of the canonical epic writer.

Milton not only champions adversity by writing an epic of unparalleled distinction in the English language; he serves as a canonical exemplum of innovative originality as well. In particular, he defies every literary convention he engaged while innovatively enriching every genre he ever dared to complete and complicate. Barbara Lewalski responds to this aspect of Milton's originality, acknowledging his "virtuoso use of the literary genre system."[22] Sonnets, lyrics, odes, masques, and epics are not the same once Milton tackles these genres. John Shawcross draws attention to a different aspect of Milton as an expression of self-made manhood. Placing emphasis on Milton's God-like proclivities, Shawcross notes that the epic writer "associates himself with the archetypal creator, God," therefore emphasizing *Paradise Lost* as "a similitude of God's creation."[23] Douglass's God-like leanings operate through a different type of literary script, however. Taking cues from an excerpt of book 6 in Milton's epic, he constructs himself as a messianic apostate. Both a messianic angel and satanic liberator, he gives rhetorical expression to a style of allusive engagement that fuses contrasting elements from Milton's epic in order to critique slavery. This same style of Miltonic engagement also underwrites Douglass's sense of literary autonomy as an expression of self-made manhood. These styles complete and complicate Milton based on Douglass's male-centered reception of the canonical poet.

Long before Douglass would explicitly identify Milton as an iconic exemplum of self-made manhood in his speeches, he would feel the spirit of the epic writer on the pages of Bingham's *Columbian Orator*. Douglass receives fragments of this spirit when he "gets hold of" Bingham's *Orator* and prizes the text because it "gave tongue to interesting thoughts on [his] own soul" (*Narrative*

32). The slave narrator continues, "What I got from [Richard Brinsley] Sheridan, was a bold denunciation of slavery, and a powerful vindication of human rights" (33). An infernal yet messianic change soon overcame Douglass the more he read and studied the selections contained within the pages of the *Orator*. He explains, "the more I read, the more I was led to abhor and detest my enslavers." Shortly thereafter, he describes himself as being "tormented" and "stung" in his soul. He also "writhe[s]" under his "unutterable anguish," eventually "preferring the condition of the meanest reptile to [his] own." Two paragraphs later, he has learned to identify acts of antislavery rebellion as "the fruit of *abolition*" (33). These responses to his abject condition suggest the narrative aftereffects of his critical intertextual encounter with Milton's satanic epic.

William Andrews argues that Douglass's emphasis in the *Narrative* focuses on associating himself with a resurrected savior and "without the satanic attributes of defiance that *My Bondage and My Freedom* claims for its hero."[24] However, the excerpted Miltonic passage in Bingham's *Columbian Orator* presents alternative possibilities for understanding the satanic epic as a two-faced intertext of literary influence. Specifically, Douglass's fusion of infernal and supernal elements in the *Narrative* signals aggregate effects of Miltonic influence. That influence necessitates a deeper intertextual analysis on the part of readers and critics especially because "many allusions," as Machacek argues, often "have no local significance."[25] Thus, the aggregate effects of Miltonic influence in the *Narrative* especially require considerations of book 6. That book acquaints Douglass with an exemplum of infernal vices and supernal virtues that stimulate an enhanced affiliation with Milton's satanic epic as a tropological code for critiquing slavery.

Douglass's fragmented exposure to book 6 of *Paradise Lost*, as Melissa Shields Jenkins comments, provides valuable insights into the various rhetorical possibilities available to him. By quoting lines 824–93 in his primer, Bingham creates an interpretive event that, according to Jenkins, allows Milton's poem to "offer a panorama of complex yet representative characters [who] navigate a landscape described primarily through dichotomies of heaven and hell, dark and light, righteousness and sin."[26] Early chapters of the *Narrative* evidence Milton's panoramic influence on Douglass. Troping with

Milton's hell and Eden to autobiographical effect, Douglass plays mischievously with the satanic epic against the grain of orthodox receptions. This form of mischievous play with Milton codes his autobiography as a satanic narrative. Such a narrative empowers Douglass to preach a gospel of black revolt while, at the same time, underwriting both his self-made status and literary manhood.

The fragmentary encounter with book 6 is no trivial instance of literary influence. As Machacek explains, books 5 and 6 of *Paradise Lost* have generated much debate in terms of "the war in heaven episodes" and their artistic and generic qualities. Machacek resolves this debate by exploring the "double-edged quality" of Milton's Homeric echoes, which ultimately signal his precursor's epics function as negative exempla. Negative exempla, according to Machacek, require belated authors to "negotiate contradictory demands." In terms of books 5 and 6, Milton must negotiate the task of making Satan "appear to be an epic threat" while also treating him "with mock-epic scorn."[27] These compositional demands similarly inform Douglass's reception of Milton in his *Narrative*. According to Robert G. O'Meally, the *Narrative* is in many respects informed by the African American sermons Douglass would have heard on the plantation. Thus, his *Narrative* is more than a slave narrative, but a text "meant to be mightily preached."[28] This sermonic feature connects Douglass to Milton's Christian epic, making book 6 of *Paradise Lost* even more attractive to the slave narrator.

Because of this sermonic connection, Douglass never really loses sight of his rhetorical attraction to the Son and Satan as presented in book 6. His attraction to the Son establishes Douglass as being on the Lord's side of righteousness and justice. At the same time, Douglass's rhetorical attraction to Satan amplifies the denunciatory tenor of his antislavery message. He blends these contrasting personas to produce a satanic narrative that positions him to navigate the conflicting demands of his writing situation. As an antislavery writer and black male seeking to validate his manhood in the literary arena of arts and letters, Douglass turns to Milton's satanic epic as an instructive exemplum and (w)rite of passage that assist him in navigating the specific demands attending his writing situation. The epic offers Douglass two particular characters "who exemplify various virtues and vices" with whom he expressly identifies on his own terms.[29] These interpretive possibilities ultimately inspire him to play mischievously with slavery and slaveholders while troping allusively with *Paradise Lost* in his quest for manhood within his *Narrative*.

Douglass "plays the mischief with the characters of slaveholders" and slavery throughout his *Narrative* by engaging with Milton's satanic epic on the demonic grounds of a resistant masculinity.[30] "Play[ing] the mischief" is Douglass's humorous appellation for his subversive style of troping with the characters of slaveholders. As he explains to William A. White in a letter written from Edinburgh, Scotland, "slave holders "will find the atmosphere very hot here for them" because of the orator's infernal rhetoric and argumentative style.[31] Denouncing slavery from this rhetorical posture serves as a demonic ground of contention because it plays with *Paradise Lost* by celebrating rhetorical fusions of the infernal and supernal, vice and virtue, to subversive political effect. Forsyth, examining the structures of the epic, finds that *Paradise Lost* "works by means of extended and echoing airs within its own world. So the Hell of Book 2 and the Heaven of Book 3 are brought into troubling parallel."[32] Douglass performs a variation of this aesthetic in his *Narrative*. Gleaning these parallels from the excerpted passage of book 6 as presented in Bingham's *Columbian Orator*, this feature enables him to playfully intervene in the slavery question in addition to underwriting his infernal yet messianic embodiment of self-made manhood.

Milton hovers about Douglass's *Narrative* as an intertextual exemplum as early as chapter 1. Allusions to Miltonic topographies accentuate Douglass's moments of antislavery critique in these early stages of his text where he searches to establish himself as his own self-made man. His quest begins when he confesses ignorance of his birthdate. Douglass's unknown origins contribute to his anxieties of alienation and homelessness in the nation. Valerie Smith describes this dilemma in origins as "offering counterevidence of his humanity, for his very existence derives from the conflation of sexual and property rights that slavery endorsed."[33] Douglass underscores his sense of alienation by mentioning his mother in three scant sentences in the opening paragraphs of his *Narrative*.

Because she lives apart from him on a distant plantation, Douglass has few memories of her and barely remembers her face. Douglass knows considerably less about his father. Other than the rumor that his father is a white man and presumably his slaveowner, he knows very little else.

Ignorance of his father's identity was a nagging concern for Douglass throughout his life. It encouraged an Oedipal complex, leading Gwen Bergner to argue his "lack of established paternity compounds his distance from the Father's name, [ultimately] frustrating his claim to masculine identification and his ability to speak from within his oppressive social order."[34] Compounding this dynamic, Douglass also feels like a motherless child. For instance, he admits, "I never saw my mother, to know her as such, more than four or five times in my life" (*Narrative* 13). Upon learning of her death, he receives that information "with much the same emotions I should have probably felt at the death of a stranger" (13). Alone in the world with no origins of note to speak of, Douglass begins his *Narrative* on the grounds of ontological nothingness. Rather than immediately chart his narrative ascent to self-made manhood, Douglass takes a rhetorical detour. Invested in presenting a second critique of slavery, he journeys to the demonic grounds of hell. This downward journey functions as an allusive means for introducing additional fragments of Miltonic presence into his *Narrative*.

This first of several Miltonic fragments in the *Narrative* occurs on the demonic grounds of hell, a faint allusion to the satanic epic that coincides with the filial anxieties of ontological nothingness Douglass has already expressed. In this early stage of his narrative, Douglass searches for coping mechanisms that might legitimate him as human to members of his reading audience. This search is necessary, for, as Valerie Smith recognizes, Douglass "possesses origins that offer counterevidence of his humanity."[35] Therefore, he attempts to re-member a stable sense of his humanity, one that ultimately inspires him to identify with his Aunt Hester in chapter 2 of his *Narrative*. Focusing on a barbaric scene involving his Aunt Hester and their slaveowner, Captain Anthony, Douglass narrates a "pornographic spectacle" that recounts a merciless whipping Hester endures for defying her owner's commands to resist seeing another male slave. Douglass is a child at the time the event occurs and is, therefore, "doomed to be a witness and a participant" (*Narrative* 15). Again, feeling a sense of ontological nothingness, he finds himself incapable of exercising a brand of patriarchal masculinity that would problematically confirm the sense of heroic manhood that slavery denies him.

Building upon his anxieties of paternal and maternal loss, Douglass reveals his angst concerning an inability to intervene and protect his female kin. An "impotent onlooker [who is] condemned to watch the abuse," Douglass suffers from a frustrated sense of manhood.[36] This dilemma motivates him to embrace the "fulfillment of [a] patriarchal masculine ideal," one fiercely rooted in internalized "phallocentric idealizations" of white maleness.[37] If he could intervene on Aunt Hester's behalf, Douglass would accrue to himself the honor of a heroic manhood. Instead, he finds himself incapable of fulfilling the tenets of "rugged individuality, physical strength, and geographical mobility" that Smith notes have tended to "enshrine cultural definitions of masculinity" throughout history.[38] These patriarchal impulses occasion Deborah McDowell's astute critique of the *Narrative*'s treatment of women. Douglass's narrative presentation of Hester's sufferings, she argues, actually works to uphold his interest in projecting himself as a heroic male. More specifically, "black women's backs become the parchment on which Douglass narrates his linear progression from bondage to freedom."[39] Ironically, Hester's back also becomes the parchment upon which Douglass first writes and affirms his literary quest for manhood through allusive scripts of Miltonic intertextuality.

Powerless to intervene on Aunt Hester's behalf, Douglass substitutes for this lack by journeying to the gates of hell in order to establish an allusive affiliation with Milton on the demonic grounds of contention. Douglass's hell does not instantly evidence its rhetorical affiliation with Milton. That relationship becomes especially evident as his critiques of slavery increasingly signify on Milton's descriptions of heaven and hell with greater intertextual clarity. This strategy allows him freedom to pursue a "literary autonomy" capable of supplying him "with the ability to purge himself of some pain."[40] If Hester's sufferings bring readers to the gates of hell, then Douglass's ability to generate his first allusive association with Milton on demonic grounds contributes to the literary autonomy he strives to obtain and perform. This achievement comes at the expense of Hester's scarred back, a parchment of flesh that subsequently renders Milton as a legible presence throughout the remainder of Douglass's *Narrative*.

Paradise Lost is the canonical work in English tradition that concentrates its theme on the contrasting topographies of heaven and hell toward justifying Christian principles. For this reason Milton's epic enjoys prestige as an exemplum for descending and journeying through hell then winging flight up to light in heaven. Milton leaves this rhetorical imprint to aftertimes such that Douglass cannot adopt a similar interpoetic route without prompting recalls of his precursor's satanic epic. These contrasting topographies and the journeys of descension and ascension function like so many figures, schemas, and concepts in literary tradition whose interpretive origins "inevitably carry Miltonic associations" regardless of the belated writer's literary ancestry.[41] Douglass intensifies this recall of Miltonic presence in the succeeding paragraph of chapter 2 where he describes Captain Anthony's treatment of Aunt Hester as indicative of the slaveowner's "infernal purpose." With this hellish modifier, Douglass begins to play with Milton's rhetorical fire. The following two chapters continue in this allusively rhetorical vein by sometimes equating Colonel Lloyd's plantation with Milton's hell and Edenic paradise at other moments.

Chapter 2 opens with descriptions of Colonel Lloyd's plantation. Situated on close to 12 miles of land in northern Talbot County, its principal products consist of tobacco, corn, and wheat, which according to Douglass "were raised in great abundance" (*Narrative* 16). A full operation that ran on the forced labor of "three to four hundred slaves," Lloyd's plantation, as Douglass describes it, "was the great business place," or more specifically, "the seat of government for the whole twenty farms." Describing the plantation as a "seat of government" invites a recall of Pandaemonium, the "high capital / Of Satan and his peers" (*PL* 1.756–57) where infernal affairs of state are debated. Douglass strengthens additional recalls to Milton's hell through descriptive epithets such as "fiendish barbarity" and "horrid oath," which extend his rhetorical practice of playing with fire to the detriment of slavery (*Narrative* 17).

He is not merely playing mischief with infernal and hellish diction. Rather, he is guiding readers well within the gates of Milton's hell by mischievously punning on Pandaemonium through artful descriptions of Colonel Lloyd's plantation.

His most direct rhetorical affiliation with Pandemonium occurs when he compares Lloyd's "*Great House Farm*" to U.S. Congress (*Narrative* 18). Douglass explains: "Few privileges were esteemed higher, by the slaves of the out-farms, than that of being selected to do errands at the Great House Farm. It was associated in their minds with greatness. A representative could not be prouder of his election to a seat in the American congress, than a slave on one of the out-farms would be of his election to do errands at the Great House Farm." Several lines later, he observes: "The competitors for this office sought as diligently to please their overseers, as the office-seekers in the political parties seek to please and deceive the people. The same traits of character might be seen in Colonel Lloyd's slaves, as are seen in the slaves of the political parties." Douglass's congressional similes plunge readers to deeper infernal depths as he continues to play mischief with slavery through practices of intertextual critique. His interpretation of slaves' attitudes concerning their election to serve at the Great House Farm reflects a rhetorically loaded reading of Lloyd's plantation and its hellish operations. In particular, he depicts this demonic seat of government as an infernal capitol/capital that commodifies and capitalizes upon enslaved laborers who are anything but a political electorate. This mischievous and playful critique of slavery continues to make Milton intertextually relevant and visible in the *Narrative*. Through his congressional similes, Douglass castigates national politicians whom he regards as slaves to their respective political parties. Since, from Douglass's perspective, they lack the courage to overturn national policy, this clever fugitive of arts and letters refashions the demonic grounds of Milton's hell by remastering them into subversive similes and figures that further establish his place among canonical men in Western literature.

Chapter 3 temporarily detours from this poetics of infernal description. Douglass suddenly depicts Lloyd's farmhouse in Edenic terms. His survey of the plantation emphasizes Lloyd's "finely cultivated garden" (*Narrative* 20). Described as "the greatest attraction of the place," the garden poses a temptation for hungry slaves who are tantalized by its attractive fruit. According to Douglass, the garden "abounded in fruits of almost every description, from the hardy apple of the north to the delicate orange of the south. This garden was not the least source of trouble on the plantation. Its excellent fruit was quite a temptation to the hungry swarms of boys, as well as the older slaves, belonging to the colonel, few of whom had the virtue or the vice to resist it." Douglass's lavish description immediately conjures images of the garden of Eden "with its 'excellent fruit' and its thematic recall of forbiddenness and punishment."[42] The allusive imprint of biblical tradition certainly informs this Edenic passage, as Shaindy Rudoff correctly observes. However, Douglass's mention of the "hardy apple" expressly locates Milton as an allusive presence who does not fall too far from Douglass's tree of knowledge. The Bible never specifies the forbidden fruit that leads to Adam and Eve's spiritual downfall. Rather, it is Milton's epic that takes poetic license in naming the apple as the fruit of interdicted knowledge. That Douglass identifies apples, and before oranges, in his update of the temptation scene intensifies Milton's literary presence in the *Narrative*. Milton's presence remains visible as Douglass's *Narrative* progresses, repeatedly playing mischief with slavery through contrasting allusions to hell and Eden.

Douglass's interest in heaven and hell stems from the poetic workings of his antislavery vision. Blyden Jackson maintains Douglass's *Narrative* works by "dichotomizing the people it portrays, and most of the action it presents, quite symmetrically according to a formula which surrounds with a bright and presumably celestial light all that is antislavery, including the slaves, and shrouds within a Stygian gloom the exact opposite of a heavenly radiance everything and anything of supposed aid to slavery."[43] Douglass's symmetrical formula shifts between these supernal and infernal expressions. Often this rhetorical vacillation gestures toward pronouncing and reiterating his knowledge of good and evil in unequivocal terms. A rhetorical by-product of this dual interest is that it solidifies Milton's presence as an interpretive code within the *Narrative* in addition to keeping the satanic epic at the forefront of readers' consciousness.

Examples of this dynamic include a wealth of phrases that identifies slavery as a satanic practice. When recounting Mr. Bondly's payment of restitution for mercilessly killing one of Colonel Lloyd's slaves, for instance, Douglass interprets the deed as a "fiendish transaction" (*Narrative* 25). Later, he refers to the "fatal poison of irresponsible power" consuming Mrs. Auld, his mistress, who begins to "commence its infernal work" (29). This poisonous work alters a voice "of sweet accord" and changes it to "one of harsh and horrid discord." Moreover, her "angelic face gave place to that of a demon." These numerous infusions of satanic energy appear so frequently throughout the *Narrative* such that each additional reference further intensifies Douglass's rhetorical practice of troubling the demonic grounds of Miltonic contention. Douglass troubles these grounds because he remains invested in playing mischievously with the "peculiar institution" in order to bring about its demise.

A second phase of completing and complicating Milton through his mischievous critique of slavery emerges in chapter 4. At this stage of the *Narrative*, Douglass turns to "play[ing] the mischief" with slavery through a series of rhetorical tautologies that are allusively reminiscent of Satan's resolve to "make a Heaven of Hell, a Hell of Heaven (*PL* 1.255). Like Satan, Douglass manipulates language into rhetoric that perverts demonic grounds into topographies of freedom. For instance, in *Paradise Lost*, Satan makes evil his good, reasoning, "Here at least / we shall be free," and subsequently affirming "Better to reign in Hell than serve in Heaven!" (*PL* 1.258–59, 263). Douglass's mischievous wordplay with rhetorical tautologies, by contrast, perverts the satanic vices of slaveholders and overseers unto a good work. Occupying the office of the pulpit as a "man of God... furnished unto all good works," Douglass serves humanity in the soul-stirring capacity of a devout preacher (2 Tim. 3:17). He assumes and performs this messianic posture through a series of rhetorical tautologies inflected with satanic resonances of "implacable hate" that Percy Bysshe Shelley considered "venial in a slave [but] not to be forgiven in a tyrant."[44]

One of Douglass's satanic tautologies involves a sarcastic description of his overseer, Mr. Gore. Mocking his adversary, Douglass notes, "He was just the man for such a place, and it was just the place for such a man" (*Narrative* 23). Several lines later, he critiques Gore's character by artfully employing a string of sentences composed of parallel structures. These structures establish a poetic rhythm that extends an unfavorable depiction of Gore. According to Douglass, Gore "was just proud enough to demand the most debasing homage of the slave, and quite servile enough to crouch, himself, at the feet of the master." He strengthens this rhetorical structure by adding two additional "was/and" constructions. Immediately following these constructions, Douglas asserts, "His words were in perfect keeping with his looks, and his looks were in perfect keeping with his words" (23). Douglass's satanic tautologies and parallel structures represent a few scathing examples of his rhetorical skill in playing the mischief with slavery and slaveholders. What appears a positive description in the first half of the tautology, is perverted in the balance of the line. Rhetorically, then, Douglass makes evil his good, playing mischief with slavery and railing against the institution while occupying the messianic office of an antislavery preacher.

His tautologies express a hatred for slavery, thereby aligning him paradoxically with the Son in book 6 of *Paradise Lost*. Satan's mutinous revolt in that book incites the Son's divine wrath and spurs him to messianic action. Forsyth notes the satanic undertones motivating the Son's messianic wrath as an expression of hate that also doubles as divine vengeance. This ironic phenomenon manifests when the Son responds to God's directive that he drive the infernal host from heaven. The Son responds, "whom thou hat'st, I hate, and can put on / Thy terrors, as I put thy mildness on, / Image of thee in all things" (*PL* 6.734–36). "Hate itself is heavenly," Forsyth explains, an interpretation of hatred that subsequently marks Satan as one who "expresses and performs what is already God's."[45] Emulating aspects gleaned from the Miltonic passage he studied in the *Columbian Orator*, Douglass likewise verbalizes sentiments of passionate hatred through his various tautological expressions. These rhetorical figures operate as infernal and supernal signs and assist Douglass in denouncing slavery through a messianic posture of revolutionary dissidence.

One of Douglass's most famous rhetorical tautologies in the autobiography is the statement that reads: "You have seen how a man was made a slave; you shall see how a slave was made a man";

this prefaces a major shift in the author's narrative arc (*Narrative* 47). This tautological expression registers as an amplified expression of Douglass's self-made manhood in that it blatantly communicates his "epistemic upsurge" and rupture of a system like slavery that "denies the slave any status as an Other or a self."[46] Alerting readers that he will now narrate his resurrection from a slave to a man, Douglass puts readers on existential notice. This notice marks a new beginning for the rhetorical trajectory of his narrative. From this point forward, Douglass becomes narratively self-possessed to the extent of signaling an obverse of black passivity that "debunks the Eurocentric notion of an agentless, passive, docile African."[47] Forbes notes that history has often demonized black leaders possessed of this constitution. Labels like "*activist, radical,* [and] *militant,*" she explains, are not negative attributes, but "indicate that the persons so labeled labor on behalf of full citizenship rights for African Americans."[48] Douglass embodies this spirit of self-possession and black manhood from this point forward in the *Narrative*. Preaching his narrative with intensified registers of infernal yet divine hate, Douglass sustains Milton's relevance as a hovering presence and admirable exemplum of resistant masculinity.

Chapter 7 is noteworthy in this regard because Douglass begins charting his ascent by introducing the word "brute" into his narrative. "Brute" appears more frequently as the *Narrative* progresses, and Douglass increasingly relies on the word in order to confront "problems of [black] existence [that] address the human confrontation with freedom and degradation."[49] Throughout the remainder of his text, "brute" specifically refers to an enslaved individual who is deprived of reasoning faculties and is ultimately reduced to an existential state of figurative nothingness. Douglass introduces the term when recounting his experiences living with "Master Hugh's family" in Baltimore (*Narrative* 31). While living with the family, Douglass learns to read under Mrs. Auld's private instruction, unbeknownst to her husband. When Mr. Auld learns about these private teaching sessions, he immediately commands his wife to cease these periods of instruction. Mrs. Auld "did not adopt this course of treatment immediately," Douglass explains. He continues, "She at first lacked the depravity indispensable to shutting me up in mental darkness." Only after receiving adequate instruction "in the exercise of irresponsible power" does Mrs. Auld learn how to treat her slave "as though [he] were a brute" and not a man.

This passage is rhetorically significant because Douglass associates brute existence with states of ignorance expressive of mental darkness. These rhetorical associations signal a distinct instance of Miltonic engagement. Through an allusive identification with Milton's blindness, Douglass adds layers of rhetorical complexity onto his sense of literary autonomy. Specifically, this allusive moment forges a more direct affiliation with the blind epic writer on demonic grounds that prove equally existential. Gordon helps to explain the complexity of Douglass's demonic existentialism by building off of Frantz Fanon's idea that "a black who quotes Montesquieu had better be watched...in the sense that he is starting something" relatively close to a revolution.[50] This "'starting something,'" Gordon continues, expresses "an assertion of [one's] humanity," which for blacks in Douglass's time signals transgression and a radical rupture of hegemonic systems.[51] Douglass, in equating his brute existence on account of his ignorance with Milton's blindness, becomes existentially self-possessed in himself.

If Milton can overcome blindness, write a canonical epic, and achieve high literary acclaim in aftertimes, then Douglass intuitively reasons he can similarly aspire to feats of epic heroism. Heroism for Douglass means triumphing in the adversity of his enslavement and mental blight. To facilitate the actualization of these aims, Douglass "imagines himself beyond his condition" and in Miltonic terms. This understanding of his being underwrites his sense of literary autonomy by allusively equating himself with his precursor through acts of self-made manhood and Miltonic reception.[52] This existential upsurge coincides with the self-made Milton Douglass was increasingly coming to know on the pages of his autobiography. It is this intertextual understanding of himself that leads him to express his translation from brute existence to liberated manhood. This mode of Miltonic reception aids Douglass in seeing aspects of himself in England's epic poet of liberty.

In chapter 8 and immediately after Captain Anthony's death, Douglass and his fellow slaves are assembled as property to be "equally divided between Mrs. Lucretia and Master Andrew" (*Narrative* 35). Douglass explains, "we were all ranked together at this valuation," noting they "had no more voice in that decision than the brutes among whom we were ranked" (35, 36). The brutes in this statement literally refer to horses, cattle, and pigs. Thus, Douglass again indicts slavery for depriving blacks of formal literacy and subordinating them to an existence of human chattel blighted in mental darkness. Images of darkness and brute existence surface in chapter 10 also. In this chapter, Douglass describes Mr. Covey's tyrannical success in annihilating his rebellious spirit. He relates: "I was broken in body, soul, and spirit. My natural elasticity was crushed, my intellect languished, the disposition to read departed, the cheerful spark that lingered about my eye died; the dark night of slavery closed in upon me; and behold a man transformed into a brute!" (45). Earlier in the narrative, Douglass mentioned how Sheridan's selection on "Catholic emancipation" in the *Columbian Orator* proved to be a "choice document" (33). He read it and other selections "over and over again with unabated interest," which soon motivated his resolve "to run away" and be free (34). By chapter 10, however, the "cheerful spark" that once "lingered about [his] eye [had] died" as "the dark night of slavery closed in upon [him]" and blighted his will to become free. By the close of the chapter, Douglass has learned the secret that enabled slaveholders to transform men into brutes. He understands "that, to make a contented slave, it is necessary to make a thoughtless one. It is necessary to *darken* his moral and mental vision, and, as far as possible, to annihilate the power of reason. He must be able to detect no inconsistencies in slavery; he must be made to feel that slavery is right; and he can be brought to that only when he ceases to be a man" (64–65; my emphasis). Once again, Douglass perceives mental darkness as a sign of ignorance and the lack of intellectual reasoning. This reading of himself as existing in a landscape of mental darkness heightens the Miltonic presence in the *Narrative* by prompting readers to perform an advanced literacy and cultural kinship with Milton's spirit of self-made manhood as it is conveyed in key moments of blindness in *Paradise Lost* and *Samson Agonistes*.

Douglass's *Narrative* especially generates this interpretive dynamic at this stage of his autobiography because the interpoetic gesture reinforces how far he has grown in stature as his own self-made man. The focus on blindness as a metaphor for brute ignorance in the narrative necessitates an advanced literacy informed by an "indirect or learned reference."[53] For Machacek, this term identifies the "shar[ing] of a tradition with the author," one that is steeped in a "form of a body of knowledge with which both poet and reader are acquainted."[54] Douglass's thoughts on mental darkness as an indirect reference to Milton's blindness enrich an appreciation for traces of the epic poet's hidden identity within his great poems. Joseph Wittreich, commenting on the "fabric of narration" in *Paradise Lost,* asserts, "details of autobiography like blindness, fearful circumstances, and treacherous enemies link the narrator of [Milton's epic] and its author."[55] Douglass, particularly when discussing Milton's blindness, links up with his precursor by prompting recalls of critical incidents in the epic writer's oeuvre. Since issues of freedom are so closely bound with Douglass's conceptions of blindness and brute ignorance, and because his epic already evidences an intertextual affiliation with Milton, both features bring the epic narrator in book 3 of *Paradise Lost* to mind. Such a recall inevitably validates the epic heroism he wishes to be remembered by on the pages of his narrative.

For instance, book 3 begins with an apostrophe that hails "holy light," the "offspring of Heav'n, first born" (*PL* 3.1). Interestingly, the apostrophe recounts the epic narrator's performance of self-made manhood. Subsequent lines reveal he has "escaped the Stygian pool, though long detained / In that obscure sojourn, while in my flight / through utter and through middle darkness borne" has surfaced to sing "of Chaos and eternal Night" (*PL* 3:14–16, 18). That he has been "Taught by the Heav'nly Muse to venture down / the dark descent, and up to reascend, / Though hard and rare" (*PL* 3:19–21) testifies to a heroic triumph that overcomes trial and adversity. This triumph reflects a literary feat worthy of epic heroism. Not only does the blind epic narrator "revisit safe" the abode of his celestial muse, he does so "having equaled...Blind Thamyris and blind Maeonides, / And Tiresias and Phineus prophets old" in poetic renown (*PL* 3:21, 33–36). These heroic accomplishments triumph over adversity, reflecting modes of self-made manhood that Douglass himself displays in that self-defining moment when he dares to resist Covey's tyrannical authority.

Douglass's conception of himself also aligns with *Samson Agonistes,* a text that presents a second Miltonic example of blindness that intertextually underwrites Douglass's reflections on mental darkness. In Milton's closet drama, Samson, a slave under "Philistian yoke," bemoans an ocular infirmity that leaves him "dark in light expos'd" and situated within a world that has now become "Irrecoverably dark" to his visual sense.[56] Ever despondent, he can find no solace during his opening soliloquy, for the "tender ball" or orb of sight that is robbed of its kinetic movement deprives him of an ability to "look at will through every pore" of the universe (SA 94). His despondence makes his chance of spiritual recovery far less likely, for he has not yet reconciled the ignominy associated with having been "Designed for great exploits" with the mockery of being "debas't / Lower then [a] bondslave" (SA 32, 37–38).

Whether Douglass read *Samson Agonistes* or not, his meditations on ignorance as emblematic of mental darkness spurs a recognition of the closet drama as intertextually relevant to the *Narrative* since both chronicle slow yet steady transitions from states of debased abjection to heights of heroic triumph. Douglass and Milton's Samson achieve self-made manhood by overcoming the trials of physical, spiritual, and/or states of mental darkness. In Douglass's case, he has achieved such "monumental status" within the tradition of African American autobiography that literary criticism, as Deborah McDowell astutely explains, has often "privileged and mystified" the 1845 narrative "as a beginning text" based on male-centered examinations that fail to address feminist concerns.[57] These "monumental" receptions of Douglass's *Narrative* and heroic image are reminiscent of *Samson Agonistes'* conclusion.

Milton's closet drama concludes by celebrating its hero as a monumental hero of self-made manhood. After his strength has been renewed in order to exact divine revenge upon the Philistines, Samson's father expresses his intentions to

> build him
> A Monument, and plant it round with shade
> Of Laurel ever green, and branching Palm,
> With all his Trophies hung, and Acts enroll'd
> In copious Legend, or sweet Lyric Song   (SA 1733–37)

This monument honors Samson for overcoming his darkest trial of spiritual experience and existence. It is interesting to note that

Douglass's 1893 version of his "Trials and Triumphs of Self-Made Men" speech likewise memorializes Samson as a heroic legend. Expressing his high regard for Milton and Stowe, Douglass acknowledges that both are worth "more than a thousand Sampsons." In regarding both as worthy of Samson's *kleos*, Douglass intensifies an affiliation with Milton as an expression of self-made manhood in his later years. Understanding the biblical hero as one who has been tried in the fire of adversity and, therefore, is worthy of the moniker "self-made man," Douglass indirectly voices *Samson Agonistes* as an intertext. *Samson Agonistes* serves as a semiotic territory through this indirect style of allusion. Intertextuality of this type, as Machacek argues, "designates not so much a study of the relations *between texts* as a study of the semantic and cultural presuppositions that lie *between* two *texts* and allow both of them to have the meaning that they do."[58] Even if Douglass is unacquainted with *Samson Agonistes* at the time of composing his autobiography, his equating mental darkness with Milton's blindness spurs readers who are familiar with the closet drama to read additional texts from the epic writer's canon into the *Narrative*'s rhetoric of resistant masculinity.

Satan is another Miltonic character who rhetorically underwrites how Douglass wishes to be remembered on the pages of his narrative. This satanic affiliation with Milton as an expression of self-made manhood proves especially significant, since Douglass's narrative reveals his penchant for playing with fire as a mischievous art form of antislavery rebellion. One of the ways Satan corresponds to Douglass as an indirect or learned Miltonic reference concerns the pair's existential origins on the demonic grounds of self-begottenness. This topography of ontological rootedness forms the basis for reading both as analogous expressions of self-made manhood.

During a contentious debate, Satan, responding to Abdiel, claims he and his crew are "self-begot" and "self-raised / By [their] own quick'ning power" (*PL* 5:860–61). Rejecting Abdiel's claim that God "made / Thee what thou art, and formed the pow'rs of heav'n / Such as he pleased, and circumscribed their being" (*PL* 5:823–25), Satan challenges his supernal rival to declare when such doctrine was learned and to pinpoint the specific moment when the angels were created. He later contends, "Our puissance is our own" and declares "our own right hand / Shall teach us highest deeds, by proof to try / Who is our equal" (*PL* 5:864–66). Because Douglass's will to freedom so closely resembles Satan's sentiments of ontological rootedness and based on his repeated tropes with infernal and Edenic elements throughout his *Narrative,* his text reflects an image of himself as a self-made man that is congruent with the various fragments informing his male-centered reception of Milton's satanic epic.

The epic narrator of book 3, Milton's Samson, and Satan contribute to different projects of autobiographical intertextuality that underscore how Douglass wishes to be remembered on the pages of his narrative. As these indirect learned references indicate, Douglass aspires to a self-made manhood that will solidify an image of himself through no less than three rhetorical affiliations with Milton and his canon. Of the three indirect references, Milton's Satan holds intertextual preeminence. This is not surprising, for Forsyth, in considering Satan's literary appeal, notes "how entangled is the narrator with his hero, and how alike they are." Additionally, Satan functions "as equivalent or double of the Son," performing a salvific role that causes the downfall of humanity yet providing the impetus that leads God to forgive the first couple.[59] Nor is Satan's attractiveness lost upon Milton. As Wittreich explains, Milton expressly "underscores the autobiographical impulse within" *Paradise Lost,* where "autobiography is invented by Eve, perfected by Adam, and parodied by Satan."[60] If Satan functions as autobiographical parody for Milton, Douglass likewise gravitates to this aspect of satanic energy in his narrative. However, he perverts this state of intertextual attraction. Inverting this Miltonic paradigm for messianic purposes, Douglass radically appropriates fragments from *Paradise Lost* as a means for turning his preacherly text into a satanic narrative expressive of self-made manhood.

His satanic narrative forges additional rhetorical affiliations with Milton's epic by triumphing and overcoming the challenges imposed on him by Covey. For John Seeyle, Douglass's *Narrative* constitutes a "*black* book in Gothic characters," a text that puts "forth the outlines of the Protestant epic in reverse, being not a record of essays to do good, but attempts to be bad." Seeyle elaborates upon this Miltonic reading of *Narrative*, equating Douglass with Milton's Satan and interpreting both as operating from rebellious impulses that "invent virtue from an evil necessity."[61] Andrews, building upon Seeyle, reads this Miltonic interpretation as instructive for assessments of Nat Turner's autobiography. Another rebellious slave whose radical politics buck against the godlike authority of white hegemony, Turner is equally in need of intertextual assistance. According to Andrews, "Turner needs [Thomas R.] Gray as much as Gray needs Turner, in the sense that Milton needs Satan as much as he needs Christ, or rather, in order that he may identify Christ as he does in his narrative poem."[62] Douglass needs Milton's intertextual assistance as well. Like the Son in book 6 of Milton's satanic epic, he must vanquish a demonic adversary with the messianic might of self-made manhood. Unwilling to choose between the infernal and the messianic, Douglass synthesizes the two, forging a rhetorical affiliation with Milton as a messianic apostate filled in and with the spirit of a radical self-made manhood.

At one of his lowest points in chapter 10 while narrating his experiences with Covey, Douglass laments and wonders, "why was I born a man, of whom to make a brute!" (*Narrative* 46). Looking out on the Chesapeake Bay, he observes sailing vessels and bemoans his fate "in the hottest hell of unending slavery." It is at this moment that Douglass resolves to run away and secure freedom. Later, while working for Mr. Freeland, Douglass considers his "treatment" under this new overseer as "heavenly compared with what I experienced at the hands of Mr. Edward Covey" (54). The implication, of course, associates life with Covey as a living hell. If Douglass interprets his existence under Covey's tyrannical rule as a living hell, defeating his satanic adversary inverts an identification with the Son, who, according to the heading in Bingham's reader, reigns "triumphant over the Apostate Angels." Douglass, by contrast, reigns by liberating himself out of hell.

Immediately following this passage, Douglas comments on the effects produced by his epistemic upsurge of self-made manhood. According to him, the "battle with Mr. Covey rekindled the few expiring embers of freedom, and revived within me a sense of my own manhood. Furthermore, it recalled the departed self-confidence, and inspired me again with a determination to be free" (*Narrative* 50). A few sentences later, Douglass describes this pivotal moment of existential transition as a "glorious resurrection, from the tomb of slavery, to the heaven of freedom. My long-crushed spirit rose, cowardice departed, bold defiance took its place; and I now resolved that, however long I might remain a slave in form, the day had passed forever when I could be a slave in fact. I did not hesitate to let it be known of me, that the white man who expected to succeed in whipping, must also succeed in killing me" (50–51). Douglass's "rekindled" spirit revives a fire that had been all but extinguished before he finds an existential path to ontological rootedness. Prior to coming into a fuller knowledge of himself as a man and not a brute, Douglass understood his wretched condition in slavery as blighted and darkened. Immediately after beating Covey, however, embers of freedom begin reviving his greater sense of manhood. His translation from states of abject darkness to liberated enlightenment continues to highlight his ascension to self-made manhood. For example, his "glorious resurrection" and triumph over the trials of death and the grave is tantamount to a metaphorical journey through darkness up to light. Such a voyage is no less heroic than those undertaken by Satan at the conclusion of book 2 in *Paradise Lost* or the epic narrator at the opening of book 3. These infernal impulses intensify Douglass's rhetorical attraction to Milton's satanic epic, all the while underwriting and solidifying his existential actualization into self-made manhood.

After narrating his defeat of Covey and firmly establishing his sense of self-made manhood, Douglass's rhetoric of resistant masculinity increases in infernal pitch. For example, his diction becomes more boldly defiant as his ornamental epithets intensify in sarcastic severity. If he appears more brazen in this latter stage of his *Narrative*, he also tends to temper this satanic ethos by identifying and associating himself with a meek and lowly Christian Savior. This messianic identification contrasts a more brazen ethos used to underwrite his denunciations of slavery. Speaking in these dual tongues of infernal militance and messianic lowliness, Douglas performs another iteration of his male-centered engagement with book 6 from *Paradise Lost*. Most important, blending the epic's exemplum of contrasting vices and virtues, Douglass performs his greatest expression of the self-made Milton, whose allusive spirit permeates the fugitive slave's satanic narrative.

By 1834, Douglass worked for William Freeland. While working for Freeland, Douglass formed a Sabbath school where he taught more than "forty scholars" who were slaves "how to read the will of God" (*Narrative* 55). This rebellious practice defies the slave codes that forbid the teaching of slaves to read and write. Notwithstanding these infernal inclinations, Douglass considers this missionary work of "instructing [his] dear fellow slaves...the sweetest engagement with which [he] was ever blessed" to serve. Because this engagement contributes to "bettering the race of [his] people," he is loath to leave them at the close of the Sabbath and even more so prior to his escape from slavery. Leaving them proves "a severe cross indeed," he explains. His diction speaks in rhetorical tongues by likening his salvific ministry to Christ, who willingly carries the sins of the world on his shoulders and makes his way to Golgotha's mountain to be crucified.

Lisa Zeitz notes the Christological parallels between Douglass's rhetorical self-fashioning and the martyred Messiah. Citing another instance in the *Narrative* where Douglass presents a battered image of himself as bruised, bloodied, and tattered in briars and thorns, she argues that "the resemblance to the crucified Christ is unmistakable," which facilitates the recognition of a "self-prophetic, millennial, or missionary ideology" at this moment in Douglass's satanic narrative.[63] Douglass twins this messianic image of a martyred Christ with that of a salvific warrior to embody tenets of black messianism. This synthesis of a "masochistic martyr and retributive messiah," according to Wilson Jeremiah Moses, proved a popular identificatory source for "Black Christians during the ante-bellum decades."[64] Douglass aligns himself with this tradition in his satanic narrative. In this latter stage of his autobiography, he embraces a messianic posture while carrying out an infernal ministry dedicated to speaking out against slavery in more radical tones of black revolt.

After revealing his plan to escape with several of his fellow slaves, Douglass reports, "my tendency was upward" (*Narrative* 56). Immediately thereafter, he connects this resolved ascendency to an actualization of manhood. Recounting his increasing dejection of his paradoxical circumstances, Douglass notes, "I was fast approaching manhood, and year after year had passed, and I was still a slave." These conflicting emotions do not simply rouse the discontented slave to action. They particularly signal his coming into a fuller knowledge of himself as a man worthy of controlling his fate. This demonic ground of self-affirmation leads Douglass to classify his resolution to become free as a "life-giving determination," one that liberates his "being for [him]self" rather than leaving that responsibility to someone else's benevolent act. This will to revolt, according to Sartrean principles, evidences Douglass's existential moment of rebirth. Reborn and re-created by his own quickening power, he, like Milton's Satan, renews himself by boasting new origins of "self-begottenness" as the *Narrative* progresses to its conclusion.

However much Douglass may regard himself as a messianic figure, he is well aware that proslavery proponents are apt to interpret him as demonic. Earlier in his narrative, he asks readers, "does a slave look dissatisfied? it is said, he has the devil in him, and it must be whipped out" (54). When he and his fellow comrades' plan for escape is discovered and thwarted, Mr. Freeland's mother excoriates Douglass in satanic terms. Holding him responsible for leading this revolt, she berates Douglass, saying, *You devil! You yellow devil! It was you that put it into the heads of Henry and John to run away. But for you, you long-legged mulatto devil! Henry nor John would never have thought of such a thing"* (60). Douglass gives no indication how he interprets this tirade, but he does turn the use of the demonic against itself for his rhetorical benefit two paragraphs later.

Continuing his rhetorical strategy of playing the mischief with slaveholders through satanic rhetoric, he begins applying demonic epithets to several of his adversaries. For instance, when visiting agents for slave traders heckle him while held captive in a local jail, Douglass identifies them as "fiends from perdition," underscoring their demonic character further by mentioning "a band of pirates never looked more like their father, the devil." This demonic language surfaces at the conclusion of the paragraph as well. According to Douglass, the insolent crew cursed, swore, and laughed at him and his comrades, "telling us that they could take the devil out of us in a very little while, if we were only in their hands" (*Narrative* 61). These three instances, in particular, reveal that Douglass also has a little of the devil in him. Appropriating demonic language and turning it against himself, he intensifies intertextual affiliations between his *Narrative* and Milton's satanic epic by speaking a language of hate from a messianic posture of antislavery rebellion.

These affiliations are especially recognizable in the final sections of the *Narrative* where Douglass increasingly amplifies his style of blending infernal and supernal figures together. In this regard, Milton's "seductive text" continues to evidence its shaping influence on Douglass's quests to secure freedom, manhood, and literary autonomy.[65] As Forsyth explains, Milton's epic emphasizes Satan's dual role as "angel and serpent." Additionally, "Satan seduces the reader in several ways: first he has an interior, a private self, recognizably close to ours, and it is here rather than in a literal Hell that he is so intelligently, self-consciously damned—he has that hollow depth that texts seem to share with people; and second, well, he is a good speaker, both in the public scenes of the early and middle books, and in the more intimate dialogue of Book 9."[66] Satan's interiority, frustration with his hellish state of abjection, his "hollow depth," and infernal eloquence appeal to a slave like Douglass, who desires and wills himself to become free. A satanic primer of sorts, book 6 of *Paradise Lost* provides Douglass with an intertextual road map for synthesizing infernal and supernal elements as a means for propagating his gospels of freedom and manhood. These gospels highlight his male-centered receptions of Milton's Son as both serpent and spiritual liberator.

As his narrative ascension to self-made manhood continues to explore new heights, Douglass yet tropes with figures of heaven and hell in his *Narrative*. In chapter 11 and after his owner, Mr. Thomas, chides him for wanting to hire his time then exhorts him to remain contented as a slave, Douglass "resolves" to flee. As September 3, 1838, draws nigh, Douglass considers his lot and contemplates whether his attempt to escape will fail or prove successful. He explains, "the wretchedness of slavery, and the blessedness of freedom, were perpetually before me. It was life and death with me" (*Narrative* 69). This statement weighs his tautological diction with signifiers suggestive of hell and heaven, respectively. Next, he reflects upon slavery as a site of exile and abjection, contrasting its connotative geography against a landscape of freedom, which he regards as a sign of spiritual blessedness. In hallowing freedom as a sacred and consecrated state of blessedness, Douglass perceives and balances his disconsolate musings on slavery's wretchedness with diction reflective of God's perfect peace. This tautological balancing act rescues the utterance from its initial sense of infernal gloom.

In the chapter's next to last paragraph, Douglass discusses the significance that Garrison's *Liberator* held for him as a free man in a slaveholding republic. Having escaped to New York and settled in New Bedford, Massachusetts, Douglass recalls that Garrison's paper "became my meat and my drink" (74). Additionally, he informs readers his "soul was set all on fire" as a result of the antislavery paper's emancipatory gospel. Douglass's allusion to scriptural tradition in this statement inflects his supernal utterance with sentiments of infernal eloquence. For instance, in 1 Corinthians 3:1, Paul, a preacher of the Gospel, addresses his Christian brethren "as unto babes in Christ." Paul addresses his audience in this manner because he recognizes that their interpretive understanding of Christian principles is limited by a carnality that overwhelms an ability to comprehend complex spiritual teachings. Deeming them spiritually immature, Paul also admits he has hitherto fed them "with milk, and not with meat" (1 Cor. 3:2). He uses this same metaphor in Hebrews 6:12 in a discussion concerning the ministry of priesthood. Again, recognizing his audience as "dull of hearing" concerning Christ's high priesthood, Paul explains, "ye have need that one teach you again which *be* the first principles of the oracles of God; and are become such as have need of milk, and not of strong meat" (Heb. 6:12). Douglass alludes to both scriptural metaphors when he extols Garrison's *Liberator* as his "meat and drink." Finding doctrinal sustenance in this antislavery weekly that sets his soul on fire, he depicts himself as fluently conversant in supernal and infernal rhetoric. This remastery with contrasting rhetorical figures of heaven and hell fortifies his Christian sense of self-made manhood through additional performances of literary autonomy.

In particular, Douglass extols the newspaper for its "scathing denunciations of slaveholders—its faithful exposures of slavery—

and its powerful attacks upon the upholders of the institution" (*Narrative* 74). Douglass's incendiary rhetoric indicates that he delights in the newspaper's infernal currents. Additionally, the *Liberator* sets his soul aflame because its discourse attacks the institution in bitterly severe terms. He relates that its vituperative messages send "thrill[s] of joy through [his] soul, such as [he]... never felt before." The final paragraph of the narrative briefly chronicles Douglass's impromptu decision to mount the rostrum of public oratory. Narrating the inaugural event of his oratorical career in Nantucket allows Douglass to end his *Narrative* with a Christian image of his self-made manhood intact. Doubtful that he is eloquent enough to address this audience, he explains that Mr. William C. Coffin urged him to speak at the convention. "It was a severe cross, and I took it up reluctantly," he explains, again associating himself with an image of a crucified Christ (75).

Douglass addresses the audience with ease, feeling "a degree of freedom" that spurs him to develop an oratorical career that would span more than 40 years. The *Narrative* ends with a completed image of Douglass as a self-made man. He has successfully preached his translation from brute existence to manhood while spreading the gospels of Milton and black revolt in the process. The appendix that follows extends Milton's presence and influence into the final pages of the *Narrative* as Douglass turns to playing the mischief with slaveholding religion. Douglass condemns slaveholding religion through allusive figures that echo and are influenced by Milton's satanic epic. Specifically, his sarcastic blending of vices and virtues correspond to an ongoing aesthetic that mischievously fuses infernal and supernal attributes together.

By blending these attributes, Douglass privileges "the unity of opposites" which, according to Moses, "characterizes [a style of] Christian doctrine" and rhetoric that likewise "encourages assertiveness as well as submission."[67] The Christ of black messianism emerges from this unity of opposites. The salvific and retributive figure surfaces with increased fervor throughout Douglass's appendix. Moses associates the opposing personalities of this messianic figure with the "apocalyptic tradition of the New Testament," which was further developed and elaborated upon "by the Puritan poets John Milton and Edward Taylor, and by the evangelical Julia

Ward Howe."⁶⁸ As Douglass's satanic narrative reaches its conclusion, these warring opposites figure more prominently as his gospel of black revolt focuses on the evils of slaveholding religion. This focus eventually leads to the *Narrative*'s final intertextual engagement with Milton and the theme of self-made manhood.

Having played the mischief with slaveholding religion, Douglass includes an appendix in the hopes of removing all doubt that he is "an opponent of all religion" (*Narrative* 75). A Miltonic highlight in this appendix concerns his allusive reference to the epic poet through an overlooked intermediary text of the early nineteenth century. In reviewing his *Narrative*, Douglass recognizes that certain readers might misinterpret his stance on religion given the vituperative tone of his rhetoric. Douglass makes it clear that his intent expressly focuses on his intention to denounce "the *slaveholding religion* of this land," not "Christianity proper." According to Douglass, "the Christianity of Christ" appeals to him, but he despises the corrupted and hypocritical version that leads tyrants to debase themselves through such heathenish practices as "slaveholding, women-whipping, [and] cradle-plundering." Even referring to this religion as a corrupted form of Christianity sets Douglass on edge. To him, linking these heathenish practices to Christianity sullies the term. Thus, he considers the reference "deceitful," the "climax of all misnomers, the boldest of all frauds, and the grossest of all libels." These accumulating epithets inflect Douglass's denunciatory rhetoric with amplified levels of vehement censure to the point of hallowing the demonic grounds of his rhetoric as a preparatory stage for infusing this satanic narrative with the spirit of Milton's intertextual influence.

Immediately following his denunciatory assessments of slaveholding religion, Douglass allusively channels the dissident spirit of Milton's Satan. In a surprising moment of allusive Miltonic intertextuality, he declares, "Never was there a clearer case of stealing the livery of the court of heaven to serve the devil in." This quote, with its synthesis of infernal and supernal elements, appropriates a line from Robert Pollok's epic, *The Course of Time* (1827). "Immensely popular for several decades" after its publication, Pollok's epic, according to Julie Nall Knowles, referred to *Paradise Lost*, quoted it periodically, and rewrote it "into a narrative of 'things to come / As past.'" Knowles describes the epic as a "Calvinistic version of *Paradise Lost* that "rejected the formulas for epic poetry that Milton used." Pollok's epic also focused its action on "'the final doom of man'" rather than the first fall, and "replaced Milton's conception of the Trinity with essentially Calvinistic theological ideas."[69] Douglass, in appropriating these lines and situating their satanic ideas into his appendix, hallows the demonic grounds of Miltonic interpretation through processes of intermediary influence. *The Course of Time* as intermediary influence extends Milton's afterlife and his satanic epic to nineteenth century audiences in early African American tradition. More importantly, Pollok's epic ingeniously finds its way into antislavery discourse under the erudite auspices of an early African American writer and self-made man like Douglass.

This playful erudition with slaveholding religion through Pollok and Milton amplifies the denunciatory power of Douglass's infernal rhetoric. Stealing the livery of heaven's celestial courts to serve infernal religious purposes performs an intertextual revision of Milton's satanic epic by altering one of Satan's most familiar phrasings. Interpretively, Pollok's line refers to false prophets who steal heaven's livery in order to deceive others to acts of ungodliness. As a result, Pollok's descriptive line of religious cross-dressing faintly alludes to Satan's tautological expression, "make a Heaven of Hell / A Hell of Heaven" (*PL* 1.255). Because Pollok's line places descriptive emphasis on perverting good to achieve satanic ends, it likewise prompts a recall of Satan's resolution, "Evil, be thou my good" (*PL* 4.110). Douglass's appropriation of Pollok's language once again incorporates Milton into his *Narrative* through an allusive style of phraseological adaptation that glories in blending infernal and supernal elements as a means of playing the mischief with different aspects of slavery. In Douglass's appendix, Milton's influence by way of Pollok signals a scathing indictment of slaveholding religion by textually cross-dressing Christianity in the false garments of religious blasphemy. Douglass underscores his loathing for this form of religious tyranny, stating, "I am filled with unutterable loathing when I contemplate the religious pomp and show, together with the horrible inconsistencies, which everywhere surround me" (75). That loathing stems from his intertextual ability to read slaveholding religion with Milton's satanic energy in mind.

Douglass's disdain for religious hypocrisy continues in the Miltonic vein of textual cross-dressing. Performances of textual cross-dressing involve acts of appropriation that subversively cloak orthodox meaning ascribed to a precursor text with interpretive shades of figurative differences. When it comes to considering the paradox of slave traders and dealers who likewise serve in or support the pulpit, Douglass again discusses this infernal dichotomy in Miltonic terms that cross-dress slaveholding religion as a queer perversion of Christian righteousness. He recalls: "The dealer gives his blood-stained gold to support the pulpit, and the pulpit, in return, covers his infernal business with the garb of Christianity. Here we have religion and robbery the allies of each other—devils dressed in angels' robes, and hell presenting the semblance of paradise" (76). On the one hand, Douglass's queering of slaveholding religion by covering it in the rhetorical garb of Christianity extends a cultural practice that mischievously signifies upon Pollok's epic. On another level, Douglass is also signifyin(g) or playing the mischief with slaveholding religion by inverting Miltonic topographies. Within the subversive context of his intertextual engagement with Pollok's epic, Douglass's references to "hell" and "paradise" immediately continue to prompt readers to recall *Paradise Lost* as a shaping influence in the satanic narrative. This intertextual recall occurs not only because these terms are so rhetorically loaded and associated with Milton, but mainly because *The Course of Time* is itself derivative of the literary precursor's epic poem. This direct affiliation with Milton strengthens Douglass's intertextual relationship to the seventeenth century poet, capping his *Narrative* with Miltonic presence through Pollok's intermediary epic of antislavery indictment.

With its numerous allusions to Miltonic iconography, borrowed rhetorical figures, and appeals to intermediary texts that are also influenced by *Paradise Lost*, Douglass's satanic narrative underwrites the fugitive slave's sense of literary autonomy. This autonomy punctuates the fulfillment of Douglass's narrative quest for self-made manhood. Milton's autobiographical spirit of self-made manhood contributes to Douglass's quest, infusing the autobiography with resonances of resistant masculinity that the fugitive slave author identifies in himself. Milton's autobiographical spirit continued to be evident in Douglass's second autobiography, *My*

Bondage and My Freedom. A text that heralds the second coming of Douglass's self-made manhood, *My Bondage* presents a subsequent (w)rite-of-passage for the fugitive slave who gloried in his ascension to self-made manhood.

My Bondage heralds Douglass's second coming as his own self-made man by chronicling the author's successful efforts in liberating himself from Garrison's abolitionist and literary paternalism. By the summer of 1847, Andrews notes, "Douglass found himself increasingly at odds with William Lloyd Garrison and the ideology of the Garrisonians."[70] For example, they disagreed upon whether the *Constitution* was a proslavery or antislavery document and held opposing views concerning the best political methods for abolishing slavery. In *My Bondage,* Douglass explains to his readers that he had early on sensed a growing discord between Garrison and himself. Moreover, he became increasingly aware that their professional relationship began to mirror that of a master and servant. Douglass provides examples of this turn in his relationship with Garrison, which, to his mind, is evidence of his sponsor's abolitionist paternalism.

For instance, Douglass admittedly delivers a flawed speech at a rally and is eclipsed by Garrison's more seasoned oration. According to Douglass, Garrison "followed me, taking me as his text" and delivering a speech "never to be forgotten by those who heard it."[71] In co-opting Douglass's body to oratorical success, Garrison appropriates and mutes Douglass's voice, effectively speaking for and through him. By chapter's conclusion, Douglass narratively intuits he has once again been reduced to a *"thing,"* something akin to a brute (*My Bondage* 366). The Garrisonians further remind Douglass of their low estimation of his self-sufficiency once he returns from his 21-month anti-slavery tour of Great Britain. Douglass returns to the states with the ambition to start his own antislavery newspaper independent of Garrison's *Liberator*. The Garrisonians "earnestly oppose" this enterprise, according to Douglass. Their attempts to quell his spirit encourage a renewal of his self-made manhood (389).

Concerning this dilemma as it plays out in his *Narrative,* Bergner notes, the white master as "overdetermined...oedipal father" especially prohibits Douglass from "achieving basic autonomy, normative masculinity, self-determination, and access to language (literacy)."[72] Douglass responds to these impositions on his self-made manhood once again in *My Bondage* by extricating himself from Garrison's paternal governance. Eric J. Sundquist, writing about Douglass's responses to these politics in the revised autobiographies, explains them as indicative of how well the former slave learned the "subversive lesson...that literacy is power."[73] For Andrews, *My Bondage* renders "a greater testimony of freedom" because Douglass is more than an "abolitionist mouthpiece" for Garrison, the "alpha and omega of the 1845 *Narrative*."[74] If Garrison figures as a god to Douglass, he rejects his sponsor's monarchial authority by reprising his role as a messianic apostate who remains grounded in the spirit of self-made manhood and a love for liberty.

Douglass narrates this second coming of his self-made manhood according to this Miltonic paradigm that pits heaven against hell through rhetorical tones of messianic apostasy. Having caught the "spirit of the [abolitionist] movement" while living in New Bedford, Douglass finds that his heart "burns at every true utterance against the slave system" and credits "the truths which burned in [his] breast" (*My Bondage* 363). These impulses of infernal eloquence, when contrasted against Garrison's godlike authority, complete a picture of Miltonic intertextuality that Douglass is only too willing to portray himself as in the spirit of manly independence from tyrannical rule.

The structural logic of this section of *My Bondage*, then, takes poetic liberties with Miltonic strains of satanic energy. This energy especially increases its tones of messianic apostasy in chapter 17, where Douglass narrates the second coming of his self-made manhood in a manner suggestive of a rebellious state of "hellish interiority."[75] Forsyth uses this term to connote Satan's inner mode of self-exploration, self-examination, and self-invention. These facets of selfhood enable marginalized individuals like Douglass to "emerge into full subjectivity," even though this coming into one's self may require one to esteem hell's degraded landscape and becoming one with it.[76] Douglass reprises this role of existential liberty in *My Bondage* by once again summoning a spirit of a hellish interiority.

In chapter 17, for instance, Douglass revisits his rebellious disposition in narrating the Covey incident. This time, he amplifies his spirit of hellish interiority by contrasting it against several references to paradise. Failing to receive a reprieve from his owner, "Master Thomas," and given Covey's tyrannical abuse, Douglass confesses to his "extinguished" hope in his owner's willingness to "protect [him] as a *man*" (*My Bondage* 277). Forlorn, he returns to Covey's "den of horrors," further "doubting" that he has a "friend in heaven." The contrast between his den and a hope in heaven reestablishes the hell/paradise paradigm that keeps Milton's epic intertextually alive for readers. A few lines later, Douglass contrasts Covey's "snakish habits" against the life of servitude he endures under his owner, Hugh Auld in Baltimore (278). For instance, he considers Baltimore "a paradise" compared to that of his present situation.

By chapter 18, Douglass gloats in his hellish interiority. Specifically, he relays, "I sometimes '*got the devil in me*'" (*My Bondage* 288). From this point onward, he promotes himself as a defiant leader every bit as satanic as Milton's infernal hero. In one passage, he distinguishes his devilish ways from the complacency he observes in his "servile brethren." Soon thereafter, he elevates his diction to incendiary levels of rhetorical resistance. Assured that slavery keeps slaves servile by keeping "their minds occupied with thoughts and aspirations short of the liberty of which they are deprived," he proudly asserts that the "south would blaze with insurrections" if these prohibitive practices were not vigorously kept intact (290, 291).

In chapter 19, he comments that a "desire for freedom only need[s] a favorable breeze to fan it into a blaze at any moment" (*My Bondage* 304). This statement precedes Douglass's concentration on the image of paradise in order to critique America as a hell for black people. For instance, he charges a "slaveholding priestcraft" with propagating a litany of false doctrines and is particularly incensed by an insistence that slaves "esteem [their] condition, in this country a paradise to that from which [they] had been snatched in Africa" (306). In addition to drawing upon the tradition of Ethiopianism with this quote, Douglass also implies that American soil represents a hellish landscape for African Americans. These Miltonic representations extend Douglass's mischievous play with slavery to his second autobiography, eventually contributing to a heroic stature that exceeds the confines of enslaved imprisonment. In particular, Douglass finds he has "become altogether too big for [his] chains," with the added knowledge that he is "fast verging toward manhood [with] the prophecies of [his] childhood...still unfulfilled" (*My Bondage* 306). Blending images of hell and paradise together and fusing them with an attention to fulfilling a spirit of self-made manhood reiterates Milton's relevance as an autobiographical intertext of satanic influence. Ever motivating Douglass's messianic impulses of antislavery justice, Milton's satanic energy leads the slave narrator to a deeper and more heroic understanding of himself on the pages of black autobiography.

Andrews interprets Douglass's affiliations with the demonic as the author's rhetorical attempt to assume the role of "the Rebel, the essential character of the Christian devil."[77] This continued affiliation with tenets of black messianism keeps Douglass in dialogue with God and Satan alike. More important, Douglass's rhetorical perversion of negative signs figures as an attempt to "confront his reader with an image of himself as both savior and devil whose gospel threatens order throughout the plantation, whose leadership is shot through with the motives of hatred and the methods of violence, and whose unshakeable pride refuses to accept any status or seek any outside justification that conflicts with the desire of self."[78] Andrews's interpretation of Douglass's satanic affiliations reveals the latter's tendency to imagine political rebellion as being congruent with messianic deliverance and in racialized contexts. Moses explains this impulse of black messianism as motivated by a people's need to "develop a messianic view of themselves because of the historical experience of being oppressed as a group." Ultimately, as Moses explains, "messianic traditions persist because the heritage of oppression persists."[79] Douglass reflects this tendency in his *Narrative* and *My Bondage*. Serving infernal yet messianic purposes, he fuses Christological images with satanic ones in order to produce an antislavery rhetoric of resistant masculinity and self-made manhood.

Until now, the rhetoric of self-made manhood and resistant masculinity in the literature and oratory of Frederick Douglass and many of his contemporaries has existed as a veiled Miltonic presence. Several of Douglass's orations contain Miltonic allusions.[80] Yet, his famous speeches on self-made men provide the strongest context for locating and theorizing about the seventeenth century writer's rhetorical presence in Douglass's writing and oratory. Milton's literary persona, his use of satanic energy, as well as the Romantics' unorthodox readings of *Paradise Lost* all contribute to Douglass's emphasis on might and manly rhetoric. Douglass's self-made manhood and brand of resistant masculinity have afforded him prestige in literary criticism as a kind of cultural hero in early African tradition. Feminist criticism has rightly called Douglass's gendered politics into question, emphasizing patriarchal blind spots that have negative repercussions for black women and the issues pertinent to their well-being. Given these patriarchal blind spots, Miltonic receptions of self-made manhood could not effectively suit their gendered cases. Thus, they developed strategies for completing and complicating Milton on distinct grounds of contention. Preaching Milton and gospels of black revolt in tones of tempered assertiveness, they contributed to the ministry of racial uplift "not by might nor by power" (Zech. 4:6), but by an effectual spirit of feminist self-invention.

5

BREAKING NEW GROUNDS WITH MILTON IN FRANCES ELLEN WATKINS HARPER'S *MOSES: A STORY OF THE NILE*

While a militant ministry of "self-made men" preached Milton's satanic epic as a symbolic expression of resistant black masculinity, a collective of "self-invented women" labored in the vineyard of racial and social uplift, operating in the spirit of a tempered assertiveness. Self-invented women, as defined by Mary Helen Washington, constitute the scores of early African American female authors who have fallen outside literary history because they or their works have been neglected or dismissed by patriarchal critics. These women, according to Washington, constitute "the disinherited." More important, they are literary artists who "do not fit in" because their "ritualized journeys, ... articulated voices, ... [as well as their] symbolic spaces are rarely the same as a man's."[1] Frances Ellen Watkins Harper, the most prolific African American writer of the nineteenth century, qualifies as a self-invented woman in her own right. Affectionately known as the "Bronze Muse," Harper is also a prominent member of Milton's early black sisterhood. Completing and complicating Milton after slavery was abolished and Abraham Lincoln's assassination, Harper engages the epic poet in her own time and on her own rebellious grounds of intertextual waywardness and remastery.

Later works in Harper's canon reveal she knew Milton well as early as 1869. This acquaintance with Milton is not surprising, given her privileged educational background. Harper, according to Maryemma Graham, was "born free in Baltimore in 1825," orphaned at three, and raised by her maternal uncle, William Watkins.[2] According to Melba Joyce Boyd, Watkins was "the most influential person during Harper's early development."[3] For instance, he founded the school for free blacks where Harper received her formal education. Watkins ran the William Watkins Academy for Negro Youth and trained students in "the classics, rhetoric, and the Bible."[4] This curriculum was specifically designed to prepare students for teaching or the ministry. With this type of educational mission, Harper would have definitely encountered Milton in her studies. Her formal education at the academy ended in 1839, but she would have been reacquainted with Milton as a result of gaining employment as a domestic for a Mr. Armstrong, the owner of a local bookshop. Mr. Armstrong granted Harper "access to the family library," and it was around this time that her poetry began appearing in various newspapers.[5] The quality of Harper's earliest poetry was exceptional enough to cause various readers to doubt its originality.[6] By 1846, Harper had published her first collection of poetry, *Forest Leaves*, of which no surviving copies exist.

In 1850, Harper relocated to Ohio, where she taught sewing at Union Seminary in Wilberforce, Ohio. Two years later, she secured a different teaching position in Pennsylvania. In 1853, the Maryland legislature "enacted a law whereby any person of color who entered via the northern border of the state could be sold into slavery."[7] Exiled from her kin as a result of its enactment, Harper relocated to Philadelphia, served on the Underground Railroad under William Still, and wrote and published poetry in Garrison's *Liberator* as well as the *Frederick Douglass' Papers* prior to moving once again to Boston. "Warmly received by the Anti-Slavery Office and Y. B. Yerrinton and Sons," who subsequently published her second collection of verse, *Poems on Miscellaneous Subjects*, Harper went on to pursue a career as an antislavery lecturer in Maine, various northern states, and Canada. She proved an instant success and capitalized upon her favorable reception by selling "several thousand copies of her books" while on these lecture tours and contributing "a generous portion of the proceeds to the Underground Railroad."⁸

When she returned to Philadelphia in 1857, Harper had established herself as a "prominent lecturer and the author of a book of poetry that had sold more than 10,000 copies."⁹ Throughout her career, Harper wrote almost exclusively in the ballad form. Frances Smith Foster explains Harper's popularity, noting that "during the antebellum period," Harper's "first two volumes reportedly sold over 50,000 copies." *Poems*, in particular, "merited at least twenty printings before her death" in 1911. These statistics indicate nineteenth century audiences did not deem Harper's poetry as inferior. Her predilection for ballads evidences her understanding "that nineteenth-century popular audiences preferred poems with rhythms and rhymes that were easy to memorize and to recite."¹⁰ Like her U.S. contemporaries the Fireside Poets, Harper greatly appealed to audiences whose literary tastes appreciated artistic sentiment. According to Thomas Wortham, the aesthetics governing the Fireside Poets included "clarity and even simplicity of expression, good feeling, and hopeful expectations, [which] were the virtues celebrated in good writing and right thinking" among this group.¹¹ Harper meets these aesthetic demands on her own grounds of literary style, then takes a wayward departure from that tradition in 1869 when she uncharacteristically forges a rhetorical affiliation with Milton through her brief epic, *Moses: A Story of the Nile*.

Despite her earlier acquaintances with Milton, the intertextual shadow of the epic writer's presence does not appear anywhere in *Poems*. Though this collection "attacks racist and sexist beliefs" and is thematically devoted to "confronting American social, political, and cultural systems of repression," Milton proves strikingly absent.¹² Only after the Emancipation Proclamation and Abraham Lincoln's death does Harper incorporate Milton into her canon. With *Moses*, Harper makes an innovative contribution to epic tradition. Moreover, this deviation from ballads finds her "abandon[ing] for the first and only time her characteristic heavily metered and rhymed lyric form."¹³ Written in blank verse and containing various rhetorical structures and themes borrowed from *Paradise Regained* and *Paradise Lost*, *Moses* conveys Harper's allusive familiarity with England's epic poet of liberty. Her uncharacteristic if not untimely affiliation with Milton positions Harper on demonic grounds that complete and complicate him through her wayward intertextual aesthetic. Additionally, her temporary break with literary tradition also ruptures temporal configurations and conventional arrangements of geographical space. More specifically, Harper produces a poem that radically deterritorializes Milton for the express purpose of memorializing and consecrating the U.S. landscape as a terrain of struggle and reconstituted site of freedom.

With *Moses*, her groundbreaking poem in epic tradition, Harper deviates from various conventional standards while preaching a radical messianic gospel in a distinct style of feminist self-invention. Her rather distinct epic exists within a "radical tradition that supports a pronounced negation of selfhood yet reinforces the nationality and liberation of black people."[14] Boyd also regards *Moses* as a radical text that bears the influence of one of the most incendiary works within the early African American literary tradition. Specifically, Boyd argues, "the conceptual underpinning of Frances Harper's poetic vision literarily and autobiographically connects to David Walker's *Appeal*." According to Boyd, this connection can be seen based on Harper's characterization of the biblical hero and his style of spiritual leadership. Furthermore, Harper's Moses "acts as the revolutionary metaphor for Afroamerican character, an example for individual guidance out of the depths of complicity with the forces of slavery."[15] These interpretations of Harper's *Moses* generate a deeper appreciation for her intertextual engagement with Milton, since he too writes from a rebellious posture.

Harper's epic registers as a groundbreaking literary performance in terms of her canon and the Western literary tradition more generally. For the first and only time in her literary career, she deviates from the ballad form to compose in a variation on epic. Her contribution to epic tradition is groundbreaking in another way as well. In composing *Moses* as an allegory of African Americans' pilgrimage from enslavement to freedom, Harper, in effect, troubles and pacifies the U.S. landscape by memorializing and consecrating it into two distinct dispensations. By poetically reviving and elaborating upon Moses's story in 1869, Harper memorializes the U.S. landscape as a terrain stained by slavery. She simultaneously consecrates that landscape, heralding the promise of a "brighter coming day" that has dawned in the years following the Emancipation Proclamation. To enrich this groundbreaking exercise in literary achievement, Harper appropriates fragments of Miltonic presence. Renowned as England's epic poet of liberty, his presence in Harper's poem breaks new ground relative to interpreting the U.S. landscape before and after 1869.

Moses is not only a groundbreaking literary performance; it also proves to be an untimely one. Harper's sudden decision to compose a work inflected with Miltonic presence and influence signals an untimely event in literary history because her formal education would have acquainted her with Milton prior to the abolition of slavery. That she does not bother to incorporate fragments of Milton anywhere in her canon prior to *Moses* levies a palpable critique concerning the seventeenth century writer's relevance for Harper's canon at that temporal moment of her literary career. Since Milton does not appear in her canon until she decides to compose an epic that pays homage to African American freedom, Harper's intertextual engagement with England's epic poet of liberty sends a clear message concerning his interpoetic relevance for her writing. For Harper, Milton is not an appropriate intertext in her canon as long as the peculiar institution exists, therefore making it impossible for the Bronze Muse to be buried in a free land. By engaging him in 1869, Harper preaches a gospel of black revolt that legitimates Milton's relevance and appropriateness in her canon. This belated yet (w)rite on time engagement with the epic poet of liberty ruptures intertextual temporalities of literary decorum by making Milton a fit and appropriate interpoetic source according to Harper's sense of demonic timing.

One of Harper's first groundbreaking methods for signaling her rhetorical affiliation with Milton occurs by publishing *Moses* in a two-text format. Unlike her earlier collection of poetry, which contains 18 poems, *Moses* consists of one poem and an allegorical story, "The Mission of the Flowers." This two-text format echoes Milton's final publication, which contains *Paradise Regained* and the closet drama *Samson Agonistes*. Twinning her brief epic with an accompanying allegorical story, Harper performs an instance of generic reprise expressive of Miltonic influence. In *Milton and Homer*, Machacek references a mode of intertextual allusion that works by "help[ing] to establish a work's genre."[16] Alice Rutkowski explains Harper's "seemingly strange pair[ing] of texts" as constituting Harper's "very public rejection of the benevolent maternalism of white, middle-class feminism and a powerful assertion of black self-determination."[17] In addition to asserting an allegorical voice of black self-determination, Harper pairs both texts together, thereby coding her epic with a distinct allusive character reminiscent of Milton's *Paradise Regained*.

Moses is a brief epic containing more than 700 lines of blank verse interspersed with two ballad poems. Its story, like each of Milton's great poems, elaborates on biblical narrative for the politicized purpose of engaging with themes of liberty. Harper writes under the auspices of Miltonic influence in this way by revisiting the book of Exodus and exploring cultural parallels between the leader of a chosen but oppressed people and African Americans at the dawn of the Reconstruction era. A little more than midway into the epic, her narrator identifies what constitutes "the central and the primal truth" of the work.[18] Its primal truth preaches a gospel of black revolt that centers on the unity of God and the author's conviction that all members of his creation are "co-heirs / With Christ" (*Moses* 161). Both works in Harper's collection perform variations on this thematic gospel of racial inclusion. *Moses*, in particular, gravitates to Miltonic forms and motifs to strengthen this claim more emphatically.

Apart from its Christian themes and elaboration on Scripture, *Moses* first communicates Harper's interest in epic convention through rhetorical acts of wayward versification. Because this brief epic is the only poem in her canon not written in ballad or hymn forms, this radical break from the conventions of literary form she obviously preferred translates to a wayward artistic approach. Barbara Christian, in her examination of the poetics of contemporary black women authors like Alice Walker, identifies a "wayward" aesthetic as an expressive style of literary communication where one willingly embraces the forbidden or unconventional. Undergirded by a womanist or type of black feminist spirit, a wayward aesthetic reveals creative impulses that privilege contrariness.

A wayward aesthetic also calls attention to an author's "peculiar sound [as well as] the specific mode through which her deepening of self-knowledge and self-love comes." For Christian, these characteristics in Walker's earliest works "seem to have much to do with [that author's] contrariness, her willingness at all turns to challenge the fashionable belief of the day," ultimately, as a "possible route to truth."[19] In consideration of early African American writers' Miltonic engagements, Harper's wayward affiliation with epic tradition and Milton especially proves contrary.

As a mode of cultural geography, moreover, Harper's wayward or contrary epic spirit achieves demonic status. Specifically, it goes against the grain of unorthodox receptions yet operates within them. This feminist approach to Miltonic intertextuality artfully renegotiates the demonic grounds of contention as charted by male writers and orators in early African American tradition. To renegotiate Milton within these feminist parameters of "paradoxical space" is to map an intertextual cartography that, according to Gillian Rose, "would be mutually exclusive if charted on a two-dimensional map," and, therefore, "occupied simultaneously" as in center/margin or inside/outside configurations.[20] Troping with Milton through wayward means and on demonic grounds unorthodoxly yet toward orthodox ends exposes the subversive nature of paradoxical space and its "radically heterogeneous geometries." For Harper, Milton provides the occasion for a (w)rite of passage that empowers her to preach a gospel of black revolt through phraseological adaptations of tempered assertiveness as opposed to a rhetoric of militant might. This demonic status inflects Harper's unconventional and contrary approach to Miltonic epic with heightened feminist subversiveness, for her allusive strategy of phraseological adaptation ultimately enables her to forge intertextual routes of literary affiliation with her precursor as a means for documenting her rebellious truths. Similarly, this approach enables contemporary audiences to interpretively navigate the fugitive routes and demonic pathways she charts in and out of time and geographical space throughout *Moses*.

One of these fugitive routes pertains to the epic's uncharacteristic rhythm and the liberty Harper derives from it. These wayward deviations underscore Harper's freedom aesthetic wherein she uses blank verse as poetic license for a "shifting of the caesura...from place to place within the line;...the stress among syllables; or the use of the run-on line, which permits thought-grouping in large or small blocks."[21] Throughout *Moses,* Harper's poetic lines often exceed the rhythmic feet proscribed for blank verse. Usually written in iambic pentameter, blank verse, according to Harper's freedom aesthetic, often fails to adhere to this convention. For instance, a given line may contain 11, 12, or sometimes 14 syllables. In other instances, Harper routinely limits the syllabic count to 8 or 9. A representative example of her verse gives contemporary readers a sense of her wayward deviation from ballad form coupled with her contrary epic spirit in blank verse.

Harper's epic begins with a series of dramatic dialogues between Moses and Charmian, the Egyptian princess who rescued the Hebrew leader from the Nile when he was an abandoned infant. In the opening stanza of dialogue, Moses thanks this surrogate mother, alerting her of his intention to forsake a life of royalty in Egypt and return home to his people in Israel.

> Kind and gracious princess, more than friend,
> I've come to thank thee for thy goodness,
> And to breathe into thy generous ears
> My last and sad farewell. I go to join
> All other bright advantages, save
> The approval of my conscience and the meed
> Of rightly doing.

Charmian responds:

> What means, my son, this strange election?
> What wild chimera floats across thy mind?
> What sudden impulse moves thy soul? Thou who
> Hast only trod the court of kings, why seek
> Instead the paths of labor? Thou, whose limbs
> Have known no other garb than that which well
> Befits our kingly state, why rather choose
> The badge of servitude and toil? (*Moses* 139)

Despite the syllabic irregularity of these unrhymed lines, they in no way resemble the meter and form associated with ballads or hymns. Harper composes several of these lines using iambic pentameter; however, 7 of the 16 exceed or fall short of the meter.

This rhythmic irregularity continues throughout the entirety of Harper's epic. It further evidences a wayward tendency that proceeds as a willful violation of blank verse, though not from ignorance or from poetic ineptitude.

Rather, this wayward approach to epic blank verse allows Harper to rupture poetic time. Because her sense of rhythmic irregularity of cadence and metrical lines defies sustained temporal patterns, this rebellious approach produces a subsequent rupture of poetic untimeliness. By rupturing poetic time in this manner, Harper expresses a willfully demonic deviation in epic temporality that destabilizes and disorients her readers from any consistent or verifiable pattern. Moreover, Harper refuses to be poetically bound by the rigid demands of epic convention while writing within it. Thus, her sense of poetic untimeliness encourages her to compose a dissident epic whose temporal ruptures ultimately communicate a thematic homage to liberty. This rebellious (w)rite of passage in epic tradition charts demonic and fugitive pathways, a mode of intertextual engagement that proves particularly salient in a poem devoted to celebrating black liberation and freedom.

Another instance of demonically rupturing time pursuant to epic convention and the use of blank verse occurs when Harper intersperses ballad forms within *Moses*. The conclusion of chapter 6, for instance, ends with a four-stanza ballad poem entitled "Miriam's Song." The first two stanzas read:

> A wail in the palace, a wail in the hut
> > The midnight is shivering with dread,
> And Egypt wakes up with a shriek and a sob
> > To mourn for her first-born and dead.
> In the morning glad voices greeted the light,
> > As the Nile with its splendor was flushed;
> At midnight silence had melted their tones,
> > And their music forever is hushed.   (*Moses* 161)

The following two stanzas continue with this four-line *abcb* rhyme scheme. Interspersing a ballad poem within her blank verse is Harper's way of reiterating her self-invented womanhood as an artist in her "own write."[22] To compose and pioneer literature under the auspices of self-invented womanhood in her "own write" is to "nurture the black women's literary tradition" and code it with distinct resonances of matrilineal difference.[23] These resonances have been passed down in African American women's literature through an ancestral line beginning with Wheatley. Harper enriches this tradition of matrilineal difference by interspersing a ballad within her epic as a means for celebrating the freedom enjoyed by the Israelites after they successfully made their way across the Red Sea. In addition to radically rupturing the rhythmic cadence of her poem, Harper's inclusion of a ballad poem references her wayward aesthetic as she breaks from the chains of epic convention while author-izing her literary identity through a tradition of verse closely associated with her poetic style. This defiant rupture of epic time proves politically salient, for Harper's deviations make it known that she would rather remain true to her poetic calling in ballad tradition than to slavishly and wholly submit herself to the strict meter demanded of blank verse.

This wayward expression of self-invented womanhood produces another reverberation in Harper's groundbreaking epic indicative of Milton's interpoetic presence. By daring to rhyme at all in her epic, Harper expressly announces her wayward deviation from Miltonic influence. In "The Verse" prefacing *Paradise Lost*, for instance, Milton states his unequivocal position on rhyme as a counterproductive element in heroic poems. "Vulgar readers" might take his "neglect of rhyme" as a "defect," Milton explains. Nevertheless, he "esteems" his deviation from the "troublesome and modern bondage of rhyming" as a canonical example for others to emulate in aftertimes.[24] For most of her epic, Harper respects these rigid conventions that Milton regards and ordains as a liberating aesthetic. Not content to slavishly resign herself to his canonical authority, she unequivocally occupies demonic grounds of contention and interpretation by waywardly leaning[25] toward her own understandings and occasionally "esteeming" the "example set" in her canon.

Because Harper's success as a poet rests upon her skill in rhyming within the ballad form, to fully comply with Milton's canonical commands would be tantamount to enslaving herself to her precursor's literary demands. Rather than betray her aesthetic entirely, Harper pioneers epic tradition in her own right. That is, she exercises her poetic liberties while working within the literary conventions Milton bequeaths to belated poets. *Moses* results from this wayward or demonic approach to Miltonic engagement. An innovative variation on epic, this groundbreaking poem in literary tradition ever ruptures the Western canon, subverting Milton while extending his originality within paradoxical spaces reflective of Harper's wayward spirit of intertextual engagement.

Far from being unskilled in blank verse or ignorant that this form of versification is an epic convention, Harper crafts her poem in such a way as to express a willful disobedience to what is expected of her as a writer within this genre. The second ballad in her epic especially highlights this demonic rupture with Miltonic blank verse. *Moses* ends uncharacteristically with an enjambed, unrhymed ballad. This rebellious feature signals Harper's ability to compose Miltonic epic in conventional blank verse as if she were interested in fully complying with conventional rules. Although Milton's "The Verse" extols unrhymed blank verse as heroic and suitable to epic and its composition, Harper again remains true to her own poetic calling within the paradoxical spaces of feminist difference. Preaching a gospel of black revolt that announces she can and will write within these strict parameters according to her own authorial desires and not as epic prescriptives and conventions demand, Harper concludes her epic in modified blank verse:

> Oh never on that mountain
> Was seen a lovelier sight
> Than the troupe of fair young angels
> That gathered 'round the dead.
> With gentle hands they bore him
> That bright and shining train,
> From Nebo's lonely mountain
> To sleep in Moab's vale.   (*Moses* 165)

Throughout the 25 lines of this concluding poem, Harper relies upon a rhythmic cadence evocative of ballads. The rhythmic weight accorded to each of the alternating lines produces a cadence that encourages expectations of a sustained rhyme pattern. Specifically, readers are led to anticipate an *abcb* rhyme scheme.

Harper ruptures this expectation by dispensing with rhyme altogether. Unlike the earlier rhymed ballad, "Miriam's Song," Harper's concluding ballad includes this wayward metrical variation to highlight her willful deviation from blank verse and Miltonic epic. Keeping in mind Milton's wayward aesthetic of using unrhymed blank verse in epic, Harper adapts this contrary spirit of literary innovativeness to her own poetics of self-invented womanhood. Unwilling to abandon her poetic calling in the ballad tradition outright, Harper retains its measure while dispensing with rhyme. Thus, she composes her variation of Miltonic epic on demonic grounds of contention that further underscore her awareness of generic convention and her insistence upon achieving poetic liberty within it. If, as John Shawcross demonstrates, a form of Miltonic presence exists that encourages readers to see a "poet in the poem through the decisions [belated authors] have made in forms or structures, language and imagery, [or] the craft and the ideas or emotions that that craft sustains," then *Moses* offers a distinct glimpse into this allusive phenomenon of intertextual engagement within African American tradition.[26] In her own (w)rite of tempered assertiveness, Harper completes, complicates, and remasters Milton by deciding to trope with him as she sees fit.

Harper's wayward or demonic deviations in literary form reiterate her numerous efforts to preach a gospel of black revolt that highlights her poetic calling as a self-invented woman. Addressing these radical deviations in literary form, Boyd recognizes the poet's wayward style as "underscor[ing] her versatility as an artist and craftsperson."[27] This interpretive reading of Harper coincides nicely with her poem's thematic focus, which celebrates African American freedom indirectly by chronicling the Israelites' rise from slavery to freedom. In keeping with this interpretation, Patricia Liggins Hill specifically identifies *Moses* as an "apologue of the Black race's struggle for Emancipation."[28] Harper, no doubt, recognized this aspect of Moses's experience as one that is exceptionally worthy of epic treatment. As Boyd notes, Harper's poetic enterprise serves as "the most appropriate response for a shared legacy of spirituality and struggle" in the African American tradition.[29] Both the Emancipation Proclamation and Abraham Lincoln's assassination facilitated a need for the poetic documentation of both legacies. Harper attended to this need by composing an African American epic inspired by Miltonic tradition that memorializes and consecrates this groundbreaking moment in U.S. history.

Harper moves beyond literary form as a rhetorical device for establishing the genre of her groundbreaking poem through ruptures of Miltonic influence and intertextual interaction. Throughout *Moses*, she tropes with generic structures and themes derivative of *Paradise Regained* and *Paradise Lost* but out of their publication sequence. In structure and thematic focus, *Moses* most resembles *Paradise Regained*. Images of *Paradise Lost* do not surface until later in her epic, producing another rupture of intertextual untimeliness by troping with two of Milton's great poems out of their chronological sequence. This element of waywardness confirms her dedication to uncharacteristically naming and ordering experience through rituals entrenched in the demonic grounds of "deep time" and "deep space." She continues to rupture conventional time arrangements through Milton by writing in what was then the historical present of emancipation while poetically and allegorically reflecting on the past when her people were yet enslaved. Reaching back in time from the vantage of her future present, Harper, through her intertextual engagements with *Paradise Regained*, retrieves demonic geographies of history in order to reclaim, then hallow, those grounds as consecrated terrain. This wayward mode with Milton destabilizes multiple dispensations in and out of time by reversing chronological orderings in literary history. Moreover, it produces a subversive poetics of untimeliness and ordered chaos as Harper preaches her gospel of black revolt on demonic grounds in and out of multiple time zones simultaneously.

Moses best facilitates this aspect of Harper's wayward rupture of time through a generic structure reminiscent of *Paradise Regained*. This freedom poem especially qualifies as an innovative rendition of brief biblical epic. Barbara Lewalski defines this subgenre as a form of writing more substantive than the convention of brevity. She explains that the genre "is not merely any narration told in briefer compass...but that it is rather a significant condensation and epitome of the vast span of history treated in *extenso* in the diffuse epic."[30] Milton's and Harper's brief epics adhere to these formulas in different ways. *Paradise Regained* achieves this approach to epic by highlighting the Son's heroic resistance while fasting in the wilderness to Satan's temptations. *Moses* similarly focuses on an exiled figure's wilderness experience, capitalizing upon that moment as the transformative event responsible for making a hero of biblically epic stature out of a servant who needs to endure God's divine chastening before fulfilling his leadership potential.

Of equal intertextual importance, *Moses* recalls the genre of brief biblical epic and Milton's *Paradise Regained* based on Harper's stylistic preoccupation with the theme of inward spiritual heroism. Both epics engage this theme through a portrayal of exiled leaders modeled on a more passive type of Christ, who, according to Erik Gray, conducts himself nobly by exercising the "might of weakness" through expressions of "perfect passivity."[31] Additionally, Harper's use of the journey motif, epic battles, and her commitment to chronicling the trials and triumphs of spiritually noble heroes connotatively enrich instances of literary interaction between her poem and Milton's. These components further establish *Moses* as an innovative poem influenced by Milton's revolutionary approach to the genre of brief biblical epic. Although significantly briefer than *Paradise Regained* at only 700 lines, *Moses* establishes generic parameters that alert discriminating readers to the precise literary tradition within which Harper writes according to her own wayward designs.

Harper's brief biblical epic deviates from Milton's innovative treatment of the genre by further reducing the poem's already compact structure. Rather than divide her epic into books, her wayward aesthetic leads her to section *Moses* into chapters. This literary deviation infuses her brief biblical epic with a greater sense of intimate immediacy, therefore, reducing its scope to a more condensed narrative format than the four books comprising *Paradise Regained*. Harper economizes her epic structure further by limiting her story to nine chapters. Since she often performed *Moses* in churches and other public platforms, Harper may have found it expedient to downsize her brief biblical epic in this manner. In light of the demands associated with public performance, reducing the divisions of her poem to chapters augments her need to instantly captivate, enlist, and sustain her audience's attention over the course of a specific allotment of time.

Moses also deviates from conventional epic by dispensing with an invocation to muses. As mentioned above, by this time in her literary career Harper was known as the Bronze Muse. Thus, she could afford to dispense with this convention and fulfill the poetic office in her own (w)rite as an expression of self-invented womanhood. Dispensing with this convention, Harper begins her poem *in media res*, presenting Moses and Charmian in dramatic dialogue at the moment the former plans to return to his race rather than enjoy the privileges of royalty accorded to him in Egypt. The characters' opening dialogue immediately promotes the gospel of inward spiritual heroism, presenting Moses as a selfless racial other based on his steadfast spiritual convictions. For instance, after the Egyptian princess responds to his decision to rejoin members of his race, Moses replies,

> Let me tell thee, gracious princess; 'tis no
> Sudden freak nor impulse wild that moves my mind.
> I feel an earnest purpose binding all
> My soul unto a strong resolve, which bids
> Me put aside all other ends and aims,
> Until the hour shall come when God—the God
> Our fathers loved and worshipped—shall break our chains,
> And lead our willing feet to freedom.   (*Moses* 139)

Harper's Moses sounds a lot like Milton's Samson in this opening statement. Toward the end of Milton's closet drama and prior to Samson's reviving spirit, the exiled slave experiences the internal workings of an inward spiritual heroism. He admonishes the chorus: "Be of good courage, I begin to feel / Some rousing motions in me which dispose / To something extraordinary my thoughts."[32]

Moses's earnest purpose and Samson's rousing motions reflect both exilic leaders' recognition that they are chosen vessels operating under the unction of a divine spiritual calling. In both instances, the mind coupled with an intensity of soul-stirring emotion reinforces attributes of inward spiritual heroism that shall lead them to deliver their people through acts of holy faith. With this allusive diction to *Samson Agonistes*, the text Milton pairs with *Paradise Regained*, Harper reestablishes another wayward method for signaling an echoic connection between her brief biblical epic and that of her precursor. In this instance, Moses resembles Milton's Samson, who through a "series of willing surrenders"[33] extends the acts of perfect passivity so heroically exercised by the Son in *Paradise Regained*.

Harper regards Moses's decision to give up royalty as an embodiment of inward spiritual heroism. She makes this reading of Moses's character evident in her 1859 essay, "Our Greatest Want." In that essay, she regards the biblical hero as "the first disunionist we read of in the Jewish Scriptures" and one who would "have no union with the slave power of Egypt."[34] Based on this interpretation of the Old Testament hero, Moses serves as a typological symbol who further reiterates an intertextual investment by thematically privileging *Paradise Regained* over *Paradise Lost*. The inward heroism of Harper's Moses parallels the spiritual character exhibited by Milton's Son, who possesses "firm obedience fully tri'd" and performs deeds "above Heroic, though in secret done."[35] The emphasis on "firm obedience" and deeds done in secret expresses a moral character that heroically resists public displays of physical valor. Harper similarly interprets Moses according to this understanding of the Son as Milton characterizes him in *Paradise Regained*.

For instance, in his examination of Milton's Son, Burton O. Kurth identifies one of these virtues as the hero's ability to withstand the trials and sufferings he experiences in the epic. According to Kurth, Christ's victory against Satan ultimately amounts to an exercise of heroic spirituality. The Son's spiritual and moral victories further constitute the "most significant experiences for the Christian hero," which subsequently delineates the "chief measures of his faith, virtue, and fortitude."[36] Given these virtues, Milton's Son does not conform to conventional epic heroes. Rather, as Richard Burton Jordan has noted, the Son epitomizes the "quiet hero par excellence," who engages Satan in what amounts to a "war game, not a real battle."[37] When Harper characterizes Moses's adherence to his inward spiritual calling, she presents an epic hero whose moral valor reiterates Milton's mediated influence in her poem.

Moses's explanation for why he forsakes royal life in Egypt for the poverty of kin likewise communicates the valor of inward spiritual heroism. His earnest purpose compels him to surrender the spoils of his lavish lifestyle because he so values God's higher calling for his life. Ever mindful of "the grand traditions of [his] race" generated by holy men like Abraham, Isaac, Jacob, and Joseph, he epitomizes "earnest faith" in the work and workings of the Lord (*Moses* 143, 145). The conclusion of this first chapter reveals the extent of Moses's spiritual heroism. In response to Moses's convictions, the epic narrator relates how "God poured the chrism of a holy work" upon the Israelite leader's head (145). The divine ritual suggests that this Christ-like figure finds and receives God's holy favor. Additionally, God's anointing empowers Moses to stand as "a bright / Ensample through the changing centuries of time" (145). By exalting Moses as a shining example throughout the ages, Harper preaches a gospel of black revolt that espouses inward spiritual heroism as opposed to more physically abrasive manifestations of epic strength.

The narrator of Harper's poem continues to extend this intertextual theme of inward spiritual heroism through rhetorically loaded diction. Words like "grand" and "grandeur" convey these themes of epic heroism. Collectively, both words appear a total of 10 times throughout this brief poem. Examples include references to the "grandeur of [Moses's] will," the "grand traditions of [his] race," as well as the hero's "calm, grand patience" (*Moses* 143, 152). Later, the narrator acquaints readers with the "grandeur" of Moses's "mission" and the "grandeur of [his] heroic triumph," ultimately emphasizing the "grand," "central," and "primal truth of all / the universe—the unity of God" (154, 160, 161). Interestingly, Harper would later apply the word "grand" to her description of Moses in a speech entitled "Factor in Human Progress," which appeared in an 1885 edition of the *African American Methodist Episcopal Church Review*. In that speech, she credits the biblical hero's display of "self-sacrifice" as teaching humanity "the grandest of all sciences, the science of a true life of joy and trust in God, of God-like forgiveness and divine self-surrender."[38] These assessments of Moses's inward spiritual character emphasize the biblical hero's God-like nature in ways that serve as ornamental epithets and intertextual connectives that further activate associations with Milton's Son.

Connotatively, the words "grand," "grandeur," and "heroic" share lexical relationships that make it possible to locate Miltonic presence as a feature implicated in Harper's rhetorically loaded diction. The *Oxford English Dictionary*, for instance, defines and associates the word "grand" with notions of eminence, either in "reputation," "position," or "scale of operations."[39] Milton's Son exhibits these attributes throughout his dealings with Satan. For example, when the Son rejects Satan's offer to "hearken" to him that he might receive the demon's riches and fortunes, the Messiah shuns wealth in a manner consistent with Harper's reading of Moses (*PR* 2.428). According to Milton's Son, wealth without "virtue, valour, [and] wisdom" prove "impotent" (*PR* 2.431). Thus, he acknowledges these spiritual attributes as superior to wealth.

After making this statement, the Son reflects on history and notes how "men endu'd with [wealth] have oft attain'd / In lowest poverty to highest deeds" (*PR* 2.437–38). In fact, he performs the very form of heroism he extols. Nobly enduring Satan's temptations throughout the work, the Son performs a valiant heroism predicated upon his even-tempered logic against the deceptive and alluring wiles of his foe. Commenting on this measure of heroic conduct, Jordan argues, quiet heroes "achieve important successes" not by expressions of physical valor but by "waiting" or "undertaking" some "climactic action that has a symbolic relationship to the outcome rather than being a major cause of it."[40] In *Paradise Regained*, the Son teaches Milton's readers how to withstand the wiles of demonic powers not by force or might but through a mastery of words, logic, and sound reasoning. Hence, Kurth asserts, "for Milton the real victory over evil was to be won in the individual human spirit, not in the larger area of worldly pomp and glory."[41] Harper entertains this same ideal in her characterization of Moses and his epic display of grand heroism.

Another telling instance concerning Harper's wayward aesthetic with Milton and the theme of inward spiritual heroism involves the politics of naming the Egyptian princess Charmian. This instance of demonic naming survives as a mediated influence of Shakespeare's tragedy, *Antony and Cleopatra*, an intertext Milton draws upon when creating a "scene of seduction" that reintroduces Dalila in the latter stages of *Samson Agonistes*.[42] By naming the Egyptian princess Charmian, Harper, perhaps intuiting this Shakespearean connection through Milton, primes a recollection of Cleopatra's attendant in Shakespeare's tragedy. This style of indirect Miltonic allusion mirrors Matthew Arnold's and Lord Alfred Tennyson's interpoetic practices, which, according to Gray, "frequently embeds allusions to Milton within allusions to other, often older writers."[43] Harper's practice of naming also survives as a "signature of derivation,"[44] generating literary interactions of frenzied chaos between and among multiple texts simultaneously. In keeping with her wayward approach of engaging with Milton, Harper signs an intertextual signature on demonic grounds of contention that leads readers to Shakespeare.

Harper's literary interaction with Shakespeare through Milton appropriates Charmian's name to signify racial and spiritual otherness. As an Egyptian princess, Charmian signifies a spiritual otherness that is at enmity with Harper's racial project of allegorically siding with Moses and Hebrew traditions. Typologically, the Cleopatra and Charmian characters are directly connected to serpents. Both commit suicide in Shakespeare's drama by applying venomous asps to their persons rather than suffer the ignominy of being captured by imperialist Rome. This serpentine connection imbues Harper's "signature of derivation" through intertextual naming with infernal rhetorical resonances. Specifically, this process underscores the degree to which the Egyptians are at enmity with God's chosen people. Associating Charmian with the demonic in this manner ultimately undermines the heroic role of maternal surrogacy that she remembers once the dramatic dialogue progresses.

When Charmian responds to Moses's opening assertion that he is called to an earnest spiritual purpose, readers gain an intimate understanding of the future leader's heroism. To her carnal mind, Moses's decision to renounce his royal stature amounts to a foolish act of self-abnegation. Thus, she vainly implores,

> Listen to me, Moses: thou art young,
> And the warm blood of youth flushes thy veins
> Like generous wine; thou wearest thy manhood
> Like a crown; but what king e'er cast
> His diadem in the dust, to be trampled
> Down by every careless foot? Thou has
> Bright dreams and glowing hopes; could'st thou not live
> Them out as well beneath the radiance
> Of our throne as in the shadow of those
> Bondage-darkened huts?   (*Moses* 139)

Charmian's queries provide the story with its immediate conflict, distancing her from Moses on the grounds of racial identity. As

Moses explains, his mother, siblings, and people reside "within those darkened huts" (139). To renounce his royal status is to claim his racial heritage and give himself to the earnest purpose that ultimately positions him as a spiritual liberator of his people. Because he is so aware of their sufferings and his mission to liberate them, Moses can no longer abide life with Egypt's royal courts. Underscoring the measure of his inward spiritual heroism relatively early in chapter 1, Moses further relates,

> When I gaze upon their cruel wrongs
> The very purple on my limbs seems drenched
> With blood, the warm blood of my own kindred race;
> And then thy richest viands pall upon my taste,
> And discord jars in every tone of song.
> I cannot live in pleasure while they faint
> In pain.   (*Moses* 140)

Moses continues to conduct himself as a quiet hero despite Charmian's mockery of his noble calling. In choosing to follow the promptings of his inner spirit, he, like Milton's Son, evidences a heroic ability to remain spiritually committed to a stern resolve for some holy purpose. This spiritual resolve further epitomizes the Son's philosophy as articulated in book 4 of *Paradise Regained*. Remaining steadfast to his divine calling, Moses preaches in action words uttered by the Son, who makes it known that he cannot be lured by the "grandeur and majestic show / Of luxury, though called magnificence" (*PR* 4.110–11). Substituting this temptation with the spiritual power of a "constant love for kindred, tribe / And race" on the one hand, and a "loving trust and lofty faith" (*Moses* 151, 164) on the other, Harper portrays Moses as one who heeds the call of his great commission in a spiritually elevated manner.

For instance, Moses responds to his spiritual calling as "the quickening of a higher life as if his soul had wings and he were conscious of their growth" (*Moses* 146). As Harper's epic progresses, Moses goes "forth a strong man, girded with lofty / Purposes and earnest faith" (146). When confronting Pharaoh with God's decree to release the Israelites from bondage, he follows divine instruction and displays an "earnest faith in God" (*Moses* 158). These acts of spiritual heroism resemble those performed by Milton's Son, who, marked by "perfect absolute, graces divine, and amplitude of mind to greatest deeds," respects the will of his sovereign as well (*PR* 2.137–39). In both cases, Harper and Milton's quiet heroes emanate from a Christianizing of the "Aristotelian ideal of the magnanimous man" where inward virtue equates to a grand and noble heroism.[45] Interestingly, Harper and Milton's epic treatment of quiet heroes and inward heroism is not limited to the male characters whose spiritual strength dominates both poems' thematic focus. In yet another thematic parallel between both works, Harper and Milton extend these virtues of inward spiritual heroism to female characters. Their quiet female heroes are likewise endued with epic might, transmitting spiritual strength to their sons who shall one day lead a chosen race out of the house of bondage.

Harper and Milton give intertextual expression to the role of heroic mothers and their maternal strength by appealing to the use of typological symbols as units of extended meaning. Symbols of heroic motherhood, in particular, function in the interest of rhetorically highlighting the Son and Moses's inward spiritual heroism. As such, these typological symbols emphasize the degree to which both texts parallel one another. For instance, Lewalski finds Milton "develop[ing] further ranges of meaning through typological symbolism," where his "allusions to the standard Old Testament and classical types of Christ" serve as models for reiterating his theme of inward spiritual heroism.[46] In both poems, it is the maternal strength of epic mothers that establishes the precondition responsible for making these inward heroes and spiritual liberators magnanimous. This same motif further reestablishes *Moses* as Harper's innovative contribution to the genre of brief biblical epic à la Milton's *Paradise Regained*.

Maternal heroism in both poems plays a vital role in the lives and development of the Son's and Moses's moral valor. More accurately, it is their mothers' expressions of holy faith that influence their noble acts of inward heroism. Directing their sons' respective paths, Mary and Jochabed prepare the way for both liberators to walk nobly according to God's divine purpose. Marjorie O'Rourke Boyle addresses the significance of maternal heroism in Milton criticism, identifying the "Catholic and medieval *Meditationes vitae Christi*" as the literary "source of Milton's closure" in *Paradise*

Regained.⁴⁷ Her examination of Marian presence specifically unravels the philological contexts surrounding the Son's return to his mother at epic's end.

Boyle's examination relies upon these philological origins in order to identify the Son's virtue of meek humility as derivative of his mother's holy disposition. She observes, "the meaning of humility became a philological issue of Renaissance humanism, which devolved around the person of Mary."⁴⁸ This interpretation of Mary's humility makes it possible to recognize the Son's inward virtue as flowing directly from his mother. These insights relative to Marian presence in Milton's epic paved the way for recent discussions concerning "literary representation of heroism during the long seventeenth century in England."⁴⁹ According to Mary Beth Rose, such representations "reveal an accelerating idealization of passive fortitude" in contrast to martial displays of valor and heroism that often dominated the poetic imagination during the period.⁵⁰ New heroic figures evolve from the ruptures created by this poetic intervention. For instance, Rose classifies the Son's "female heroism" in *Paradise Regained* as not only constitutive of "Milton's representation of motherhood," but a strong indicator that "the Son's heroic identity in the present moment of the poem involves accepting his [maternal] origins."⁵¹ Milton, therefore, constructs his characterization of the Son as a model of inward spiritual heroism by paying respect to Mary's spiritual virtue.

In book 1 of *Paradise Regained*, Milton allows the Son to recount how when he was a child his mother taught him that he was the messiah of an enslaved people. Perceiving the young Messiah's desire to "rescue Israel from the Roman yoke" through the power of "winning words" as opposed to brute violence, Mary nourishes her son with knowledge concerning his spiritual destiny (*PR* 1.217, 222). She teaches him that he is "no Son of mortal man" and apprises him that he shall "be great and sit on David's Throne, / And of [his] Kingdom there should be no end" (234, 240–41). She continues by recounting the events associated with the night of his birth so that he knows he is to assume the title of "King of Israel" (253). Having heard his mother's words, Christ relates that he straightaway sought and engaged "the Law and Prophets, searching what was writ / Concerning the Messiah," that he might walk pursuant to his God-given purpose (260–61). As these passages indicate, the Son learns who he is and the spiritual destiny he has been preordained to fulfill through his mother's holy faith in the words of God.

Moses similarly learns of his origins through the dynamics of maternal transmission, a detail that has not gone unnoticed in literary criticism devoted to Harper's brief biblical epic. Displays of a surrogate maternal heroism in *Moses* surface as early as chapter 1 in Harper's poem. Harper introduces the theme early in the chapter when Charmian recalls the day she found and rescued an infant Moses from the Nile River. Charmian's reverie replays the bold steps she took to save this racial other from being killed by her father. Her dream-within-a-dream sequence recalls her bathing in the Nile and finding Moses in "that little ark which floats beside / The stream" (*Moses* 140). Before discovering her new charge, Charmian sits down "to weave a crown of lotus leaves / And lilies fair" (140). The floral imagery proves significant because it crowns Charmian with a laureate of heroic motherhood. Such imagery relies upon the Victorian language of flowers to underscore the heroic grandeur of maternal nurturing.

Catherine H. Waterman's *Flora's Lexicon*, a popular 1863 resource devoted to the interpretation of floral language, associates lotus flowers with conceptions of "estranged love" and "recantation." Waterman bases these interpretations of floral language on the Greek lexicon, which recognizes those who eat the leaves of this flower as "preferring a foreign country to their own."[52] Charmian's circlet symbolizes these aspects of her character, for in rescuing the child of a despised and "Hated race," the princess defies "the oracles" predicting "the pyramids shall wane before [Israel's] shadow, / And from them a star shall rise whose light shall / Spread over earth a baleful glow" (*Moses* 142). In contributing to her culture's undoing, Charmian exhibits heroic motherhood. Rescuing this abandoned child is tantamount to betraying her race. Therefore, she participates in an act of selflessness that communicates a treasonous estrangement from her culture and a preference for the enemy. Her crown of lotus leaves signals a kind of maternal heroism that comes at the expense of a cultural betrayal. Thus, Harper's language of flowers communicates an even greater sense of irony since Charmian ultimately becomes estranged from her surrogate charge when Moses departs to return to his biological kin at chapter's end.

The lilies decorating Charmian's crown also symbolize heroic motherhood by alluding to the surrogate's innocence, purity, and modesty.[53] Both interpretations prove symbolically appropriate within the poetic context of Charmian's storytelling. For instance, the narrative structure of Charmian's story proceeds from a dreamlike state. "How like a dream the past floats back," she recalls, vividly remembering that day when she "lay tossing upon / [her] couch of pain" and seeking refuge in the Edenic beauty of the Nile. Commenting on the "bright, glad hopes, that give to early life / Its glow and flush," Charmian remembers the "breath of lilies, fainting on the air," the "cooling flood," and "the sacred stream" that induced her to sit "in a sweet revery," where she "dream[t] of life and hope" (*Moses* 140). Here, Harper re-creates a setting of innocence not unlike the purity and serenity associated with Eden as an unfallen paradise.

Harper's epic narrative intensifies its focus on deeds of maternal heroism with a second instance of motherly valor. This instance occurs when Charmian explains her insubordinate behavior toward her father when interceding on Moses's behalf. When Pharaoh, her father, discovers she has been caring for baby Moses, he chides her for "bring[ing] a member / Of that mean and servile race within [his] doors" (141). Next, he "sends for Nechos, whose / Ready sword shall rid [him] of [Moses's] hateful presence." Charmian intercedes on the infant's behalf and falls to Pharaoh's feet in lowly submission. "Catching / Hold of his royal robes," she exclaims, "'Not so, / Oh! Honored Father, he is mine; I snatched / Him from the hungry jaws of death, and foiled / The greedy crocodile of his prey" (142). Her physical and vocal responses to Pharaoh exhibit a sacrificial display of heroic motherhood. Having already risked her own life by rescuing Moses from the jaws of serpentine death, she now tempts and courts her father's wrath.

Though Pharaoh instantly commands, "give me up the child, and let him die," Charmian defiantly responds, "clasping the child closer to [her] heart" and exclaiming, "the pathway to his life is through my own; / Around that life I throw my heart, a wall of living, loving clay." Even in the midst of her father's wrathful countenance, Charmian remains undeterred from her convictions and unmoved by her father's imposing authority. Moreover, her pleading countenance of defiance suddenly works maternal wonders. With her penetratingly defiant gaze, Charmian proves powerful enough to soften her father's hardened disposition. As her narrative relates, a "sudden change" befalls her father once he recognizes her dead mother's visage in the pleading eyes of his daughter.

The power of her defiant countenance moves Pharaoh to grant Charmian's prayer. Consequently, he allows her to "claim" and "nurse" Moses as "doubly" hers. By concentrating on Charmian's countenance and its resemblance to her mother, Harper subtly invokes the theme of inward spiritual heroism, focusing on the princess's tempered assertiveness as a maternal virtue. Harper conveys this theme still further by acknowledging Asenath, Pharaoh's deceased wife, as "the light of my home; the star that faded out too / Suddenly from my dwelling, and left my life / To darkness, grief and pain." His homage to Asenath indicates the deceased mother's powerful role within the domestic sphere. The visage of motherhood proves so heroic, in fact, that the mere reflection of Asenath in Charmian's countenance effects a power to move and persuade Pharaoh to concede to his daughter's defiant petition.

Charmian's maternal heroism precedes that of enlightened biological motherhood and its "grandly constructive" work. Once again, Harper's poem parallels Milton's, for like Mary in *Paradise Regained*, Moses's biological mother instructs her son concerning his heroic lineage. Upon Moses's return to his mother Jochabed's home in chapter 2, Harper replays the extent to which the hero's maternal education has contributed to his actions thus far in the epic. His mother's narrative and that of her son evidence the power of his mother's distinctly quiet heroism, which she passes along to Moses. Boyd recognizes this motif of maternal legacy in Harper's epic when she credits Moses's mother as the "key molder of his political and religious consciousness."[54] Evidence of Jochabed's influence reveals itself immediately after Moses greets her with tidings that he has "come to share the fortunes of [his] race / [and] dwell within these lowly huts, — to wear / The badge of servitude and toil" (*Moses* 146). His mother responds to this greeting with a story chronicling the strength of her maternal and resolute faith in God (146).

As this story indicates, Jochabed's faith stands in stark contrast to that of her husband's. According to her narrative, Amram, her husband and Moses's father, "bowed his head upon his staff and wept" upon hearing the false report that his son had "forsworn [his] kindred, tribe and race" in order to be "engrafted in Pharaoh's regal line" (146, 147). Unlike her husband, Jochabed does not share this measure of weakened faith. Possessing a "stronger faith than that," she enumerates a series of heroic acts dramatizing her inward spiritual heroism (147). Moreover, her testimony resounds with the majestic cadence resonant in Hebrews 12, a scriptural passage that is sometimes hermeneutically referred to as the "roll call of faith" in contemporary black preaching. Rather than believe the circulating rumor that Moses has rejected his people, his mother recalls:

> But I had stronger faith than that. By faith
> I hid thee when the bloody hands of Pharaoh
> Were searching 'mid our quivering heart strings,
> Dooming our sons to death; by faith I wove
> The rushes of thine ark and laid thee 'mid
> The flags and lilies of the Nile, and saw
> The answer to that faith when Pharaoh's daughter
> Placed thee in my arms, and bade me nurse the child
> For her; and by that faith sustained, I heard
> As idle words the cruel news that stabbed
> Thy father like a sword. (147)

Moses's mother emulates the rhetorical style of this New Testament passage by generating a string of anaphoric phrases beginning with the words, "by faith." Moses has learned the faith of his mother well, for he responds to her in kind.

In addition to echoing his mother's speech pattern, Moses credits her holy teachings as the source of his spiritual valor. According to him, when faced with the critical decision of renouncing allegiance to his race,

> Then, mother
> Dear, I lived the past again. Again I sat
> Beside thee, my lips apart with childish

> Wonder, my eager eyes uplifted to thy
> Glowing face, and my young soul gathering
> Inspiration from thy words. Again, I heard
> Thee tell the grand traditions of our race,
> The blessed hopes and glorious promises
> That weave their golden threads among the sombre
> Tissues of our lives, and shimmer still amid
> The gloom and shadows of our lot. Again
> I heard thee tell of Abraham, with his constant
> Faith, and earnest trust in God, unto whom
> The promise came that in his seed should all
> The nations of the earth be blessed. (148)

Moses continues to extol the Hebrew roll call of faith in this passage by reciting the spiritual heroism of his ancestral line. He links this narrative of Hebrew faith with his mother's using anaphoric phrases containing "of" constructions. Whereas his mother's passage emphasizes the phrase "by faith," Moses resorts to phrasal strings like "Of Isaac," "Of Jacob," and "Of Joseph." These connectives coupled with biographical qualifiers that further characterize the faith of these holy men unite both recitations, ultimately revealing the transmission of a distinct type of inward spiritual heroism from mother to son.

This variation on his mother's speech act presents a second instance where Moses speaks in the tongues of his mother's holy faith. Earlier, when discussing his lineage with Charmian, Moses recounts "the grand traditions of [his] race," explaining that his biological mother taught him the importance of remembering "the past, [which are] hallowed by deeds / Of holy faith and lofty sacrifice" (143). Speaking in an anaphoric chain suggestive of his mother's roll call of faith, he reiterates the phrase, "she would tell us," reducing its use to multiple phrasal iterations beginning with the word "that." Through this verbal pattern, Moses preaches a historical gospel that showcases his faith as a verbal expression of inward spiritual heroism. These internal structures enable Moses to retell the story of Abraham hearing the voice of God, the shrinking of his heart as he prepared to offer up his only son to him as a sacrificial offering, the "uplifted knife [that] glittered in the morning / Sun," God's intervention, and ultimately, "how his faith, like gold / Tried in the fiercest fire, shone brighter through / Its fearful test" (143–44). Following this internal anaphoric narrative, Moses returns to the larger repetitive structure:

> *And then she would tell us*
> Of a promise, handed down from sire to son,
> *That* God, the God our fathers loved and worshiped,
> Would break our chains, and bring to us a great
> Deliverance; *that* we should dwell in peace
> Beneath our vines and palms, our flocks and herds
> Increase, and joyful children crowd our streets;
> *And then she would* lift her eyes unto the far
> Off hills and tell us of the patriarchs
> Of our line, who sleep in distant graves within
> That promised land; and now I feel the hour
> Draws near which brings deliverance to our race.   (144; my emphasis)

Moreover, in the moment of heroic trial, his mother's "words / Came back as messengers of light to guide / [His] steps" (148–49). As he explained to Charmian earlier in the epic, it was through his biological mother that he "learned the grand traditions of our race" along with his people's "wrecked and blighted fortunes" (143). Although he does not rely on the phrase "by faith," as his mother does, Moses speaks in the tongues of his mother's spiritual beliefs, marking her speech through anaphoric chains of maternal reverie. Sometimes using "of" constructions and in other instances remembering how often his mother led Moses and his siblings "through / The distant past" or "how she would tell [them] of Abraham, / The father of [their] race," Moses makes it evident that his inward spiritual heroism is a testament to his mother's holy influence. A child called by God, Moses is indeed his mother's son, the quiet hero she carried in her womb then nurtured by the inward maternal strength of her spiritual faith.

Moses's chain of anaphoric statements reiterates his mother's inward spiritual heroism and the maternal influence she transfers to him. Foster and Valerie L. Ruffin make this point when they recognize "Moses's birth mother [as] not only nursing him physically but also nurturing his spirit and sense of morality and social justice."[55] They even extend this reading of maternal influence to a wider circle of female participants. According to their reading of *Moses*, women as birth and surrogate mothers, wives, and sisters are collectively "responsible for giving Moses life, for saving his life, and for helping him lead the oppressed toward a new land of liberty."[56] This reading of the role of women in Harper's brief epic coincides with resonances of maternal heroism that appear in her later oratory. In these later works, Harper refers to these feats of inward spiritual valor as virtuous examples of "elevated womanhood."[57]

Chapter 4 enlarges on the theme of inward spiritual heroism when Moses, like the Son in *Paradise Regained*, exiles himself in the wilderness to emerge as a quiet hero. The desert holds symbolic significance in *Moses* and *Paradise Regained*. Its setting provides an arena where the spiritual fitness of both emancipators is to be tried and tested for the fulfillment of some later and greater heroic act. In *Moses*, Harper identifies the significance of this exilic setting as a place of solitude where her biblical hero experiences spiritual transformation. Moses's spiritual transformation accords with Christ and the Son's spiritual transfigurations in the wilderness as recorded in the New Testament and Milton's epic. Harper introduces Moses's spiritual transfiguration at the beginning of her chapter. For instance, her epic narrator asserts that "men grow strong in action, but in solitude / their thoughts are ripened" (*Moses* 151). Moses's seclusion mirrors the Son's, who similarly isolates himself while attending to the Spirit,

> And his deep thoughts, the better to converse
> With solitude, till far from track of men,
> Thought following thought, and step by step led on,
> He entered now the bordering Desert wild,
> And with dark shades and rocks environ'd round,
> His holy meditations thus persu'd.   (*PR* 1.190–95)

In keeping with the Son's virtue of quiet reflection, Harper transforms Moses into a quiet hero whom God grooms for holy purposes of racial uplift.

For instance, at this stage in her epic, Moses has adopted the vocation of a shepherd. He tends his sheep and leads his flock among "the solitudes and wilds of Midian." He also "nurse[s] in silent loneliness his earnest faith / In God" as well as his "constant love for kindred, tribe / And race." Though he advances in age and experiences changes to his physical body, time takes "no atom from his strength, nor laid one heavy weight / Upon his shoulders." These changes in his inward character manifest as instances of quiet heroism and tempered assertiveness. Moses continues to experience spiritual transfiguration as Harper's epic narrator begins reporting the physical changes overtaking his body. The "down upon his face" has "ripened to a heavy beard" while the "fire" that once glowed within his youthful eye" has "deepened / To a calm and steady light." These physical changes affect his inward character as well. The ripening of his visage, for instance, conveys he is maturing into wisdom. Essentially, Moses' inward and outer transfigurations reveal his change from a kind of youthful intemperance to that of a tempered or settled assertiveness. No longer given to impulsive retaliatory acts, this spiritually transfigured Moses composes himself in a "calm" but "steady" manner.

Moses not only looks the part of a quiet hero; he conducts himself as one. Harper's epic narrator adds the heart of this transfigured hero yet proves "just as faithful to his race as when he had / Stood in Pharaoh's courts and bade farewell / Unto [the tyrant's] daughter" (*Moses* 151–52). This qualifying description re-presents Moses as one who still possesses the measure of epic faith demonstrated in the first chapter. After describing Moses's spiritual transfiguration, Harper's chapter progresses then shifts to another pivotal moment in the life of this quiet hero. Commenting on the look of "grand patience" Moses's visage now communicates, the epic narrator relates:

> But the hour came when he must pass from thought
> To action,—when the hope of many years
> Must reach its grand fruition, and Israel's
> Great deliverance dawn. (152)

"Action," in this instance, refers to the holy orders Moses receives from God during his burning-bush experience. Commanded by God to approach "Egypt's guilty king, and bid him let / The oppressed go free," a spiritually transfigured Moses is poised to faithfully execute a ministry of quiet heroism in the remaining lines of Harper's brief biblical epic (153).

It is at this juncture in the poem that Harper's brief biblical epic produces its rupture of "deep time" by suddenly troping with *Paradise Lost* contrary to its chronological publication in literary history. Neil Smith discusses ruptures of "deep time" as breaks with conventional temporalities that have significant impact on the ways we come to understand and theorize about geographical arrangements. According to this theoretical framework, "space becomes [and serves as] the metaphorical bearer of time's meaning."[58] Smith also defines deep space as "the relativity of terrestrial space, the space of everyday life in all its scales from the global to the local" to include the "different layers of life and social landscape [that] are sedimented onto and into each other."[59] Understandings of geographical and social space pursuant to this definition can refer to a range of complex dynamics impacting the worlds of social space and their attendant loaded meanings.

Harper's decision to trope with Milton's first epic midway into her poem and out of chronological sequence presents another deep and wayward rupture of time in literary history. Ironically, engaging Milton in and out of conventional time in this manner mirrors the chronological ruptures occurring throughout *Paradise Lost*. Mary Nyquist calls attention to these temporal ruptures in Milton's epic on the basis of its "complicated relations between a presumed chronological and a narrative ordering of events." Nyquist's concern specifically entertains the dynamics of gendered subjectivity that complicate Milton's decision to order Eve and Adam's narratives of their origins in reverse chronology. As Nyquist explains, *Paradise Lost* "would seem to use both retrospective and prospective narratives in a more systematic and motivated manner than does any of its predecessors [in epic tradition], in part because it is so highly conscious of the problematical process of its consumption."[60] Like Milton, Harper reverses the chronological arrangement of Milton's publication record. First, she establishes *Moses* as derivative of brief biblical epic and *Paradise Regained* specifically. She underscores this intertextual relationship further by nurturing her quiet hero under the maternal auspices of inward spiritual heroism.

At this juncture, however, Harper suddenly goes back in Miltonic time by appropriating key figures from *Paradise Lost*.

This engagement of intertextual reversal thwarts narrative progress in her epic and dramatizes the infernal nature of the Hebrews' spiritual adversaries. Troping with these infernal mascons from *Paradise Lost* aids Harper's style of epic storytelling. This method illuminates the demonic geographies and obstacles to freedom that Moses must contend with and successfully overcome as tensions in her epic escalate.

One of the first allusions to *Paradise Lost* surfaces in chapter 5 when Pharaoh calls a "council / Of his mighty men" to order (*Moses* 154). This assembly of tyrannical rulers and advisors instantly provokes a recollection of Milton's infernal council in book 1 of *Paradise Lost*. Harper adapts Milton's infernal council in the manner of an assimilative allusion. This instance of interpoetic engagement both adsorbs and absorbs Milton's satanic epic into Harper's poem as a reprise and reminder of the demonic forces Moses must contend with and overcome in his ministry as a quiet hero. For Edward Stein, forms of assimilative allusion adsorb and absorb "the attitudes and imaginative atmosphere of preceding poets or poetic communities in order to enrich" these intertextual markers.[61] Harper's parliamentarian session, which is conducted by Pharaoh and his adversarial advisors, almost instantly brings Milton's infernal council to mind. Like Milton's devils, this adversarial group aims to overthrow God by attacking his chosen people.

Harper does not content herself with merely bringing Milton to mind at this juncture in her poem. Thus, she enriches his connotative presence, blending him into her brief biblical epic and making him "cling to the [interpretive] surface" of the familiar, then "mixing [him] in so thoroughly" that Milton becomes smoothly integrated into her poem as a "subtle essence" who remains hidden in plain sight.[62] Evidence of this style of intertextual admixture is reflected in Harper's decision to introduce two of Pharaoh's lords through phraseological instances of satanic profiling. This style of introducing infernal characters through their satanic vices borrows a rhetorical strategy practiced by Milton's narrator when presenting Moloch, Belial, and Mammon to readers of his epic. For instance, Moloch is the first to speak at the infernal council once Satan calls the demonic proceedings to order. Before Moloch proposes his case for "open war," however, Milton's narrator describes this "sceptered king" as "the strongest and the fiercest spirit / That fought in Heav'n, now fiercer by despair (*PL* 2.43, 44–45). This instance of satanic profiling alerts and cautions readers against being so easily seduced by the rhetorical sophistry that will follow. Milton continues this practice when introducing Belial. For this fallen angel, the epic narrator immediately profiles the fallen angel, paying particular attention to his "false and hollow" tongue, which counsels "ignoble ease and peaceful sloth" (2.112, 227).

Milton abandons this practice of satanic profiling when Mammon speaks but resumes it when Beelzebub rises to address the infernal assembly. Milton's epic narrator profiles the fallen angel by describing his visage as possessing a "grave / Aspect" and by referring to him as one who rises as "A pillar of state" given his "sage" posture and those "Atlantéan shoulders fit to bear / The weight of mightiest monarchies" (*PL* 2.300–01, 302, 306–07). Harper adsorbs and absorbs this practice of satanic profiling when introducing Pharaoh's infernal advisors. Relying on prefatory epithets as well, she profiles these advisors in a style that triggers parallels to the infernal council in book 2 of *Paradise Lost* in order to position these adversarial characters at enmity with her readers. Since their works can mean no good for God's chosen people, Harper introduces them by satanically profiling them as religious others.

When introducing Amorphel, for example, Harper delineates this Egyptian advisor by delineating his wickedness. Before allowing him to speak, she intrudes upon the narrative and provides details that expose his satanic or infernal traits. As a result, Harper's audience learns that Amorphel is not only a "Keeper of the palace and nearest lord / unto the king" but an individual who is a "crafty, treacherous man, / With oily lips well versed in flattery / and courtly speech." Additionally, he is "a supple reed ready / To bend before his royal masters lightest / Breath" (*Moses* 154). Harper repeats this pattern of demonic profiling several lines later when introducing Rhadma, the "oldest lord in Pharaoh's court" (155). Again, the epic narrator intrudes upon the narrative to give a satanic account of Rhadma's character. Before he offers his venomous council, the narrator describes him as "an aged man, whose white / And heavy beard hung low upon his breast" and whose visage reveals a "hard cold glitter in his eye" (155).

Pharaoh may trust these spiritual advisors, but Harper sets them at interpretive enmity with her readers, bringing Milton to mind as a mode of enriching the drama of her narrative moment with the satanic energy of her literary precursor.

Harper further enriches Milton's satanic presence with assimilative allusions by subversively manipulating demonic tropes and rhetorically restoring them to coincide with orthodox interpretations of *Paradise Lost*. Earlier in the epic, Harper has already portrayed and marked Pharaoh as possessing satanic characteristics. During Charmian's narrative in chapter 1, for instance, the Egyptian princess allusively describes the ruler's countenance as satanic. When revealing to Pharaoh that the baby she has been nursing is a "Hebrew child," he responds by "suddenly recoil[ing] as if an adder / Had stung him" (*Moses* 141). This serpentine characteristic assumes greater satanic tenor as Charmian's narrative continues. For instance, after declaring her intentions of laying down her life in order to save her adopted child, Pharaoh's visage turns "dark as the thunder / Clouds of distant lands" and his "eyes flash with the fierce lightnings / Of his wrath" (142). This darkened description of Pharaoh's countenance allusively references Milton's depiction of Satan in book 1 of *Paradise Lost*.

From the outset of *Paradise Lost*, Milton's readers learn Satan's form "had yet not lost / All her original brightness" (*PL* 1.591–92). Furthermore, the epic narrator specifies that the fallen angel's "darkened" face bears "deep scars of thunder" (*PL* 1.599, 600–01). Later, the narrator reports that "revenge" lurks and waits beneath those brows "Of dauntless courage and consid'rate pride" (*PL* 1.603–04). Pharaoh continues to assert an allusive resemblance to Milton's Satan in chapter 5 when he "hiss[es] / A taunt into [the] ears" of the groaning Israelites who succumb to their "added tasks" under the tyrannical monarch's oppressive rulership (*Moses* 156). Additionally, his brow grows "dark with wrath" when Moses enters his royal courts to advocate for the Israelites' freedom. These assimilative allusions accumulate with greater satanic intensity as Harper's brief biblical epic progresses.

For instance, her use of thunder as yet another assimilative allusion of satanic profiling and characterization reveals another Miltonic overtone that invites intertextual comparisons between

Satan and Pharaoh and the infernal temperaments they share. The recurrent use of thunder in *Paradise Lost*, as Elton D. Higgs examines, involves tripartite levels of rhetorical complexity primarily signifying God's omnipotence and wrathful vengeance. According to Higgs, the use of thunder "illuminates the psychology of the fallen Satan, foreshadows the compounding of the devils' damnation, and ties the fall of man poignantly to that of the rebellious angels."[63] Milton ultimately refers to his devils as being "thunderstruck" in book 4 of the epic where they are driven to the edge of heaven's precipice and made to suffer their hellish downfall. Too fallen to accept God's omnipotence as factual, they are made to suffer ruin at the rhetorical expense of Milton's "hellish reversal of values which obscures the devils' perception of what is going on" relative to their cosmic existence within the epic.[64] Harper adapts this rhetorical use of thunder as an assimilative allusion in her epic. Its signifying force especially surfaces in her recounting of the perilous moment when the drowning Egyptians suddenly and belatedly recognize they are at enmity with God and his chosen people.

After narrating the Israelites' successful pilgrimage through the Red Sea, Harper's epic narrator looks to the heavens and appeals to nature's fury as an echoic sign of Miltonic presence. This instance of intertextuality occurs immediately prior to the collapse of the waves as the narrator asserts that it was then that "the solemn truth broke on [the Egyptians]—that God / For Israel fought" (*Moses* 159). The Egyptian soldiers' countenances reveal their fear of this solemn recognition: "With cheeks in terror / Blenching, and eyes astart with fear," they feebly attempt to return to shore though God, unbeknownst to them, "had loosened every / Axle and unfastened every wheel" (159–60). What is particularly interesting about these descriptions of martial downfall as reflected in the Egyptians' facial expressions is the kinesthetic response of shock and awe that they portray in concert with the imagery of nature's tempestuous fury. The reference to "blenching" cheeks coupled with the description of ears "astart with fear" conveys a visage of awesome wonder not unlike the thunderstruck countenance Milton's devils project in book 4 of *Paradise Lost*.

Harper solidifies this Miltonic connection even further with her appeal to nature's fury as a rhetorical sign for God's wrath and omnipotent judgment upon those he considers at variance with his chosen people. First, the narrator reports that the Egyptians' faces "did gather blackness and each heart stood still / With fear, as the livid lightnings glittered / And the thunder roared and muttered on the air" (*Moses* 160). The darkened gloom of the Egyptians' faces accented by the flashing lightning and roaring thunder coalesce to signal God's wrath as is consistent with Higgs's reading of Milton's epic. The display of nature's tempest when considered in tandem with the Egyptians' fearful countenances produces a kinesthetic image of thunderstruck awe relative to God's mighty acts of divine vengeance. By attending to nature's tempestuous fury and the Egyptians' facial expressions, Harper poetically creates an image that subsequently conveys God's divine judgment against infernal dissidents. These dissident powers frustrate the righteousness of God's chosen people "who are called according to his purpose" (Rom. 8:28).

Still another parallel to Satan and his followers' tragic downfall involves Harper's loaded phraseological adaptation of "ruin" when depicting the Egyptians' drowning. Her narration explains how the Egyptians "saw the dreadful *ruin* that shuddered / O'er their heads" (my emphasis). Interestingly, Milton's epic narrator in book 6 of his epic also references a trail of ruin. For instance, "Hell saw / Heav'n ruining from heav'n" when the Messiah routs the apostate angels out of God's celestial sphere (*PL* 6.868). That both poets reference a trail of "ruin" to describe the descent of the spiritually fallen is more than coincidental. In *Paradise Lost*, Satan and his "thunderstruck" crew are driven "to the bounds / And crystal wall of heav'n, which op'ning wide, / Rolled inward" as a "spacious gap disclosed / Into the wasteful deep" (*PL* 859–61). Soon thereafter, they are hurled "from the verge of heav'n... to [hell's] bottomless pit" (*PL* 865–66). As they fall "through [hell's] wild anarchy," the geographical space containing them "yawns [and] receiv[es] them whole" before ultimately closing in upon them (*PL* 6.873, 875).

The "dreadful ruin" overtaking the drowning Egyptians reflects a supernatural disaster involving water as opposed to fire. This Miltonic repetition with cultural difference echoes Milton so that Harper may remain faithful to dramatizing the collapse of the Red Sea as her wayward sign of God's divine judgment and the satanic ruin of those who oppress his chosen people. Harper solidifies this rhetorical connection to Milton by referencing the crashing waves as a durable structure. Similar to the "crystal wall of [Milton's] heav'n," Harper imagines the parted Red Sea as a stable fortress through which the Israelites successfully cross (*PL* 6.860). Upon their safe passage to the other side, the waves tremble as "the wall of flood [began] to bend" (*Moses* 160). The "madly dashing, wildly crashing" waves ultimately vanquish the "flower and pride / Of Egypt [who] sank as lead within the sea." Harper's water imagery vividly recaptures the trail of ruin that Milton depicts by fire. Collectively, her amplification of the fallen angels' thunderstruck awe and the trail of hellish ruin expose her brief biblical epic as a wayward reprise of *Paradise Lost*. With its infernal network of rhetorical figures *Moses* continues to showcase Harper's artistry in appropriating Milton's satanic energy for her own messianic purposes. Moses therefore memorializes and commemorates the U.S. landscape as a fallen yet regained paradise of racial equality and freedom.

Harper's inversion of the demonic in her epic performs a subversive reordering of orthodox interpretation in traditions of Milton's reception. Orthodox interpretations of Milton's epic hermeneutically cohere to the epic writer's spiritual goal to "justify the ways of God to men" (*PL* 1.26). Harper, by gravitating to Milton's satanic epic, adopts a wayward approach to justifying God's ways in an orthodox manner. She resists the militant intertextual engagements favored by self-made men like Douglass or the British Romantics who identified with the infernal hero as a political rebel. Instead, she identifies and tropes with the demonic as a negative sign of hegemonic oppression. This inversion of an unorthodox style of Miltonic appropriation reflects a wayward aesthetic that adheres to orthodox interpretations of Milton's Satan but on demonic grounds of contention as opposed to supernal ones.

According to this self-invented style of intertextual engagement, characters like Amorphel, Rhadma, and Pharaoh maintain their negative identifications with the satanic and its metaphorical tenor. For instance, Amorphel and Rhadma vocally represent this unorthodox aspect of Harper's unfit appropriations of Milton's demonic figures by separately advising Pharaoh of the potential threats the Israelites pose for Egypt. Both advisors denigrate the captive Israelites as potential rebels. Amorphel, for one, advises Pharaoh to increase the Israelites' tasks and labors so that they will "have less time to plot sedition / And revolt" (*Moses* 155). Advising Pharaoh on the dangers inherent in listening to Moses and his brother, Rhadma claims both men "mean mischief," for "sedition / And revolt are in their plans." These insurrectionary fears evidence rhetorical reversals of the infernal character displayed in books 1 and 2 of Milton's epic.

Overall, this unorthodox strategy of troping with Milton's satanic epic allows Harper to subversively tread on the demonic grounds of contention and profile infernal characters without intertextually compromising the spiritual fitness of her messianic gospel. Moreover, this self-invented mode of tempered assertiveness enables the Bronze Muse to break new interpretive grounds in Milton's canon and transform the U.S. landscape from the hell of slavery to a paradise of freedom. In this way, Harper engages with Milton as a means for memorializing the U.S. landscape and consecrating it anew. Writing the nation's passage through Milton's canonical poems, Harper, a chosen vessel for God's chosen people, preaches a poetic gospel of spiritual redemption through wayward or demonic acts of intertextual sedition.

Incorporating Milton in her canon and manipulating the rhythms of epic verse reflect upon Harper's unconventional sense of Miltonic timing. Her wayward respect for Milton's relevance within literary history and for epic timing more generally impacts geographical arrangements also. Harper would have been familiar with Milton well before 1869 given her formal education at her uncle's school, yet she chose not to trope with the epic poet until the Emancipation Proclamation rendered her people free and after Lincoln's death. Rupturing her canon with the epic poet's presence at this curious moment in her life suggests Milton and his theme of liberty are not an appropriate fit for her poetry until the U.S. landscape has been made free in/deed à la Lincoln's Emancipation Proclamation. Reading Milton's presence in her canon according to this interpretive paradigm exposes the intertextual ruptures of deep space and deep time that *Moses* frustrates as a result of Harper's groundbreaking poem in epic tradition.

Harper would continue to trope selectively with Milton in subsequent works of fiction like her serialized novels, *Sowing and Reaping* (1876–77) and *Trial and Triumph* (1888–89). In the collection of poems, *Sketches of Southern Life* (1886), she evokes Milton's presence once again in her allegorical story, "Shalmanezer, Prince of Cosman." The story invites an interesting recall of book 3 in *Paradise Regained*, which references the "golden Monarchy" and "seat of *Salmanassar*," the Assyrian king, "whose success," according to Satan, "*Israel* in long captivity still mourns" (*PR* 3.277–79). That Harper's allegory and Milton's brief epic both reference this rather obscure biblical name seems more than mere coincidence. In both instances, the authors capitalize upon the Assyrian king's name in order to preach moral and spiritual gospels of self-denial.[65] Harper even tropes with Milton in her 1893 speech, "Women's Political Future," delivered at the World's Congress of Representative Women. That speech allusively echoes the ending of book 12 from *Paradise Lost*, championing women's evangelical ministry as providing "sublimest opportunit[ies]" for helping to eradicate the "social evil" of lynching.[66] In a phraseological gloss on Adam and Eve as they "hand in hand.../ Through Eden t[ake] their solitary way," Harper reverses the theme of Edenic exile to signal her abiding rhetorical investment in regaining paradise (*PL* 12.646–49). Extolling women's purpose, Harper faintly glosses Milton's phrase by acknowledging, "With such a purpose" of sublime opportunity, "Eden would spring up in our path, and Paradise be around our way."

Ironically, Harper's abiding interest in regaining paradise would follow her even unto death. In "Bury Me in a Free Land," one of her most canonical antislavery poems, Harper reiterates the horror she would feel if her body were buried in a land where slavery yet existed. As the voice of her poem explains, she could not repose comfortably in a land where the "steps of a trembling slave" or the "tread / Of a coffle-gang" might frighteningly disturb her while in eternal slumber.[67] Nor could her soul rest contented if while buried beneath her tomb she "saw the lash" of a slaveowner "drink [a mother's] blood at each fearful gash." It is, perhaps, a providential act of poetic irony that upon her death in 1911 Harper was interred in Eden Cemetery. An African American burial ground located in Philadelphia, Pennsylvania, Eden Cemetery houses the earthly remains of various African Americans of high regard. Frances Harper, the Bronze Muse of African American tradition, is one of these interred souls. Resting in the peace of Eden Cemetery, Harper abides and is interred in a paradise hallowed by a different type of cultural interaction with Milton. As a result of being buried in Eden Cemetery, Harper may have regained paradise on subversive grounds of Miltonic contention. Additionally, she rests on a canon of wayward poems that will eternally complete and complicate Milton in new and exciting ways. Having broken new grounds in Miltonic engagement through this legacy of poetic achievement, Harper, *free* from every care, regains Edenic paradise at last, reposing in that paradoxical space of intertextual interment where "the wicked cease from troubling and...the weary [are] at rest" (Job 3:17).

6

MILTONIC SOUNDSCAPES IN ANNA JULIA COOPER'S *A VOICE FROM THE SOUTH*

In keeping with the proto-womanist spirit of tempered assertiveness, Anna Julia Cooper, another prominent member of Milton's black sisterhood, performs a series of rebellious vocal exercises with Milton in her 1892 publication, *A Voice from the South*.[1] Whereas Harper rebelliously engages Milton mostly through a subversive appropriation of literary form and theme, Cooper actually vocalizes her knowledge of the epic poet's figures, rhetoric, and literary persona through a range of allusive fragments. *A Voice from the South* is a unique text in the sense that its contents are comprised of eight essays that Cooper sets to a compositional score of literary music. Cooper divides these eight essays into two sections. One section appears under the heading "Soprano Obligato," while the second boasts the title "Tutti ad Libitum." *Soprano obligato* is Latin in derivation and is used in music to identify an indispensible component of accompaniment that is an integral part of a musical score. Because *soprano*, derived from *supra*, meaning "superior" or "highest above," typically refers to female voices, Cooper appropriates the musical term as a metonym for women. Considered alongside one another and according to Cooper's womanist logic, the term *soprano obligato* communicates the indispensability of women and their voices in public discourse.

The term *tutti ad libitum* extends Cooper's subversive interest in the womanist politics of skilled musicianship. Meaning "all at liberty" in music, the term especially commands members of an ensemble to play without restraint or imposed limitations. Such a command generally occurs at "the end of an extended solo passage when the entire ensemble enters."[2] In titling the second division of her essays with this musical reference, Cooper voices a womanist sensibility that fully integrates women in the chorus of public and philosophical opinion that has traditionally consisted of men. Because she argues the larger concerns of the race after first privileging her arguments concerning black women's indispensability to the elevation of the human race, Cooper philosophically produces a literary score that harmonizes the sexes for the betterment of Western civilization. This philosophical bridging of the sexes is at the heart of Cooper's womanist impulse throughout *Voice from the South*. To give greater literary expression and musical vocality to this impulse in the early years of the fin de siècle, Cooper vocalizes her knowledge of Milton and worries the line of epic and early African American tradition near the close of the nineteenth century.

Cooper is renowned in early African American culture as a proto-womanist, essayist, activist, educator, and high school principal, among numerous other achievements. She was born a slave in Raleigh, North Carolina, in 1858 and lived to the age of 105. By the age of 10, she had skillfully negotiated an arrangement to serve as a "peer teacher" at the St. Augustine's Normal School and Collegiate Institute in order "to supplement her tuition scholarship." A high school that enjoyed a reputation as "a hub of intellectual activity," St. Augustine's was "created under the auspices of the Freedmen's Bureau and the Episcopal Church."[3] Vivian May, one of the most recent scholars to enrich contemporary understandings of Cooper, argues that the school offered the former slave girl a liberal arts education that proved "formative in shaping [her] comparative, Black Atlantic view of race politics and history."[4] Cooper married fellow theology student George A. C. Cooper and continued her educational aspirations well after his death two years later. First, she entered Oberlin in 1881, enrolling "in the 'Gentleman's Course,'" where she "earned a classical education on par with men" and graduated among that institution's first cohort of African American women.[5] These formative years of education undoubtedly exposed Cooper to Milton, who, by the latter decades of the nineteenth century, remained popular in Victorian culture and relevant in African American tradition. Her rigorous education at St. Augustine and Oberlin would prime her for greater accomplishments throughout the remainder of her career and public life.

These accomplishments included her distinguished career as a teacher and high school principal committed to academic rigor and student excellence. Throughout her 35-year teaching career, Cooper specialized in multiple disciplines. For instance, Charles Lemert and Esme Bhan acknowledge her disciplinary specialties in "the classics, the modern and ancient languages, literature, mathematics, and the sciences."[6] A highlight of Cooper's teaching career involved her various roles at the prestigious M Street High School in Washington, D.C., where she eventually served as its principal. Dedicated to rigorous teaching standards, Cooper proved to be a "brilliant teacher and an effective school leader," enriching that school's "curriculum in classical subjects [so] that a markedly greater number of its graduates were accepted to elite colleges like Harvard."[7] Unfortunately, Cooper suffered backlash for holding students to rigorous standards of academic excellence contrary to the wishes of the school district's white superintendent. As a result, her contract was not renewed for academic year 1906–07 due to trumped-up charges that cast aspersions on her administrative leadership and personal character.

Later in life, Cooper went on to become the first African American woman to earn a Ph.D. at the Sorbonne.[8] By 1914, she "enrolled as a doctoral student in the Department of Romance Languages at Columbia University where she began her annotated translation from medieval to modern French of the epic poetry cycle *Le Pèlerinage de Charlemagne.*"[9] Unable to fulfill the one-year residency requirement in New York City due to economic circumstances and familial responsibilities, Cooper subsequently transferred to the Sorbonne. Receiving a generous fellowship from the African American women's sorority, Alpha Kappa Alpha, Cooper transferred to the Sorbonne, which accepted all of Cooper's credits from Columbia but mandated she develop an entirely different dissertation topic. In 1925 at the age of 62, Cooper completed her dissertation, *L'attitude de la France à l'égard de l'esclavage pendant la Révolution* (France's Attitude toward Slavery during the Revolution). May considers this achievement "an important intellectual and political contribution to Black modernism, to the Harlem Renaissance, and to the development of a comparative anticolonial methodology."[10] Cooper's distinguished achievement in doctoral letters helps to explain the extent and intellectual complexity of this race woman's multivoiced heritage. A visionary in women's issues, race matters, and epic tradition, Cooper vocalizes her Miltonic knowledge at different points throughout *A Voice from the South*. Through these signifying exercises, Cooper worries the lines of Miltonic reception, piercing the patriarchal soundscapes of her era and transforming the demonic geographies of her times so that black women may enter discourse when and as they please.

"Worrying the line" in African American music references an expressive style of repeating words, phrases, figures, or vocal sounds to exaggerated effect as a means for punctuating meaning. This mode of repetition operates within the expressive space afforded between rhythmic beats. Worrying the line, as Stephen Henderson explains, functions as a device that facilitates a musician's need to "alter the pitch of a note" as "ornamentation" or "for affective or didactic comment." Cheryl A. Wall, noting a variation of this musical style in African American women's literature, describes the line as "a metaphor for lineage" that likewise governs the "literary traditions in which these texts participate." More specifically, these intertextual engagements among black women writers highlights how their various approaches to this art form work "changes on literary traditions" by repeating any number of expressive figures or modalities with punctuated difference.[11] On the one hand, Cooper's intertextual engagements with Milton worry the line of Miltonic affiliation established by Wheatley and Harper specifically, and early African American literature more generally. On the other hand, *A Voice from the South* engages in this practice to amplified rhetorical effect. In her gospel of black revolt, Cooper also worries the lines of Milton's epic verse in order to promote a theme of gendered liberty. Throughout the work she vocalizes her Miltonic knowledge, piercing the patriarchal soundscape with aural tones of womanist difference.

By worrying the lines of Milton's epic verse throughout *A Voice from the South*, Cooper vocalizes a mode of "black expressive culture" that "contribute[s] to what might be considered new and contestatory geographic acts."[12] Thinking about music and its sonic effects on the landscape, Katherine McKittrick categorizes musical expressions and the technologies of music making within a paradigm of aural politics that further expands conventional ideas concerning sounds and their attendant geographical implications. McKittrick contends that the effects of music on aural geographies cannot be charted on conventional maps. Thus, she designates sonic activities or the "implicit technologies of the poetics of landscape" as "soundscapes." This reading of music and its impact on geography calls attention to the art of noise, its technologies of production, and the multiple activities or behaviors they induce. These activities and behaviors include "dancing, seeing, not listening, and (in)voluntary listening to other people's music."[13] Music, in each of these contexts, impacts the soundscape, inducing bodies to move or not as a response to sonic productions and the power of their reverberating influence on culture. Cooper performs a similar musical rupture when she worries the line of Milton's epic verse throughout *A Voice from the South*. Her Miltonic vocalizations prove satanic because they radically respatialize the spaces "when and where" black women may enter discourse "in the quiet, undisputed dignity of [their] womanhood" (*Voice* 31). Such a rupture on the soundscape of her era exercises Milton by permeating the sound waves of patriarchal thinking with the worried fragments of his epic verse.

In order to understand Cooper's approach to worrying the line with fragments of Milton's verse, it is worth noting that these intertextual re-memberings of the epic writer exercise the Miltonic recall of "fit" audiences (*PL* 7.31) who are attuned and well versed in the borrowed themes and figures of her literary precursor. As a result, this aspect of her multivocal communicative strategy especially addresses a segment of white readers she seeks to enlighten through her rebellious gospel of womanist revolt. Vivian May, drawing on Maria Lugones's theoretical understandings of the "playfulness" of language, calls for a more complex reading of Cooper's subversive way with words. For instance, she advises, "it is essential...to attend not just to what Cooper says in a literal sense, but also to trace the spirit of her words and ideas as they unfold by noticing allusions, hearing sarcasm, and unpacking allegories."[14] Cooper's Miltonic allusions throughout *A Voice from the South* underscore May's point, for they cohere to form an intertextual style of musical expression that doubles as an expressive weapon for piercing and, therefore, rupturing musical geographies of patriarchal domination. Worrying the line with Milton's fragmented influence, then, empowers Cooper to transform the patriarchal landscape of her era by inflecting her voice with the rebellious tenor of her precursor's satanic poetry.

Cooper's central theme throughout the essays punctuates her womanist goal of adding or including the black woman's voice "to the already full chorus of [male] public opinion" (*Voice* ii). By including the black woman's "muffled chord" and "mute and voiceless note" in the male chorus of public opinion, Cooper undermines a tradition of patriarchal thought that actively works to silence and repress black women (i). She recognizes that black women's philosophical theories on the issues of her day are vital to the race and Western civilization as a whole and uses her embodied womanist voice to raise consciousness concerning the shared plight of all women across the color line. If prior to her Miltonic exercise in *A Voice from the South* black women have been excluded from the male chorus of public opinion, Cooper reorders these geographical spaces of patriarchal privilege by rebelliously altering the aural landscape through her proto-womanist allusions to England's epic poet of liberty.

Cooper begins vocalizing and exercising her knowledge of Milton in the first essay, "Womanhood: A Vital Element in the Regeneration and Progress of a Race." With each subsequent allusion to his epic, Cooper worries the line with his canonical presence. Using the form of Milton's satanic poetry, her gospel of womanist revolt is imbued with themes of liberty by vocalizing rebellion on demonic grounds where issues of race and sex collide to champion a cause of gendered inclusivity. The first instance of forging a rhetorical affiliation with Milton in this essay occurs in the essay's title. The title conveys an implied reference to Milton that operates primarily on the levels of allusive and acoustic echo. Though this first echo is not readily apparent to the casual reader, it signals its implied relationship with Milton as a rearticulation of the epic writer's Edenic theme and trope of generation. As the essay progresses and its references to paradise and employment of horticultural imagery increases, it becomes apparent that Cooper's title invites readers to compare and contrast her womanist ideas against Milton's epic. Similar to Danielle A. St. Hilaire's understanding of intertextual processes within literary tradition, Cooper's essay performs a "mark of resemblance that tie[s] the new work to the old...that therefore allow[s] us to read [both] side by side."[15] Cooper's rhetorical invitation establishes an intertextual beat of Miltonic presence that she worries throughout the essay and subsequent ones throughout the book.

Milton's Edenic theme and his trope of generation figure prominently as expressions of "the beautiful" according to eighteenth century receptions of *Paradise Lost*. The reception of "the beautiful" where Milton's epic is concerned originates from Joseph Addison's *Spectator*. In *Beautiful Sublime*, Leslie Moore notes that Addison "arranges the scenes of *Paradise Lost* into a different set of categories, the great, the uncommon, and the beautiful." Addison ranks "the beautiful" as inferior in scope with its scenes of "*Pandaemonium*, Paradise, Heaven, Angels, and Adam and Eve." However, Moore's analysis reveals that women literary artists in the period favored Milton's beauty and rejected the "machining" episodes containing "celestial and infernal agents." Based on their intertextual engagement with "the beautiful" in their literary works, Moore asserts that Milton's "inferior" scene often served as a contentious ground for women readers and authors. They referred to these scenes of "the beautiful" in order to rewrite Eve in interpretive images more favorable to their conceptions of women. Thus, some of them engaged Milton's epic to "attack existing institutions or to reimagine the idea of woman" along contestatory lines.[16] Cooper stands in rhetorical solidarity with this eighteenth century sisterhood, as her ample use of the trope of regeneration suggests.

Addressing racial concerns and those of gender, the essay's primary focus establishes woman as the vital agent in uplifting the African American race and Western civilization. However,

Cooper's primary message is that of regarding the black woman as the one heroic agent powerful enough to *regenerate* the African American race. Her trope of regeneration signifies and updates Milton's figure of generation in a vocal register of womanist difference. Through this vocal exercise, Cooper "exercises the memory" to meditate on Milton's paradise and all that has been lost in the wake of patriarchal fallenness as prophesied by Michael in book 12.[17] Here, Cooper prophesies the power of womanist regeneration, associating it with a divine office that restores a lost paradise to the fallen or "benighted sons and daughters of Africa" and Western civilization as well.[18] On a more literal level yet in keeping with the disciplines of biology, physics, and theology, "regenerate" means "to reform spiritually or morally" or "to form, construct, or create anew."[19] If the black woman is "a vital element in the regeneration and progress of a race" and civilization as well, then the implication of Cooper's assertion conveys that both landscapes constitute fallenness and are, therefore, in need of restoration or rebirth. According to this logic, the race needs regeneration because it has only been two decades since its members have been emancipated. Western civilization is also in need of restoration as a result of the postlapsarian stains of slavery and racial injustice. As Cooper effectively argues, the race and Western civilization may be read as fallen. Both merit indictment for their systematic disenfranchisement of women. In these fallen times, the elevation of the race and civilization depends entirely upon the "indispensable agency of an elevated and trained womanhood" (*Voice* 29). Only she can regain paradise and restore it to greatness through the effectual exercising of her moral and spiritual strength.

The trope of Edenic regeneration establishes Milton as an intertextual beat that Cooper repeatedly worries throughout this first essay. Within the scope of the womanist author's message, Milton surfaces as an intertext that facilitates Cooper's multivocal project of "rewriting or reading the dominant story" of canonical tradition in her own write and in rebellious contrast to the patriarchal soundscapes that have worked to silence and exclude black womanhood.[20] Cooper exercises Milton's trope of generation further and allusively worries the figure by interpreting black women's strength as a heroic role worthy of epic valuation. She emphasizes women's epic strength by capitalizing upon horticultural rhetoric. Her theme of regeneration draws rhetorical strength from no less than 40 horticultural references throughout the essay; they include terms such as "germ," "seed," "plantlet," "ingrafted," "branches," "trunk," "root," and "chlorophyll." Cooper even puns on these terms, developing phrases such as "narrow, sickly and stunted growth" and "harvests from this over ripe field of home missions" to further highlight the strength of the black woman as a regenerating force in nature (*Voice* 19, 34). While the rhetorical fecundity of these horticultural references does not, at first, appear to signal an intertextual relation to Milton's trope of generation, their interrelatedness becomes evident upon an assessment of the stylistic parallels governing both writers' use of the Edenic as symbolic expression.

Cooper's horticultural rhetoric figuratively echoes Milton's poetics by exercising and worrying it as a sign of plenitude that contrasts with the masculine lack governing the epic poet's despair relative to his failing sight. As John Rumrich discovers, Milton cleaves to the trope of generation as a kind of rhetorical compensation for his failing sight while composing *Paradise Lost*. While the trope of generation in Milton's epic suggests fecundity, it also locates a traumatizing sense of lack as a motivating force for the poet's aesthetic vision. According to Rumrich, the significance of this trope directly relates to interventions made by William Harvey. A seventeenth century physician, Harvey defied Aristotelian belief by recognizing the brain and the womb as equivalent generative powers. Until then, the brain was symbolically regarded as a powerful faculty of generative creativity. Typically associated with men, its power to conceive, produce, and create profound philosophical ideas and theories encouraged men to esteem themselves a little higher than the women whose procreative abilities they may have slightly envied. Hence, this symbolic womb envy apparently generated a desire for some counterimage that might have given men the figurative potency they craved in order to feel superior along gender lines.

By resisting the notion that the brain was superior to the womb, Harvey situated women's creative faculties as equivalent to men's in the discourse of scientific thought. *Paradise Lost* contains myriad figures of womblike creation, as Rumrich shows. He regards these multiple references as signaling the blind poet's pining for maternal creative power in the absence of his own visual impairment. By implication, this rhetorical gesture conveys Milton's sense that his failing sight ultimately denies him poetic potency as a master poet of profound ideas and strong artistic vision. Rumrich, therefore, interprets Milton's trope of generation as a sign of the epic poet's "yearning for transcendence of limitations imposed by gender."[21] For instance, in book 3 of *Paradise Lost*, Milton endows his blind narrator with the poetic inspiration of channeling creative forces, often associated with women's generative capacities, into his own myth-making aesthetic. His narrator seeks light in order to conceive a grand epic and turns to various womblike figures to satisfy his poetic imagination.

Other examples of this dynamic include the pairing of hollow imagery with the darkened cavities of the poetic mind, the "strange symbolic connection between devilish artillery and Eve's Womb," the fallen angels' rape of the soil in their attempts to invent gunpowder, the effects of metallurgical transubstantiation, and the erection of Pandaemonium as well. These instances, according to Rumrich, have their origins in women's creative faculties while at the same time "disclos[ing] the manifold generative force of maternal nature in a way that allows [Milton] to participate in [woman's] realm of power."[22] In other words, Milton, in his anxiety, turns to the womb for rhetorical strength. What he expresses by this rhetorical return to the womb is his possible belief that woman's generative powers prove a poetics of restoration in times of impairment, lack, or fallenness.

Cooper, by contrast, acknowledges the humanity of woman with her trope of regeneration. Moreover, she specifically recognizes woman's moral and spiritual strength as the vital elements enabling her to advance society. A rhetorical by-product of her trope of regeneration, the emphasis on woman's moral and spiritual strength becomes a figure for recreating a fallen world anew. From here, the "Womanhood" essay takes a series of winding rhetorical turns. Complex and sophisticated (digressively so), Cooper's mode of rhetorical argumentation exercises Milton by regenerating him through an accumulation of philosophical ideas, aphorisms, intertextual echoes and allusions. Each instance of intertextual regeneration with Milton positively worries his presence in *A Voice from the South*. In turn, these vocal exercises augment Cooper's argumentative style, which rhetorically flourishes from her own Edenic sensibilities.

One of the first instances of positively worrying the line of Milton's epic in this essay occurs when Cooper identifies Christianity and the feudal system as originating sources responsible for providing modern civilization with its "noble and ennobling ideal[s] of woman" (*Voice* 9). After making this claim, Cooper segues into an examination of fallenness based on her interpretations of Asian culture, Islamic religion, and the limitations of their respective ideologies in terms of women's equality. The trope of generation as a sign of cultural fallenness emerges almost immediately as she cites the Koran as a "product and not a growth," which unlike the Bible "makes no account of woman whatever in its polity" (*Voice* 9, 10). Cooper's distinction between these scriptural traditions as a product and growth reflects the idea that anything that does not grow cannot live. The Koran, in this instance, represents a manufactured ideology of patriarchal fallenness as opposed to a more egalitarian idea that organically germinates from nature's sound principles. Furthermore, Cooper's horticultural expression denotes her feminist concept that the ideological and philosophical *products* of civilizations can have no lasting value for cultures seeking to advance themselves throughout the ages. Consequently, she regards them as fallen civilizations.

More than fallen, these civilizations position women in a hellspace of gendered inequality, therefore subjecting them to eternal damnation in a figurative sense. Cooper also considers these religious practices as having broader cultural implications. Wherever and whenever women are excluded from any material considerations, Cooper believes that those civilizations likewise relegate them to an existence that is "uniformly devoted to a life of ignorance, infamy, and complete stagnation" (*Voice* 10). Cooper emphasizes this point in Edenic terms as well. Expanding upon the trope of regeneration that has already begun establishing Milton's presence in her text, she intimates that these circumstances translate to fallenness, since there can likewise be "no hereafter, no paradise for [woman]" given these misogynist practices (*Voice* 10).[23] By explicitly equating her meditations on Eden with paradise, Cooper elaborates upon her vocal exercise of worrying the line of Milton's epic by engrafting his figures into *A Voice from the South*.

The more she worries the lines of Milton's epic by reiterating the trope of regeneration, the more her references to paradise become primed with increased and heightened Miltonic significance. Patrick Hogan describes this process of priming as a direct extension of metaphorical interpretation, where readers "transfer constituents from source to target" specifically because meaning in a given text gives them reason to.[24] This process continues to prime Milton's presence in Cooper's text with each accumulating reference to the thematic binaries of paradise and fallenness. For instance, in addressing Turkish Muslims' intellectual brilliance and their "intricacies of diplomacy and statesmanship," Cooper primes a consideration of Edenic fallenness by referring to their minds as branches that "were not the normal outgrowth of a healthy trunk" (*Voice* 11). The rhetorical implication of her reference to diseased vegetation signals an interpretive association of lack or abnormality with the theme of fallenness. In figurative terms, Cooper interprets this male sect as fallen as a result of their being generatively stunted.

At this stage of her argument, Cooper begins to intensify her vocal exercise of worrying Miltonic presence into her argument. She achieves this musical practice by combining a use of generative tropes with satanic energy that specifically echoes *Paradise Lost* and its fallen rebels. First, Cooper extends her commentary on the Turkish Muslims' diseased trunks, adding that their limbs consist of "ephemeral excrescencies which shoot far out with all the vigor and promise, apparently, of strong branches; but soon alas fall into decay and ugliness because there is no soundness in the root, no life-giving sap, permeating, strengthening and perpetuating the whole" (*Voice* 11). Initially, this statement seems to express a positive concept until Cooper reveals that the trunk produces diseased branches. According to her, its stunted growth is the consequence of her belief that no good can come from a society holding its women in such low regard. Healthy trees generate vibrant limbs and flourish because they stem from women's valuable contributions to society by way of their deep insights. Their philosophical meditations are at once the "soundness" of root and the "life-giving sap" on which civilization thrives. By contrast, where "the homelife is impure," Cooper finds a "worm [existing] at the core!" (*Voice* 11). Upon closer inspection, she finds that even the domestic sphere, where woman is believed to reign, falls into ruin. Challenging patriarchal culture within the ideologies of true womanhood discourse, Cooper ultimately advises, "when we look for fruit, like apples of Sodom, it crumbles within our grasp into dust and ashes" (*Voice* 11).

Her reference to ash-ridden apples immediately conveys her satanic reading of *Paradise Lost*. This reference echoes book 10 of Milton's epic. In this passage, Satan and his legion undergo their transformation into serpents following the infernal hero's return to Pandaemonium. As serpents, they slither along the earth, craving the "fair fruit, like that / Which grew in Paradise" (*PL* 10.550–51). They soon find a tree whose fruit seems as fair as that which grew "near that bituminous lake where Sodom flamed" (*PL* 10.562). They eat its alluring fruit, but to their dismay, they "chew bitter ashes" instead (*PL* 10.566). With this passage in mind, Cooper's Miltonic echo highlights just how fallen modern civilization has become in the wake of cultural values that deny women social equality. For Cooper, woman's "soundness" as well as her "life-giving sap" is vitally compromised when patriarchal culture hinders her social and cultural elevation. The result is indicative of a signature of derivation that yields a Miltonic image of strange fruit where a promising domestic sphere, in reality, disintegrates to a hellspace of utter ruin. Cooper re-creates satanic poetry by worrying the lines of Milton's epic through this playful appropriation of his demonic figures. Appropriating Satan's evil tendencies to critique patriarchal practices that expose the good or soundness of her womanist logic, Cooper vocalizes her knowledge of Miltonic artwork as a "positive manifestation of negativity."[25] Making good from evil in this instance pierces the patriarchal soundscape with the intellectual savvy of Cooper's spirit of womanist difference.

This satanic reading of Milton proves significant for two reasons. First, the relationship between a fallen and ruined domestic sphere with the apples of Sodom threatens the ideological structure supporting the true womanhood discourse itself. Thus, Cooper's Miltonic echo serves as a vocal weapon for subversively dismantling the patriarchal houses that attempt to confine and limit her to the domestic sphere. "Domesticity," writes Barbara Welter, "was among the virtues most prized by the women's magazines" of the nineteenth century, and it was in the home where they were "supposed to keep busy at morally uplifting tasks."[26] By threatening the structural instability of this patriarchal ideology, Cooper is able to philosophically enlarge woman's terrain. She uses the threatening image to motivate a change in the hardened hearts of men. In clear Miltonic terms, her logic suggests that woman's elevation in society will secure the domestic sphere while also affording her immense opportunities beyond its limiting walls. As this satanic reading of Milton's epic suggests, Cooper places Milton's text in collusion with patriarchal discourse in order to "justify the ways of [her feminist gospel] to men" (*PL* 1.26). This specific instance of Miltonic echo further supports critics like May and others, who interpret Cooper's investment in true womanhood discourse "as a lure, only to dispose thoroughly of its premises."[27] Likewise, Cooper's satanic appropriation of Milton verbalizes the strength of her rhetorical multivocality, for in adapting the epic poet's verse to her womanist cause, she transforms the geographic sphere by expanding its ideological dimensions to include black women within male-privileged spaces.

Yet, her rhetorical indulgence in Milton's rhetorical energy is not wholly satanic or infernal in nature. For instance, she equally draws inspiration from the epic poet's messianic poetics as well. First, manipulating the ash-ridden fruit to serve her feminist cause, Cooper reveals a poetics of messianic qualities. Operating in this mode, her rhetorical tactic qualifies as an instance of "divining the priest within."[28] Christine Froula examines this feminist mode of rebellious reading in her critique of *Paradise Lost* and patriarchal authority more generally. As she explains, the process of divining the priest within affirms a gnostic practice of privileging one's distinct interpretation of a literary work especially when such readings defy the sanctioned authority of more orthodox assessments. She emphasizes that these interpretive liberties do not reveal an envy of the priest nor a desire to obtain priestly authority. Rather, divining in this sense serves the political purpose of "debunking...the priestly deployment of cultural authority and [woman's] refusal to adopt that stance herself."[29] One has only to read Cooper's unpublished poem, "The Answer," in order to appreciate the extent to which she privileges her gnostic divinings of Milton.

In that poem, a prelapsarian spirit wanders and ponders "life's riddles," though the answer to such mysteries "no night-wind could tell."[30] Having roamed land and sea in addition to scanning celestial vistas, the "weary soul" pants, rests, and finds God in herself, asserting that the "Hereafter is here, / Eternity's new, / And *myself am Heaven or hell*" (my emphasis). By voicing Milton's Satan in this way, Cooper testifies with the epic poet in a manner that suggests a form of gnostic divining. This autonomy in voice produces a heaven on earth rather than in the afterlife. Thus, Cooper's voice proves that individual acts of gnostic divining do not exclusively translate to infernal practices. They can and do, in fact, produce effects that are supernal in nature.

The supernal nature of these gnostic divinings similarly impact theoretical readings of the demonic and contentious grounds Cooper occupies in altering our sense of orthodox Miltonic interpretations. As a demonic ground of black geography, where some unforeseeable end radically alters space and place, Cooper's gnostic divinings yield subversive benefits. For instance, it affords her the opportunity of walking within her ministerial calling as a secular womanist preacher. To apprehend such a vocation is to literally encourage women beyond the limits of the domestic sphere and into a specific public arena that was thought of as exclusively reserved for men. In this context, both the domestic sphere and the preacher's pulpit constitute "transparent space," a geography that is erroneously assumed to be "readily knowable [and] bound up with ideologies and activities that work to maintain a safe socioeconomic clarity."[31] Cooper's Miltonic voicings, which are the product of her gnostic divinings, frustrate the supposed clarity of these inhibitive and prohibitive sites. By naming the black woman's work as a secular vocation of preaching as she does throughout *A Voice from the South* and in other writings, she empowers herself to heed a divine ministerial calling "without violence and without suing or special patronage" (*Voice* 31).

The second messianic impulse located in her "Womanhood" essay develops in the next stage of argumentation where she worries the lines of Milton's epic further. Here, Cooper transitions into a primary consideration of American civilization. Her goal in this section sets about the rhetorical task of disturbing a false belief: that American civilization symbolizes an Edenic paradise in terms of women's social status. While she believes it is more advanced than other civilizations, Cooper explains that the Western world has yet to build a society that proves Edenic for women. Her discussion begins by recognizing Europe and America as symbolic of Western culture. Asserting that both contain the seeds of enlightenment within themselves, she regenerates Milton's Edenic trope of generation as an expression of woman's moral and spiritual strength.

Cooper alludes to the Edenic trope by identifying the Western world as "the European bud and the American flower of modern civilization," respectively (*Voice* 11). These floral descriptors lay the rhetorical groundwork for her extended intertextual journey with Milton. Her engagement with Milton does not materialize immediately, nor does she trope with him via direct textual references. Rather, Milton's literary presence in the following passages is mediated by tropes of the "beautiful sublime" and through Cooper's more direct engagement with Thomas Babington Macaulay and Ralph Waldo Emerson. The floral descriptors establish the rhetorical and argumentative grounds of an earthly paradise. Citing two quotes by Macaulay and Emerson, Cooper expresses her strong belief in the philosophical strength of European and American literary traditions. These appropriations likewise shade her rhetorical arguments with the sense of the Edenic. As she subsequently relates, both Macaulay and Emerson's ideas reflect the "germ of a prolific idea which in our own day is bearing such rich and varied fruit" and has been "ingrafted into European civilization" (*Voice* 13).

Macaulay's notion that one "may judge a nation's rank in the scale of civilization from the way they treat their women" epitomizes the European half of what Cooper deems a prolific feminist idea (*Voice* 12). She borrows from Emerson as well, quoting his contention that the "influence of good women" represents the best measurement for gauging any society's advanced status (*Voice* 12). In quoting these ideas, Cooper testifies that both traditions provide a canon of ideas rich in expressing a high regard for women. Considering that she has already acknowledged both civilizations in Edenic terms, her use of their respective literary traditions extends this horticultural outlook even more. A signifyin(g) effect of quoting Macaulay and Emerson's ideas, then, functions to artistically highlight the Edenic philosophical power of both civilizations' literary traditions. In rhetorical terms, they resonate as a regenerating repository for cultivating gender equality while simultaneously constituting the grounds of a womanist Eden.

Next, Cooper's line of argument proceeds by digressing into an interrogation of epic strength and heroism. Her digressive approach ultimately flows into an echoic performance of literary analysis and Miltonic criticism. A goal of these digressions is to acknowledge women's moral and spiritual heroism in contrast to the force of violence and domination, which Cooper attributes to patriarchal masculinity. Unlike the previous line of argumentation, Cooper's focus on a beautiful sublime centers on a sophisticated interplay with both infernal and supernal rhetorics. For instance, her argument pinpoints the Middle Ages as the period where barbarism "crystallized into the Feudal System" (*Voice* 13). Cooper contrasts acts of barbarism against Tacitus's "tender regard for women" and the veneration of women within the home as found in old Norse legends in order to critique the notion that brute force equals strength. Instead, she offers Christian womanhood as a strength excelling all others. What emerges is her figurative representation of the war between heaven and hell that increasingly plays itself out along rhetorical gender lines. The highlight of this gendered terrain of struggle materializes through Cooper's historical analysis of woman's moral force coupled with her metonymic reading of the church's civilizing ministry in the aftermath of the Roman Empire's fall.

According to her historical analysis, the church at this time immediately set about the "task of conquering her conquerors" (*Voice* 19). It proved mighty in battle based on an "all-compassing diplomacy" that refused to embrace a "warlike nature" (19). Additionally, Cooper personifies this metonymic church as female.

She also characterizes the institution as having contented "herself with less radical measures" (20). Having conquered her adversaries by way of nonviolent protest, the church, as seen through Cooper's historical analysis, holds meritorious distinction. She has responded to acts of institutional tyranny based on an exercising of its moral and spiritual strength. Cooper emphasizes this sign of female heroism by stating that the church "carried her point" (20). She carries her own point as well, echoing the war between heaven and hell to underscore her faith in woman as a vital element of regeneration.

Cooper's echo rests upon the poetic laurels of Lord Byron and William Wordsworth. Taking interpretive cues from John Bascom's *Philosophy of English Literature*, Cooper theorizes on the Romantic poets' infernal and supernal energies: "Byron and Wordsworth were both geniuses and would have stamped themselves on the thought of their age under any circumstances; and yet we find the one a savor of life unto life, the other of death unto death. 'Byron like a rocket, shot his way upward with scorn and repulsion, flamed out in wild, explosive, brilliant excesses and disappeared in darkness made all the more palpable'" (*Voice* 21–22). With its emphasis on heat, combustion, and explosive diction, Bascom's assessment of Byron prompts Cooper to interpret the Romantic poet as embodying the self-destructive force that, no doubt, leads one to death. To some degree, this interpretation of Byron's infernal energies recalls Cooper's own thoughts about the black woman's voice in her preface. For example, she describes the black woman's vocal "calorimeter" as a "delicately sensitive" instrument that accurately and fairly diagnoses some of the more confounding facets of "our Nation's Problem" (*Voice* iii). It is interesting to note that Cooper plays with rhetorical fire when she reads the power of black women's vocal registers as an instrument designed to measure quantities of heat. Moreover, she worries the line of *Paradise Lost* with Milton's satanic energy by analyzing Byron's poetic temperament.

Wittreich augments this reading of Byron by noting that the poet "could praise Milton for his constancy in the face of threatening opposition." Lucy Newlyn comments on this satanic impulse as well. For her, the appeal of Byron's Cain emanates from that character's "love of liberty which is recognized to be at once courageous and self-destructive."[32] Wittreich's and Newlyn's readings align with Cooper's reception and analytical exposé of Byron's Miltonic temperament. Considered collectively, these assessments stress the satanic impulses associated with militant masculinity, which is the point of Cooper's echoic reception of the Romantic poet and the very aspect of satanic poetry she seeks to subvert. What she notes in Byron's literary characters exposes her satanic orientation relative to her interpretation of the Romantic poet. This interpretation of Byron proceeds from Cooper's fluency with Satan's fallen language. St. Hilaire, theorizing on fallen language in *Paradise Lost*, recognizes such speech acts as products of self-centeredness. Unlike the angels in heaven whose divine language facilitates prayer and praise, the "performative language" of Milton's demons sings about and for the self, therefore "making their song autotelic and not aimed at some higher purpose."[33] To balance this rhetorical affiliation with Milton through Satan, Cooper worries the line of *Paradise Lost* further by reading the epic poet through Wordsworth's literary character.

With Byron, Cooper seeks to underscore woman's tempered calorimeter in the hope of effectively arguing the point that a "delicately sensitive" approach to tyranny is indeed powerful enough to alter aural geographies without having to resort to vitriol or lambaste. She makes this point by studying Wordsworth and worrying the line of Milton's epic verse through an emphasis on things supernal. If Byron signifies death by infernal association, then Wordsworth figures as an angelic force. Wordsworth, in her estimation, is more like a "savor of life unto life" (*Voice* 21). She relates that he "Lent of his gifts to reinforce that 'power in the Universe which makes for righteousness' by taking the harp handed him from Heaven and using it to swell the strains of angelic choirs." Finally, she concludes her Miltonic assessment of both poets: "Two locomotives equally mighty stand facing opposite tracks; the one to rush headlong to destruction with all its precious freight, the other to toil grandly and gloriously up the steep embattlements to Heaven and to God. Who—who can say what a world of consequences hung on the first placing and starting of these enormous forces!" (*Voice* 22).

By positioning Wordsworth and his "harp" as the angelic counterpart to Byron's force of satanic destruction, Cooper replicates the war between heaven and hell by worrying these contrasting figures metaphorically. In terms of its Miltonic cognates, Cooper's process of signification works by encouraging readers to "fill in [interpretive] slots in unusual ways."[34] By design, she uses the rhetoric of the devil's party to confound those who have yet to acknowledge the self-destructive nature of patriarchal force. This intertextual engagement with Milton, again, works by way of an interpretive principle that revolts by indulging in negative rhetorical figures that generate meaning through their relationship to positive ones.

Having carried her Miltonic point through these digressive rhetorical acts, Cooper writes her satanic passage through Milton until the essay's conclusion. She praises womanhood and motherhood as heroic offices. Epic in their scope and magnitude, these heroic responsibilities "might make angels tremble and fear to take hold!" (*Voice* 22). Her 1892 speech before the Congress of Representative Women at the World's Columbian Exposition in Chicago underscores the epic nature of their ministerial office. In that address, Cooper considers the magnitude of black women's heroic office by noting that their "history is full of heroic struggle" so much so that it "would furnish material for epics."[35] Cooper continues to dramatize the importance of epic throughout the essay. For instance, she "adds [her] plea for the *Colored Girls* of the South" in the interest of protecting a race that is only "twenty-one years removed from the conception and experience of a chattel" (*Voice* 26). No doubt, thinking of Homer's *Iliad*, she insists that "the vulnerable point" of the race's development lies "not in the heel, but at the heart of the young Achilles" (27).

The epic metaphor serves the interest of characterizing a race newly emancipated in the figure of a young but strong Achilles. Cooper provides an epic helpmeet, however, by referring to the black woman's ministry as "the Herculean task devolving upon her" (*Voice* 28). She is most likely drawing upon her literary indebtedness to Ovid and Homer in these fragments of racialized epic. Yet this assembly of intertextual sources in no way detracts from her rhetorical interest in Milton. Rather, they accentuate the extent of her vocal range in epic tradition. Subsequent essays in *A Voice from the South* exhibit the far reach of her Miltonic vocal range as she returns to the specific exercise of worrying the lines of his epic to serve her womanist cause. Through these playfully erudite exercises of Miltonic intertextuality, Cooper continues to regenerate Milton's poetics in rather revealing ways. In each instance, she pierces the patriarchal soundscape of her era by challenging fit readers to think of woman's strength along demonic grounds of Miltonic interpretation.

In "The Higher Education of Women," the book's second essay, Cooper vocalizes her knowledge of Milton and worries the line of his epic verse more directly. Instead of relying on allusive echoes, she names him in the middle of the essay, exhorting her female readers to "revel in the strength of Milton" (*Voice* 69). Although Cooper does not offer this exhortative admonition until two-thirds of the way into the essay, she has already paved the way for this direct engagement with Milton based on the "horizons of expectations" she creates in her introductory paragraph. "Horizons of expectations," as Wittreich explains, refer to any variety of cultural practices whereby a "poet has come to be 'known'—through representations by others and through self-representations."[36] These speculative or anticipatory ways of perceiving, knowing, and seeing precursor authors in belated works surface via ideological myths, truths, cultural scripts, and assumptions that impact and shape how various reading audiences might interpret writers and their works.

Milton often sets up these expectations in his prose and poetry. For example, throughout his canon, the epic poet looms as a "hidden presence—someone who must be sought out in unexpected places, usually in shadows, fragments, or glimpses, seldom in full-blown portraits."[37] In a somewhat similar vein, Mary Helen Washington calls for a practice of locating autobiographical modes of neglected black women writers within their works. To understand and appreciate these "self-invented women" whose artistic contributions have been "lost in black literary history" and the wider canonical tradition more generally, it is necessary to assess their literary productions by examining how they "name and order experience."[38] Similarly, applying these standards to Cooper's "Higher Education" enables contemporary scholars to determine the author's meaning when she encourages her Africanist sisters to "revel" in Milton's strength. By exhorting women to revel in Milton as an intertextual source of womanist strength, Cooper highlights the epic writer's "masked" or "hidden" presence within the essay.

Cooper establishes a Miltonic horizon of expectation through an intertextual exercise that vocalizes the epic writer through an intermediary source. Milton proves useful in this essay as Cooper revels in his strength in order to pierce patriarchal soundscapes on behalf of the "thinking woman" who dares to transgress the boundaries of the domestic sphere and acquire higher education. Through this vocal practice, Cooper exercises the intertextual strength she challenges women to usurp. Given the subject matter of this essay, Cooper's rhetorical strength, in tandem with Milton's poetic might, offers readers a subversive lesson in intertextual vocality. Cooper's double-voiced rhetoric ruptures the public sphere by calling for major geographical shifts within colleges and universities. Her call for educational inclusivity threatens to transform traditional spatial arrangements in multiple ways. First, a woman's access to institutions of higher learning stands to liberate her within and beyond the marriage relation. Second, this dynamic threatens patriarchal privilege, for the ideals generated through the cult of True Womanhood discredits the notion of female education. In her study of this cult, Barbara Welter explains that one reason for this disapproval of woman's intellectual development may be traced to the belief that such an enterprise may "detract from the practice of housewifely arts."[39] Cooper undertakes the womanist project to dismantle this patriarchal belief by worrying the lines of Miltonic intertextuality through an intermediary text like Silvain Maréchal's 1801 book, *Shall Woman Learn the Alphabet*.

In that work, the French theorist expresses the fear generating his disapproval of an intellectually elevated womanhood. Cooper sarcastically paraphrases Maréchal's sexist fears in Miltonic terms. According to her interpretation of Maréchal, he fears "if woman were once permitted to read Sophocles and work with logarithms, or to nibble at any side of the apple of knowledge, there would be an end forever to their sewing on buttons and embroidering slippers" (*Voice* 49). Maréchal's sarcastic reference to Milton through the figure of an apple as the fruit associated with the tree of knowledge does not escape Cooper's vocal range as a later passage will suggest. To debunk Maréchal's fallen logic, Cooper exercises her voice in the service of claiming Milton as a vital tree or "talking book" of knowledge for the regenerated woman.

True to her rebellious spirit, Cooper voices a womanist battle cry that encourages the "thinking woman" to "commune with Socrates about the *daimon* he knew and to which she too can bear witness" (*Voice* 69). That she pointedly signifies on Maréchal by specifically referencing Sophocles on her own terms reveals she has hardly forgotten the offensive nature of his fallen logic even though she does not debunk it until 40 paragraphs later. Exercising her knowledge of heroic biblical women like Ruth and Naomi, historical icons such as Spartan women, Joan of Arc, the daughters of Charlemagne, and quoting literary luminaries such as Petrarch, Ovid, Charles Dickens, Matthew Arnold, and others, Cooper progressively builds her case in opposition to Maréchal's fallen logic. Throughout her wildly digressive discourse of her subject, she plants rhetorical seeds of womanist rebellion, proudly proclaiming women can "*revel* in the majesty of Dante, the sweetness of Virgil, the simplicity of Homer, [and] the *strength of Milton*" (*Voice* 69; my emphasis).

Derived from the Latinate root, *revelere*, "revel" means to rebel with merriment or to "engage in wild or noisy recreation or festivities."[40] On a very literal level, then, to revel in the strength of Milton means to rebel in the might of his esteemed epic verse and canonical authority. This rebellious instance of worrying the line, with Milton as an intertext of strength and womanist emancipation, names and orders women's experience by referencing Milton as both a literary and artistic score of female empowerment. Since Cooper believes these readerly activities of political recreation "render women less dependent on the marriage relation for physical support," she, in essence, proposes freedom and liberation as an end goal (*Voice* 69). The blessings of womanist liberty, in this context, yield added benefits as well. For example, she notes that woman's intellectual development on these terms frees woman from feeling "compelled to look to sexual love as the one sensation capable of giving tone and relish, movement, and vim to the life she leads" (*Voice* 69–70). Through these lenses, the politics of reading and reveling in Milton's strength helps to nuance a practice that the casual reader presumably takes for granted as nothing more than recreational activity. Cooper's womanist viewpoint promotes the art of reading as expressly political. To revel in Milton's strength is to engage in a specific practice of literacy where reading constitutes political activism.

One of the rhetorical tactics Cooper employs when reveling or rebelling in Milton's strength is her strategic use of deliberate repetition in her diction and word choice. In other words, she worries the line of her essay with the word "strength," rhetorically capitalizing upon its loaded association with Milton. "Strength" appears no less than eight times throughout the text and is further complemented with words like "force" and "potent." These synonyms help to define her diction as being motivated by a rhetorical concern with the concept of might, power, and heroism. This concern becomes more evident with her critiques of patriarchal forms of dominance. As she does in the "Womanhood" essay, Cooper comments on these brute displays of force only to undermine them with depictions of women's epic female heroism. For instance, she challenges "the world of thought under the predominant man-influence," which she defines as a form of power that demands all to "fall down and worship [its] incarnation of power" (*Voice* 53). At another point in the essay, she recognizes "masculine influence" as a negative force, "which has dominated [the world] for fourteen centuries" (51). Still another critique of male dominance may be seen when she interprets the history of civilization as having suffered ever "since the idea of order and subordination succumbed to barbarian brawn and brutality in the fifth century" (51). These examples portray the mode of strength she seeks to undermine.

According to Cooper, the ideological reign of male dominance as the epitome of strength has ironically weakened society. Civilization, she asserts, has been brought up like a motherless child and without a mother's benevolent instruction and compassionate spirit. Conditioned to extol violence and domination, civilization has "needed the great mother heart to teach it to be pitiful, to love mercy, to succor the weak and care for the lowly" (*Voice* 51). Cooper is well aware that her arguments border on essentialist notions of gender, a feature in her writing that has produced grounds of interpretive contention in scholarship devoted to feminist analyses of *A Voice from the South*. Lemert and Bhan classify these "reservations toward Cooper" as owing to scholars' belief that the author "too comfortably accepted the white pieties of the true womanhood ideal."[41] May responds to this area of scholarship by emphasizing "Cooper's *manipulation* of concepts from True Womanhood discourse," which according to May "does not necessarily indicate [Cooper's] full *acceptance* of them."[42] May and other critics like Hazel Carby, whose work explains Cooper's strategic redeployment of these essentialist notions, point to instructive subversive markers in *A Voice from the South* that aid contemporary readers in understanding the full vocal range of this revolutionary author.[43]

Cooper, herself, endeavors to protect her philosophical vocalizations against a misreading of her womanist perspective when she espouses her belief that Christian mercy and meekness are not the "exclusive possession of women, or even that women are their chief and only advocates" (*Voice* 60). Acknowledging that men can and do exercise this leavening influence upon civilization, she clarifies that these expressions have their origins in maternal impulses because racist culture excludes Cooper and her sisters from the category of "woman." In addition, by engrafting men's emotional sensitivities with women's, Cooper expresses her willingness to include the former within that structure notwithstanding its negative philosophical implications on axes of gender identity. Thus, according to Cooper, men who embody these tenets of Christian heroism are "simply materializing and giving back to the world in tangible form the ideal love and tenderness, devotion and care that have cherished and nourished the helpless period of his own existence" (60). She also takes a moment to recognize the strength of male Christian heroism as anything but a sign of weakness. Rather, she critiques the "sneaking admiration we all have for bullies and prize-fighters" and defends the "so-called weak or unwarlike races and individuals" (51).

Finally, Cooper mocks detractors who might otherwise read nonviolence as passive weakness. She mocks this segment of the population by qualifying the above statement with the sarcastic rejoinder, "as if the possession of the Christian graces of meekness, non-resistance and forgiveness, were incompatible with a civilization professedly based on Christianity and the religion of love!" (*Voice* 51–52). This rejoinder in addition to her negative portraiture of patriarchal masculinity express her womanist allegiance to a mode of strength modeled on Christian fortitude. In these respects, Cooper's essay has named and indirectly defined what she means by the expression "revel in the strength of Milton." According to these Miltonic vocalizations, Cooper keenly identifies and agrees with Milton's poetics of fortitude in tandem with the Victorian sensibilities Erik Gray identifies as "perfect passivity" or "the might of weakness."[44]

John M. Steadman, Juanita Whitaker, and Stanley Fish have severally interpreted Milton's poetics of heroism as being predicated upon an ideal of strength in moral and spiritual terms. Steadman, for instance, emphasizes fortitude as virtuous heroism in Milton's writings, and he recognizes the inward virtue as constituting a primary mode of heroic action with respect to the poet's aesthetic vision. Specifically, this aspect of strength "entails other qualities—wisdom, and prudence, piety and temperance, [in addition to] charity and justice."[45] Juanita Whitaker observes a similar aesthetic pattern at play in *Areopagitica*, Milton's political tract against book censorship. In her essay, she focuses on the significance of *sapientia* and *fortitudo*, or wisdom and strength, as heroic attributes according to Milton's poetics. She further explains that the latter specifically references "moral force" or "intellectual courage."[46]

Steadman and Whitaker's assessments also recall Stanley Fish's reflections on heroism with respect to his reading of *Paradise Lost*. Fish argues that heroism does not "require a particular field of battle" but may consist of a mental fortitude that shapes one's future actions. He further asserts that "true virtue is a state of mind—loyalty to the best one knows—and true heroism is a psychic (willful) action—the decision, continually made in a variety of physical situations, to maintain that loyalty."[47] Steadman, Whitaker, and Fish's analyses about Milton's poetics of heroism ground and clarify the meaning of Cooper's Miltonic expression pursuant to the epic writer's thematic portraiture of strength. Milton's poetics in this regard serve as rhetorical grounds for more fully comprehending the concept of strength and its signifyin(g) relation to the "horizon of expectations" that Cooper sets forth in her essay.

Moreover, Cooper's vocal exercise of worrying the lines of Milton's epic in her essay come closest to forging a rhetorical affiliation with expressions of heroic quietude that surface throughout her precursor's great poems. As Gray astutely notes, "Milton's four major poems show a definite progression, or rather a recession: victory is obtained first by sitting still, then by tactical retreat, and finally by losing outright."[48] Gray understands the "Miltonic paradox of powerful resignation or retreat" as instructive for understanding the intertextual relationship that bonds a Victorian writer like Matthew Arnold to his predecessor. This same paradox clarifies an aspect of Cooper's intertextual relation to Milton, which announces itself through her strategic redeployment of Milton's strength as a regenerating source worth reveling in.

Reveling in Milton's strength to this digressive degree reveals her more subversively subtle engagements with the epic writer in her introductory paragraph. The concluding sentence of this paragraph signals the rhetorically demonic and contentious grounds of Miltonic interpretation that Cooper has been occupying all along. By framing her argument with Maréchal's thoughts on women's intellectual development, Cooper lays out the patriarchal parameters concerning the restrictive geographies that help to keep women in place. According to Cooper's reading of *Shall Woman Learn the Alphabet*, Maréchal, like Molière, believes that the art of love reflects the "ground and limit of [woman's] intuitive furnishing" (*Voice* 48). This "sayability of geography," where expressive acts communicate the variety of ways space and place prove "central to [the] kinds of geographies [that] are available to black women" in particular, becomes a ground that Cooper troubles with increased reverberations of Miltonic presence.[49] Whereas Maréchal's assertion, according to Cooper, attempts to contain woman's intellectual mobility by dehumanizing her through his poetics of landscape, she troubles this soundscape with her dissident Miltonic vocals.

By setting love as the "ground and limit" of women's use and need for books, Maréchal likewise structures strict geographical limits on the intellectual spaces they may enter. This dictum simultaneously works to tether women to the domestic sphere, since the deprivation of formal education may prove detrimental to those seeking careers within the public sector. Essentially, Maréchal's thoughts on woman's quest for intellectual development and her hopes for advancement beyond the domestic sphere bolster the inhibitive ideologies that generate "real spatial inequalities" through such discourses as true womanhood and separate spheres.[50] In order to undermine the fallacy that women are not fallen as a result of their formal intellectual development, Cooper rebels by vocalizing Miltonic dissent. Sarcastically using Maréchal's concept of woman's "nibbling at the side of the apple of knowledge" (*Voice* 49) as an argumentative foundation, she orders her rhetorical steps in the intertextual word of Milton to prove the fallenness of Maréchal's patriarchal fears.

The Miltonic echo concluding the introductory paragraph serves as an implied thesis of sorts. As such, it is the argument that generates Cooper's rhetorical activism. The chronological components of Cooper's essay move from her implied thesis to a survey of the gender landscape of nineteenth century U.S. colleges and universities. Based on her review of their admission policies and graduation rates, Cooper finds that there has been "no upheaval" and "no collapse" (*Voice* 49, 50) as a result of opening the doors of higher education to women. Furthermore, Cooper strengthens her case with the added discovery that women have even begun avoiding "Ladies" courses. She finds their increased enrollments in "Gentlemen's" courses grant them opportunities for more rigorous studies, particularly instruction in Greek and Latin. Gentlemen's courses also prepare students for theological training, therefore, granting women formal access to the office of preaching.

Cooper's proposal that women gain access to this privileged educational experience provides an occasion for black geographies to occur. Since gentlemen's courses primarily prepare men for the preaching ministry, women's navigation of this gendered public alters the patriarchal geographies of the pulpit in ways that were not available to formal preachers such as Jarena Lee and Zilpha Elaw. Cooper develops this argument by commenting on the value of these transformed black geographies. She recognizes that a result of this new spatial arrangement is that the "thinking woman" has begun to stream into "the arteries of this nation, [bringing with them] a warm, rich flood of strong, brave, active, energetic, well-equipped, thoughtful" individuals who "have given a deeper, richer, nobler and grander meaning to the word 'womanly' than any one-sided masculine definition could ever have suggested or inspired" (*Voice* 50). These surveys and commentaries betray the logic of Maréchal's fear that the intellectual woman is fallen.

Next, Cooper develops her argument by distinguishing barbarian brawn from woman's "feminine ingredient" of mercy, which she acknowledges as "the tender and sympathetic chord in nature's grand symphony" (*Voice* 53–54). The point of this emphasis is to strike a balance between barbarian brawn and woman's sympathetic tenderness, again highlighting the Miltonic tones of perfect passivity and the might of weakness. In this way, Cooper argues for an understanding of their complementary forces. Yet her focus remains that of delineating how woman specifically complements man. According to Cooper, woman's strength provides the tenderness and sympathy that man's brute prowess lacks. It is on these argumentative grounds that she believes, "Religion, science, art, [and] economics have all needed the feminine flavor and literature, the expression of what is permanent and best in all of these, may be gauged at any time to measure the strength of the feminine ingredient" (*Voice* 59–60). Likewise, apocalyptic theologies, understandings of God's governance of the universe, patriarchal laws that disenfranchise women within the marriage relation, political economics, and ultimately, the "law of love" stand to benefit from the "feminine half" whose ingredient "consummates" the union between man's "Truth" and her "Mercy" (*Voice* 57). Most important, this consummation cannot occur without making higher education for women a necessity and priority. As Cooper mentions, this opportunity endows her with an ability to "reason," "think," and voice her thoughts, that she might "administer to the world the bread it needs as well as the sugar it cries for" (57).

These discussions concerning the complementary strength of woman's added ingredient lead to the next phase of her argument, which worries the line of Milton through another intermediary source. Moving from a discussion of women's complementary strength, Cooper reveals how men expressly benefit from woman's intellectual development. She carries her point by quoting 22 lines of Alfred Lord Tennyson's blank-verse poem from canto 7 of *The Princess*. Milton's "masked" presence in Tennyson's poetry is not difficult to detect, according to Gray. Milton's presence permeates much of Tennyson's canon, emerging "at the center of a pantheon of great writers," particularly as the "first among equals." This "diffuse power," according to Gray, grants Milton a distinguished type of visibility in Tennyson's canon as he surfaces and "becomes enmeshed in an ever-expanding web of literary references."[51] Cooper, in keeping with her commitment to championing the complementary strength of women, further vocalizes Milton by cleverly appropriating Tennyson's contribution to epic tradition in blank verse.

Using Tennyson's epic blank verse to voice a rhetorical strategy of womanist dissent, Cooper summons recollections of Milton consistent with eighteenth century audiences' receptions of the canonical poet. For instance, Wittreich contends that by the eighteenth century, Milton had become so powerfully associated with blank verse and epic poetry that his form "announce[d] a politics to the poem's [*Paradise Lost*] readership."[52] Cooper's *A Voice from the South*, like Harper's *Moses*, appropriates blank verse to announce a subversive poetics steeped in an "idiom of opposition."[53] In this section of her essay, Cooper strategically voices her opposition to essentialist stereotypes concerning a presumed masculinity and femininity for men and women respectively while working within these flawed conceptions of gender performance. She astutely notes that both expressions of gender "are needed to be worked into the training of children in order that our boys may supplement their virility by tenderness and sensibility, and our girls may round out their gentleness by strength and self-reliance" (*Voice* 61). It is at this precise moment that Cooper appropriates lines from Tennyson's gender-bending epic, thereby voicing womanist dissent in an idiom of Miltonic opposition.

To emphasize her point that "woman's development and education" are needed near the end of the nineteenth century, Cooper worries the lines of Miltonic epic via Tennyson. Appropriating Tennyson's epic marks a loaded instance of intertextual irony, since the setting of *The Princess* in canto 7 takes place in an exclusive female university, a site of education Cooper champions as necessary for women to inhabit in *A Voice from the South*. The first few lines of Tennyson's appropriated text feature a wooing prince who, disguised as a woman, attempts to console a forlorn Princess Ida. The princess has previously vowed never to marry, an extension of her feminist experiment, which she is presently about to renege upon. Her disguised prince addresses the interrelated causes of man and woman and pledges to be a worthy helpmeet. To plead his case effectively, the prince reveals he

> know[s]
> The woman's cause is man's: they rise or sink
> Together, dwarfed or godlike, bond or free:
> For she that out of Lethe scales with man
> The shining steps of nature, shares with man
> His nights, his days, moves with him to one goal.[54]

To express these sentiments within a woman's university underscores the political urgency of Cooper's oppositional stance.

Because Cooper has already vocalized her knowledge of Milton throughout earlier passages in *Voice*, it is not likely that the feminist ascension from depths of enslavement to the heights of liberty represented in Tennyson's appropriated lines would escape this womanist visionary's intertextual notice. Tennyson all but primes the idea of woman's fugitive escape from hellish ignorance with the reference to Lethe, one of the rivers in classical mythology that flows through Hades and was believed to cause forgetfulness to those who drank of its waters. In rising from the Lethean depths of ignorance, Prince Vivian's hypothetical female has the potential for becoming intellectually liberated and an effective helpmeet. She may now know as much if not more than her husband. As a result, she can effectively relate to him on a variety of formal intellectual registers, which, according to the prince's logic, presumably liberates women like Ida from the fate of being consigned to the patriarchal thralldom of their husbands' edicts. As intellectual equals, they may work collaboratively toward fulfilling shared goals as one.

Cooper's appropriation of Tennyson's prince especially highlights how man may benefit from the marital consummation of equal minds. It is important to Cooper that she present the prince's reasoning, for he believes that, "If [woman] be small, slight-natured, miserable, / How shall men grow?" Later in the passage, he concludes: "For woman is not undevelopt man, / But diverse: could we make her as the man, / Sweet Love were slain."[55] His sentiments support Cooper's overall belief that equality in the matrimonial market does not solely benefit woman. As her womanist rebellion through Tennyson's epic indicates, the intellectually developed woman complements and enriches the marriage relation by making both individuals equal partners. This same rebellion occurs through Cooper's insistent practice of reveling in the strength of Milton by worrying the lines of epic tradition that are greatly influenced by his canonical authority.

Cooper's appropriation of Tennyson vocalizes and worries Milton's presence further by appealing to the latter based on the former's aesthetic interest in mock-heroism. According to Gray, Tennyson engages Milton in *The Princess* with touches of intertextual modesty by recasting "the heroism of *Paradise Lost*...in a lower tone."[56] Tennyson's engagement with Milton on this level of phraseological adaptation through literary form has intertextual implications for Cooper's style of allusively remastering Milton. Cooper, who derives rhetorical pleasure from reveling in Milton's strength, also proves adept in vocalizing her ideas with subversive tones of sarcastic wit. Thus, her allusive style of erudite playfulness with Milton and Tennyson simultaneously enables her to invoke her seventeenth century precursor on at least two distinct intertextual registers. Through Tennyson's epic blank verse, she summons Milton's presence and reminds late Victorian audiences of his continued significance as an intertext of liberty relative to her arguments for women's education. Additionally, by appealing to Milton through Tennyson's interest in themes of mock-heroism and the genre of mock-epic by default, Cooper likewise accents her argument for women's rights in education as a sarcastic undermining of patriarchy and its efforts to restrict the opposite sex to secondary status.

Most important, Miltonic engagement via Tennyson assists Cooper's womanist efforts to champion the cause of educational liberty for women. Both Milton and Tennyson are appropriate intertexts at this point in Cooper's argument, for they support the essay's interest in championing educational liberty as a public office that aids women to "fitly and intelligently stamp [their] force on the forces of her day, and add her modicum to the riches of the world's thought" (61). The conflation of these elements—Milton's theme of liberty, Cooper's appeal of higher education for women, the site of a female university in Tennyson's mock-epic, and the interrelatedness of man and woman's cause—interacts to produce a metaphorical image of advanced schooling as a paradise or intellectual bower for women. That colleges and universities still barred women from their doors at the time of Cooper's essay reveals the fallenness of a male-centered logic that satanically discriminates against the rights of women at the close of the nineteenth century. To write and right these patriarchal wrongs, Cooper brings her argument full circle, using argumentative digressions as satanic weaponry toward restoring a fallen paradise for women.

Before returning to the Miltonic resonances informing Maréchal's fallen logic in the essay's opening paragraph, Cooper further extends and worries the line of argumentative digression. As Shirley Wilson Logan observes, the essay contains four remaining argumentative proportions before it concludes. These proportions survey the history of "highly educated women throughout history," nineteenth century concerns for "valuing higher education for women," followed by a refutation that education does not prove a "deterrent to marriage," with an added emphasis on the "importance of higher education for black women."[57] These arguments coincide with the next critical moment of Miltonic engagement in the essay. At this pivotal juncture of the essay, Cooper undertakes the task of proving that education does not prove detrimental to woman's place in the matrimonial market. Her discussion constitutes the essay's final rebellion, ultimately showcasing the fruits of vocally reveling in Milton's rhetorical strength.

First, Cooper revisits Maréchal's fears by returning to the allusive echo that concludes her introductory paragraph. If Maréchal fears the consequences associated with woman's "nibbl[ing] at any side of the apple of knowledge," then Cooper capitalizes upon his anxieties by radically shifting the signifying value of the Miltonic trope altogether. At this stage of her argument, she has effectively argued for the "adaptability of the educated woman to the marriage relation," building upon her rationale that a rigorous exposure to subjects like physiology, chemistry, the natural sciences, and mathematics equip women to responsibly manage the domestic sphere (*Voice* 71). As she nears the completion of her womanist interrogation, she exploits Maréchal's Miltonic use of the apple, sarcastically making the thinking woman symbolic of the forbidden fruit itself.

In an echoic gloss on Satan's sensual temptation to Eve, Cooper describes the educated woman's virtues in somewhat similar terms. With a tinge of sarcasm, she offers: "Now the apple may be good for food and pleasant to the eyes, and a fruit to be desired to make one wise. Nay, it may even assure you that it has no aversion whatever to being tasted. Still, if you do not like the flavor all these recommendations are nothing. Is the intellectual woman *desirable* in the matrimonial market?" (*Voice* 72). With her speculations on the apple's visual appeal and her emphasis on its desirability, Cooper aligns her conceptions of the thinking woman with a satanic poetics that once again revels in the infernal energies of Milton's Satan and his art of re-creative creativity in language. Here, Cooper combines the "flavor" of woman's intellectual development with the power of the "feminist ingredient" she has been extolling throughout the essay. Since Maréchal's misogynist fears of the thinking woman snidely align her intellectual aspirations with fallenness, the consequence of tasting the fruit from the tree of knowledge conditions a line of womanist critique that likewise participates in satanic practices of Miltonic reception.

In book 9 of *Paradise Lost,* Satan baits Eve by expressing the desirability of the apple in vivid terms. He makes the fruit all the more desirable by mentioning that he acquired speech through his consumption of it. He was "at first as other beasts that graze / The trodden herb, of abject thoughts and low" (*PL* 9.571–72). However, his abject status changed when he

> Chanced
> A goodly tree far distant to behold
> Loaden with fruit of fairest colors mixed,
> Ruddy and gold: I nearer drew to gaze;
> When from the boughs a savory odor blown,

> Grateful to appetite, more pleased my sense
> Than smell of sweetest fennel, or the teats
> Of ewe or goat dropping with milk at ev'n,
> Unsucked of lamb or kid, that tend their play.   (*PL* 9.575–83)

With his striking use of visual and olfactory imagery, Satan makes Eden's "fair apples" (*PL* 9.585) seem all the more desirable. Cooper, responding to Maréchal, satanically revels in the weakness of the French writer's fallen logic and the strength of Milton's epic. Although she feigns ignorance concerning her ability to answer the question about women's desirability in the matrimonial market place, she nevertheless exploits the occasion to trope with *Paradise Lost* in her own write and on her own subversive terms. Ironically, her interpoetic exploitation of Miltonic figures resolves the dilemma Maréchal instigates. Cooper's intertextual savvy with Milton undercuts her profession of ignorance, for in revisiting the site of temptation and making women the metonymic expression of forbidden fruit, she subjects men to the position Eve experiences when Satan tempts her to eat the apple. This manipulative rhetorical strategy worries the lines of Milton's epic that men may reconsider the falsity of their patriarchal knowledge, which governs tyrannical belief systems that ultimately renders them fallen.

For instance, Cooper makes woman a metonymic expression of forbidden fruit when she speculates on the desirability of the apple and its powers to make one wise. By emphasizing the apple's visual attractiveness and the temptation it provokes to be tasted, Cooper articulates a poetics of desirability that alludes to a kind of patriarchal thinking that prizes women for their alluring bodily forms and views them as sexual objects. Cooper undercuts this carnal association with woman as a sign of sensual desirability by indicating that her physical form ultimately means nothing if men hold disdain for her intellectual "flavor." It is this tension between body image and intellect that compels Cooper to question woman's worth in the "matrimonial market." In the following paragraph, Cooper feigns ignorance to her own question, responding with the retort, "this I cannot answer. I confess my ignorance. I am no judge of such things" (*Voice* 72). These answers merely serve to promote rhetorical instances of feigned ignorance. As a rhetorical strategy, these answers concede to a line of speculative reasoning rather than presenting conclusive didactic statements that might prove too forthright for members of Cooper's patriarchal audience to accept readily. Instead, she proceeds by responding to the dilemma posed by her question based on the data informing the subsequent answers she provides. In response to her hypothetical questioning of woman's worth in the matrimonial market, she explains: "I have been told that strong-minded women could be, when they thought it worth their while, quite endurable, and, judging from the number of female names I find in college catalogues among the alumnae with double patronymics, I surmise that quite a number of men are willing to put up with them" (72). Cooper's survey of college catalogues leads her to speculate that the marital institution has not suffered any upheaval as a consequence of woman's intellectual development. She uses this speculative claim to further discredit Maréchal's sexism, which is negatively inflected with Milton's allusive presence.

Rejecting Maréchal's negative patriarchal theories relative to the positive message produced by her line of womanist reasoning worries the line of Milton's epic by default. Since Cooper's speculative argument meets Maréchal on the very demonic grounds of Miltonic contention that allow him to falsely justify his sexist philosophy concerning women, her rejection of his fallen knowledge has implications for extending the interpoetic relevance of *Paradise Lost* in this essay. At this moment in her essay, Cooper rejects Maréchal's patriarchal tyranny, differentiating herself, women, and the race from his negative thinking in an argumentative move that simultaneously performs a satanic reception of Milton. Rejecting Maréchal's fallen logic likewise extends and comments on Milton's allusive presence as a condition for her line of womanist argumentation. Consequently, her rebuttal constitutes an artistic form of criticism that doubles as satanic poetry. In the same way that Milton's Satan "differentiate[s] himself from God not as another God, but as something that is precisely not-God," so, too, does Cooper separate herself from the God-like tyranny of Maréchal's false patriarchal thinking.[58] She achieves this act through a performance of satanic re-creation that poetically differentiates women from negative patriarchal constructions that falsely define them as objectified ornaments.

Based on Cooper's womanist logic, women's intellectual "flavor" does not logically translate to forbidden fruit. Cooper justifies this affirmation in contradistinction to Maréchal by speculating on the many husbands who fail to protest their wives' elevated knowledge. Relying upon her survey of college catalogues, she speculates that the husbands of these college-educated women have seen no reason to divorce their wives. These speculations are reminiscent of Satan's aesthetic language, which St. Hilaire recognizes as speech acts that "open up possibility without presenting any positive content" in the sense that they are comprised of "question marks, uncertainty, and doubt" rather than conclusive statements.[59] It is fitting that Cooper's rhetorical strategy at this juncture of her essay justifies its line of reasoning through this satanic mode of aesthetic language, since Maréchal's fallen logic provides the occasion for troubling the demonic grounds of Milton's epic. Cooper, indeed, troubles the demonic grounds of *Paradise Lost*. Interpreting the thinking and college-educated woman as a metonymic embodiment of the forbidden fruit, temptation, and interdicted knowledge, she resolves the debate concerning women's desirability in the matrimonial market by surmising that many husbands have not been negatively impacted by their wives' elevated intellect. By concluding this section of her essay through a sarcastic line of speculative reasoning that cunningly imitates the rhetorical structures and aesthetics of Satan's fallen language, Cooper champions the cause of women's liberty by arguing for their inclusion within the academic sphere.

By starting the essay with Maréchal's fallen logic and its Miltonic resonances, Cooper reveals the argumentative scope of her essay as intertextually indebted to modes of satanic poetry and re-creation. Without appearing to engage the Miltonic tenor of Maréchal's argument directly, Cooper periodically vocalizes the range of her knowledge where England's epic poet of liberty is concerned. Whether she cites Milton by name when encouraging women to revel in his strength or appropriates his epic presence through Tennyson's use of blank verse in *The Princess*, Cooper actively responds to Maréchal's fallen logic through a wayward engagement that approximates the vocal exercise of satanic poetry and re-creation. Her most radical instance of womanist differentiation through Miltonic figures occurs when she rebelliously constructs her argumentative line of reasoning around Maréchal's declaration that the thinking woman symbolizes Edenic fallenness. Too worldly wise in her subversive knowledge of Milton and Western culture more broadly, Cooper showcases her intellectual artistry and womanist autonomy by rejecting Maréchal's patriarchal assertions on the demonic grounds of his fallen logic. Her erudite playfulness with Maréchal's patriarchal reception of Milton conforms to a style of satanic poetry where acts of creation are negatively "invested with existence in the world only through [their] relations to the very power [they] reject."[60] Cooper's argumentative style throughout this essay participates in this satanic reception of Milton where vocalizations of the epic writer exercise a facility and fluency in fallen language.

To exercise Miltonic fluency in this manner is to likewise flex and strengthen the memory of Cooper's fit male audience in particular. In *Milton and Homer*, Gregory Machacek explains the important function of certain types of allusions that function to "exercise the memory" and mental faculties, which Milton, himself, "regarded as essential to moral decision making."[61] Similarly, Cooper exercises the mental faculties of her fit audience, an exclusive aggregate of readers comprised of men who were well versed in Milton having enjoyed the patriarchal privilege of being schooled in colleges and universities. In satanic fashion and in an updated manner not unlike Wheatley's period of instruction before her privileged male pupils in "To the University of Cambridge," Cooper ends up schooling her fit audience of male students. She schools them by worrying the lines of Milton's epic through words, figures, and an aesthetics of fallen language that are spread out periodically and sometimes allusively across the expanse of a 31-page essay containing 60 paragraphs.

Spreading Milton's signifying presence across the breadth of her essay in this periodic fashion is not without interpretive significance. Consistent with practices of worrying the line in black music, skilled musicians prove themselves adept in defying space and time through their artistic manipulations of rhythm. Musical rebellions of this sort occur within the break or cut of the beat, the interval of rhythmic space where creative repetitions of difference surface. According to Wall, "African American literary tradition insinuates itself as the beat" of extended intertextual revision.[62] Within these spaces of repetition, skilled literary artists revise, repeat, and extend a long line of tradition that cuts across African American writers' double-voiced heritage in language and culture. Accordingly, these literary beats "create the safe space in which [literary] musicians [like Cooper] improvise" their aesthetic craft within multiple traditions simultaneously by worrying the lines charted by their precursors.[63] Cooper showcases her individual talent in this intertextual art form by worrying the words, figures, and lines of Milton to satanic effect. In doing so, she exposes the falsity of the cult of True Womanhood while dispelling the patriarchal myth of the thinking woman as a sign of domestic fallenness.

Cooper worries the line with Milton in subsequent essays. Milton surfaces as an allusive presence in the third essay, "'Woman versus the Indian,'" where Cooper addresses a fit audience of white women who exclude "a colored lady" and teacher from enjoying the "privileges and opportunities" provided by a "woman's culture club" (*Voices* 80, 81). Weighing in on this scandal of racial discrimination and exclusivity, Cooper argues, "Pandora's box is opened in the ideal harmony of this modern Eden without an Adam" (81). Her Edenic metaphor introduces another fragmented instance of satanic poetry indebted to *Paradise Lost*, interrogating the fallenness of exclusionary practices that desecrate what would otherwise constitute a bower of feminist paradise. Cooper challenges this fallenness of feminist ideals by lending her womanist voice toward regaining a paradise of female solidarity.

The essay "What Are We Worth" worries the line of Milton reception by considering the epic writer as a cultural analogue and example of racial value for her people. Entertaining the worth of the African American race relative to its contributions to the uplift of Western civilization, Cooper forges a political affiliation with Milton and Cromwell while rejecting the "Feudal froth and foam of the South" with its "aristocratic notions of case and class distinctions" (*Voices* 239) that bar the race from equal participation in society. Considering this feudalism in contrast to the "Puritan's sound, substantial, sanctified common sense," Cooper opines, "I have wished that it might have been ordered that as my race had to serve a term of bondage[,] it might have been under the discipline of the successors of Cromwell and Milton, rather than under the training and example of the luxurious cavaliers" (239). With this statement, Cooper worries the line of Miltonic reception by speculatively revisioning what the race's existence would be like on the grounds of English liberty as opposed to the tainted terrain of the U.S. landscape. Later in the essay, she name-drops Milton again, listing him second to Shakespeare yet above an impressive pantheon of luminaries in Western civilization who, according to Cooper, reflect a "noble army" of individuals who have "taken of the world's bread and paid for it in immortal thoughts, invaluable inventions, new facilities, heroic deeds of loving self-sacrifice; men who dignify the world for their having lived in it and to whom the world will ever bow in grateful worship as its heroes and benefactors" (273). These fragmentary examples of Miltonic engagement continue to worry the line of his canonical presence in *A Voice from the South*, further exercising Cooper's vocal dexterity with her literary precursor.

Perhaps Cooper's greatest moment of satanic reception with Milton surfaces in the essay, "One Phase of American Literature," in part 2 of *A Voice from the South*. The essay showcases what is arguably her most direct and satanic instance of reveling in Milton's strength. Here Cooper engages Milton by occupying the office of the pulpit in the manner of an astute literary critic and visionary. In keeping with her commitment to the theme of liberty, she regenerates Milton's strength for purposes of propagating an African American poetics whose tenets revolt against the gospel of black didacticism. Her womanist spirit proves to be no less vibrant in this chapter as she infuses its philosophies into a treatise that leads the African American literary tradition in new directions toward the dawn of the twentieth century. As if this bold enterprise were not daring already, Cooper amplifies her rhetorical strength by transforming the grounds of Miltonic interpretation in ways suitable to her womanist sensibilities. Specifically, she troubles the waters of his Narcissus passage (*PL* 4.450–88), daring to revise and radically alter its grounds in one of her volume's final displays of rhetorical strength and satanic creativity relative to Milton's poetics of fortitude.

Thinking about the African American literary tradition at the close of the nineteenth century, Cooper believes her contemporary age has outgrown the didactic teachings of Milton's more forceful prose. Therefore, she resists a militant reception of the epic poet favored by the self-made men I've examined in chapter 3. Instead, Cooper favors the intertextual politics of many of her black sisters in the literary tradition. Like them, she valorizes Milton's beautiful sublime with the recognition that on these poetic grounds the epic writer will always constitute a "perennial" example of poetic strength (*Voice* 183). The "beautiful sublime," as I've discussed previously, refers to the "two central oxymorons" governing eighteenth century readers' reception and evaluation of Milton's epic.[64] With respect to Milton's eighteenth century female audience, they often resisted the impulse of reifying Adam's magnanimity of character or celebrated Milton's scenes of hell. "Extended allusions to Eden," the epic's domestic scenes, and Eve's heroic yet human role tended to appeal to their intertextual engagement with the poet. Cooper reflects her similar appreciation for the "beautiful sublime" in Milton in a mode of appropriation designed to temper the didactic impulse so often practiced by black male writers in the tradition.

Cooper's appreciation for the beautiful sublime in Milton expresses her poetic attraction to the powerful force of his grand ideas that in particular instances never sacrifices the beauty attending the ethos " art for art's sake." In this way, even her aesthetic appreciations prove congruent with her commitment to the feminine ingredient of passive strength. Her argument eventually constructs a paradigm where poetic didacticism implies fallenness, the infernal, and hell. By contrast, the beautiful sublime reiterates a supernal poetics of regeneration. This dyad crystalizes through her pronouncements on didactic poetry as a kind of secular preaching that pummels the reader into submissive acceptance, agreement, or compliance. With her gnostic reading of Milton's poetic strength, Cooper continues to derive revolutionary power from his might. Moreover, she testifies that his rhetorical strength can empower black poets to achieve a tempered balance between force and heroic restraint. When blended, this complementary fusion of poetic styles produces an eternal gospel that is never bound within its moment of historical specificity. Therefore, Cooper's gospel of revolt along the lines of an African American poetics translates to a treatise of liberation for would-be future writers. She endeavors to free the literary tradition from a time-bound relevance, so that future literary productions may endure as art as opposed to historical documents.

Cooper's deviation from Milton's more didactic form of secular preaching is best understood within the context of her "rough" classificatory system of poets (*Voice* 181). She classifies poets into two distinct camps and identifies the first group as those who possess "artistic or poetic instincts" (181). These poets write with the conviction that "being true to themselves and true to nature is the only canon" (181). This variation of the beautiful sublime explains why and how artistic poets compose their literary productions. As Cooper relates, this class of poets "write[s] to please...because *they* please,...and simply paint what they see" (181). The motivating force that generates these poets' creative impulses stems from their desire to compose art for art's sake and without the agenda of preaching to their audience of readers.

Cooper acknowledges the second group of poets as "the preachers" (*Voice* 181). These writers constitute "righteousness" or "unrighteousness" (182); however, they

> have an idea to propagate, no matter in what form their talent enables them to clothe it, whether poem, novel, or sermon, all those writers with a purpose or a lesson who catch you by the buttonhole and pommel you over the shoulder till you are forced to give assent in order to escape their vociferations; or they may lure you into listening with the soft music of the siren's tongue—no matter what the expedient to catch and hold your attention, they mean to fetter you with their one idea, whatever it is, and make you, if possible, ride their hobby. In this group I would place Milton in much of his writing, Carlyle in all of his, often our own Whittier, the great reformer-poet and Lowell; together with such novelists as E. P. Roe, Bellamy, Tourgee and some others. (*Voice* 182–83)

Her classification of preacher poets—both "righteous" and "unrighteous"—is important for at least two reasons. On one level, this classificatory system establishes a critical framework for understanding how Cooper receives the didactic works of white writers who concern themselves with the "problematical position...occupied by descendants of Africans in the American social polity" (*Voice* 185). The gospels preached by these didactic poets stem mainly from a resistance on the part of Anglo Saxons to align their Christian faith with civil and political customs. In keeping with Cooper's readings of the British Romantics, the uncivil aspects of Anglo-Saxon history help to explain why the roster of African American male poets primarily consists of a chorus of Byrons as opposed to a choir of Wordsworths. Notwithstanding their good intentions, Cooper assesses the aesthetic choices these white writers make when relying too heavily upon didactic strains. She finds that almost all of their productions have been "uniformly perverted to serve their [humanist] ends" (*Voice* 185). Consequently, their secular sermons are more bombastic than artistic in their form and message.

Cooper cites another negative aspect of preacher-poets' literary productions. Most often these texts evolve from writers' "partial acquaintance with the life they wished to delineate" (*Voice* 185). That is, they write out of "sheer ignorance" and "from design occasionally," almost never "putting themselves in the darker man's place" (*Voice* 185). Cooper asserts that this long-range distance from African American life yields a class of writers who produce poetic gospels containing thunderous ideas. Unfortunately, these same literary productions do not paint nature in its true artistic beauty. Under such conditions, their literary productions are bound to rely upon didactic modes of poetic expression. Cooper supports this critique when she declares, "'thinking one's self imaginatively into the experiences of others is not given to all, and it is impossible to acquire it without a background and a substratum of sympathetic knowledge" (185). Cooper's theoretical insights promote the idea that preacher-poets who compose nature devoid of sympathetic impulses paints life violently and recklessly. She assesses their art as leaving carnage behind, for "without this power [of sympathetic knowledge] our portraits are but death's heads or caricatures and no amount of cudgeling can put into them the movement and reality of life" (185). With her use of the verb "cudgel," Cooper even proves poetically instructional; its use expressly conveys the conflicts confronting white poets who are held captive within these compromising positions. Rather than produce beautiful art, white poets find themselves consigned to a mode of literary expression dependent upon a forced acceptance of their messages even though their poetic truths lack integrity of the heart and soul of the texts' subject matter.

Cooper situates "much of [Milton's] writing" within the group of preacher-poets, who pummel their audiences into submission (*Voice* 183). When she categorizes Milton within this group of didactic poets, she at first seems to suggest an attempt to achieve some rhetorical distancing from his literary style. For instance, her line of reasoning expresses dissatisfaction with the brute force of didactic poetry. She prefers an expression of life's realities achieved by and through the beauty of art's imaginative revelations. Harriet Beecher Stowe's writings provide concrete instruction concerning the kind of literary beauty she admires most. Stowe's writing, she asserts, resonates with "humility and love," and like her thoughts concerning woman's vital element, this literary technique may be cultivated as a poetic means for regenerating the progress of the race and Western civilization (*Voice* 186). Cooper regenerates Milton along similar lines as well. As her subsequent engagement with Milton reveals, she only revels in a passage reflective of the beautiful sublime.

For Cooper, only poet-artists "will...withstand the ravages of time" (*Voice* 183). "'Isms' have their day and pass away,'" she believes, which means the texts of preacher-poets are only as good as the contemporaneity of their moment (183). Cooper astutely observes that her philosophy places the longevity and poetic sustainability of the African American literary tradition at risk. If Cooper's assessments of the African American canon prove true, then many of its texts stand to be bound in their times, since changes in the conditions of a race stand to invariably imprison those messages within the historical specificity of their composition. According to her analysis of the tradition, she is persuaded that the didactic impulse in black literature must ultimately yield its rhetorical power to transitions occasioned by evolution and societal advancements. Thus, she suspects that "the world...has outgrown...those passages of *Paradise Lost* in which Milton makes the Almighty Father propound the theology of a seventeenth century Presbyterian" (183). By contrast, Milton, as artistic-poet, endures forever. Quoting *nearly* all of the Narcissus passage, Cooper regards Eve's narrative of origins as an example of poetry that proves "as perennial as man" (183). On the strength of this analysis, she believes it will "never cease to throb and thrill as long as man is man and woman is woman" (185).

Her adaptation of Milton's Narcissus passage (*PL* 4.450–88) positions Cooper in the feminist company of her eighteenth century sisters. First, she selects a passage that highlights the "aesthetic categories defining...Eve" as opposed to celebrating one of the "machining" episodes in Milton's epic.[65] Selecting Eve's narrative of origins over the "machining" episodes, which focus on the celestial and infernal agents of Milton's poem, constitutes a feminist mode of adapted appropriation congruent with Cooper's interest in the heroic quietude of Christian valor. Based on his reading of Addison's *The Pleasures of the Imagination*, Moore states that the eighteenth century critic assigned the category of the "beautiful" as inferior to the scenes labeled as "the great" and "the uncommon."[66] If Eve figures as a representative of "the beautiful" pursuant to eighteenth century receptions of Milton's epic, then Cooper's appropriation of her narrative origins signals a poetics of appropriative subversion. By promoting Eve's narrative as a template of "perennial" poetry, she displays a commitment to the tradition of feminist receptions performed by her literary sisters in the eighteenth century. Their poems similarly explored scenes of the beautiful. They appropriate and re-create Milton's poem with the subversive outcome of "attack[ing] existing institutions" and "reimagin[ing] the idea of woman."[67] Cooper assumes a similar rhetorical position in her subversive appropriation of Milton's Narcissus passage. It is not enough to merely appropriate the passage. She dares to take gnostic liberties with his words, therefore transforming the patriarchal grounds of its rhetorical landscape.

One may logically infer that the reason Cooper takes gnostic liberties with Milton's passage is because Eve's utterance of gender subordination reflects an "archetypal instance of canonical instruction" that proves antithetical to the womanist author.[68] Froula notes the problematic nature of the passage as consigning Eve and any of the epic poet's submissive female readers to several patriarchal figures within and outside the literary text. According to Froula, Eve does not submit to Adam alone, but to "Milton's God, and thence to Milton's poem, and through the poem to the ancient patriarchal tradition" as well.[69] Given the telltale nature of her literary excisions, Cooper no doubt finds Milton's passage problematic, notwithstanding its merits as an exemplary model of the beautiful sublime.

In order to remain true to her womanist self, Cooper excises those lines she finds misogynistic. For instance, her appropriation of the passage from book 9 begins at line 449 rather than line 440, which is where Eve's narrative of her origins actually begins. That she ends the narrative prematurely again signals her art of selective appropriation as a textual moment of rhetorical activism. In this instance, Cooper limits her quotation of the passage to line 488 rather than 491, where Eve's narrative terminates. These excisions are not without feminist significance. In omitting these eight lines, Cooper radically alters the demonic and contentious grounds of Milton's poem and its meaning. By striking the "ontological debt" Eve believes she owes to Adam from the Miltonic record, Cooper abolishes the notion of woman's secondariness, thereby making the gendered grounds an even playing field.

A brief summary of the lines in question will facilitate a clearer understanding of Cooper's gnostic liberties. In the first three lines of her narrative, Milton's Eve addresses Adam accordingly:

> O thou for whom
> And from whom I was formed flesh of thy flesh,
> And without whom am to no end, my guide
> And head, what thou hast said is just and right. (*PL* 4.440–43)

Lines 488–91 contain similar expressions of woman's secondariness. At the conclusion of her narrative, having recalled the moment she first laid eyes on her helpmeet, Eve remembers that Adam "seized" her "gentle hand" and exclaims, "from that time see / How beauty is excelled by manly grace / And wisdom, which alone is truly fair" (*PL* 4.488–91). Given *A Voice from the South*'s strong womanist leanings, Cooper must, of necessity, excise these articulations or "gestures of subordination" so as not to undermine her advocacy of woman's equality.[70] If patriarchal culture assigns woman a subordinated position to men, then Cooper must rebel in a rhetorical strength that radically revises the poet's epic and the biblical script informing it. Cooper revels in this strength and in doing so "reads outside the bounds of [patriarchal] authority" and "[dis]credit[s] the imagery that Milton would make a universal currency."[71]

Of equal if not greater importance, Cooper rebels and makes her point through the art of textual silence. She does not pummel her audience with thunderous vocalizations and protestations. Instead, she speaks volumes by what she does not say. That this vocalized silence appears through the quoting or voicing of Milton's Narcissus passage only amplifies the reverberations caused by Cooper's troubling of the interpretive waters of Eve's origins. This same textual performance troubles the demonic and contentious grounds that Cooper occupies as well. Since she uses the passage to emphasize the perennial nature of Milton's "beautiful sublime," her subversive appropriation ends up fulfilling two purposes at once. On the one hand, she offers an example that validates her theory about the supernal power of poet-artists. On the other hand, on a more subversive level, her rebellion in Milton's rhetorical strength tacitly conveys the notion that one might effectively rebel in a poetics of nonconfrontational heroism without sacrificing the ideological power of her womanist ideas. Collectively, these practices reveal a poetics that glories in forging rhetorical affiliations with Milton's satanic energy but for messianic purposes.

It would seem that the implications of this poetics of liberation for the future of African American literature regenerates Milton for the express purpose of challenging black male writers to think of political art in less militant ways. With respect to her survey of black male writers, Cooper bemoans the fact that "in literature we have no artists for art's sake" (*Voice* 223). From the standpoint of the previous two decades, Cooper finds no existing authentic portrait by a black man that presents him "as a free American citizen...divinely struggling and aspiring yet tragically warped and distorted by the adverse winds of circumstance" (222–23). Only Albery A. Whitman, a black poet and minister from Kentucky, comes close to "attempting a more sustained note than the lyrics of [Frances] Harper," and Cooper laments that even his note scarcely amounts to more than "a wail" (223). Consequently, she awaits the time when the "black man's native and original flowers" might bloom instead of languishing in their present state as "hardened and sharpened into thorns and spurs" (223). Cooper's liberating poetics, therefore, preaches and sings a gospel of revolt that hopes in the day when a tradition of poetry written by black male writers might gravitate to an aesthetic of humility and love. The echo of Miltonic presence continues to lie just beneath the surface of this gnostic criticism, however, for Cooper may be seen as advocating for a kind of sermonic poetry that preaches a firm and unequivocal message yet paints nature's truths in expressions of artistic eloquence.

Up until 1892, the publication year of *A Voice from the South,* Cooper contends that secular black male preachers such as Frederick Douglass, Alexander Crummell, Edward Wilmot Blyden, and Timothy Thomas Fortune have left a literary legacy but not a tradition of poetry that might prove eternal for the ages. This is not to suggest that she does not esteem them at all. For instance, she recognizes them as those black "champions" of the polemic class of writers who "stand ever at the forefront dealing desperate blows right and left, now fist and skull, now broad-sword and battle-axe, now with the flash and boom of artillery" (*Voice* 200). Though she applauds their martial heroism, the force and strength of their words continue to make her point about the Byronic or self-destructive force of patriarchal masculinity. Literary cadences of this type may prove heroic; however, Cooper ultimately concludes that this incendiary way with words makes for "interesting history" but not literary art (201).

As *A Voice from the South* has articulated on nearly every page, the black woman constitutes the vital element of regeneration for the race and civilization as a whole. Indeed, Milton constitutes a valuable component of Cooper's rhetorical activism. On the literary pages of the African American tradition, it may very well be that his "masked" and "hidden" presence offers rhetorical space for black women and men to enter a variety of prohibitive and inhibitive spaces through a strength keenly attuned to the "quiet, undisputed dignity" of one's selfhood (*Voice* 31). On the strength of these womanist convictions, Cooper's combined choir of black men and women are poised to sing gospels of black revolt that affirm a gnostic word of Miltonic interpretation. Her womanist interpretations of Milton and his gospel of liberty "make a joyful noise unto the Lord" on humanity's behalf that all men and women might "enter his gates with thanksgiving, and into his courts with praise" (Ps. 100:1, 4).

7

RETURNING TO MILTON'S HELL WITH WEAPONS OF PERFECT PASSIVITY IN SUTTON E. GRIGGS'S *IMPERIUM IN IMPERIO*

In 1899, the last year of what is known as the long nineteenth century, Sutton E. Griggs brought the tradition of early African American engagement with Milton to a fitting satanic close. His novel, *Imperium in Imperio,* or *State within a State,* focuses on warring black politics that pits ideologies of black nationalism and accommodationalism against each other relative to the mounting acts of terrorism perpetrated against blacks on the cusp of a new century. In this novel, Griggs tropes with Satan in double vision. Developing a double plot that presents readers with two race leaders of contrasting political persuasions, Griggs combines artistic modes of characterization and setting to herald the second coming of a new messianic rebel whom the author re-creates in stark contrast to Satan's militant spirit. The Miltonic tenor of both characters' political differences is especially evident in the climax and denouement stages of plot structure, where Griggs intertextually revisits *Paradise Lost* by returning to the demonic grounds of hell. This revisitation of Milton's epic coupled with Griggs's return to hell brings the tradition of Miltonic engagement in early African American literature to a satanic close. For these reasons, *Imperium in Imperio* represents a climax of intertextual tradition relative to early African American writers' interpoetic engagements with Milton. Its satanic politics with Milton chart new intertextual lines for subsequent members of Milton's black sisterhood and brotherhood to extend and enrich in the centuries that follow.

Literary criticism has only recently begun to pay renewed interest in Griggs who has fallen outside of literary history as a result of his unpopular political views concerning race and the problem of the color line. An accomplished writer, preacher, and activist of the African American nadir, Griggs has fallen into a virtual hellspace of forgotten oblivion. A. J. Verdelle, noting "time and criticism have sometimes been harsh" to the author, further explains that Griggs's work "has been ignored, and when it has been considered or visible, he has often been labeled polemical." Hugh Gloster, in his assessments of *Imperium in Imperio*, notes that the novel is "weakened by melodramatic situations, idealized characters, and stilted conversation." Finnie D. Coleman, one of the most recent critics to present a comprehensive examination of Griggs as an author and literary figure, enriches contemporary understandings of the author's fallen status in history. For example, in *Sutton E. Griggs and the Struggle against White Supremacy*, he states: "Widely criticized for its implausible plot, lofty romanticism, and at times heavy-handed didactism, *Imperium in Imperio* is most often discussed as it complements earlier nineteenth-century Black nationalist literature. Rarely is the text approached as the first of five novels that offered 'conservative action' as an alternative to the 'militant rhetoric' that pervaded much of Black nationalist literature in the nineteenth and early twentieth centuries." Coleman's account of Griggs's reception in history synthesizes cultural responses to the author's literary art and political views. Understood from these vantage points, Griggs's literary aesthetic is found wanting and artistically inferior, and his political ideologies are considered unsuitable for a race struggling to overcome tyrannies such as lynching and voting discrimination.[1]

Griggs's literary aesthetic coupled with his racial politics partially explain why *Imperium in Imperio* and its author "remain at the margins of critical discourse" throughout much of the twentieth and twenty-first centuries.[2] As a result of these cultural responses to his work, Griggs has suffered indignity in a cultural hellspace of darkened (in)visibility. Commenting further on his abject status in literary history, Coleman asserts, "by the time of Griggs' death in 1933, members of popular literary circles had practically forgotten him and his five novels."[3] In this respect, Griggs stands on equal footing with his heroic protagonist, Belton Piedmont, who returns to Milton's hell at the site of a black Pandaemonium and dies a noble death for rejecting a racial politics of militant rebellion. Ironically, it is on these demonic grounds of rebellion and literary tradition that Belton and Griggs simultaneously extend Milton's relevance in African American literary tradition beyond the nineteenth century. Emerging as lords of satanic re-creation, both differentiate themselves from more popular beliefs in black political thought in their times. These acts of satanic re-creation complete and complicate Milton's poetry, casting both personalities in their intertextual roles as fallen stars of racial uplift at the dawn of a new century.

Griggs occupies the controversial office of a lord of satanic re-creation by espousing gospels of black revolt that selectively and strategically vacillate between militant and conservative politics. Because he straddled the line between these contrasting political viewpoints, many saw him as espousing a passive gospel of accommodationalism. Randolph Meade Walker, addressing this misperception of Griggs's politics, notes that the author "merely was a reflection of the age in which he lived," astutely recognizing that he wrote at a "time when answers were being sought." In *The Metamorphosis of Sutton E. Griggs*, Walker describes the author as "less well known than [W. E. B.] Dubois or [Carter G.] Woodson, but more direct in his reaction to the anti-black propagandists" of his era.[4] Given the strong intellectual tenor of Dubois and Woodson's political leanings, Walker's understanding of Griggs asks for a nuanced reconsideration of misperceptions that have unjustly reduced the author to that of a passive accommodationalist rather than a lord of satanic re-creation, as his intertextual engagements with Milton would otherwise suggest.

Griggs was born in Chatfield, Texas, in 1872. He attended school in Dallas before graduating from Bishop College in 1890. The son of a Baptist clergyman, Griggs furthered his education from 1890 to 1893 "in preparation for a ministerial career at the

Richmond Theological Seminary." Upon graduation, he began a ministerial career in Berkley, Virginia, for two years before relocating to Nashville, Tennessee, where he served as pastor at the First Baptist Church of East Nashville. In 1899, he published *Imperium in Imperio*, which was followed by four more novels between 1901 and 1908. His "primary motivation" in these novels was to "rebut the distortions presented by [Thomas Nelson] Page and [Thomas] Dixon and others" whose literary works negatively portray the race as intellectually inferior. Because Griggs actively undertook this endeavor, Walker recognizes him as a "literary crusader for black justice" and a "courageous original thinker" who served as a literary respondent to the racist propagandistic literature generated by Dixon and Page. Moreover, in responding to these authors and other intense political situations throughout his lifetime, Griggs, according to Walker, "wrote his African American apologetics during an era in which intolerance, economic intimidation, and physical violence against blacks were every day occurrences in the South."[5]

These literary preoccupations especially afforded Griggs opportunities to re-create himself through (w)rites of passage that staunchly opposed his "father's stark conservatism, the conservatism espoused by Booker T. Washington."[6] Coleman explains that Griggs "never departed wholly from this ideology, but to the degree possible, he expressed the concerns of Black America through the narrative voices of both conservative and militant characters."[7] This tension between political conservatism and militant rebellion produce a kind of writing situation where struggling writers are forced to forge their own literary identities. Because Griggs makes these tensions between political conservatism and militant rebellion a central component of *Imperium in Imperio*, the conflicts posed by his writing situation function as a ground of demonic contention and warring opposition for an author searching for answers to problems of the color line at the end of the nineteenth century. It is on these demonic grounds that Griggs becomes his own lord of re-creation, in part, due to Milton's satanic poetry.

By 1907, Griggs, a licensed preacher and author of four novels, turned to pamphlet writing. His *The One Great Question: A Study of Southern Conditions at Close Range* (1907) exposed and examined the tyrannies of racial violence perpetrated against black citizens in Nashville by their white oppressors. Its fiscal success encouraged Griggs to understand "that he could state the case of the Black community more clearly and concisely with political tracts than he could with his novels." This recognition of the power of the literary pen motivated Griggs to publish "more than thirty nonfiction pamphlets and book-length political tracts" in the years following his last novel, *Pointing the Way* (1908).[8] In light of his ministerial vocations as a preacher and novelist, this new literary vocation establishes Griggs as a Miltonic heir in the sense that he, too, pursues a (w)rite of passage that occupies the office of a Christian pulpit through poetry and political writings.

Griggs's political tracts reveal closer ties of rhetorical kinship with Milton based on the intertextual relationships he forged with Thomas Jefferson and the Bible. "The complexity of [Griggs's] beliefs," according to Walker, "can be seen in [the author's] synthesis of Thomas Jefferson, Charles Darwin, and the Bible."[9] Jefferson appealed to Griggs, in particular, because the author valued the former president "as an authority on what was proper and just in both the fiction and nonfiction writings."[10] In "rever[ing] 'Jeffersonian' ideals of personal freedom and independence," Griggs likewise pays homage to Milton.[11] Since Jefferson's political philosophies on the creation of the U.S. republic and themes of liberty were similarly influenced by Milton as has been discussed in chapter 2, Griggs becomes a lord of satanic re-creation and Miltonic heir by intertextual default through intermediary sources penned by one of the nation's more prominent founding fathers. The Declaration of Independence was of particular interest to Griggs. He frequently quoted the document, regarding its self-evident truths concerning the equality of all "as sacred as any of the scriptures."[12] Griggs highly regarded Jeffersonian principles in his fictional and nonfictional writings even though he recognized that their political ideals did not always extend to blacks. Inspired to intervene in this political paradox on behalf of his race while operating from an authorial impulse to respond to negative portrayals of African Americans, Griggs wrote *Imperium in Imperio* as a rebuttal to the limitations of Jeffersonian principles inscribed on the nation's juridical instruments of liberty and freedom. Responding to that document and giving fictional reality to the African American condition aided Griggs in advancing the cause of liberty for his people, obliquely referencing Milton as well.

The Bible is another text that indirectly ties Griggs to Milton. Even though he was a preacher, Griggs relied on scriptural texts as an earthly guide for living in moral harmony with nature. He was no Bible fanatic, as Walker explains, yet extolled its virtues as justificatory tools that aided the exercise of superior reasoning. In synthesizing his biblical views with various Jeffersonian insights, Griggs wrote in an idiom of Miltonic influence without directly appropriating any of the epic writer's language. Because he was a preacher-poet and statesman for liberty, these elements of his literary persona combined to strengthen his rhetorical kinship with Milton. He intensifies this Miltonic relationship in *Imperium in Imperio* when he presents Belton as a model of "perfect passivity"[13] who returns to demonic grounds reminiscent of Milton's hell but with a geographical repetition of political and racialized difference. These intertextual technologies perform what Edward Stein identifies as an "enrichment of connotation." *Imperium in Imperio* enriches connotative expressions of Miltonic presence and influence by blending Belton's positive and heroic characterization with the fallen geographical setting of hell in *Paradise Lost*. This synthesizing of a positive and negative relationship under the intertextual auspices of Milton's satanic poetry crowns Griggs and his heroic protagonist as lords of satanic re-creation. This distinction reflects the connotative value of Milton's allusive presence in *Imperium in Imperio*, an aspect of Griggs's literary art that has been overlooked by previous scholars in literary history.

An examination of this neglected aspect of Miltonic engagement in *Imperium in Imperio* corroborates Gabriel A. Briggs's conclusion that "the time for revaluation of Griggs' intellectual contribution to southern literature and culture has come."[14] Taking up the call proposed by Briggs continues the rupture of Milton's realigned originality and the Western canon that Wheatley inaugurated with her *Poems on Various Subjects*. If in the past Griggs has fallen outside of literary history because *Imperium in Imperio* appears to preach a social gospel that is accommodationist in tone and in philosophical outlook, it is only because critics have overlooked the allusive significance of Milton's presence in the novel. Milton's allusive presence through characterization and geographical setting empowers Griggs to re-create carnal understandings of epic heroism in black political thought. Revisioning epic heroism according to his assessments of black experience at the close of the nineteenth century motivates Griggs to indulge in intertextual acts of satanic poetry. In his novel, these acts privilege the spiritual weaponry of perfect passivity over that of militant strength. *Imperium in Imperio*, then, constitutes a climax in intertextual tradition, re-creating a different aspect of what it means to complete and complicate Milton as a call to arms in literary projects devoted to addressing the complexities of black life in 1899 and beyond.

A poetics of perfect passivity governs Griggs's depiction of militant strength throughout his novel. This model of strength manifests through exercises of restraint and inaction where the "might of weakness" trumps more carnal performances of heroic might. Erik Gray identifies this poetics of strength operating throughout Milton's canon, which likewise influences the poetry and prose of Victorian writer Matthew Arnold. According to Gray, Milton's perfect passivity represents a "Miltonic paradox of powerful resignation or retreat."[15] As a poetics of Christian heroism, the technique measures strength in proportion to epic displays of inaction in physical, spiritual, or moral terms. Griggs's novelistic gospel of black nationalism promotes this idea of a firm and unyielding passivity based on the political vision of rebellion espoused by the favored protagonist, Belton Piedmont. Although Belton dies by novel's end, his example invites Griggs's white and black readership to reconsider their political situatedness relative to the problems of the color line at the close of the nineteenth century.

In Griggs's novel and according to Belton, his favored protagonist, one may exercise the might of weakness through perfect passivity by drawing political strength from the power of the pen. More important, one may derive this power through a strategic literary companionship with Milton and a variety of writers in the Western canon. The return to Milton's hell in the novel's third section provides the oratorical platform for preaching the controversial benefits of this strategic companionship with the epic writer. By this point in the novel, Griggs has traced the rise and trajectory of two political rivals who become "young rebels" in the political service of their race.[16] Rivals from the time they meet, Belton Piedmont and Bernard Palgrave reunite in the final five chapters on the demonic grounds of the Imperium in Imperio, a secret black society devoted to radical projects of racial uplift. This secret society "reflects the vexed relation of African Americans to their national government," according to Caroline Levander.[17] As a result, blacks within the Imperium in Imperio constitute a "nation within a nation," a phrase Martin Delaney, a popular midcentury black emigrationist, used a few decades earlier to describe African Americans' curious existence within U.S. policy. Located outside Waco, Texas, the Imperium convenes its meetings on a palatial estate in an assembly room situated four stories beneath ground level. Its secret existence and subterranean headquarters, coupled with the society's revolutionary aims, instantly prompts a consideration of Milton's hell and Pandaemonium more specifically. At the end of the novel, Belton espouses his gospel of black revolt on the demonic grounds of the Imperium's congressional floor, where Griggs's favored lord of re-creation establishes his satanic "companionship" with Milton and the epic writer's infernal hero.

While preaching this gospel of black revolt at the Imperium, Belton endorses a form of cultural paternalism that recognizes the "arts of civilization [and] knowledge of the English language" as beneficial by-products of slavery (*Imperium* 155). He takes particular pride in "the great fact" that blacks may presently "enjoy the companionship of Shakespeare, Bacon, Milton, Bunyan, together with the favorite sons of other nations adopted into the English language such as Dante, Hugo, Goethe, Dumas and hosts of others" (155–56). To Belton, this pantheon of literary greats functions as a signifier of a civilization whose canonical authority can attest to African American intellect and their rights to equality. Furthermore, listing Milton in this pantheon of canonical heavyweights simultaneously places Belton and Griggs on par with Lord Tennyson and the seventeenth century epic writer, as Gray has shown. According to Gray, listing Milton as one among many canonical authors in the Western tradition connotes how later writers often "resembled Milton in precocious learning" in addition to "show[ing] how largely [he] figured" in the "erudite imagination" of these lords of creation.[18] Belton puts this display of erudite imagination to political use with the Imperium's Congress when he acknowledges "instruction in the arts of civilization, a knowledge of the English language, and a conception of the one true God and his Christ" as valuable payment for African Americans' "years of toil" in the United States. Here, Belton adheres to a line of reasoning that considers the African past as pagan and primitive, reminding his audience that "it was the Anglo-Saxon who snatched from our idolatrous grasp the deaf images to which we prayed, and the Anglo-Saxon who pointed us to the Lamb of God that takes away the sins of the world" (156). For Belton, "enslavement in America" caused African Americans to "come into possession of the great English language," which positions his people to become "heir[s] to all the richest thoughts of earth" (155).

Belton preaches this seditious gospel of cultural paternalism on demonic grounds modeled after Milton's hell. Because his speeches occur on demonic grounds, they are reminiscent of the infernal council in book 2 of Milton's epic. Like his protagonist, then, Griggs advocates companionship with Milton by journeying to subterranean depths and preaching a gospel of black revolt in a congressional setting derivative of Pandaemonium. Griggs's authorial descent to the capital of the underworld for purposes of racial uplift presents Belton as a fallen star of political righteousness whose gospel of black revolt preaches a message of perfect passivity in the fight for liberty, justice, and social equality for African Americans in this turbulent era of race relations. In espousing this gospel, Griggs and Belton seek strategic companionship with Milton, confident that this literary relationship will provide possibilities for "conquering [the] Anglo-Saxon" without having "to wade through blood to achieve their freedom" (*Imperium* 164).

Moreover, and in a rhetorical posture suggestive of Moloch's speech during the infernal council, Belton rejects open war and the carnage that accompanies it. In *Paradise Lost*, Moloch, one of the fallen angels, who the epic narrator acknowledges as "the strongest and the fiercest spirit," declares, "My sentence is for open war: of wiles, / More unexpert" (*PL* 2.51–52). Belton opposes this aggressive display of physical violence. Instead, he celebrates the art of a linguistic might forged in the companionship with Milton. For him, strategic companionship with Milton produces the desired results of war but on a battlefield of literacy where one's casualties occur on the cognitive terrains of philosophy and critical thinking as opposed to promoting bodily injury at the risk of physical death. By rejecting Moloch's radical politics, Belton re-creates himself as a fallen star distinct from those who open Milton's epic. Instead of rebelling against forms of monarchial tyranny through militant violence, Belton allows the light of his nonviolent politics to shine before a host of delegates who have yet to comprehend the might of Miltonic weakness as a penultimate expression of epic strength and heroism.

Belton preaches the nonviolent benefits of Miltonic companionship as literary warfare when he speaks before the Imperium and asserts that one "can by means of the pen force an acknowledgment of equality from the proud lips" of one's adversaries (*Imperium* 164). If this pandering to cultural paternalism seems problematic from a contemporary standpoint, Wilson Jeremiah Moses notes that such reactions were typical of black nationalists in the mid-nineteenth century. "Despite their fierce rhetoric of independence," he asserts, they "were hardly eager to remove themselves from white society, and were reluctant to contemplate a future severed from the values of Anglo-American civilization."[19] This is so because many of this ideological persuasion recognized literacy as a cultural marker that accrued political benefits of social mobility and racial uplift for an oppressed and marginalized people. These viewpoints would remain popular throughout post-Reconstruction as writings by Alexander Crummell, another proponent of education as a racial sign of civilization, indicate. For Belton, using the power of the pen as effective weaponry for successfully "accomplishing revolutions" provides his people with an alternative technology of militant rebellion. Specifically, this form of intellectual warfare uses literacy and the power of words as a strategic means for effectively dealing with the various socio-political "forces of the American capitalistic dynamic" that black intellectuals throughout history have had to learn to "control and channel."[20]

Griggs promotes this gospel of black revolt by favoring Belton's political philosophy over Bernard's. Thus, he anticipates Harold Cruse's examinations of the crises suffered by black intellectuals.

As Belton's oratorical performance on the floor of this black Pandaemonium suggests, Griggs constructs a poetics of characterization that promotes a distinct type of fallen rebel. Belton is militant-minded in his political thinking but through a nonthreatening arsenal of complex philosophical ideas. This performance of satanic re-creation through Griggs's aesthetic of differentiated characterization is especially evident upon reconciling interpretive understandings of Belton's character at this late stage in the novel alongside descriptions of him during the exposition stage of plot. In chapter 1, entitled "A Small Beginning," the narrator introduces Belton, who as a listless juvenile has yet to appreciate the benefits of education. The opening paragraph conveys a setting of humble origins as Belton's mother addresses the lad through low diction as she prepares him for school. She tells Belton, "Cum er long hunny an' let yer mammy fix yer 'spectabul, so yer ken go to skule. Yer mammy is 'tarmined ter gib yer all de book larning dar is ter be had eben ef she has ter lib on bred an' herrin's, an' die en da a'ms house" (7). Following her instructions, the narrator explains, "these words came from the lips of a poor, ignorant negro woman, and yet the determined course of action which they reveal vitally affected the destiny of a nation and saved the sun of the Nineteenth Century, proud and glorious, from passing through, near its setting, the blackest and thickest and ugliest clouds of all its journey; saved it from ending the most brilliant of brilliant careers by setting, with a shudder of horror, in a sea of human blood." The narrator's commentary extols the mother's heroic vision of racial uplift. Determined to provide her son a first-rate education even if doing so means she is driven to the almshouse, Mrs. Piedmont, Belton's mother, regenerates the race and guides its future by instilling the importance of education in black youth. Of particular importance, her "determined course of action" saves the "Sun of the Nineteenth Century." A metonym for Western civilization and its trajectory of universal progress, the sun's rising and setting is connected to Belton's future achievements. Furthermore, his future contributions to civilization save the sun from becoming eclipsed by the racial strife that would otherwise obscure its shining glory. According to the narrator's poetic observations, if not for Belton, the sun would decline and set in a "sea of human blood" and carnage.

In other words, Belton's little light allows the sun's glory to shine as brilliantly as it does at the close of the nineteenth century. The narrator justifies this idea by adding, "Those who doubt that such power could emanate from such weakness; or, to change the figure, that such a tiny star could have dimensions greater than those of earth, may have every vestige of doubt removed by a perusal of this simple narrative." Belton, a weak and "tiny star" according to the narrator, possesses a light so powerful that it positively affects the brilliance of the sun's universal light. Interestingly, this weak and tiny star shines its illuminating light in the subterranean darkness of the Imperium's capital by championing the might of weakness and perfect passivity to an army of delegates beholden to militant violence. Because he illumines his positive light by descending to the geographical darkness reminiscent of Pandaemonium, Belton re-creates himself in the satanic image of a fallen star, yet differentiates himself from Milton's infernal hero by emerging as his own lord of creation.

The novel casts Belton as a "conservative assimilationist," pitting his character against Bernard, a "militant separatist."[21] Presenting readers with competing protagonists provide the novel with its major conflict. When Belton and Bernard engage in oratorical battle on the Imperium's demonic grounds, they highlight the very dilemma Griggs faced as a prolific writer hurled outside of literary history. Belton, according to Briggs, "insists upon patience and passive resistance, while Bernard...argues in favor of war."[22] Jane Campbell recognizes a similar dilemma impacting Griggs's protagonists. For her, Griggs's dual protagonists "occupy the two horns of the dilemma faced by blacks in turn-of-the century America," that of choosing between militant and accommodationist models of revolt as effective political strategies of liberation.[23] Griggs's novel entertains this dilemma by contrasting these poles of political rebellion through the lens of black nationalism and by establishing Belton's character as the embodiment of a "good" protagonist with Bernard serving as his antithesis.

Broadly defined, black nationalism refers to Africanist political movements grounded in principles designed to unify "the black racial family" pursuant to a collective understanding and shared sense of oppression and institutional disenfranchisement.[24] On occasion, black nationalist proponents have promoted quests for nationhood predicated on geographic separation from the imperialist state in the hopes of resettling either domestically or abroad where black governments might be formed. Both of these tenets appear in *Imperium in Imperio*, therefore, prompting Cornel West to recognize the work as "the first major political novel written by an African American" and "the first literary portrait of a black revolutionary movement in violent revolt against white supremacist America."[25] The novel also finds Griggs espousing a black literary nationalism as well, for as Moses explains, the author conceived the crafting of a black literary tradition as a political investment that would ultimately produce and establish "a national Negro literature."[26] A tradition of this type addresses multiple and intersecting aspects of black culture while simultaneously serving as nationalist repositories of intellect, civilization, and, therefore, racial equality.

Given its black nationalist impulses, *Imperium in Imperio* instantly invites an intertextual association with Milton's first epic because *Paradise Lost* engages a similar political project. From the moment Milton's readers encounter Satan in book 1 of *Paradise Lost*, they come into immediate contact with nationalist themes of subterranean rebellion and liberty. For instance, in his opening passage from the depths of Milton's burning hell, Satan revives Beelzebub into political consciousness, reminding his peer of their recent defeat as a result of God's omnipotence. According to Satan, it was his vehement dislike for God's monarchial rule in heaven that enflamed the fallen angel's "unconquerable will" (*PL* 1.106). Even in this early passage from the epic, the urge to reestablish a new government yet consumes Satan.

For example, he aspires to the "study of revenge, immortal hate / And courage never to submit or yield" (*PL* 1.107–08); hence, he ends his introductory speech by seeking yet again to enact revenge against God's celestial empire. With an emboldened sense of hope, he resolves

> To wage by force or guile eternal war
> Irreconcilable to [their] grand Foe
> Who now triumphs and in th' excess of joy
> Sole reigning holds the tyranny of Heav'n.   (*PL* 1.121–24)

If, as Moses asserts in another context, "nationalism has often been bred by evil circumstances," then Milton's Satan offers an intertextual touchstone for the infernal political movement that proves central to *Imperium in Imperio*.[27] Since the Imperium remains dedicated to securing civil rights for blacks in an age where lynchings and other racial tyrannies are rampant, the secret underground society, like Milton's devils, may be interpreted as resorting to nationalist enterprises in the cause of freedom.

Imperium in Imperio takes the nationalist enterprises a controversial step further by having the Imperium execute Belton at the denouement. Until this climactic moment in the novel, Belton and Bernard, according to Coleman, have "vie[d] for ascendency in this text." With Belton's execution, the plot promotes his more conservative political vision as the favored approach for negotiating problems of the color line. More importantly, his death "signals the death of a particular brand of conservative voice [that] warns of the potential ascendency of another."[28] For Coleman, Griggs's amiable approach to resolving tensions of the color line gave dangerous rise to the ascendency of more militant voices of rebellion by those who more readily endorsed Bernard's style of political agitation.

Since Belton's willingness to die for his strong political beliefs actually inspires the narrator to expose the Imperium's secret identity, the novel ends by extolling the protagonist as a heroic martyr. The political implications of this ending partly explain critics' dismissal of Griggs as a militant writer. However, Robert Bone recognizes the profundity of Griggs's literary dilemma for what it was within the historical time of cultural production. In *The Negro Novel in America*, he contends, "Militancy is one thing; translating it into effective political action is another."[29] His statement alludes to the challenges black literary crusaders confronted in their quest to rupture hegemonic structures and systems by radical and militant means. Theirs was a crisis that ultimately asks the black intellectual to discover solutions for rupturing hegemonic systems without killing one's self off in the process. If, as Bone points out, literary works too "uncompromising" in this radical direction are "bound to have a certain Utopian ring," then such a crisis necessitates more sophisticated strategies for regaining paradise through the power of the pen.[30] In *Imperium in Imperio* at least, Griggs resists this utopian impulse. Instead, he regains paradise by seeking companionship with Milton on the demonic grounds of Milton's hell and through an unconventional mode of militant poetics and Christian heroism.

Griggs's strategic companionship with Milton first announces its militant poetics through a novelistic manipulation of literary form that preaches a political gospel of black revolt from the demonic grounds of Milton's hell. The author of myriad political tracts, Milton, as E. M. W. Tillyard notes, expresses themes of patriotism to such a high degree "that there is no need to emphasize its presence" in the early pamphlets.[31] Similarly, Griggs's novel announces a love for black patriotism by rendering its story through an infernal legal instrument that equally serves as a secular gospel of political revolt. *Imperium in Imperio* begins with Griggs's authorial intrusion into the novel's plot structure. In a prefatory address, "To the Public," Griggs identifies himself as the editor of Berl Trout's manuscript. According to Griggs, Trout, a deceased member of the Imperium in Imperio, bequeaths his "Dying Declaration" and personal papers to the author with instructions to edit and publish his manuscript. Trout's personal papers tell the story of Belton's and Bernard's origins in addition to chronicling the events leading to the former's execution. In the role of Trout's editor, Griggs positions himself as qualified to attest to Trout's personal character and the veracity of his private papers. Assuring readers that the incidents contained in Trout's papers "will speak for themselves," Griggs, as authenticator of these narrated events, also acknowledges the novel as a talking book of sorts (*Imperium* 3).

Because this incendiary talking book documents the Imperium's political and underground existence, Trout's novelistic narrative may be understood as speaking from demonic grounds and in an infernal or satanic register. Already functioning as a legal instrument, that Trout is the Imperium's former secretary of state lends his narrative an added political quality. His high-ranking position coupled with his treasonous decision to divulge the existence of the secret society and its history legitimates his talking book as a highly incendiary text of political revolt. Trout's high-ranking position within the Imperium's cabinet brings to mind Milton's political assignment as Secretary for the Foreign Tongues by Council of State. When considered in tandem with his cabinet position, Trout's novelistic manipulation of his "dying papers" lends his narrative a heightened sense of political urgency. A political tract of sorts, Trout's papers recall one of the many genres associated with Milton. Because Griggs would write more than 30 political tracts throughout his literary career, his novelization of this genre in *Imperium in Imperio* functions as another instance of achieving states of Miltonic companionship in this first fictional work.

Though Griggs cites Milton directly only once in the novel and delays this intertextual companionship until chapter 15 by venturing to Pandaemonium, the epic poet's presence remains virtually (in)visible across the entirety of the text. Gray, remarking on this type of Miltonic (in)visibility in Victorian texts refers to this allusive form of intertextual engagement as "'dark with excessive bright,'" where Milton exists as "a blind spot" or "something so patent as to go unnoticed" as a result of being "hidden in plain sight."[32] Trout's dying declaration represents such an instance of Miltonic (in)visibility where the epic writer begins to surface in the novel as a "diffusive power" of salient intertextual engagement.[33] As in Tennyson's poetry, Milton's (in)visible presence in *Imperium in Imperio* signifies "latency" through any number of scattered indirect echoes that ultimately refer to the epic poet without dominating a given literary text. In fact, Gray's overarching argument centers on his contention that Victorian writers saw little need to make multiple direct references to Milton in their works because they regarded him as a "classic" and a "Bible."[34] In other words, it was a foregone conclusion that Milton epitomized the summit of poetic achievement even in the declining years of the Victorian era. For this reason, Griggs could seek companionship with Milton through subtle yet sophisticated modes of intertextual complexity as opposed to simply relying upon a series of direct phraseological adaptations.

Writing near the end of this era, Griggs draws upon Milton's "diffusive power" in *Imperium in Imperio* in styles other than literary form. Another iteration of this appeal to Miltonic influence through a militant poetics of Christian heroism involves his literary style of fusing infernal deeds with divine attributes of supernal glory. This mode of engagement with Milton specifically incorporates Satan's poetry into Griggs's narrative framework. Cognizant that his papers will betray the Imperium's insurrectionary interests, Trout openly acknowledges himself as a race traitor. He is also aware that the Imperium will execute him for this treasonous deed. Yet, he glories in the supernal reward he expects to receive as a result of his martyrdom. He interprets his treason beyond race loyalty and "pronounce[s] [himself] a patriot" beyond its "nation within a nation" agenda (*Imperium* 6). His personal political convictions not only express an emphatic recognition of his Americanness, they also inaugurate a fundamental motif regarding Griggs's militant poetics of Christian heroism. Through this motif, Griggs lays a rhetorical foundation for the entrance of his peculiar infernal hero who, in the role of a messianic rebel, must be purged of his infernal qualities and saved by supernal grace.

Trout's purgation works as a result of his choosing himself for himself. He chooses himself as a satanic particular, "revolt[ing] into negativity by rejecting" the militant ideals of the Imperium and the godlike authority this institution lords over his subjectivity and the political allegiance he owes to this nation within a nation.[35] In essence, Trout re-creates himself by conceiving possibilities for a different kind of tradition in black political thought. According to Danielle A. St. Hilaire, when an individual dares to "preserve difference and particularity" instead of remaining in league with ideals of sameness, they re-produce acts of satanic re-creation.[36] Satan inaugurates this tradition of fallenness in poetry by remaking himself as self-begotten and self-raised in ways that have "real consequences in Milton's universe."[37] Trout replicates this practice when he differentiates himself from the Imperium by becoming a political apostate and publishing his private papers. Their contents betray the goals of his militant government, which are to distance himself from the kinds of political activism that whites have traditionally coded as demonic in response to black men's militant vocalizations. In eschewing this so-called demonic posture, Trout, who has been persuaded by Belton's call for perfect passivity, re-creates himself and furthers a gospel of black revolt that he deems supernal in its political ideology.

This motif of satanic differentiation relies heavily upon the warring angelic forces depicted in *Paradise Lost*. In drawing upon this schema, Griggs alters the rhetorical significance of his descent to the site of Milton's hell. Synthesizing these warring angelic forces in the development of Belton's heroic character, the protagonist navigates problems of the color line as a peculiar type of infernal hero whose militant assertiveness has been tempered by the supernal grace of restraint and political conservatism. Trout operates in this subversive mode when he confesses his race betrayal as a political act performed "in the interest of the whole human family—of which [his] race is but a part" (*Imperium* 6). For this reason, he takes solace in knowing that while his race may "shower curses upon" him for his act of treason, "eventually[,] all races, including [his] own, shall call [him] blessed" (6). The implication of such a political stance asks for a reconsideration of what it means to navigate white hegemonic spaces *effectively*. Trout's understanding of the black intellectual's crisis encourages a strong sensitivity to acts of Christian heroism where one's "strength is made perfect in weakness" (2 Cor. 12:9).

Trout's dying declaration echoes this scriptural referent through a vivid metaphor that synthesizes infernal deeds with supernal glory. Vividly extending the motif of warring angelic forces, he anticipates that the earth will eventually "belch forth [his] putrid flesh with volcanic fury" (*Imperium* 6) while resigning himself to the heavenly thought that God will ultimately receive him with "out-stretched arms" (6) of divine approval. This resolute spiritual conviction informs his refusal to "shrink" (6) from his radical decision even though his betrayal to the Imperium exacts death. Dying in the faith that the future shall one day call him blessed, Trout reinterprets his treasonous deed as a mixed Miltonic blessing. Though a member of a secret organization patterned after the infernal crew in *Paradise Lost*, Trout embraces a strategic companionship with Milton that enables him to rest content in knowing his more conservative politics shall one day yield supernal or messianic glory.

In this way, Trout functions as a type of John the Baptist, a spiritual forerunner who precedes Belton and the messianic glory the protagonist eventually comes to symbolize by the end of the novel. Since readers encounter Trout before becoming acquainted with Belton, his dying declaration foreshadows and paves the way for

Belton's triumphant arrival. As Belton's humble beginnings will indicate, the protagonist does not instantly surface as a quiet hero. Rather, he must grow into his messianic role having been groomed for it as a result of his mother's epic strength. The novel traces Belton's humble origins up to that moment where he becomes a differentiated version of Milton's infernal hero, a character who must be saved by God's supernal grace before he can be successful within the conservative model Griggs provides. This differentiated model of political engagement seems destined to emulate those associated with Milton's Satan by eventually deviating from an infernal temperament of militant violence. Initially, when he is inducted into this secret nation within a nation, Belton actively participates in league with that organization's political mission and expresses his rhetorical companionship with Milton. By the later stages of the novel, however, Belton preaches and embodies a gospel of revolt contrary to the Imperium's aims. In other words, he knowingly sides with the devil's party but on his own peculiar though supernal terms.

To show the successive stages of Belton's development as a peculiar infernal hero, Griggs, as editor of Trout's manuscript, constructs the novel's plot by sequencing its narrative episodes in 20 chapters that mostly alternate between both protagonists. Coleman recognizes the novel as being comprised of "three distinct sections: early childhood in Virginia, young adulthood in Virginia and Louisiana, and the Imperium in Imperio chapters."[38] In the first section, Griggs's character development of his dual protagonists sustains Milton's unstated presence through an oppositional schema reminiscent of the war between heaven and hell in *Paradise Lost*. In a rhetorical mode suggestive of Anna Julia Cooper's Miltonic descriptions of Wordsworth and Byron in her essay "Womanhood" in *Voices from the South*, Griggs constructs Belton and Bernard as angelic rivals. Cooper's essay, as has been discussed in chapter 5, tropes with Milton and the war between heaven and hell by interpreting Wordsworth and Byron as ideological adversaries who possess supernal and infernal temperaments, respectively.

Griggs characterizes Belton and Bernard similarly. For instance, Coleman reads Belton's character as "a soft-spoken conservative" in contrast to Bernard, whom he considers "a hot-blooded radical."[39] Described at one point in the novel as "the morning star[,] which told by its presence that [the] dawn [of liberty] was near at hand," Belton, while a student, shows early signs that he is destined to fulfill the role of a political angel or celestial light (*Imperium* 34). Much later in the novel, the narrator refers to Belton as "the acknowledged guiding star that had led the Imperium to the high point of efficiency where Bernard found it" (153). Given his role as a "soft-spoken conservative" in contrast to Bernard, the "hot-blooded radical," Belton rhetorically and politically embodies the characteristics associated with supernal angelic forces. That he likewise refers to his audience in the Imperium as "Holy Angels" while delivering his messianic oration on the demonic grounds of the institution's congressional floor, amplifies the rhetorical salience of Milton's warring angelic forces in the novel (164).

Belton's and Bernard's extreme oppositional politics, coupled with a variety of incidents in the plot, often places these political messiahs at enmity with each other throughout the novel. Griggs's use of dual protagonists makes the point further, as Verdelle notes: "This kind of character arrangement was often used in nineteenth-century literature—often with one 'son' of the story being fine and good, and the other being the personification of some opposite, some evil."[40] *Imperium in Imperio* indulges in this form of character arrangement while simultaneously amplifying the novel's Miltonic overtones relative to the war between heaven and hell. The plot particularly capitalizes upon this style of oppositional characterization by contrasting the protagonists through various rhetorical means, namely, narrative structure and socioeconomic class.

Structurally, the novel vacillates between Belton's and Bernard's individual lives. The first two chapters deviate from this structure, introducing the protagonists and acquainting them in the school setting where their rivalry begins. Chapter 3 deviates from this narrative structure, focusing solely on Belton and the importance of his need to secure a formal education. Belton struggles to achieve a quality education due to the mistreatment and marginalization he experiences from his white teacher, who favors Bernard. Griggs does not devote a special chapter to Bernard's character development. This glaring instinct of character neglect and atypical break in narrative structure signals Belton's significance as the novel's good son or favored protagonist. Belton specifically benefits from this preferential treatment in Griggs's narrative as chapter 3 presents his character as a kind of underdog figure, calling attention to the numerous disadvantages he suffers.

Chapter 4 returns to a dual focus on the paired protagonists, chronicling their educational experiences while heightening their academic rivalry. Subsequent chapters return to an alternating narrative structure. For instance, chapters 5–7 focus solely on Belton. Chapters 8 and 9 feature Bernard as the focal character. Chapters 10–12 revisit Belton's trials, with chapters 13 and 14 returning to examinations of Bernard's tribulations. By chapter 15, Griggs reunites his protagonists and remains devoted to a style of narrative structure that includes both. By this stage in the novel, Griggs's alternative narrative structure has solidified both characters' oppositional standpoints into an image of warring angelic forces reminiscent of Milton's epic.

One of the techniques Griggs uses to mark Belton as a "good" or favored son involves his use of folk dialect and low diction. The first chapter opens by privileging the dialect of the protagonist's mother, Hannah Piedmont. Her words motivate the plot's narrative trajectory and communicate her "determined course of action" to make Belton presentable for his first day of school (*Imperium* 7). Her dialect and low diction critically impacts Belton's characterization, for her speech patterns signify the family's lack of formal education and its members' low socioeconomic status. Physical aspects of setting serve as markers of Belton's disadvantaged status, therefore endearing him to readers even more. As the narrator tours the Piedmont home, which is located in the "humble and commonplace surroundings" of Winchester, Virginia, readers gain a sense of the Piedmont's abject poverty (8). For instance, they live in a "low and squatty house" built of rock consisting of one room, a loft, and a single window (8). Sleeping arrangements are modest at best. Belton sleeps at the foot of a bed he shares with two of his sisters.

As for his apparel, Belton's attire consists of mismatched scraps, which his mother stitches together from various donated garments. Hannah also struggles to head her six-member household unassisted by the husband who abandoned the family long ago. Struggling to live out the meaning of freedom in 1867, a few years after emancipation, Belton and his family come from "small beginning[s]," as the chapter's title indicates. Yet, by chapter's end, Belton's only saving grace results from his fortune in having the opportunity to attend school with the hope of transforming himself into an intellectual citizen of political influence on the world's stage. This importance is not lost on the narrator, who describes the schoolroom as Belton's "royal court" where the favored protagonist will one day emerge as "an uncrowned king" (*Imperium* 10). Projecting that Belton will elevate beyond his state of abject poverty to political fame works in the interest of establishing him as a character to root for and support. To move beyond such dire economic limitations is to begin developing his character through an archetype of the good son.

Bernard, on the other hand, reflects the antithesis of the good son archetype. Through no fault of his own, he immediately falls subject to the politics of infernal characterization on account of his mother's phenotype, beauty, and upper-class standing. Griggs manipulates these characteristics in such a way as to directly inform the preferential treatment Bernard receives at Belton's expense. The moment his mother, Fairfax Belgrave, enters the schoolhouse with Bernard in tow, she receives an entirely different treatment from both the narrator and the white schoolteacher, Tiberius Gracchus Leonard. Unlike Hannah Piedmont, who is described solely on the basis of her dialect and meager household furnishings, Fairfax is introduced to readers by way of the narrator's emphasis on her complexion, hair, and facial beauty. She is so beautiful that the narrator makes time to dote on her "flawless" physical features. Her flawless beauty is not lost upon Mr. Leonard either, who ingratiates himself to exaggerated excess before her presence. He politely removes his hat in her company, honors her with the salutation "madam" in another instance, and wastes no time or effort in deferring to her wishes to have Bernard educated at his school.

Mr. Leonard does not extend this same treatment to Hannah Piedmont. In his interactions with her, he contemptuously agrees to enroll Belton in his school, referring to her son as a "brat" and in a tone "accompanied by a lurking look of hate that made Mrs. Piedmont shudder and long to have her boy at home again" (*Imperium* 13). His unequal treatment of both women indicates biases predicated upon colorism, a psychological politics of color discrimination governed by "a matrix of attitudes about skin color and features in which color, not character, evolve to form a prejudicial sign system."[41] Because Bernard's privileged treatment from Mr. Leonard benefits from this prejudicial sign system, Belton's underdog status is significantly heightened. Made to endure the politics of Mr. Leonard's colorism and preferential treatment for Bernard's intellectual welfare, Belton suffers acts of educational violence.

That violence proves more severe once Mr. Leonard accepts Bernard to his school. As Mr. Leonard returns to his desk to enter his newest student in his register, he unconsciously sits on a "crooked pin" placed in the chair by some mischievous student. Having made a spectacle of himself "before his charming visitor," Mrs. Belgrave, Mr. Leonard reacts by making "an internal oath to exact revenge out of Mrs. Piedmont and her son, who had been the innocent means of his double downfall that day" (*Imperium* 15). Mr. Leonard's oath provides the novel's complication relative to Belton's character development. Setting Belton and Bernard on a collision course, Mr. Leonard generates a rivalry that pits both protagonists as metaphorical expressions of Milton's war between heaven and hell.

Chapter 4 elevates this rivalry further. Specifically, the chapter underscores Mr. Leonard's mistreatment of Belton as a biased force of satanic energy. It is his satanic mistreatment of Belton that motivates the good son's emerging transition into an infernal hero who will later be saved by supernal grace. Once Belton successfully vanquishes this formidable foe, he slowly transitions into a militant infernal hero in the cause of liberty. Entitled, "The Turning of a Worm," chapter 4 directly alludes to Mr. Leonard as a satanic force while indirectly reflecting upon Belton's rebellious spirit. From the chapter's outset, Mr. Leonard is described as both "an infamous scoundrel" and intellectual who possesses a laudatory amount of "brain power" (*Imperium* 23). He proves especially detrimental to Belton's development by choosing "Bernard [as] his pet and Belton as his "pet aversion" on whom "he might expend his spleen" (23.) As the student rivals mature into late adolescence, Mr. Leonard soon discovers both possess extraordinary measures of intellectual talent and ambition. Consequently, he intervenes to Belton's detriment, bending "all of his energies to improve Bernard's mind" and leaving Griggs's favored protagonist to fend for himself. Undaunted by Mr. Leonard's neglect, Belton meets the academic challenges before him and refuses to allow Bernard to "gain an inch on him" by the time of high school graduation.

With commencement approaching, Mr. Leonard exploits the occasion in the hopes of publicly exalting Bernard at the expense of humiliating Belton. He challenges his "two oratorical gladiators" to compose and deliver commencement addresses which will be judged by public officials. As is to be expected, Mr. Leonard coaches and prepares Bernard for victory while neglecting Belton altogether. After Belton and Bernard successfully deliver their speeches, the judges have difficulty declaring a winner. Even though they recognize Belton's oration as superior to Bernard's, their colorism makes it difficult for them "to see nigger blood triumph over any Anglo-Saxon blood" (*Imperium* 29). Unable to resolve their prejudicial dilemma, Mr. Leonard solves the problem by unscrupulous means. He declares Bernard the winner "on the ground[s] of good behavior" to the vehement displeasure of the audience. Consequently, he serves as the worm and foil to Belton's academic ambitions (30).

Despite Mr. Leonard's wicked intervention, Bernard fails to receive the prized gold medal because Belton anticipates he will be slighted and has acted accordingly. In an act of preemptive revenge, Belton rigs the dais the night before commencement. When Mr. Leonard attempts to bestow the prized medal upon Bernard, he suffers a second public humiliation. He falls through a trap door into a pit of cold water and loses the medal, to the amusement of the audience. Mr. Leonard's literal and figurative fall "from the sublime to the ridiculous" critically impacts Belton's characterization. First, it points to Belton's transition into a militant or infernal hero, who conducts himself by doing evil unto others as they have unto him. As Briggs expresses, Belton is "no longer a passive observer" but a character who "shows that he has learned how to meet prejudice with subversive, even vengeful action."[42]

In response to Belton's subversive deed, Mr. Leonard draws his pay and leaves town. The narrator, commenting on Mr. Leonard's humiliating departure, sarcastically concludes: "Sometimes, even a worm will turn when trodden upon." Worm, in this context, conveys a serpentine connotation, allusively punning on the patriotic motto "Don't Tread on Me." By signifying on the Gadsden flag's serpentine image and motto, Trout, the narrator, caricatures Mr. Leonard in a symbolic image of satanic energy. This pun also identifies Belton as a victor who has slowly begun his transition into an infernal hero who bears a resemblance to Milton's Satan.

The rattlesnake depicted on the Gadsden flag is poised in the position of self-defense, and this loaded rhetorical symbol relates to Belton as much as it specifically refers to Mr. Leonard's undoing. Here, word and image symbolically convey resistance to political tyranny analogous to Belton's act of revenge. Associated with the original 13 colonies as far back as the mid-seventeenth century, the rattlesnake increasingly came to serve as a loaded visual symbol of colonial America by the time of the American Revolution. Benjamin Franklin explains the symbolic metaphor in a 1775 article from the *Pennsylvania Journal*, reconciling its loaded political meaning in tandem with the patriotic spirit of the times. According to Franklin, the serpent's symbolic meaning signifies the "temper and conduct of America," specifically epitomizing unparalleled courage in that it "never begins an attack, nor, when once engaged, ever surrenders."[43] When the narrator puns on the resilient nature of the national symbol by mocking Mr. Leonard at the end of the chapter, he similarly identifies Belton as an aspiring political rebel who instigates the teacher's demise and ruin. Even more ironic, Belton vanquishes his foe and aspires to the office of political rebellion as a direct extension of his educational tyrant's infernal curriculum. Though uncited in Mr. Leonard's curriculum, it is virtually impossible not to consider Milton as an influential companion informing Belton's militant response to his teacher's acts of educational violence.

Mr. Leonard's curriculum may be regarded as infernal since its pedagogical values stem from political gospels that preach revolt against tyrannical abuses. Interestingly, the bulk of Mr. Leonard's curriculum derives from sources by and about patriotic rebels.

Here, Milton constitutes an (in)visible presence in much the same way that Toni Morrison finds it impossible to dismiss the range of Africanisms present in literary works devoid of black characters. Pursuant to Morrison's assertions, black absence legitimates the very presence that is seemingly invisible. Milton's absented presence announces itself similarly within the context of literary traditions where writers preach political rebellion in the pursuit of liberty.

It is hardly coincidental that Mr. Leonard's curriculum places such a strong emphasis on U.S. history and the art of rhetoric. Additionally, it cannot be surprising that Griggs's protagonists are greatly invested in this knowledge. According to the narrator, Belton and Bernard "throw their whole souls into" this canon of literature that gives "coloring to the whole of their lives" (*Imperium* 25). They specifically enjoy studying the American Revolution as evidenced by their willingness to immerse themselves "in the spirit of [the] heroic age" in addition to taking delight in "the story of the rebellion against the yoke of England" (25). They also share a fascination for the study of rhetoric. Thus, they learn the art of declamation by turning their minds "to the sublime in literature" (25). Texts that appeal to them most include those recording "the most heroic deeds of man, of whatever nationality" (25). Leonidas, Louis Kossuth, Robert Emmett, Martin Luther, and Patrick Henry represent several of the revolutionary writers informing these aspiring political rebels' infernal education.

Given this impressive pantheon of freedom writers, Milton's literal absence seems suspect. Indeed, it calls such great attention to itself as to make him a very present help in times of political trouble. Gilbert and Gubar offer a precedent for just this form of Miltonic presence when in their reading of *Wuthering Heights* they recognize the epic writer's "absence [as] itself a presence."[44] Gray pushes the boundaries of Milton's (in)visibility in literary texts still further when he acknowledges Milton as shining "'dark with excessive bright'" in various Victorian texts.[45] An example of how Milton's presence can materialize under such circumstances occurs on the signifying levels of word usage that prove so rhetorically loaded in their associations with the epic writer that they mark his presence without directly naming him in the texts of later writers.

Gray makes another significant contribution concerning routes of transmission and literary influence relative to Milton. As has been discussed in previous chapters, Milton's influence is so wide and predominant within the English language that it is somewhat impossible for later writers to refer to certain words, images, or modes of innovative form without at the same time performing homage to him. Themes of warring angels, rebellious political orators, or the focus on cultivating a first-rate education in the classics or canonical literature are just a few additional examples that could be added to Gray's catalogue of "devils," "snakes," "temptation," "creation," "wandering," and others.[46] Furthermore, in some instances, later writers may not even be aware of an intertextual indebtedness to Milton. As Cheryl A. Wall notes, "some texts circulate so widely in a culture that people do not need to have read them to quote them. Even the illiterate may make literary allusions."[47] In other words, certain themes, concepts, and rhetorical figurations are so intensely associated with Milton as to infuse later works with his presence even when he is not directly or expressly named. This system of absented presence informs a tropological network of profound (im)possibilities where Milton's uncited influence in literary works proves so (in)visible because certain ideas, themes, and poetic conceits are so biblically Miltonic that to deny him as an intertext would in and of itself prove irresponsible.

In keeping with Gray's equation of Miltonic influence, the epic writer enjoys preeminent status as a political rebel in the cause of liberty. Like his figures of paradise, warring images of heaven and hell, or poetics of fallenness, his devotion to themes of liberty in concert with these loaded signifiers reflects one of any given number of tropological (im)possibilities that call his presence into being, existence, or recollection. Such is the case where Mr. Leonard's curriculum is concerned. That Milton goes uncited in this curriculum devoted to patriotism, liberty, scholarly elocution, and rhetorical training appropriated from "the sublime in literature" that instructs pupils in declaiming "the most heroic deeds of man, of whatever nationality," reflects a profound impossibility of Miltonic influence (*Imperium* 25). Especially given Belton's and Bernard's subsequent political trajectories, it is virtually impossible to conceive that they could go on to distinguish themselves as race leaders without Milton's instructional influence.

Their satanic companionship with Milton manifests almost immediately in terms of their political aspirations. For example, both begin to feel the flames of political dissent and crave opportunities to emulate the political heroes they have been studying. Their respective speeches at commencement evidence this desire. For instance, Belton delivers his speech, "The Contribution of the Anglo-Saxon to the Cause of Human Liberty," and its message enflames the hearts of his audience and induces them to "burst forth in applause" once he concludes (*Imperium* 27). Bernard selects a theme devoted to "Robert Emmett," another dissident political writer. His speech strikes an emotional chord with his listeners as well but has an opposite rhetorical effect that moves them to tears. These distinct responses to their respective speeches underscores Belton and Bernard's angelic rivalry through embedded rhetorical codes that showcase Griggs's rich intertextual heritage.

The audience's contrasting receptions to the speeches parallel Plutarch's description of the declamatory eloquence of Tiberius Gracchus and Tiberius Gaius. In *Roman Lives*, Plutarch, notes Tiberius Gracchus's "features, expression, and bearing were calm and unassuming whereas Gaius was lively and intense." These features impact both brothers' styles of oratorical delivery. Concerning these oratorical styles, Plutarch adds, "the way Gaius spoke was emotive and designed to provoke indignation in his audience, whereas Tiberius was less harsh and aimed more at arousing pity."[48] That Belton's eloquent delivery mirrors Tiberius Caius's aggressive flair, whereas Bernard's recalls the refined restraint synonymous with Tiberius Gracchus proves particularly interesting since Griggs names Mr. Leonard after one of these brothers of Roman antiquity. In naming Mr. Leonard after Tiberius Gracchus, Griggs subtly inflects Belton's character with an aggressive militant temperament.

Griggs complicates this subtle aspect of character development even more when the plot journeys to Milton's hell on the demonic grounds of the Imperium. At that stage of the novel, Belton's and Bernard's political temperaments are reversed. The reversal of their character traits suggests that Belton, in particular, has undergone some radical transformation in between this stage of plot and the novel's third section. While also highlighting the pair as Miltonic opposites, Griggs's mediation of their personalities by naming Mr. Leonard after Tiberius Gracchus further attests to Meade's assertion that the author "was a scholar who was well read in many fields."[49] These signs of fragmentary influence also reveal the complex subtleties of Griggs's intertextual artistry. As a result, these subtle codes of influence reiterate the need to examine the embedded traces of early black writers' "double-voiced" companionship with writers in the Western literary tradition such as Plutarch, Milton, and others.

This subtle example of Griggs's double-voiced companionship with Plutarch suggests the author's rhetorical affiliation with Milton and his satanic energy as an expression of political rebelliousness are not merely coincidental. Griggs's companionship with Milton as a demonic sign system plays a critical role at this stage of the novel, for it is the point at which Belton is poised to evolve into a militant infernal hero whose words and deeds underscore a dissident temperament given to militant displays of heroic leadership. Over the course of the next few chapters, Belton shows signs of this militant edge. That is, he transforms into a young political rebel for racial justice. In chapter 5, he encounters and is befriended by a benefactor who recognizes "the flame of liberty" existing within the protagonist's heart (*Imperium* 34). Belton's commencement speech appears in the "leading journals of England" to wide acclaim, eventually garnering the attention and favor of Mr. V. M. King (32). From the moment he reads Belton's speech, Mr. King is convinced that God has sent a black messiah who will effectively champion the cause of racial uplift.

The introduction to Mr. King's character calls attention to the narrative's heightened interest in the rhetoric of liberty. Griggs uses the word no less than seven times throughout the chapter, a shift in rhetoric that emphasizes the messianic role Belton will fulfill once his character development reaches completion. Meanwhile, Mr. King values education as a vital enterprise for struggling blacks during the Reconstruction era. He believes that "the young negro" will soon catch "that most contagious of diseases, [a] devotion to liberty [that will subsequently] infect his soul" (*Imperium* 33). He further believes the race will, in time, "deify liberty as the Anglo-Saxon had done." He predicts liberty will prove so vital that

African Americans will risk martyrdom to attain it. These assessments lead him to conclude that they will ask for liberty and "if refused, to slay or be slain" shall become their revolutionary creed (34). Recognizing Belton's messianic potential in the cause of liberty, Mr. King decides to pay for Belton's college expenses at the fictional Stowe University. Named after Harriet Beecher Stowe, the university provides the demonic training grounds where Belton fully transforms into and practices the militant vocation of Milton's infernal hero.

Stowe University serves as an infernal training ground. It trains and prepares students for political warfare against hegemonic practices of racial tyranny and injustice. Moreover, its student body is comprised of "an immense army of young men and women...being trained in the very best manner" as stewards who would subsequently "go forth to grapple with the great [racial] problems before them" (*Imperium* 40). This mission critically shapes Belton's aspirations to serve his people as a political rebel and hero dedicated to liberty and racial equality, and it is on the institution's demonic grounds where the militant activist enjoys his first taste of political success. Referred to as "a young rebel" in the chapter's title, Belton fulfills the expectations of an infernal hero by leading a revolution for racial equality against the university's white administration. Upon his discovery that the black "vice-president of the faculty" is barred from dining at the same table as his white colleagues, Belton leads a revolt in order to rectify this instance of racial discrimination (42). That the thought of racial discrimination "burned him," indicates the intensity of his infernal passions for justice (44). Furthermore, in leading this black revolt, Belton prefigures his membership in the Imperium near the end of the novel. His passions inspire him to create a secret organization of black revolt. He adopts the motto Equality or Death as the group's password, a phrase echoing Patrick Henry's famous outcry, "Give me liberty or give me death."

Interestingly, Satan in *Paradise Lost* lives by a similar rebellious creed. In his contentious argument with the archangel Michael in book 6, Satan refuses to surrender at the prospect of his utter ruin. Michael, while in the midst of celestial battle, admonishes Satan to return to hell with his infernal crew before "this avenging sword begin thy doom / Or some more sudden vengeance winged from God / Precipitate thee with augmented pain!" (*PL* 6.278–80). Satan ignores Michael's threat and warning of impending doom, declaring his intention to "style / The strife of glory, which we mean to win / Or turn this Heav'n itself into the Hell / Thou fablest" (*PL* 6.289–92). Nor does he relinquish his obstinate stance when in battle he suffers pain from Michael's mighty sword. Though "his pride [was] / Humbled by such rebuke so far beneath / His confidence to equal God in power," Satan remains committed to devising new schemes of warfare against heaven's monarch instead of retreating or surrendering in defeat (*PL* 6.341–43). His do-or-die mentality obviously wins him favor among his legion, for even in book 1 he has no problem reviving their abject spirits into action. Acknowledged as a "general," "their great sultan," "great commander," and "great emperor" within a space of 40 lines, Satan, an infernal hero who is sold out to martyrdom, operates by the very dissident spirit of rebellion Belton embraces in his revolt at Stowe University (*PL* 1.337, 348, 358, 378).

Trout gives some indication of Belton's rebellious spirit and its impact upon the youth's student legion. For instance, the narrator reveals Belton "swept the students away from the lethargic harbor in which they had been anchored" (*Imperium* 45). When the university president reads the students' complaint, dismisses their petition, and orders them to retire from the assembly at the conclusion of the service, Belton assumes command and leads the student body to successful revolt. Under his leadership, "not a student moved," and when the president dismisses them a second time, they respond, "at a signal from Belton," by raising signs that read Equality or Death (45, 46). The administration ultimately relents to the students' demands. Their victory inspires the narrator to reflect that then, "a new Negro, self-respecting, fearless, and determined in the assertion of his rights was at hand" (46). This pivotal moment crystalizes Belton's political transition into an infernal hero.[50]

Despite Belton's political success, Griggs does not limit the protagonist's characterization by making him a static resemblance to Milton's infernal hero. Instead, he differentiates his protagonist from Satan, tempering Belton's infernal impulses with characterizations of supernal grace. Belton undergoes this gradual metamorphosis as he learns to embrace a Christian heroism grounded in acts of perfect passivity and the "might of weakness." His metamorphosis begins in chapter 7 under the sermonic wisdom of Dr. Lovejoy, the university president and commencement speaker (*Imperium* 64). This moment of spiritual transfiguration holds political implications for Belton's future greatness. On one interpretive level, it guides his political vision and political transition into his becoming a so-called accommodationist leader. On still another interpretive plain, Belton's willful subjection to Dr. Lovejoy's divine supernal wisdom contributes to his differentiation from Milton's Satan even though both leaders figure as fallen stars and lords of satanic re-creation.

Dr. Lovejoy's address, "The Kingdom of God Is within Us," resonates strongly with Belton and plants the seeds of Christian heroism in the young rebel's heart. Lovejoy's message begins by acknowledging that the students' collective responsibility will play an integral "part in the adjusting of positions between the negro and Anglo-Saxon races of the South" (*Imperium* 49). While society may designate them heroes for their courageous acts, he advises them not to "play with fire, merely for the sake of the glare that it may cast upon" them individually (50). Doing so, he believes, will compromise the efficacy of their social and political ministries as race leaders. He also adds they "shall become true patriots" provided they live their lives according to this supernal gospel. Because "none more readily incorporated the principles enumerated as a part of their living lives" than Belton did, Dr. Lovejoy's sermon plants the first seeds of Christian heroism in the protagonist's heart (51). He is inspired to walk boldly and circumspectly within a political calling that eschews militancy as a feasible gospel of black revolt. He has, in effect, been saved by supernal grace and born again into a doctrine of perfect passivity that exemplifies heroism through the "might of weakness."

Belton's might of weakness is perfected when an "insanely jealous" classmate humiliates him by substituting a putrid-smelling sock for the stylish silk handkerchief he planned to use as a fashion accessory. As class valedictorian, Belton intends to give "the speech of his life" on this occasion (*Imperium* 53). Contrary to his hopes, he experiences a loss of paradise in the sense that the room where he delivers his address is "decorated with choice flowers" and presents the "appearance of the Garden of Eden" (54). Overcome with emotional pride while delivering his valedictory address, Belton wipes away his tears with the odious sock instead of his "supposed handkerchief" (55). Shamed by the audience's uproarious laughter, he storms from the platform, vowing to "find and kill the rascal who had played that trick on him" (55).

If not for Dr. Lovejoy's intervention, Belton would have made good on this vow. He purchases a pistol, intent upon seeking out the roommate who he correctly believes orchestrated his loss of paradise. However, Dr. Lovejoy's tender chastening tempers Belton's rage and helps the young graduate to recognize revenge as an "unholy passion" that should be rejected (*Imperium* 56). Because Dr. Lovejoy specifically references Christ's humility in dying on the cross for others, his message serves as Belton's second salvific moment, amounting to what the narrator describes as Belton's "narrow escape" from suffering the consequences of militant revenge. Moreover, Dr. Lovejoy's gospel doubles as a redemptive lesson in perfect passivity.

Perfected by these Christian ethics of supernal grace, Belton learns to leave vengeance to God. To underscore how critical this intervention is in terms of the plot, the narrator predicts the world will ultimately be made to see "how much it owes to God for planting that lesson in Belton's heart." Chapter 1 has already indicated that Belton will save the Sun of the Nineteenth Century from setting in the carnage of human casualties. As a result, this latest prophecy concerning the value of Dr. Lovejoy's instructional lesson enriches the intertextual importance of Belton's differentiation from the infernal hero he resembles in terms of his militant temperament. Dr. Lovejoy's lesson, with its spiritual and messianic gospel, directly relates to Belton's metamorphosis of character by the time the latter rejects a strategy of open war on the Imperium's demonic grounds in the final stages of the novel. This spiritual change in his character complicates static readings that would simply interpret Belton as an accommodating embodiment of political weakness and enervated manhood.

Rather, Belton's perceived weakness identifies him as a Miltonic heir who subscribes to the perfect passivity exhibited by characters such as the Lady in Milton's *Comus*, the Son in *Paradise Lost* and

Paradise Regained, and the hero of *Samson Agonistes.* Situated among these Miltonic companions, Belton exemplifies a Christian heroism that differentiates his character from Satan and undermines previous readings of the protagonist as a political accommodationist. These moments further identify Belton's peculiar character as an infernal hero who has been saved by supernal grace. Griggs's narrator capitalizes upon this moment, using it as a rhetorical bridge for understanding Belton's political vision in the last third of the novel. This chapter marks the completion of Belton's character development. Accordingly, it ends by asking readers to consider, "what will he do with it?" (59).

The novel's third section takes place on the Imperium's demonic grounds following a series of events that try Belton's salvation by supernal grace. Married to Antoinette Nermal, Belton struggles to secure gainful employment commensurate with his academic credentials. Rather than conforming to the militant stance adopted by the "army of educated malcontents and insurrection breeders" of his race who share his same experience, he leaves town and disguises himself as a female nurse in order to financially provide for his family (*Imperium* 91). Belton has also survived a lynching and a white surgeon's attempts to cut him open on a dissecting board, presumably for the purpose of advancing research in the interest of scientific racism. When Belton kills the surgeon in self-defense, he is subsequently tried for murder. The case reaches the Supreme Court and Bernard, who has suffered personal tragedies of his own, successfully delivers "the speech of his life" before the nation's highest tribunal. The Supreme Court reverses the lower court's decision and Belton is soon acquitted. This "tragic experience...burned all the remaining dross out of Belton's nature and prepared him for the even more terrible ordeal to follow in after years." Thus, Belton appears at the Imperium as a metallurgically purified hero. "Tried in the fire" of several challenging experiences, he lives by a political philosophy governed by a Christian heroism of spiritual restraint and inaction.

Chapter 15 marks the novel's descent into hell by reuniting Belton and Bernard on the fictional campus of Thomas Jefferson College. The college is situated within a "high stone wall enclosure" and structure that stands "four stories high" and spans "two hundred feet long and one hundred and eighty feet wide" (*Imperium* 122). Described as the "Capitol of [the Imperium's] Government," the Imperium's palatial headquarters echo Milton's Pandaemonium in terms of the building's imposing size and the society's political mission and underground proceedings (133). For instance, the Imperium convenes its sessions in "a large room containing [145] desks arranged in a semi-circular form" located four stories underground (127). Its representative membership is "modeled after that of the Unites States" and consists of "one member for every fifty thousand citizens," with branch legislatures in each state. Logistically, the room's semicircle arrangement bears a striking resemblance to the U.S. Congress. At the same time, the Imperium's subterranean location, coupled with the secret society's commitment to rebellion in the cause of liberty, generates an allusive parody of Pandaemonium.

More important, the Imperium's ideological origins and affiliations with Thomas Jefferson's writings reference Milton's absent but "diffuse" presence in this latter stage of the novel. From its inception, the Imperium embraced a twofold mission of nationalist rebellion and racial uplift. Its political agenda sought to "secure for the free negroes all the rights and privileges of men, according to the teachings of Thomas Jefferson" (*Imperium* 130). As author of the Declaration of Independence, and therefore one of the nation's foremost founding fathers, Jefferson holds the political distinction of creating the early republic's political gospel of liberty. Jefferson definitely exerted a significant degree of influence upon Griggs. Embracing Jefferson's political ideals at this stage of the novel continues to strengthen Griggs's intertextual relationship with Milton. As John Shawcross notes, Jefferson unequivocally ranks as one of Milton's heirs. Traces of Milton's influence in his writings surface particularly in the years "from 1776 through 1791, yield[ing] extensive notes from *Of Reformation* and *Of Prelatical Episcopacy, Reason of Church-Government* and *An Apology for Smectymnuus*, and of course various sections of *Paradise Lost*."[51] Shawcross's findings reveal the extent to which Milton found favor with Jefferson pursuant to his thoughts about liberty and government. That the Imperium expressly identifies ideologically with the founding father's writings likewise translates to its author's forging of an allusive companionship with Milton on the demonic grounds of hell.

When Belton invites Bernard to Jefferson College, he intends to test his former rival's race loyalty before apprising him of the Imperium's existence and its "holy mission" (*Imperium* 153). The test involves Belton apprising his former rival about the existence of a hypothetical black nationalist organization devoted to unifying blacks and redressing their political grievances. Belton explains his intentions to betray this race conspiracy and solicits Bernard's support. Bernard refuses, dubbing Belton an "infernal scoundrel" and referring to members of this hypothetical society as "sublime patriots" (125). Bernard's ornamental epithets articulate an understanding of political war that invests in and inverts Milton's satanic motifs as a militant politics of racial uplift. His rejoinder tropes with infernal and supernal language, inverting these denotative signifiers as a rhetorical means for classifying what he interprets as competing political orientations. By recognizing Belton's feigned race treason as infernal, Bernard realigns interpretations of seditious acts that would typically register as demonic for orthodox readers. By contrast, his acknowledgment of the hypothetical society's members as "sublime patriots" communicates his endorsement of militant rebellion as a celestial activity of racial uplift. Even when Belton threatens Bernard with death, the latter refuses to comply with his former rival's infernal plot. Ultimately, Bernard's Miltonic interpretation of the hypothetical society's political mission proves he can be trusted as a prospective member of the Imperium. It also proves he possesses the demonic attributes required for siding with the devil's party without knowing that such a society actually exists.

Bernard's race loyalty facilitates his formal introduction to the Imperium's actual existence and its membership. Satisfied that Bernard has successfully passed the test of race loyalty, Belton escorts the Imperium's newest member to its demonic grounds. There, Bernard meets a cheering crowd consisting "of the conspirators whom [he] would not betray" (*Imperium* 127). After this greeting, Belton, who holds the demonic office of "arch conspirator," apprises Bernard of the Imperium's mission, historical origins, and political philosophies. This indoctrination into the Imperium's political structure prepares Bernard for his inauguration as president of this infernal society committed to the messianic liberation of the racially oppressed (127).

The subsequent chapter, "Crossing the Rubicon," exposes the Imperium's insurrectionary labors on behalf of the race within a setting reminiscent of Milton's infernal council. For instance, an act of terrorism against a black postmaster and his family "by a mob of white demons" arouses the Imperium to righteous and political indignation. In the interest of developing insurrectionary strategies, the Imperium's members call for an infernal council. The purpose of this meeting is to address the accumulation of tyrannical practices pervading the nation. Bernard inaugurates this series of oratorical resolutions with a speech that calls for "open war" not unlike Moloch's radical political vision as expressed in book 2 of *Paradise Lost*. Bernard's physical disposition strengthens this rhetorical affiliation with Milton's infernal crew, for his countenance bears "latent fires" and he speaks in tones of "biting sarcasm," "withering irony," and with a "swelling rage" and "glowing fervor" (*Imperium* 139–40). Finally, his infernal eloquence matches the militant gospel he preaches. His political sermon advocates the motto We Must Be Free and urges the Imperium's members to "strike a blow for freedom" even if doing so results in death (148).

That Bernard's militant gospel rhetorically coincides with the chapter's title intensifies Griggs's efforts to strengthen a satanic companionship with Milton on demonic grounds. An idiom designating the passing of a point of no return, the phrase "crossing the Rubicon" specifically refers to the river in Italy that Julius Caesar crossed with his army in 49 BC. His passage across the Rubicon "violated the law that forbade a general to lead an army out of the province to which he was assigned."[52] Thus, Caesar's actions constituted an insurrectionary act or "declaration of war against the Roman Senate."[53] Within this context, Trout's nautical metaphor of crossing the Rubicon translates to Moloch's call for "open war," racializing and adapting the phrase to fit the Imperium's rebellious mission. At one point during Bernard's speech, the race leader refuses to believe those who "tell us that a sea is in our way, so deep that we cannot cross" (*Imperium* 149). Insisting that crossing the sea of tyranny and racial injustice is a doable process, he incites the audience to adopt a do-or-die commitment to freedom. These expressions of radical rebellion pave the way for Belton's differentiated politics of satanic re-creation. His political speech act preaches a gospel of black nationalism and Christian heroism that have been perfected by the supernal grace of Milton's perfect passivity and purged of a satanic desire to pursue open war.

To underscore this attribute of Miltonic differentiation in black political thought, Trout narratively titles the subsequent chapter, "The Storm's Master" as an ornamental epithet for describing Belton's heroic passivity in the midst of political turbulence. Extending the series of speeches associated with Milton's infernal council, two speakers precede Belton before he addresses the Imperium and exercises the "might of weakness" that marks him as a peculiar infernal hero. The first speaker to follow Bernard's radical gospel champions the cause of staying on U.S. soil rather than emigrating or undertaking a "wholesale exodus" to some other country (*Imperium* 150). He also rallies for amalgamation with whites, an argument that again echoes Pandaemonium in book 10 since it incites the audience to respond with a "storm of hisses." This latter speech hints at the "intellectual metamorphosis" Griggs would adopt in his later writings.[54] According to Meade, this radical change in the prolific author's political stance resulted in a more strategically conciliatory tone and rhetoric. Specifically, "Griggs no longer was preoccupied with fighting, but rather now he sought interracial cooperation."[55] The Imperium's response to this more conciliatory political stance meets with vehement disapproval. Their reaction, therefore, indicates that Belton will tread in dangerous waters should he preach a similar gospel of political conciliation.

A second speaker addresses the Imperium and advocates emigration to the African Congo. His gospel of revolt is met with a modicum of success. Thus, Belton finds himself in a precarious situation by the time he mounts the political rostrum. Conscious of the oratorical dynamics and the dangerous waters he will tread with his gospel of differentiated revolt, he begins in an oratorical strain consistent with Moloch's declaration for open war. This opening message allows him to establish an ethos that can appease his audience long enough for him to gain their support as Satan must do when he has to follow the rebellious speeches rendered by Moloch, Belial, Mammon, and Beelzebub in *Paradise Lost*. Commenting on Belton's rhetorical effectiveness here, the narrator describes the effect of the race leader's oratory. Belton's infernal eloquence struck "a match to the powder magazine which Bernard had left uncovered in all their bosoms" (*Imperium* 151). This description of martial weaponry evidences Belton's success as a hero whose differentiated gospel of black revolt rides the storm of political controversy as he successfully delivers a "defense of the south" to the consternation of his listening audience (153).

When he announces his intention to defend the South, the audience expresses disapproval. They respond to his radical plan as a "current [that] was so strong that it was death to all future usefulness to try to breast it" (*Imperium* 153). Belton withstands this storm of controversy, however, intent upon gleaning good from the negative response he receives from his audience. This rhetorical move equates to Satan's creed, "Evil be thou good," for it itemizes what Belton sees as the beneficial by-products of slavery and other racial injustices borne by African Americans throughout history. Concerning "the labor question," for example, he expresses an optimistic outlook on "the prejudice and pride" that prohibits blacks from leaving lower forms of labor yet excludes them from securing more professional jobs (*Imperium* 156). For Belton, this paradox leaves blacks "in undisputed possession of a whole kingdom of labor" where they may successfully "furnish labor for [their] own talent" (156, 157). Instead of viewing these injustices negatively, Belton recognizes opportunities for blacks to enjoy the blessings of a freedom that will compel them to become entrepreneurs in a range of vocations and professions previously denied them.

His discourse on civil rights takes a similar stance. He asserts that blacks were unprepared to responsibly enjoy the rights pertaining to citizens "when they first belonged to us" (*Imperium* 157). Now, he takes pride in the advancements his race continues to make in the name of civilization (157). Belton also sees it as futile to complain about the schools "maintained by the Southerner," since the curriculum of these institutions introduced the Imperium to such "apostles of human liberty" as Washington, Jefferson, and Patrick Henry. This is the same line of thinking that informs

Belton's championing of cultural paternalism and his emphasis on forging a literary companionship with Milton and other canonical writers in the Western tradition. Subsequent discussions pertaining to the "courts of justice," "mob law," and "politics" sustain his more conservative line of political reasoning that differentiates its ideas from militant ideas of open rebellion. With each topic, Belton either mitigates the injustices perpetrated by flawed hegemonic systems or asks listeners to assume an "impartial view" of their disenfranchised circumstances in the interest of some better good (160). These conciliatory observations provide the political backdrop for his five-point resolution that lays the groundwork for his peculiar gospel of black nationalism.

Belton's resolution is peculiar in the sense that it makes the bold recommendation that the Imperium become transparent and "no longer conceal" its identity from whites. This recommendation gestures toward a social amalgamation of the races that will subsequently enable whites to recognize the need for black equality in interacting with them and discovering their commitment to attaining liberty. Only if these measures fail to secure civil rights does Belton propose the taking over of state government and the creation of a separatist state on Texan soil. This alternative measure indicates Belton's willingness to consider separatist aims. According to this proposal, he is willing to concede to a political vision where blacks will live peaceably as a separate nation and defend themselves against anyone attempting to invade their land or encroach upon their efforts to exist as a sovereign state.

In espousing a gospel of social amalgamation and black separatism, Belton articulates a political vision comprised of infernal and supernal motivations. Briggs is not totally incorrect when he regards Belton's stance as indicative of the peculiar infernal hero's "final lesson in passive resistance."[56] However, Belton views this same stance of passivity as a mark of strength. Recognizing this blend of infernal and supernal heroism, he classifies his political standpoint as "primarily pacific" with the added disclaimer that it proves "firm and unyielding" (*Imperium* 164). Ultimately, Belton refutes Bernard's declaration for open war based on his firm but assertively tempered argumentation. It "blasted away all opposition," enabling the Imperium's "ship of state [to] sail placidly on the bosom of the erstwhile troubled sea" (165). With Belton at its helm, the Imperium has an opportunity to stage a form of black revolt that calms the troubled sea of race injustice but according to the political tenets of a gospel of perfect passivity. The Imperium's members swiftly adopt Belton's resolutions, but the quiet hero's greatest challenge yet awaits him.

The novel ends with Belton's execution following the tendering of his resignation from the Imperium. Bernard, unsatisfied with Belton's resolutions, enjoins his compatriot to adopt a newly drafted plan of action that proves more militant in its political scope. Bernard remains pessimistic that whites will ever admit blacks as equals. Thus, he drafts a proposal recommending that the Imperium remain a covert insurrectionary government. He further recommends the "quiet purchase of all Texas land contiguous to states and territories of the Union" for the express purpose of building fortifications and mounting a seditious plot against the United States (*Imperium* 167). Ultimately, his plan endeavors to seize the state capitol with the added hope of demanding the surrender and ceding of Texas and Louisiana to blacks for the creation of a separate empire of their own. Belton is the only member who rejects this proposal once it is brought before the Imperium. He rejects this plan because he finds it treasonous to U.S. nationhood.

Belton's execution facilitates Trout's political conversion, leading this "apostle of liberty" within the Imperium to bemoan the hero's martyrdom in the novel's final chapter. According to Trout, when Belton fell, "the spirit of conservatism in the Negro, race fell with him" also (*Imperium* 175). More important, Belton's political influence saved the race from Miltonic ruin. His passively firm political convictions "snatched [the race] from the edge of the precipice of internecine war, from whose steep, heights we had in our rage, decided to leap into the dark gulf beneath." Given the several allusions to Milton throughout the novel, Trout's reference to the precipice points to another profound (im)possibility of Miltonic influence. The series of Miltonic allusions thus far make it impossible to overlook this figurative phrase as an allusive echo to the geographical spot that Satan and his peers are hurled from when the Messiah drives them out of heaven. Satan instigates this intertextual relationship when he remembers "the fiery surge that from the precipice / Of Heav'n received [them] falling" (*PL* 1.172–74). His account of their fall from grace also recalls Raphael's recounting of the same event.

In addition, Trout's consideration of the sacrifice Belton pays for his rebellious political ideology alludes to Raphael's account of the overthrow from heaven. His language pays intertextual homage to "the dark gulf beneath" while echoing the "bottomless pit" and "dark foundations" mentioned by Raphael (*PL* 6.866, 870). In snatching the race from the precipice of "internecine war," Belton differentiates himself from the fallenness Satan represents in book 6, performing what is arguably his most heroic act of perfect passivity in the novel. It especially facilitates Trout's political conversion in light of Bernard's radically distinct proposal. From Trout's perspective, the contrast between both protagonists' political outlooks makes Belton's gospel of black revolt a more feasible and less destructive means for leveling systems of uneven development at the close of the nineteenth century.

When he considers what was lost through Belton's sacrifice in relative contrast to Bernard's militant style of political leadership, Trout considers it a necessity to "reveal the existence of the Imperium that it might be broken up or watched." Because he believes Bernard's satanic temperament shows every sign that the militant race leader means to seek violent retribution against whites, Trout believes the Imperium constitutes "a serious menace to the peace of the world." Indeed, Bernard's lusts for carnage prove great, as evidenced by his expressed desire to have whites serve as "richer food for the buzzards to whom [he has] solemnly vowed to give [their] flesh" (*Imperium* 176). This statement of radical intent convinces Trout that a new political vision is in order. He comes to recognize the Imperium as a potentially "serious menace to the peace of the world" under Bernard's militant leadership.

Finally, his realization inspires supernal knowledge concerning the limitations associated with Bernard's infernal politics. Trout articulates this realization in satanic language by itemizing the potential threats the Imperium poses to society. He uses words such as "spark," "dynamite," "lighted fuses," "ignite," and "terrific explosion" as signifiers of the doom that awaits larger society beyond the veil of the Imperium's insurrectionary strategies. Trout extinguishes these infernal possibilities by rejecting Bernard's proposal and exposing the Imperium's existence to the world through the manuscript he bequeaths to Griggs. As a novel, *Imperium in Imperio* preaches a gospel of black revolt that warns whites of the doom they stand to suffer when a class of "educated malcontents" rejects the Christian heroism of perfect passivity as a political model for successfully transforming by any means necessary the national landscape and its systems of uneven development. For Coleman, the novel's ending leaves whites with two proposals: "End the violence and oppression that threatens to nullify the calming voice of Back conservatism as represented by Belton Piedmont, or face a proud and eloquent New Negro who would be much more likely to resort to internecine warfare if the disputation did not change."[57]

Returning to the site of Milton's hell at the close of the nineteenth century relies upon a companionship with the epic writer based on "the great consult" known as the infernal counsel (*PL* 1.798). This prophetic strain of satanic intertextuality warns the nation at large of the structural changes that will need to occur if paradise is ever to be regained on terrains of racial struggle. Stephen Knadler's interpretation of the novel as "sensationalizing patriotism" echoes these sentiments by focusing on the "particular moments of psychological and emotional shock or spectacles of horror that, in the end, put back into play the meaning of an African American citizenship" at the close of the nineteenth century and beyond.[58] Griggs's return to Milton's hell serves as a site of horror and spectacle in the interest of prophesying doom should white readers, in particular, fail to recognize blacks as citizens and treat them accordingly.

At the same time, Griggs's gospel of revolt, through Belton's martyrdom, asks his black readership to reconsider the pitfalls associated with militant rebellion as a political weapon for leveling the playing field of racial equality. Relative to the novel's plot, insurrectionary politics of the kind Bernard promotes potentially produce outcomes that ultimately marginalize blacks as outcasts within the nation at large. Belton may die a martyr, but the potential outcome for Bernard and the Imperium, as Griggs's novels suggest, do not provide viable outcomes either. Thus, Griggs would, in later years, advocate a gospel of "social [or] collective efficiency."

This gospel of interracial harmony asked citizens to reject individualism and self-interests in exchange for a consideration of larger group concerns. While these thoughts would lead many to view him as a "tool of the white South," Griggs held to these convictions and retained his belief "in a rational instead of a violent solution to the South's race relations."[59]

Griggs's companionship with Milton in *Imperium in Imperio*, the last novel in early African American literature to trope substantively with England's epic poet of liberty, predates what has amounted to a controversial gospel of black revolt in literary criticism. Though the novel rejects militant rebellion as a viable weapon for leveling unequal playing fields at the close of the nineteenth century, it still uses the sword of the pen as a civilizing instrument of martial warfare. With Belton as an embodiment of a peculiar infernal hero saved by supernal grace, Griggs heralds a new kind of strength. Emblematic of such Miltonic poetics as perfect passivity and the "might of weakness," Griggs's engagement with these forms of Christian heroism in his novel preaches an artistic gospel for art's sake. It rejects the kind of preaching poetry that "pommels" its audience into submission, as Anna Julia Cooper associated with much of Milton's poetry (*Voice* 182).

Instead, Griggs forged a kind of intertextual companionship with Milton that asked white readers, in particular, to perform political introspection relative to race relations at the dawn of a new century. He facilitates this effort by returning to the demonic grounds of Milton's hell in an attempt to reach across the literary color line in the hopes of appealing to the consciences of white audiences on the level of a shared canonical heritage. Appealing to this segment of his audience through strategies of fragmentary and allusive appropriation produces a (w)rite of passage through Milton that authorizes Griggs's status as a lord of satanic re-creation.

Griggs re-creates himself in satanic fashion by daring to promote a gospel of black revolt that cleaves to Milton's Satan but in ways that seem politically accommodationalist to casual readers. His *Imperium in Imperio* strikes a blow for freedom by intertextually engaging *Paradise Lost* on the demonic grounds of Milton's hell while at the same time performing satanic differentiations from the fallen revolutionary. In differentiating his satanic politics from that of Milton's infernal hero, Griggs achieves something more than merely protesting the wrongs perpetrated against his people. By reaching across the literary color line through uncharacteristic affiliations and rejections of *Paradise Lost* and its satanic poetry, Griggs compels his fit audience of white readers at the turn of the century to journey within the veil of racial interpretation and participate in revolutionary acts of differentiation. *Imperium in Imperio* leads members of this fit audience through some of the horrors of black existence before returning them to the demonic grounds of Milton's hell, where they are forced to consider the lesser of two ideological evils in black political thought. They may choose to be passive bystanders and suffer the carnage of militant violence that Bernard's character heralds or become joint heirs with leaders like Belton whose political ideologies offer the hope of more peaceful resolutions. By heralding Belton as a political martyr at the end of the novel, Griggs suggests that the race leader's rebellious passivity offers a more civilizing solution for easing tensions along the lines of racial-sexual displacement and disenfranchisement.[60] Belton embraces this ethos of rebellious passivity through intertextual performances that complete, complicate, and remaster the word of Milton and other canon makers as political weaponry of racial uplift. This linguistic armament specifically uses the Miltonic gospel of freedom as an intertextual "sword of the [Holy] Spirit," a sacred yet secular variant on the spiritual weapon that Paul, writing unto the Church of Ephesus, declares is the "word of God" (Eph. 6:17).

In other words, Griggs's political engagement with Milton offers opportunities for readers of his era to choose a black God of the oppressed and reject a white God of tyranny. This rupture of the Western canon and literary tradition performs a variation on the various intertextual acts of satanic differentiation with Milton by writers like Wheatley, Equiano, Douglass, Harper, Cooper, and others yet to be named in forthcoming scholarship. According to their individual talents, all have rebelled against Milton's God, siding with a God of the oppressed who sanctions rebellion from monarchial tyranny in its variety of hegemonic manifestations. Ultimately, the practice of offering white readers the God of black liberation theology while embracing Milton on the demonic grounds of contention models a mode of "skinwalking" useful for readers of various persuasions who wish to navigate the literary color line relative to both traditions. Appropriating the term from Judy Scales-Trent and Navajo tradition, Gary L. Lemons applies the term to his pedagogical practices. Relative to his teaching, skinwalking becomes a practice for engaging "the notion of students' emotionally committing to understanding the life experiences of individuals living on the color line as if the experiences were their own."[61] His pedagogical goal is to "challenge students continually [by] evoking personal memories of having been marginalized, discriminated against, ostracized, hated for being different—for being an Other."[62] Lemon's pedagogical practice is instructive for inaugurating a new kind of criticism in Milton and African American studies.

This new criticism, existing in an age Joseph Wittreich identifies as "Milton's (Post) Modernity," attends to the artistic complexity of "a very different Milton."[63] This Milton enables and/or inhibits at the discretion of African American writers according to the complexities of their individual needs as artists. For this audience, Milton sometimes figures as "the liberationist poet," whereas on other occasions he may loom large as a "subversive cultural presence."[64] Until readers from diverse backgrounds are equipped to skinwalk in the intertextual footprints of early African American writers, knowledge of the Western canon and those of Milton and African Americans in particular, will remain incomplete. That is, all areas of literary study will remain uncomplicated by the repetitions of racial-sexual difference that have reproduced new meanings in the English language unbeknownst to our age of (post)modernity.

As the tradition of fragmentary appropriations examined in this book indicate, early African American literature reflects a canon of skinwalkers who learned to complete and complicate Milton's originality through their remastery of the English language. They achieved this art form according to various intertextual persuasions with Milton's satanic epic and its poetry of satanic fallenness. While in the not-so-distant past certain strands of criticism might have dismissed scholarly annotations of cross-cultural influence between African American authors and their white precursors as ornamental imitation, it is no longer tenable to pander to such assertions. Tracy Mishkin makes a similar assertion more emphatically when she advances the claim that "it is time to stop taking overgeneralized, negative approaches for granted and, instead, to listen to what the authors have to say."[65] Heeding Mishkin's call allows contemporary readers to map and retrace the intertextual footprints of "writers who cleared a path for others to follow headed toward freedom."[66] By writing themselves rebelliously into a tradition of poetic fallenness, these "Seraphic Lords" who re-create Milton's epic and Satan's poetry radically shift and rupture the canon on demonic grounds of contention (*PL* 1.794). Their canon of Miltonic engagement justifies England's epic poet of liberty as a satanic intertext, that is, a sacred yet secular talking book second only to the Holy Bible. Troping with Milton and the Bible empowered these early African American authors to preach their own sacred yet secular gospels of black revolt. They preached Miltonic gospels of freedom by finding subversive refuge in a range of satanic intertexts. Accordingly, they completed, complicated, and remastered the sacred yet secular words of Milton for messianic purposes of racial uplift "that the world through [them] might be saved" (John 3:17) unto greater works and higher callings in Jesus' name.

Epilogue

MALCOLM X, *PARADISE LOST*, AND THE TWENTIETH CENTURY INFERNAL READER

Preaching the Gospel of Black Revolt originated from my awareness of my status as an "outside" reader. Upon reading *Paradise Lost*, it did not take long for my lived experiences as an African American to begin informing my responses to the poem. Specifically, books 1 and 2 led me to consider how nineteenth century African American readers might have responded to Milton's epic, particularly those who suffered the horrors of slavery. Given nineteenth century protest writers' and orators' attraction to the epic's infernal language, imagery, and themes, we might argue not only that *Paradise Lost* fired the African American literary imagination, but also that it spoke directly to "the tragic but heroic story of black people's lot in America."[1]

Paradise Lost informs the radical political ideology and ministry of Malcolm X (1925–65). *The Autobiography of Malcolm X* represents one of several twentieth century African American texts expressing admiration for the epic as a type of sacred text for political purposes. Malcolm reads his personality in Satan and in the language and imagery of hell. Consequently, he too, performs infernal readings of *Paradise Lost*. If Milton's epic spoke to radical male writers like David Walker, Henry Highland Garnet, and William Wells Brown amid the horrific social climate of U.S. slavery, it certainly appealed to the racial and political outsiderness

Malcolm and other African Americans experienced throughout much of the twentieth century. Like his nineteenth century predecessors, Malcolm capitalizes upon his infernal and outsider readings by shaping them to conform to the demands of his radical theology of black power.

Malcolm's reading of *Paradise Lost* especially mirrors his predecessors', who likewise read Milton in the tradition of the black preacher's folk art. In "Saved," Malcolm presents his radical interpretation of *Paradise Lost* as a foundation for his theology: "I read Milton's *Paradise Lost*. The devil kicked out of Paradise, was trying to regain possession. He was using the forces of Europe, personified by the Popes, Charlemagne, Richard the Lionhearted, and other knights. I interpreted this to show that the Europeans were motivated and led by the devil, or the personification of the devil. So Milton and Mr. Elijah Muhammad were actually saying the same thing."[2] Here, Malcolm clearly reads Satan as a metaphor for whiteness. His recent indoctrination in Muslim teachings validates his belief that whites indeed personify the devil. Malcolm's nascent acquaintance with "the glorious history of the black man" facilitates this interpretation (195). Books as diverse as Dubois's *The Souls of Black Folk*, Carter G. Woodson's *Negro History*, and Will Durant's *Story of Civilization* promote his "sensitivity to the deafness, dumbness, and blindness that was afflicting the black race in America" (186). Ultimately, this "homemade education" illuminates the extent to which American history has been whitened. It affords Malcolm knowledge of the "monstrous" enormity of crimes committed by "the white man's hands" (191). For these reasons, he rejects occidental philosophers, believing they suffer from a "neurotic necessity to hide the black man's true role in history" (196).

Given this perspective, we might expect Malcolm to interpret *Paradise Lost* in the manner he does, but we are surprised when he also fashions himself after Satan. Unlike Milton, Malcolm is of the devil's party and *knows* it. Interestingly, Satan's view of God as tyrannical and heaven as oppressive complements Malcolm's assessment of America. Even the punishment for Satan's rebellion closely mirrors African Americans' experience in racist America, which amounts to a hell-like sentence. Malcolm's imprisonment at the time of his reading *Paradise Lost* only reinforces the epic's charged language and prison imagery, given the corollary between imprisonment and enslavement. No wonder, then, that Malcolm's autobiography and fiery political messages thereafter abound with the American Africanisms registered in Milton's epic.

Black orality, specifically the speech act of "calling a spade a spade," animates Malcolm's infernal reading of *Paradise Lost*, Malcolm's speeches and his *Autobiography* indicate how closely this speech act is aligned with his personality. In his 1964 address on "The Harlem 'Hate-Gang' Scare," for instance, he declares, "whenever you have something to say and you're not afraid to say it, I think you should go ahead and say it, and let the chips fall where they may. So I take advantage of all platforms to get off my mind what's on it."[3] He "learned early that crying out in protest could accomplish things" (*Autobiography* 10), and so believed "that if you want something, you had better make some noise."[4]

Satan's predilection for speaking his mind in *Paradise Lost* seems to be an extension of his creator's personality. Milton's outspokenness resonates in tracts such as *Reason of Church-Government*, *Areopagitica*, and *Doctrine and Discipline of Divorce*. While book 1 of *Paradise Lost* introduces Satan's dissident voice, book 5 demonstrates its boldness. Following the news of the Son's promotion to Messiah, Satan insists that the angels are "Natives and Sons of Heav'n possest before / By none, and if not equal all, yet free" (*PL* 5.790–91). He then claims that "We know no time when we were not as now" (5.859), denying their created nature. Notwithstanding Abdiel's reputation as the angel "then whom none with more zeale ador'd / The Deitie" (5.805–06), Satan remains nonplussed. He mocks Abdiel's stern reminder that God "made / Thee what thou art, and formd the Pow'rs of Heav'n / Such as he pleasd" (5.823–25) as a "strange point and new!" (5.855). What matters here is not whether Satan's position is sound, but that he boldly voices his opposition. Malcolm, no doubt, delights in this passage as his "Saved" chapter suggests. Throughout the course of his "homemade" education, he gravitates to radical thinkers like himself. Already shaped by Elijah Muhammad's radical interpretations of white people, Malcolm respects revolutionaries like Nat Turner, particularly because he "wasn't going around preaching pie-in-the-sky and 'non-violent' freedom for the black man" (*Autobiography* 191). This Satan who defies God, successfully entices a third of God's angelic host, then wages war against his creator, typifies the militancy Malcolm promotes in his campaigns against white power structures.

From the standpoint of racial subjectivity, Satan's plight, compounded by Milton's language and prison imagery, captivates the sensibilities of "outsiders" like Malcolm. Satan's experiences in heaven and hell mirror African Americans' victimization in America. As with Malcolm's attraction to Satan on the level of black orality, language and narrative function akin to those "energizing agents in the symbolic universe that issues forth out of black expressive culture, which is dominated by the emotional sovereignty of the black folk sermon."[5] Dolan Hubbard's elaboration upon Stephen Henderson's definition of "mascons" proves pertinent here because Satan's fall together with Milton's infernal language indeed carry an "inordinate charge of emotional and [spiritual] weight... setting all kinds of bells ringing [and] all kinds of synapses snapping" in the outsider reader.[6]

Early in "Saved," Malcolm ponders Mr. Muhammad's theory that the black prisoner symbolizes "white society's crime of keeping black men oppressed and deprived and ignorant, and unable to get decent jobs, turning them into criminals" (*Autobiography* 184). He comes to believe that "the American black man [epitomizes] the world's most shameful case of minority oppression" (195), which accounts for Malcolm's identifying the "white man" as a devil nine times in the chapter. Despite Malcolm's tendency to associate whiteness with the devil, Satan's prisonlike surroundings and his disdain for servility, coupled with Milton's liberal use of enslavement language, encourage an association of things infernal with blackness. Increasingly, nonwhites' "sufferings of exploitation" come to be seen as resembling the oppression under the tyranny of Milton's God. Malcolm pursues his atypical reading of *Paradise Lost* by denigrating what Albert J. Raboteau considers America's "myth of national identity."[7] Steeped in the belief that "European migration across the Atlantic" figuratively constitutes an "escape from Egyptian bondage to the Promised Land of milk and honey," this myth undergoes radical change from the perspective of African

Americans. Inverted, the myth reads America as resembling an enslaving Egypt rather than a chosen or paradisiacal Israel.

Malcolm does not specifically refer to America as an antiparadise, but his sarcasm desecrates America's identity myth. In the *Autobiography*'s "Harlemite" chapter, for instance, Malcolm equates the self-contained world of African American nightlife with paradise in declaring, "New York was heaven to me," with the added comment that "Harlem was Seventh Heaven" (*Autobiography* 86). New York (and Harlem more specifically) stand isolated, in a sense, from the tyranny of larger American culture. As havens of blackness, meccas like Harlem afford a lifestyle relatively free from white power. It is not likely that the notion of America as a city upon a hill escapes Malcolm, as his rhetoric consistently contrasts this tradition in American literature with his own definition of America's racial climate. Both in his narrative and in political speeches, Malcolm undercuts America's myth of Edenic self-identity by referring to the national landscape as "the wilderness of America." His negative depictions of American democracy and its attendant distortion of Christianity contrast with Satan's description of heaven as a place of "celestial light" (*PL* 1.245), comprised of "happy Fields / Where Joy for ever dwells" (1.249–50). For Malcolm, America, with its "disguised hypocrisy" and its vainglorious rhetoric of "beautiful preaching" simply represents "white nationalism."[8]

Malcolm's undercutting of America as Eden shares an affinity with Satan's ultimate indictment of heaven, which, of course, stems from what seem to be the stifling demands of submission and abject servility. Satan's refusal to "bow and sue for grace / With suppliant knee" (*PL* 1.111–12) correlates with his view of the "Tyranny of Heav'n" (1.124). Since Malcolm believes revolutions are "based on land...[and that they represent]...the basis of freedom, justice, and equality," we would be hard-pressed not to imagine him transferring this same ideology to Satan's predicament in heaven. Revolutionaries, he continues, "want land so [they] can set up [their] own...independent nation."[9] Satan, content in his "infernal world" (*PL* 1.251) and satisfied that in it "we shall be free" (1.259), speaks Malcolm's revolutionary language, especially when he claims "To reign is worth ambition though in

Hell" (1.262). This reversal of geographical fortune hardly escapes Malcolm's imagination. If Satan intends to "make a "Heav'n of Hell, a Hell of Heav'n" (1.255), Malcolm finds no less value in appropriating the infernal hero's stratagem. With rhetorical wit, he identifies America as "white man's heaven [and] black man's hell" (*Autobiography* 228).

Malcolm's life experiences prompt identifications with hell. He expresses African Americans' oppression in terms of their "catching hell." His idiom of choice for articulating African Americans' material existence, again, highlights the "emotional and spiritual charge" carried by Milton's poetry. As ideological metaphor, Malcolm constantly references Satan's punishment. But whereas Satan's punishment derives from his crime of rebellion, African Americans' predisposition to "catch hell" results solely from the perceived criminality of their black complexions. Satan's torments in hell range from physical suffering to psychological and emotional torture. He physically suffers from the ravages of "penal fire" as hell, "waste and wilde, /... on all sides round / As one great Furnace flam'd (*PL* 1.60–62). Psychological and emotional suffering are evidenced by Satan's "lost happiness and lasting pain" (1.55). To a degree, these torments figuratively correspond to the tragic incidents outlined in the *Autobiography's* preincarceration narrative. Racism confronts young Malcolm with one hellish crime after another. Chapters 1 through 4 of the *Autobiography*, for example, emphasize the psychological and sociological hellspaces defining his adolescence. The racially motivated murder of his father, the institutionalization of his mother, the fragmentation of the Little's nuclear family, even the thwarting of Malcolm's childhood aspiration to become a lawyer, all combine to amplify the hellish and existential absurdity of African Americans' existence in a racist America. These factors likewise affect his withdrawal from society. They further contribute to the moral degeneracy chronicled in chapters 6 through 9. By chapter 10, Malcolm directly associates himself with Satan. In titling the chapter "Satan," he embraces his newly acquired moniker, confessing he is "physically miserable and as evil-tempered as a snake" (*Autobiography* 166). Fellow inmates call him Satan as well, responding to his "anti-religious attitude" (167).

That Milton's epic describes hell as a prison only reinforces similarities between Malcolm and Satan's experiences. For instance, the epic voice considers hell a "dungeon horrible" (*PL* 1.61). Moloch extends the motif by describing hell as a "Den of shame / The Prison of [God's] Tyranny" (*PL* 2.58–59). When Satan assumes the heroic task of sojourning through hell's abyss, he, too, expresses the confining nature of the infernal. Referring to hell as "our prison strong" (2.434), he further impresses the image upon readers' psyches by noting that the "gates of burning Adamant / Barr'd over us prohibit all egress" (2.436–37). While prison, like Satan's hell, might seem daunting to Malcolm, he, too, makes a heaven of his hell-like environment. A ten-year prison sentence places him in Charlestown and Concord prisons, but eventually he is transferred to the Norfolk Prison Colony. Malcolm describes the new venue as a "most enlightened form of prison" (*Autobiography* 171). Featuring such amenities as toilets that flush and rooms devoid of bars, these delights pale in comparison to the prison library's vast holdings. Largely comprised of the Parkhurst Collection, containing materials "any college library would have been lucky to get," Malcolm achieves salvation, resolving to "devote the rest of [his] life to telling the white man about himself—or die" (201). In a sense, Malcolm experiences a kind of paradise within the confines of the Norfolk Prison Colony. His political ministry, in fact, evolves from this "homemade education" (186). Each book he reads obviously shapes his radical ideology, but no text more so than the Harvard Classics volume containing *Paradise Lost* profoundly influences the direction his life will take. Milton's epic essentially "saves" Malcolm. Complementing an acquaintance with "the glorious history of the black man," *Paradise Lost* replays the absurdity of African American experience, summoning Malcolm's literary imagination and eliciting his dissident voice in the service of a politically motivated theology of black power.

As Malcolm's *Autobiography* and political ideology indicate, the themes, language, and imagery of *Paradise Lost* speak to the "black consciousness" well into the twentieth century.[10] In Milton's Satan, Malcolm finds the mirror image of his dissident self. Ossie Davis's epilogue to the *Autobiography* best characterizes Malcolm's infernal personality. Davis praises Malcolm's inclinations always to call a spade a spade. He describes Malcolm's upfront manner of speaking as a "shocking *zing* of fire-and-be-damned-to-you rhetoric" (*Autobiography* 500). It possessed that tendency to "scare the hell out of the rest of us," he adds, even as it "kept snatching our lies away" (498). Instead, Malcolm continued to articulate his views even when he knew, as all African Americans themselves knew, "what happened to people who stick their necks out and say them" (499). Davis's literary eulogy of Malcolm capitalizes upon that same quality that makes Milton's Satan such an engaging and attractive literary character in his own right. For Davis, such heroic spirit merits a "final salute" to the "brave, black, ironic gallantry, which was [Malcolm's] style and hallmark" (500). As we shall see in future scholarship devoted to Milton's afterlife beyond the nineteenth century, fragments of satanic poetry and fallenness continue to exalt a nation by reproaching it in African American literature and culture with literary righteousness.

Notes

Notes to Chapter 1

1. Joseph Wittreich, *Why Milton Matters* (New York: Palgrave Macmillan, 2006), 186.
2. Ibid., 186.
3. Mark R. Kelley, Michael Lieb, and John T. Shawcross, eds., "Introduction," *Milton and the Grounds of Contention* (Pittsburgh: Duquesne University Press, 2003), 1.
4. Katherine McKittrick, *Demonic Grounds: Black Women and the Cartographies of Struggle* (Minneapolis: University of Minnesota Press, 2006), xxv.
5. Ibid., xxv–xxvi.
6. Thomas Jefferson, *Notes on the State of Virginia*, ed. Frank Shuffelton (New York: Penguin, 1999), 147.
7. John C. Shields, *Phillis Wheatley's Poetics of Liberation* (Knoxville: University of Tennessee Press, 2008), 1.
8. Henry Louis Gates Jr., "Foreword: In Her Own Write," *Complete Poems of Frances E. W. Harper* (New York: Oxford University Press, 1988), x.
9. Ibid., xxiv.
10. Frances Smith Foster, *Written by Herself: Literary Production by African American Women, 1746–1892* (Bloomington: Indiana University Press, 1993), 2.
11. Mary Nyquist and Margaret W. Ferguson, eds., "Preface," in *Re-membering Milton: Essays on the Texts and Traditions* (New York: Methuen, 1987), xii.
12. Henry B. Wonham, ed., introduction to *Criticism and the Color Line* (New Brunswick, NJ: Rutgers University Press, 1996), 6.
13. Henry Louis Gates Jr., *The Signifying Monkey: A Theory of Afro-American Literary Criticism* (New York: Oxford University Press, 1988), 118.
14. Frances Smith Foster, ed., introduction to *Minnie's Sacrifice; Sowing and Reaping; Trial and Triumph: Three Rediscovered Novels by Frances E. W. Harper* (Boston: Beacon Press, 1994), xxiii.
15. Ibid., xxiii.

16. Gilles Deleuze and Félix Guattari, "What Is a Minor Literature?," in *Out There: Marginalization and Contemporary Cultures*, ed. Russell Ferguson, Martha Gever, Trinh T. Minh-ha, and Cornel West, 59–69 (Cambridge: MIT Press, 1990), 63, 61.

17. Carolivia Herron, "Milton and Afro-American Literature," in Nyquist and Ferguson, *Re-membering Milton*, 280.

18. Ibid., 280.

19. Wonham, "Introduction," 6.

20. Gates, *The Signifying Monkey*, 122.

21. Aldon L. Nielsen, *Writing between the Lines: Race and Intertextuality* (Athens: University of Georgia Press, 1994), 24.

22. Neil Forsyth, *The Satanic Epic* (Princeton, NJ: Princeton University Press, 2003), 17.

23. Ibid., 17.

24. Danielle A. St. Hilaire, *Satan's Poetry: Fallenness and Poetic Tradition in "Paradise Lost"* (Pittsburgh: Duquesne University Press, 2012), 19.

25. Ibid., 107.

26. Ibid., 107.

27. Nyquist and Ferguson, "Preface," xii.

28. Ibid., xiii.

29. Gregory Machacek, *Milton and Homer: "Written to Aftertimes"* (Pittsburgh: Duquesne University Press, 2011), 96.

30. Ibid., 96.

31. Sylvia Wynter, "Beyond Miranda's Meanings: Un/Silencing the 'Demonic Ground' of Caliban's Woman," in *Out of the Kumbla: Caribbean Women and Literature*, ed. Carole Boyce Davies and Elaine Savory Fido (Trenton, NJ: Africa World Press, 1990), 364.

32. Machacek, *Milton and Homer*, 120.

33. Ibid., 8.

34. Ibid., 28.

35. Ibid., 28.

36. Richard Wright, *12 Million Black Voices* (New York: Thunder's Mouth Press, 1941), 40.

37. Ibid., 40.

38. Nielsen, *Writing between the Lines*, 5.

39. Machacek, *Milton and Homer*, 120.

40. Ibid., 102.

41. Ibid., 102.

42. John Milton, *The Reason of Church-Government*, in *The Riverside Milton*, ed. Roy Flannagan (Boston: Houghton Mifflin, 1998), 923.

43. Nielsen, *Writing between the Lines*, 3.

44. J. B. Savage, "Freedom and Necessity in *Paradise Lost*," *ELH* 44, no. 2 (1977): 286.

45. Ibid., 286.

46. Henry Louis Gates Jr., "Preface to Blackness," in *African American Literary Theory: A Reader*, ed. Winston Napier (1979; repr., New York: New York University Press, 2000), 163.

47. Henry Louis Gates Jr., "James Gronniosaw and the Trope of the Talking Book," in *African American Autobiography*, ed. William L. Andrews (Englewood Cliffs, NJ: Prentice Hall, 1993), 11, 12.

48. Ibid., 12.

49. John Milton, *Paradise Lost*, ed. Scott Elledge, 2nd ed. (New York: W. W. Norton, 1993), 1.26; hereafter cited in the text.

50. Henry H. Mitchell, *Black Preaching: The Recovery of a Powerful Art* (Nashville: Abingdon Press, 1990), 56.

51. Ibid., 56.

52. St. Hilaire, *Satan's Poetry*, 139.

53. Ibid., 139.

54. Ibid., 17, 139.

55. Allen Dwight Callahan, *The Talking Book: African Americans and the Bible* (New Haven, CT: Yale University Press, 2006), xi.

56. Toni Morrison, "Unspeakable Things Unspoken: The Afro-American Presence in American Literature," in *Criticism and the Color Line: Desegregating American Literary Studies*, ed. Henry B. Wonham (New Brunswick, NJ: Rutgers University Press, 1996), 23.

57. Ibid., 23.

58. Toni Morrison, *Playing in the Dark: Whiteness and the Literary Imagination* (New York: Vintage Books, 1993), 38.

59. Charles Whitney, "Appropriate This," *Borrowers and Lenders: The Journal of Shakespeare and Appropriation* 3, no. 2 (Spring/Summer 2008).

60. W. E. B. Dubois, *The Souls of Black Folk* (New York: W. W. Norton, 1999), 5.

61. Ibid., 11.

62. Herron, "Milton and Afro-American Literature," 280.

63. Dubois, *Souls of Black Folk*, 10, 11.

64. Charles Mills, "White Ignorance," in *Race and the Epistemologies of Ignorance*, ed. Shannon Sullivan and Nancy Tuana (Albany: State University of New York Press, 2007), 16.

65. Peter C. Herman, *Destabilizing Milton: "Paradise Lost" and the Poetics of Incertitude* (New York: Palgrave Macmillan, 2005), 4.

66. Mills, "White Ignorance," 13.

67. Ibid., 13.

68. Ibid., 23.

69. Gates, *The Signifying Monkey*, 92.

70. Ibid., 124.

71. Ibid., 103.

72. Henry Louis Gates Jr., ed., "Criticism in the Jungle," in *Black Literature and Literary Theory* (1984; repr., New York: Routledge, 1990), 3.

73. Michael Riffaterre, "Compulsory Reader Response: The Intertextual Drive," in *Intertextuality: Theories and Practices*, ed. Michael Worton and Judith Still (Manchester: Manchester University Press, 1990), 56.

74. Machacek, *Milton and Homer*, 34.

75. Ibid., 35.

76. Ibid., 35.

77. Riffaterre, "Compulsory Reader Response," 62.

78. Ibid., 57.

79. Gates, *The Signifying Monkey*, 90.

80. Henry Louis Gates Jr., *Loose Canons: Notes on the Culture Wars* (New York: Oxford University Press, 1992), 69.

81. Ibid., 44, 45.

82. Zora Neale Hurston, "Characteristics of Negro Expression," in *Sweat / Zora Neale Hurston*, ed. Cheryl A. Wall (New Brunswick, NJ: Rutgers University Press, 1997), 61.

83. Ibid., 61.

84. Zora Neale Hurston, *Mules and Men* (Philadelphia: J. B. Lippincott, 1935), 305.

85. Ibid., 306.

86. Melville J. Herskovits, *The Myth of the Negro Past* (Boston: Beacon Press, 1941), 252.

87. Forsyth, *The Satanic Epic*, 1, 310.

88. Ibid., 13.

89. Ibid., 15.

90. Hurston, *Mules and Men*, 306.

91. St. Hilaire, *Satan's Poetry*, 38–39.

92. Patricia Robinson Williams, "Poets of Freedom: The English Romantics and Early Nineteenth-Century Black Poets" (PhD diss., University of Illinois at Urbana-Champaign, 1974), 6.

93. Marlon B. Ross, *The Contours of Masculine Desire* (New York: Oxford University Press, 1989), 3.

94. Lucy Newlyn, *"Paradise Lost" and the Romantic Reader* (Oxford: Clarendon Press, 1993), 20.

95. Ibid., 121, 122.

96. William Blake, *The Marriage of Heaven and Hell*, in *William Blake: Selected Poetry*, ed. W. H. Stevenson (London: Penguin Books, 1988), 68.

97. Newlyn, *"Paradise Lost" and the Romantic Reader*, 39.

98. St. Hilaire, *Satan's Poetry*, 16.

99. Ibid., 17.

100. Newlyn, *"Paradise Lost" and the Romantic Reader*, 144.

101. Blake, *Marriage of Heaven and Hell*, 68.

102. Joseph Wittreich, *Romantics on Milton* (Cleveland: The Press of Case Western Reserve, 1970), 518.

103. Frank D. McConnell, *Byron's Poetry* (New York: W. W. Norton, 1978), 159.

104. Adriana Craciun, "Romantic Satanism and the Rise of Nineteenth-Century Women's Poetry," in *New Literary History* 34, no. 4 (2003): 700.
105. Ibid., 718.
106. Percy Bysshe Shelley, *Prometheus Unbound*, in *Shelley's Poetry and Prose*, ed. Donald H. Reiman and Neil Fraistat (New York: W. W. Norton, 2002), 207.
107. Ibid., 207.
108. Percy Bysshe Shelley, "A Defence of Poetry," in Reiman and Fraistat, *Shelley's Poetry and Prose*, 526.
109. Ibid., 526.
110. Newlyn, *"Paradise Lost" and the Romantic Reader*, 145.
111. Ibid., 146.
112. Williams, "Poets of Freedom," 25, 33.
113. Forsyth, *The Satanic Epic*, 311.
114. Ibid., 311.
115. Wilson Jeremiah Moses, *Black Messiahs and Uncle Toms* (University Park: The Pennsylvania State University Press, 1982), 1.
116. Ibid., 5.
117. Sacvan Bercovitch, *The American Jeremiad* (Madison: University of Wisconsin Press, 1978), 11.
118. Ibid., 33.
119. David Howard-Pitney, *The Afro-American Jeremiad* (Philadelphia: Temple University Press, 1990), 186.
120. Ibid., 186.
121. James H. Cone, *Black Theology and Black Power* (New York: Seabury Press, 1969), 6.
122. Ibid., 6.
123. James H. Cone, *A Black Theology of Liberation* (Maryknoll: Orbis Books, 1990), 5.
124. Nielsen, *Writing between the Lines*, 12.
125. Ibid., 12.
126. Dustin Griffin, *Regaining Paradise: Milton and the Eighteenth Century* (Cambridge: Cambridge University Press, 1986), 35, 39.
127. Phillis Wheatley, "Philis's [sic] Reply to the Answer . . . ," in *Complete Writings: Phillis Wheatley*, 4th ed., ed. Vincent Carretta (New York: Penguin Books, 2001), 87.
128. Griffin, *Regaining Paradise*, 33.
129. Leslie E. Moore, *Beautiful Sublime* (Stanford, CA: Stanford University Press, 1990), 5.
130. Ibid., 3–4.
131. Ibid., 12.
132. Charlotte Forten Grimké, *The Journals of Charlotte Forten Grimké*, ed. Brenda Stevenson (New York: Oxford University Press, 1988), 144.
133. Ibid., 144.
134. Griffin, *Regaining Paradise*, 33.

135. Frances Ellen Watkins Harper, "The Mission of the Flowers," in *A Brighter Coming Day: A Frances Ellen Watkins Harper Reader*, ed. Frances Smith Foster (New York: The Feminist Press, 1990), 232.

136. Anna Julia Cooper, *A Voice from the South* (1892; repr., New York: Oxford University Press, 1988), 9.

137. K. P. Van Anglen, *The New England Milton* (University Park: The Pennsylvania State University Press, 1993), 45.

138. Lydia Dittler Schulman, *"Paradise Lost" and the Rise of the American Republic* (Boston: Northeastern University Press, 1992), 4.

139. Van Anglen, *The New England Milton*, 58–59.

140. David Boocker, "Garrison, Milton, and the Abolitionist Rhetoric of Demonization," *American Periodicals: A Journal of History, Criticism, and Bibliography* 9 (1999): 23.

141. Erik Gray, *Milton and the Victorians* (Ithaca, NY: Cornell University Press, 2009), 8.

142. Ibid., 9.

143. James G. Nelson, *The Sublime Puritan: Milton and the Victorians* (Madison: University of Wisconsin Press, 1986), 84, 85.

144. Ibid., 41.

145. Ibid., 43.

146. Reginald Wilburn, "When Milton Was in Vogue: Cross-Dressing Miltonic Presence and William Craft's Slave Narrative," in *Milton Now: 25 Years after "Re-membering Milton,"* ed. Catharine Gray and Erin Murphy (New York: Palgrave Macmillan, forthcoming).

147. C. S. Lewis, *A Preface to "Paradise Lost"* (London: Oxford University Press, 1961), 94.

148. Ibid., 94, 101.

149. William Empson, *Milton's God* (London: Chatto and Windus, 1961), 37.

150. Ibid., 42, 88.

151. Ibid., 88.

152. Stanley Fish, *Surprised by Sin*, 2nd ed. (Cambridge, MA: Harvard University Press, 1998), 21.

153. Ibid., 49, 62.

154. Forsyth, *The Satanic Epic*, 4.

155. John P. Rumrich, *Milton Unbound* (Cambridge: Cambridge University Press, 1996); Peter C. Herman, *Destabilizing Milton: "Paradise Lost" and the Poetics of Incertitude* (New York: Palgrave Macmillan, 2005).

156. Herman, *Destabilizing Milton*, 5, 6, 7.

157. St. Hilaire, *Satan's Poetry*, 2.

158. Ibid., 22.

159. Ibid., 124.

160. Ibid., 106.

161. Machacek, *Milton and Homer*, 26.
162. Gray, *Milton and the Victorians*, 8.
163. Stephen Henderson, *Understanding the New Black Poetry* (New York: William Morrow, 1973), 44.
164. Gray, *Milton and the Victorians*, 46.
165. McKittrick, *Demonic Grounds*, xiv.
166. Ibid., xxiii.
167. Wittreich, *Why Milton Matters*, xxii.
168. Ibid., xxii.
169. Henry Louis Gates Jr., "Introduction: The Talking Book," in *Pioneers of the Black Atlantic*, ed. Henry Louis Gates Jr. and William L. Andrews (Washington, DC: Civitas, 1998), 2.
170. Gates, "Criticism in the Jungle," 2.
171. Frances Harper, "Bury Me in a Free Land," in *A Brighter Coming Day: A Frances Ellen Watkins Harper Reader*, ed. Frances Smith Foster (New York: The Feminist Press, 1990), 177.
172. Cooper, *A Voice from the South*, 183.
173. Gray, *Milton and the Victorians*, 64.

Notes to Chapter 2

1. Thomas Jefferson, *Notes on the State of Virginia*, ed. William Peden (Chapel Hill: University of North Carolina Press, 1995), 140.
2. Gregory Machacek, *Milton and Homer* (Pittsburgh: Duquesne University Press, 2011), 28.
3. J. Saunders Redding, *To Make a Poet Black* (Ithaca, NY: Cornell University Press, 1988), 8.
4. Blyden Jackson, *A History of Afro-American Literature*, vol. 1, *The Long Beginning, 1746–1895* (Baton Rouge: Louisiana State University Press, 1989), 39.
5. *Complete Writings: Phillis Wheatley*, 4th ed., ed. Vincent Carretta (New York: Penguin Books, 2001), 8. Quotations from Wheatley's works are from this volume, hereafter cited in the text by page number unless otherwise indicated.
6. I use the term "beautiful science" to refer to the seamless blend of artistry and scientific technique that governs the aesthetic design of any skill, but in this case, literary production.
7. Carolivia Herron, "Milton and Afro-American Literature," in *Re-membering Milton: Essays on the Texts and Traditions*, ed. Mary Nyquist and Margaret W. Ferguson (London: Methuen, 1987), 283.
8. Ibid., 283.
9. Donald B. Gibson, "Literature: Poetry," in *Encyclopedia of Black America*, ed. W. Augustus Low and Virgil A. Clift (New York: McGraw-Hill, 1981), 519.

10. Joseph Wittreich, *Why Milton Matters: A New Preface to His Writings* (New York: Palgrave Macmillan, 2006), 95.

11. Reginald A. Wilburn, "Malcolm X and African-American Literary Appropriations of *Paradise Lost*," in *Milton in Popular Culture*, ed. Laura Lunger Knoppers and Gregory Colón Semenza, 199–210 (New York: Palgrave Macmillan, 2006), 206.

12. Erik Gray, *Milton and the Victorians* (Ithaca, NY: Cornell University Press, 2009), 33.

13. George Sensabaugh, *Milton in Early America* (Princeton, NJ: Princeton University Press, 1964), 3–4. For instance, Sensabaugh argues, "so great was Milton's stature from colonial years through the first quarter century of the Republic that his shadow eclipsed even Homer and Virgil."

14. Herron, "Milton and Afro-American Literature," 283.

15. Karen Baker-Fletcher, *A Singing Something: Womanist Reflections on Anna Julia Cooper* (New York: Crossroad, 1994), 197.

16. Barbara Kiefer Lewalski, *Milton's Brief Epic: The Genre, Meaning, and Art of "Paradise Regained"* (Providence, RI: Brown University Press, 1966), 39, 129.

17. Robert Kendrick, "Re-membering America: Phillis Wheatley's Intertextual Epic," *African American Review* 30, no. 1 (1996): 72. Also, John C. Shields, *Phillis Wheatley's Poetics of Liberation* (Knoxville: University of Tennessee Press, 2008), 118–19, recognizes a thematic similarity between "Goliath" and "Niobe," noting the protagonists rebel against God or gods for reasons rooted in pride.

18. R. Kendrick, "Re-membering America," 107.

19. John Milton, *Paradise Lost*, ed. Scott Elledge, 2nd ed. (New York: W. W. Norton, 1993), 1.301–03; hereafter cited in the text.

20. Shields, *Wheatley's Poetics of Liberation*, 80.

21. Ibid., 17.

22. Henry Louis Gates Jr. and William L. Andrews, eds., *Pioneers of the Black Atlantic* (Washington, DC: Civitas, 1998), 3.

23. Mary Helen Washington, "These Self-Invented Women: A Theoretical Framework for a Literary History of Black Women," in *Politics of Education: Essays from Radical Teacher*, ed. Susan Gushee O'Malley, Robert C. Rosen, and Leonard Vogt, 89–98 (Albany: State University of New York Press, 1990).

24. Shields, *Wheatley's Poetics of Liberation*, 22.

25. Ibid., 17.

26. Hilene Flanzbaum, "Unprecedented Liberties: Re-Reading Phillis Wheatley," *MELUS* 18, no. 3 (1993): 75.

27. Ibid., 78.

28. John C. Shields, "Phillis Wheatley's Subversive Pastoral," *Eighteenth-Century Studies* 27, no. 4 (1994): 635.

29. Dwight A. McBride, *Impossible Witness* (New York: New York University Press, 2001), 118.

30. Shields, *Wheatley's Poetics of Liberation*, 129.
31. Sondra O'Neale. "Wheatley's Use of Biblical Myth and Symbol," *Early American Literature* 21 (1996): 147.
32. Mae G. Henderson, "Speaking in Tongues: Dialogics, Dialectics, and the Black Woman Writer's Literary Tradition," in *Changing Our Own Words: Essays on Criticism, Theory and Writing by Black Women*, ed. Cheryl Wall (New Brunswick, NJ: Rutgers University Press, 1989), 22.
33. Ibid., 20.
34. Katherine McKittrick, *Demonic Grounds: Black Women and the Cartographies of Struggle* (Minneapolis: University of Minnesota Press, 2006), x.
35. Washington, "These Self-Invented Women," 93.

Notes to Chapter 3

1. Dickson D. Bruce Jr., *The Origins of African American Literature, 1680–1865* (Charlottesville: The University of Virginia Press, 2001), 66.
2. Joseph Wittreich, *Visionary Poetics: Milton's Tradition and His Legacy* (San Marino, CA: Henry E. Huntington Library and Art Gallery, 1979), 4.
3. Ibid., 4.
4. Joseph Wittreich, *Why Milton Matters: A New Preface to His Writings* (New York: Palgrave Macmillan, 2006), 48.
5. Wittreich, *Visionary Poetics*, 9.
6. Danielle A. St. Hilaire, *Satan's Poetry: Fallenness and Poetic Tradition in "Paradise Lost"* (Pittsburgh: Duquesne University Press, 2012), 18.
7. Ibid., 107.
8. Katherine McKittrick, *Demonic Grounds: Black Women and the Cartographies of Struggle* (Minneapolis: University of Minnesota Press, 2006), 140.
9. Henry Louis Gates Jr., "Preface to Blackness," in *African American Literary Theory: A Reader*, ed. Winston Napier, 147–64 (1979; repr., New York: New York University Press, 2000), 163.
10. James H. Cone, *A Black Theology of Liberation*. (Maryknoll: Orbis Books, 1990), 17.
11. Ibid., 4, 5.
12. Ibid., 18, 20, 27.
13. Wittreich, *Visionary Poetics*, 4.
14. Ibid., 4.
15. Ibid., 4–5.
16. Ibid., 26.
17. Lydia Dittler Schulman, *"Paradise Lost" and the Rise of the American Republic* (Boston: Northeastern University Press, 1992), 3.
18. Ibid., 100.

19. Ibid., 101.
20. Bruce, *Origins of African American Literature*, 40.
21. Ibid., 40.
22. K. P. Van Anglen, *The New England Milton: Literary Reception and Cultural Authority in the Early Republic* (University Park: The Pennsylvania State University Press, 1993), 41.
23. Ibid., 42, 44.
24. John S. Tanner and Justin Collings, "How Adams and Jefferson Read Milton and Milton Read Them," *Milton Quarterly* 40, no. 3 (2006): 207.
25. Ibid., 212.
26. Gregory Machacek, *Milton and Homer: "Written to Aftertimes"* (Pittsburgh: Duquesne University Press, 2011), 38.
27. George Sensabaugh, *Milton in Early America* (Princeton, NJ: Princeton University Press, 1964), esp. 186–95.
28. Bruce, *Origins of African American Literature*, 76.
29. Ibid., 76.
30. Othello, "Essay on Negro Slavery, No. I," *American Museum*, May 10, 1788, as quoted in Othello's "What the Negro Was Thinking during the Eighteenth Century: Essay on Negro Slavery," *Journal of Negro History*, no. 1 (1916): 49; hereafter cited in the text.
31. Sharon Achinstein, *Milton and the Revolutionary Reader* (Princeton, NJ: Princeton University Press, 1994), 202.
32. Wittreich, *Why Milton Matters*, 117.
33. Ian Smith, *Race and Rhetoric in the Renaissance* (New York: Palgrave Macmillan, 2009), 140.
34. John Milton, *Paradise Lost*, ed. Scott Elledge, 2nd ed. (New York: W. W. Norton, 1993), 1.44–48; hereafter cited in the text.
35. Diana L. Hayes, *And Still We Rise: An Introduction to Black Liberation Theology* (New York: Paulist Press, 1996), 106.
36. Ibid., 106.
37. See John T. Shawcross, *John Milton and Influence: Presence in Literature, History and Culture* (Pittsburgh: Duquesne University Press, 1991), 139–55; and Carolivia Herron, "Milton and Afro-American Literature," in *Re-membering Milton: Essays on the Texts and Traditions*, ed. Mary Nyquist and Margaret W. Ferguson, 278–300 (New York: Methuen, 1987).
38. Blyden D. Jackson, *A History of Afro-American Literature*, vol. 1, *The Long Beginning, 1746–1895* (Baton Rouge: Louisiana State University Press, 1989), 60.
39. Ibid., 60, 61.
40. Olaudah Equiano, *The Interesting Narrative of the Life of Olaudah Equiano; or, Gustavus Vassa, the African. Written by Himself*, in *The Classic Slave Narratives*, ed. Henry Louis Gates Jr. (New York: Mentor, 1987), 61; hereafter cited in the text.

41. Ibid., 61.
42. Phillis Wheatley, "On being brought from Africa to America," in *Complete Writings: Phillis Wheatley*, ed. Vincent Caretta (New York: Penguin Books, 2001), 12.
43. Machacek, *Milton and Homer*, 29.
44. Elton D. Higgs, "The 'Thunder' of God in *Paradise Lost*," *Milton Quarterly* 4, no. 2 (1970): 24.
45. Ibid., 24.
46. Wittreich, *Visionary Poetics*, 24.
47. Ibid., 24.
48. David Howard-Pitney, *The Afro-American Jeremiad* (Philadelphia: Temple University Press, 1990), 5, 15.
49. Ibid., 8.
50. Jackson, *History of Afro-American Literature*, 69.
51. Ibid., 69.
52. Ibid., 70.
53. Ibid., 71.
54. Philip S. Foner and Robert James Branham, eds., *Lift Every Voice: African American Oratory, 1787–1900* (Tuscaloosa: University of Alabama Press, 1998), 60.
55. Ibid., 60.
56. As quoted in Lemuel Haynes, "Universal Salvation," in Foner and Branham, *Lift Every Voice*, 60; hereafter cited in the text.
57. Henry H. Mitchell, *Black Preaching: The Recovery of a Powerful Art* (Nashville, TN: Abingdon Press, 1990), 63.
58. Ibid., 63.
59. Wittreich, *Visionary Poetics*, 36.
60. Ibid., 35–36.
61. Foner and Branham, eds., *Lift Every Voice*, 59.
62. Machacek, *Milton and Homer*, 89.
63. Wittreich, *Visionary Poetics*, 32.
64. Jackson, *History of Afro-American Literature*, 70.
65. Timothy Mather Cooley, *Sketches of the Life and Character of the Rev. Lemuel Haynes, A.M., for Many Years Pastor of a Church in Rutland, Vt., and Late in Granville, New-York* (New York: Harper & Brothers, 1837), 105.
66. Similarly, slave narratives were often preceded by prefaces in which white attesters authenticated that the texts were indeed written by black authors themselves.
67. Charles Mills, "White Ignorance," in *Race and Epistemologies of Ignorance*, ed. Shannon Sullivan and Nancy Tuana, 13–38 (Albany: State University of New York Press, 2007), 31.
68. Ian Smith, *Race and Rhetoric*, 4.
69. Kim F. Hall, *Things of Darkness: Economies of Race and Gender in Early Modern England* (Ithaca, NY: Cornell University Press, 1995), 6–7.

70. Ian Smith, *Race and Rhetoric*, 13.
71. Albert J. Raboteau, *A Fire in the Bones: Reflections on African-American Religious History* (Boston: Beacon Press, 1995), 24.
72. Ibid., 26.
73. Foner and Branham, eds., *Lift Every Voice*, 66.
74. Jackson, *History of Afro-American Literature*, 81.
75. John Hope Franklin and Alfred A. Moss Jr., *From Slavery to Freedom: A History of African Americans*, 7th ed. (New York: McGraw-Hill, 1994), 102.
76. Jackson, *History of Afro-American Literature*, 81.
77. Peter Williams Jr., "Abolition of the Slave Trade," in Foner and Branham, *Lift Every Voice*, 67; hereafter cited in the text by page number.
78. Bruce, *Origins of African American Literature*, 58.
79. Wittreich, *Visionary Poetics*, 36.
80. Williams substitutes "woe" for Milton's "sorrow."
81. Wittreich, *Visionary Poetics*, 88.
82. Wilson Jeremiah Moses, *Black Messiahs and Uncle Toms: Social and Literary Manipulations of a Religious Myth* (University Park: The Pennsylvania State University Press, 1982), 38.
83. Wilson Jeremiah Moses, *The Golden Age of Black Nationalism, 1850–1925* (New York: Oxford University Press, 1978), 24.
84. Machacek, *Milton and Homer*, 89.
85. Ibid., 89.
86. Sacvan Bercovitch, *The American Jeremiad* (Madison: University of Wisconsin Press, 1978), 9.
87. Leslie M. Alexander, "William T. Hamilton," in *Encyclopedia of African American History*, ed. Leslie M. Alexander and Walter C. Rucker, 144–45 (Santa Barbara, CA: ABC-CLIO, 2010), 144.
88. Foner and Branham, eds., *Lift Every Voice*, 80.
89. Leslie M. Harris, *In the Shadow of Slavery: African Americans in New York City, 1626–1863* (Chicago: University of Chicago Press, 2003), 86, 87.
90. William Hamilton, "Mutual Interest, Mutual Benefit, and Mutual Relief," in Foner and Branham, *Lift Every Voice*, 81, hereafter cited in the text.
91. Zora Neale Hurston, "Characteristics of Negro Expression," in *Sweat / Zora Neale Hurston*, ed. Cheryl A. Wall, 55–72 (New Brunswick, NJ: Rutgers University Press, 1997), 55.
92. Ibid., 55.
93. William Hamilton, "O! Africa," in Foner and Branham, *Lift Every Voice*, 91–97; hereafter cited in the text.
94. Moses, *Black Messiahs and Uncle Toms*, 38.
95. Ibid., 46.
96. *Columbian Centinel*, January 16, 1830, quoted in Clement Eaton, "A Dangerous Pamphlet in the Old South," *Journal of Southern History* 2, no. 3 (1936): 328.

97. Sean Wilentz, "Introduction: The Mysteries of David Walker," in *Appeal in Four Articles; Together with a Preamble, to the Coloured Citizens of the World, but in Particular, and Very Expressly, to Those of the United States of America,* by David Walker, vii–xxiii (New York: Hill and Wang, 1995), viii, xi, xv. Walker's *Appeal* is hereafter cited in the text.

98. Jackson, *History of Afro-American Literature,* 101.

99. Sensabaugh, *Milton in Early America,* 185.

100. Sterling Stuckey, *Slave Culture: Nationalist Theory and the Foundations of Black America* (New York: Oxford University Press, 1987), 101.

101. "Infernal" also appears twice in book 4, twice in book 6, once in book 7, once in book 9, and three times in book 10.

102. *Oxford English Dictionary,* s.v. "abject."

103. *OED Online,* 2nd ed. (1989), s.v. "wretch" and "wretched."

104. The word "tyrant" merits recognition as well. There are 44 variations of the word throughout the *Appeal.* While this word may be considered too general a term and may not necessarily be considered Miltonic, it is nonetheless important to recognize its fairly significant presence in *Paradise Lost,* especially given its satanic resonance in relation to the other words I have examined.

105. Herbert Aptheker, *One Continual Cry: David Walker's "Appeal to the Colored Citizens of the World" (1829–1830)* (New York: Humanities Press, 1965), 54.

106. E. N. S. Thompson, "The Rebel Angel in Later Poetry," *Philological Quarterly* 27, no. 1 (1948): 2.

Notes to Chapter 4

1. David Walker, *Appeal to the Colored Citizens of the World, but in Particular, and very Expressly, to those of the United States of America* (New York: Hill and Wang, 1965).

2. Neil Forsyth, *The Satanic Epic* (Princeton, NJ: Princeton University Press, 2003), 3.

3. J. Saunders Redding, *To Make a Poet Black* (Ithaca, NY: Cornell University Press, 1988), 20.

4. Jean-Paul Sartre, "Freedom to Have, to Do, to Be: Being and Nothingness," in *Of Human Freedom,* ed. Wade Baskin, 32–98 (New York: Philosophical Library, 1966), 35.

5. Ibid., 34.

6. Ella Forbes, "Every Man Fights for His Freedom: The Rhetoric of African American Resistance in the Mid-Nineteenth Century," in *Understanding African American Rhetoric: Classical Origins to Contemporary Innovations,* ed. Ronald L. Jackson and Elaine B. Richardson (New York: Routledge, 2003), 155.

7. Gregory Machacek, *Milton and Homer: "Written to Aftertimes"* (Pittsburgh: Duquesne University Press, 2011), 65.

8. William Andrews, *To Tell a Free Story: The First Century of Afro-American Autobiography, 1760–1865* (Urbana: University of Illinois Press, 1986), 127.

9. Frederick Douglass, *Narrative of the Life of Frederick Douglass, an American Slave, Written by Himself*, ed. William L. Andrews and William S. McFeely (New York: Norton, 1997), 32; hereafter cited in the text.

10. Machacek, *Milton and Homer*, 37.

11. J. Saunders Redding, *To Make a Poet Black* (Ithaca, NY: Cornell University Press, 1988), 31.

12. Caleb Bingham, *The Columbian Orator* (Kila, MT: Kessinger Press, 1811).

13. Wolfgang Mieder, "'Paddle Your Own Canoe': Frederick Douglass's Proverbial Message in His 'Self-Made Men' Speech," *Midwestern Folklore* 27, no. 2 (2001): 24.

14. Originally the Halifax Mechanics Institute, built in 1857.

15. Erik Gray, *Milton and the Victorians* (Ithaca, NY: Cornell University Press, 2009), 22, explains this phenomenon of Miltonic presence in Victorian culture as "dark with excessive bright," which is to acknowledge the pervasiveness of the epic writer's influence as "something so patent as to go unnoticed" in surface readings of belated texts of this period.

16. Frederick Douglass, "The Trials and Triumphs of Self-Made Men: An Address Delivered in Halifax, England, on 4 January 1860," in *The Frederick Douglass Papers*, ed. John W. Blassingame and C. Peter Ripley et al. (New Haven, CT: Yale University Press, 1985), 3:290.

17. Ibid., 291.

18. Ibid., 293.

19. John W. Blassingame and John R. McKivigan, prefatory notes to Frederick Douglass, "Self-Made Men: An Address Delivered in Carlisle, Pennsylvania, in March 1893," in *The Frederick Douglass Papers*, ed. John W. Blassingame and C. Peter Ripley et al. (New Haven, CT: Yale University Press, 1992), 5:546. This version of Douglass's speech of "Self-Made Men" is hereafter cited in the text by volume and page number.

20. Carolivia Herron, "Milton and Afro-American Literature," in *Re-membering Milton*, ed. Mary Nyquist and Margaret W. Ferguson (New York: Methuen, 1987), 280.

21. Mieder, "'Paddle Your Own Canoe,'" 21.

22. Barbara K. Lewalski, "Genre," in *A Companion to Milton*, ed. Thomas N. Corns, 3–21 (Oxford: Blackwell, 2001), 4.

23. John T. Shawcross, *With Mortal Voice* (Lexington: University Press of Kentucky, 1982), 1, 2.

24. Andrews, *To Tell a Free Story*, 228.

25. Machacek, *Milton and Homer*, 85.

26. Melissa Shields Jenkins, "'The Poets Are with Us': Frederick Douglass and John Milton," *Modern Language Studies* 38, no. 2 (2009): 16.

27. Machacek, *Milton and Homer*, 56–57.

28. Robert G. O'Meally, "Frederick Douglass' 1845 *Narrative:* The Text Was Meant to Be Preached," in *Afro-American Literature: The Reconstruction of Instruction*, ed. Dexter Fisher and Robert B. Stepto, 192–211 (New York: Modern Language Association, 1978), 210.

29. Ibid., 65.

30. Frederick Douglass, "Frederick Douglass, [Letter], Edinburgh, Scotland, 30 July 1846. To William A. White," in *Life and Writings of Frederick Douglass*, vol. 1, ed. Philip Foner (New York: International Publishers, 1950), 181.

31. Ibid., 181.

32. Neil Forsyth, *The Satanic Epic* (Princeton, NJ: Princeton University Press, 2003), 22.

33. Valerie Smith, *Self-Discovery and Authority in Afro-American Narrative* (Cambridge, MA: Harvard University Press, 1987), 22.

34. Gwen Bergner, "Myths of the Masculine Subject: The Oedipus Complex and Douglass's 1845 *Narrative*," *Discourse: Berkeley Journal for Theoretical Studies in Media and Culture* 19, no. 2 (1997): 59.

35. Valerie Smith, *Self-Discovery and Authority*, 22.

36. Deborah E. McDowell, "In the First Place: Making Frederick Douglass and the Afro-American Narrative Tradition," in *African American Autobiography*, ed. William L. Andrews, 192–214 (Englewood Cliffs, NJ: Prentice Hall, 1993), 48.

37. bell hooks, *Black Looks: Race and Representation* (Boston: South End Press, 1992), 88, 98.

38. Valerie Smith, *Self-Discovery and Authority*, 34.

39. McDowell, "In the First Place," 48.

40. Michele A. Henkel, "Forging Identity through Literary Reinterpellation: The Ideological Project of Frederick Douglass's *Narrative*," *Literature and Psychology* 48 (2002): 98.

41. Gray, *Milton and the Victorians*, 46.

42. Shaindy Rudoff, "Tarring the Garden: The Bible and the Aesthetics of Slavery in Douglass's *Narrative*," *ESQ: A Journal of the American Renaissance* 46, no. 4 (2000): 229.

43. Blyden D. Jackson, *A History of Afro-American Literature*, vol. 1, *The Long Beginning, 1746–1895* (Baton Rouge: Louisiana State University Press, 1989), 111.

44. Percy Bysshe Shelley, *A Defence of Poetry*, in *Shelley's Poetry and Prose*, ed. Donald H. Reiman and Neil Fraistat, 509–38 (New York: W. W. Norton, 2012), 526.

45. Forsyth, *The Satanic Epic*, 215, 216.

46. Lewis R. Gordon, *Existentia Africana* (New York: Routledge, 2000), 47.

47. Forbes, "Every Man Fights," 169.
48. Ibid., 168–69.
49. Gordon, *Existentia Africana*, 7.
50. As quoted in ibid., 51.
51. Ibid., 51.
52. Ibid., 51.
53. Machacek, *Milton and Homer*, 28.
54. Ibid., 28.
55. Joseph Wittreich, *Why Milton Matters: A New Preface to His Writings* (New York: Palgrave Macmillan, 2006), 10.
56. John Milton, *Samson Agonistes*, *The Riverside Milton*, ed. Roy Flannagan (Boston: Houghton Mifflin, 1998), lines 75, 81; hereafter cited in the text.
57. McDowell, "In the First Place," 37, 38.
58. Machacek, *Milton and Homer*, 21.
59. Forsyth, *The Satanic Epic*, 4, 13, 17.
60. Wittreich, *Why Milton Matters*, 10.
61. Joseph Seeyle, "The Clay Foot of the Climber: Richard M. Nixon in Perspective," in *Literary Romanticism in America*, ed. William Andrews, 109–34 (Baton Rouge: Louisiana State University Press, 1981), 125, 126.
62. William L. Andrews, *To Tell a Free Story: The First Century of Afro-American Autobiography, 1760–1865* (Urbana: University of Illinois Press, 1986), 76. Turner dictated his autobiographical experiences to Thomas R. Gray, who subsequently published the work as *The Confessions of Nat Turner*.
63. Lisa Zeitz, "Biblical Allusion and Imagery in Frederick Douglass' Narrative," *College Language Association Journal* 25, no. 1 (1981): 62.
64. Wilson Jeremiah Moses, *Black Messiahs and Uncle Toms: Social and Literary Manipulations of a Religious Myth* (University Park: The Pennsylvania State University Press, 1982), 65.
65. Forsyth, *The Satanic Epic*, 7.
66. Ibid., 6, 7.
67. Moses, *Black Messiahs and Uncle Toms*, 54.
68. Ibid., 54.
69. Julie Nall Knowles, "*The Course of Time:* A Calvinistic *Paradise Lost*," in *Milton Studies*, vol. 18, ed. James D. Simmonds, 173–93 (Pittsburgh: University of Pittsburgh Press, 1983), 174, 179.
70. Andrews, *To Tell a Free Story*, 214.
71. Frederick Douglass, *My Bondage and My Freedom*, in *Douglass Autobiographies*, 103–452 (New York: Library of America, 1994), 364–65; hereafter cited in the text.
72. Bergner, "Myths of the Masculine Subject," 62.
73. Eric J. Sundquist, "Frederick Douglass: Literacy and Paternalism," in *Critical Essays on Frederick Douglass*, ed. William L. Andrews, 120–32 (Boston: G. K. Hall, 1991), 121.

74. Andrews, *To Tell a Free Story*, 217.
75. Forsyth, *The Satanic Epic*, 150.
76. Ibid., 150.
77. Andrews, *To Tell a Free Story*, 228.
78. Ibid., 228.
79. Moses, *Black Messiahs and Uncle Toms*, 8.
80. These speeches include, but are not limited to, "The American Apocalypse"; "The Douglass Institute: An Address Delivered in Baltimore, Maryland, on 29 September 1865"; "Henry Clay and Colonization Cant, Sophistry, and Falsehood"; "Slavery and the Slave Power"; and "There Was a Right Side in the Late War." All may be found in Blassingame and Ripley, *The Frederick Douglass Papers*.

Notes to Chapter 5

1. Mary Helen Washington, "These Self-Invented Women: A Theoretical Framework for a Literary History of Black Women," in *Politics of Education: Essays from Radical Teacher*, ed. Susan Gushee O'Malley, Robert C. Rosen, and Leonard Vogt, 89–98 (Albany: State University of New York Press, 1990), 90.
2. Maryemma Graham, ed., "Introduction," in *Complete Poems of Frances E. W. Harper* (New York: Oxford University Press, 1988), xxxiv.
3. Melba Joyce Boyd, *Discarded Legacy* (Detroit: Wayne State University Press, 1994), 36.
4. Graham, "Introduction," xxxiv.
5. Boyd, *Discarded Legacy*, 38.
6. This idea comes from William Still's *The Underground Railroad*, a late nineteenth century text, which Boyd quotes.
7. Ibid., 40.
8. Ibid., 42.
9. Frances Smith Foster, ed., "Introduction," in *A Brighter Coming Day: A Frances Ellen Watkins Harper Reader* (New York: The Feminist Press, 1990), 15.
10. Ibid., 26, 28.
11. Thomas Wortham, "William Cullen Bryant and the Fireside Poets," in *Columbia Literary History of the United States*, ed. Emory Elliott (New York: Columbia University Press, 1988), 284.
12. Boyd, *Discarded Legacy*, 58.
13. Foster, *A Brighter Coming Day*, 136.
14. Graham, "Introduction," xli.
15. Boyd, *Discarded Legacy*, 81.
16. Gregory Machacek, *Milton and Homer: "Written to Aftertimes"* (Pittsburgh: Duquesne University Press, 2011), 37.

17. Alice Rutkowski, "Leaving the Good Mother: Frances E. W. Harper, Lydia Maria Child, and the Literary Politics of Reconstruction," *Legacy* 25, no. 1 (2008): 83, 85–86.

18. Frances Ellen Watkins Harper, *Moses: A Story of the Nile*, in *A Brighter Coming Day*, ed. Frances Smith Foster, 138–65 (New York: The Feminist Press, 1990), 161; hereafter cited in the text.

19. Barbara Christian, "The Black Woman Artist as Wayward," in *Alice Walker*, Modern Critical Views, edited by Harold Bloom (New York: Chelsea House, 1989), 40.

20. Gillian Rose, *Feminism and Geography: The Limits of Geographical Knowledge* (Minneapolis: University of Minnesota Press, 1993), 140.

21. William Harmon and C. Hugh Holman, *A Handbook to Literature*, 11th ed. (Upper Saddle River, NJ: Prentice Hall, 2008), 62.

22. Henry Louis Gates Jr. uses this phrase in "Foreword: In Her Own Write," in *Complete Poems of Frances E. W. Harper*, ed. Maryemma Graham (New York: Oxford University Press, 1988). The phrase alludes to performances of agency as performed by early black women authors who often wrote, composed, and produced literary works under arduous circumstances.

23. Ibid., xvii–xviii.

24. John Milton, *Paradise Lost*, 2nd ed., ed. Scott Elledge (New York: W. W. Norton, 1993), 6.

25. Proverbs 3:5–6 reads: "Trust in the Lord with all thine heart; and lean not unto thine own understanding. In all thy ways acknowledge him, and he shall direct thy paths."

26. John Shawcross, *John Milton and Influence* (Pittsburgh: Duquesne University Press, 1991), 149–50.

27. Boyd, *Discarded Legacy*, 92.

28. Patricia Liggins Hill, "Frances Watkins Harper's *Moses: A Story of the Nile:* Apologue of the Emancipation Struggle," *AME Zion Quarterly Review* 95 (January 1984): 11.

29. Boyd, *Discarded Legacy*, 109.

30. Barbara Kiefer Lewalski, *Milton's Brief Epic* (Providence, RI: Brown University Press, 1966), 104.

31. Erik Gray, *Milton and the Victorians* (Ithaca, NY: Cornell University Press, 2009), 64.

32. John Milton, *Samson Agonistes*, lines 1381–33, in *The Riverside Milton*, ed. Roy Flannagan, 783–844 (Boston: Houghton Mifflin, 1998); hereafter cited in the text.

33. Erik Gray, *Milton and the Victorians*, 73.

34. Frances Ellen Watkins Harper, "Our Greatest Want," in Foster, *A Brighter Coming Day*, 103.

35. *Paradise Regained* 1.4, 15, in *The Riverside Milton*, ed. Roy Flannagan, 720–82 (Boston: Houghton Mifflin, 1998); hereafter cited in the text by book and line number.

36. Burton O. Kurth, *Milton and Christian Heroism* (Hamden: Archon Books, 1966), 29.

37. Richard Douglas Jordan, *The Quiet Hero: Figures of Temperance in Spenser, Donne, Milton, and Joyce* (Washington, DC: Catholic University of America Press, 1989), 29, 142.

38. Frances Ellen Watkins Harper, "Factor in Human Progress," in Foster, *A Brighter Coming Day*, 279.

39. *OED Online*, 2nd ed. (1989), "grand," adj., def. 3b.

40. Jordan, *The Quiet Hero*, 1.

41. Kurth, *Milton and Christian Heroism*, 128.

42. John Guillory, "Dalila's House: *Samson Agonistes* and the Sexual Division of Labor," in *Rewriting the Renaissance: The Discourses of Sexual Difference in Early Modern Europe*, ed. Margaret W. Ferguson, Maureen Quilligan, and Nancy J. Vickers, 106–22 (Chicago: University of Chicago Press, 1986), 112.

43. Gray, *Milton and the Victorians*, 94.

44. Guillory, "Dalila's House, 94. Guillory coins this undefined phrase, which I take to mean a style of allusively marking the origins of an inter-poetic source by belated writers and according to their distinct literary personalities.

45. Merritt Y. Hughes, "The Christ of *Paradise Regained* and the Renaissance Heroic Tradition," *Studies in Philology* 35, no. 1 (1938): 258.

46. Lewalski, *Milton's Brief Epic*, 106.

47. Marjorie O'Rourke Boyle, "Home to Mother: Regaining Milton's Paradise," *Modern Philology* 97, no. 4 (2000): 502, 504.

48. Ibid., 506.

49. Mary Beth Rose, "Why Is the Virgin Mary in *Paradise Regained*," in *Visionary Milton: Essays on Prophecy and Violence*, ed. Peter E. Medine, John T. Shawcross, and David V. Urban (Pittsburgh: Duquesne University Press, 2010), 196.

50. Ibid., 196.

51. Ibid., 200, 203.

52. Catherine H. Waterman, *Flora's Lexicon: An Interpretation of the Language and Sentiment of Flowers with an Outline of Botany, and a Poetical Introduction* (Boston: Crosby and Nichols, 1863), 132. This is one of a myriad of books devoted to the symbolic etymology of floral language.

53. Waterman identifies four types of lilies in *Flora's Lexicon*. While it is difficult to identify with any certainty which genus specifically appeals to Harper's sense of floral symbolism, her plot brings to mind the *Convallaria majalis* or *Lilium candidum* varieties. The former, according to Waterman, should "form a part of every wreath that crowns the happy, the innocent, the gay." The latter proves equally appropriate as it is recognized as a universal symbol of "purity and modesty" (ibid., 125).

54. Boyd, *Discarded Legacy*, 80.

55. Frances Smith Foster and Valerie L. Ruffin, "Teaching African American Poetry of the Reconstruction Era: Frances E. W. Harper's 'Moses: A Story of the Nile,'" in *Teaching Nineteenth-Century African American Poetry*, ed. Paula Bernet, Karen L. Kilcup, and Philipp Schweighauser (New York: Modern Language Association of America, 2007), 149.

56. Ibid., 149.

57. In an 1888 speech entitled, "Enlightened Motherhood," Harper announces the role of motherhood as a heroic and majestic calling. She apprises Christian women to esteem the grandness of this social ministry, challenging them to serve Christ by "ministering to his little ones and striving to make their homes the brightest spots on earth and the fairest types of heaven." See "Elevated Womanhood," in Foster, *A Brighter Coming Day*, 285–92.

58. Neil Smith, "Afterword to the Second Edition," *Uneven Development: Nature, Capital, and the Production of Space*, 3rd ed. (Athens: University of Georgia Press, 1990), 214.

59. Ibid., 214.

60. Mary Nyquist, "The Genesis of Gendered Subjectivity in the Divorce Tracts and in *Paradise Lost*," in *Re-Membering Milton: Essays on the Text and Traditions*, ed. Mary Nyquist and Margaret W. Ferguson, 99–127 (New York: Methuen, 1987), 115.

61. Edward Stein, *Wordsworth's Art of Allusion* (University Park: The Pennsylvania State University Press, 1988), 142.

62. Ibid., 142.

63. Elton D. Higgs, "The 'Thunder' of God in *Paradise Lost*," *Milton Quarterly* 4, no. 2 (1970): 24.

64. Ibid., 25.

65. Harper's novel, *Iola Leroy* (Boston: Beacon Press, 1987), also reveals an epic trace of Miltonic presence. Chapter 30 is entitled, "Friends in Council." Bearing an uncanny resemblance to the structure and themes of Milton's "infernal council" in *Paradise Lost*, the chapter involves a meeting of black intellectuals who are "deeply invested in the welfare of the race" (246). In chapter 32, Iola requests Dr. Latimer to consider "what it must have been to be hurled from a home of love and light into the dark abyss of slavery; to be compelled to take your place among a people you have learned to look upon as inferiors and social outcasts" (273). These satanic echoes to books 1 and 2 of *Paradise Lost* are further accented by the presence of other epic signifiers such as Iola's desire to write a book of lofty imaginative verse, an attention to developing heroic characters, and the novel's concluding note, which contains what may be interpreted as Harper's epic theme and invocation.

66. Frances E. W. Harper, "Woman's Political Future," in *World's Congress of Representative Women*, ed. May Wright Sewell, 433–37 (Chicago: Rand McNally, 1984), 439.

67. "Bury Me," in Foster, *A Brighter Coming Day*, 177.

Notes to Chapter 6

1. Anna Julia Cooper, *A Voice from the South* (New York: Oxford University Press, 1988); hereafter cited in the text by page number.
2. Lindsey C. Harnsberger, *Essential Dictionary of Music* (Los Angeles: Alfred Publishing, 1997), 138.
3. Vivian M. May, *Anna Julia Cooper, Visionary Black Feminist* (New York: Routledge, 2007), 15.
4. Ibid., 15.
5. Ibid., 17.
6. Charles Lemert and Esme Bhan, eds., *The Voice of Anna Julia Cooper* (Lanham, MD: Rowman & Littlefield, 1998), 5.
7. Ibid., 9.
8. Ibid., 33.
9. May, *Anna Julia Cooper*, 32.
10. Ibid., 33.
11. Stephen Henderson, *Understanding the New Black Poetry* (New York: William Morrow, 1973), 41; Cheryl A. Wall, *Worrying the Line: Black Women Writers, Lineage, and Literary Tradition* (Chapel Hill: University of North Carolina Press, 2005), 8.
12. Katherine McKittrick, *Demonic Grounds: Black Women and the Cartographies of Struggle* (Minneapolis: University of Minnesota Press, 2006), 138.
13. Ibid., 138.
14. May, *Anna Julia Cooper*, 77.
15. Danielle A. St. Hilaire, *Satan's Poetry: Fallenness and Poetic Tradition in "Paradise Lost"* (Pittsburgh: Duquesne University Press, 2012), 105.
16. Leslie E. Moore, *Beautiful Sublime* (Stanford, CA: Stanford University Press, 1990), 11, 10, 58.
17. Gregory Machacek, *Milton and Homer: "Written to Aftertimes"* (Pittsburgh: Duquesne University Press, 2011), 37.
18. The phrase is by Maria Stewart, who referred to African Americans in this way in her speech; see "Religion and the Pure Principles of Morality, the Sure Foundation on Which We Must Build," in *Maria Stewart, America's First Black Woman Political Writer*, ed. Marilyn Richardson (Bloomington: University of Indiana Press, 1987), 34.
19. *American Heritage Dictionary*, 5th ed. (New York: Houghton Mifflin, 2012).
20. Wall, *Worrying the Line*, 16.
21. John P. Rumrich, *Milton Unbound: Controversy and Reinterpretation* (Cambridge: Cambridge University Press, 1996), 102.
22. Ibid., 94–95, 115.
23. Cooper does acknowledge the existence of *houri* in Islamic religion but notes that these deities only reflect "a figment of Mahomet's

brain" as opposed to real constructions of women as found in Christianity (*Voice* 10).

24. Patrick Colm Hogan, *Cognitive Science, Literature, and the Arts* (New York: Routledge, 2003), 91.

25. St. Hilaire, *Satan's Poetry*, 39.

26. Barbara Welter, *Dimity Convictions* (Athens: Ohio University Press, 1976), 31, 33.

27. May, *Anna Julia Cooper*, 69.

28. Christine Froula, "When Eve Reads Milton: Undoing the Canonical Economy," *Critical Inquiry* 10, no. 2 (1983): 322.

29. Ibid., 322–23.

30. Anna Julia Cooper, "The Answer," Anna Julia Cooper Papers, Box 23–4, courtesy of the Moorland-Spingarn Research Center.

31. McKittrick, *Demonic Grounds*, 5.

32. Joseph Wittreich, *The Romantics on Milton* (Cleveland: The Press of Case Western Reserve University, 1970), 11; Lucy Newlyn, *"Paradise Lost" and the Romantic Reader* (Oxford: Clarendon Press, 1993), 115.

33. St. Hilaire, *Satan's Poetry*, 49.

34. George Lakoff and Mark Turner as cited in Hogan, *Cognitive Science, Literature*, 99.

35. Anna Julia Cooper, "The Intellectual Progress of the Colored Women in the United States since the Emancipation Proclamation: A Response to Fannie Barrier Williams," in Lemert and Bhan, *Voice of Anna Julia Cooper*, 202.

36. Joseph Wittreich, *Why Milton Matters: A New Preface to His Writings* (New York: Palgrave Macmillan, 2006), 102.

37. Ibid., 49.

38. Mary Helen Washington, "These Self-Invented Women: A Theoretical Framework for a Literary History of Black Women," in *Politics of Education: Essays from Radical Teacher*, ed. Susan Gushee O'Malley, Robert C. Rosen, and Leonard Vogt, 89–98 (Albany: State University of New York Press, 1990), 89, 93.

39. Welter, *Dimity Convictions*, 34.

40. *OED Online*, 2nd ed. (1989), "revel," v., def. 1a.

41. Lemert and Bhan, *Voice of Anna Julia Cooper*, 3.

42. May, *Anna Julia Cooper*, 69.

43. Ibid., 69, and Hazel Carby, *Reconstructing Womanhood: The Emergence of the Afro-American Woman Novelist* (New York: Oxford University Press, 1987).

44. Erik Gray, *Milton and the Victorians* (Ithaca, NY: Cornell University Press, 2009), 64.

45. John M. Steadman, *Milton and the Renaissance Hero* (Oxford: Clarendon Press, 1967), 161.

46. Juanita Whitaker, "'The Wars of Truth': Wisdom and Strength in *Areopagitica*," in *Milton Studies*, vol. 9, ed. James D. Simmonds, 185–201 (Pittsburgh: University of Pittsburgh Press, 1976), 187.

47. Stanley Fish, *Surprised by Sin*, 2nd ed. (Cambridge, MA: Harvard University Press, 1998), 184.
48. Gray, *Milton and the Victorians*, 65.
49. McKittrick, *Demonic Grounds*, xxiii.
50. Ibid., xxiii.
51. Gray, *Milton and the Victorians*, 93, 92.
52. Wittreich, *Why Milton Matters*, 95.
53. Ibid., 95.
54. Alfred Lord Tennyson, *The Princess*, canto 7, as quoted in Cooper, *A Voice from the South*, 61.
55. Ibid., 62.
56. Gray, *Milton and the Victorians*, 106.
57. Shirley Wilson Logan, *"We Are Coming": The Persuasive Discourse of Nineteenth-Century Black Women* (Carbondale: Southern Illinois University Press, 1999), 122–23.
58. St. Hilaire, *Satan's Poetry*, 65.
59. Ibid., 43.
60. Ibid., 38.
61. Machacek, *Milton and Homer*, 37.
62. Wall, *Worrying the Line*, 16.
63. Ibid., 16.
64. Moore, *Beautiful Sublime*, 12.
65. Ibid., 12.
66. Ibid., 11.
67. Ibid., 58.
68. Froula, "When Eve Reads Milton," 327.
69. Ibid., 327.
70. Ibid., 327.
71. Ibid., 329.

Notes to Chapter 7

1. A. J. Verdelle, Preface to *Imperium in Imperio*, vii–xiii (New York: Modern Library, 2003), xi; Hugh Gloster, "Sutton E. Griggs: Novelist of the New Negro," *Phylon* 4 (1943): 337; Finnie D. Coleman, *Sutton E. Griggs and the Struggle against White Supremacy* (Knoxville: University of Tennessee Press, 2007), ix.
2. Coleman, *Sutton E. Griggs*, xxii.
3. Ibid., 16.
4. Randolph Meade Walker, *The Metamorphosis of Sutton E. Griggs* (Memphis: Walker Publishing, 1991), 41, 16.
5. Ibid., 17, 36, 91, 18–19.
6. Coleman, *Sutton E. Griggs*, 18.
7. Ibid., 18.

8. Ibid., 23, 35.
9. Randolph Meade Walker, *Metamorphosis of Sutton*, 35.
10. Ibid., 35.
11. Coleman, *Sutton E. Griggs*, 19.
12. Randolph Meade Walker, *Metamorphosis of Sutton*, 36.
13. This term is used by Erik Gray, *Milton and the Victorians* (Ithaca, NY: Cornell University Press, 2009).
14. Gabriel A. Briggs, "*Imperium in Imperio:* Sutton E. Griggs and the New Negro of the South," *Southern Quarterly* 45, no. 3 (2008): 171.
15. Gray, *Milton and the Victorians*, 63.
16. Sutton E. Griggs, *Imperium in Imperio* (New York: Modern Library, 2003), 38; hereafter cited in the text.
17. Caroline Levander, "Sutton Griggs and the Borderlands of Empire," *American Literary History* 22, no. 1 (2009): 73.
18. Gray, *Milton and the Victorians*, 93.
19. Wilson Jeremiah Moses, *The Golden Age of Black Nationalism, 1850–1925* (New York: Oxford University Press, 1978), 45–46.
20. Harold Cruse, *The Crisis of the Negro Intellectual* (New York: William Morrow, 1967), 451.
21. Coleman, *Sutton E. Griggs*, 34.
22. Briggs, "New Negro of the South," 154.
23. Jane Campbell, *Mythic Black Fiction* (Knoxville: University of Tennessee Press, 1986), 50.
24. Ibid., 50.
25. Cornel West, Introduction to *Imperium in Imperio*, xv–xviii (New York: Modern Library, 2003), xvi.
26. Moses, *Golden Age of Black Nationalism* 171.
27. Ibid., 17.
28. Coleman, *Sutton E. Griggs*, 42, 56.
29. Robert Bone, *The Negro Novel in America* (New Haven, CT: Yale University Press, 1968), 34.
30. Ibid., 35.
31. E. M. W. Tillyard, *Milton* (New York: Collier Books, 1966), 102.
32. Gray, *Milton and the Victorians*, 22.
33. Ibid., 122.
34. Ibid., 25.
35. Danielle A. St. Hilaire, *Satan's Poetry: Fallenness and Poetic Tradition in "Paradise Lost"* (Pittsburgh: Duquesne University Press, 2012), 99.
36. Ibid., 110.
37. Ibid., 18.
38. Coleman, *Sutton E. Griggs*, 42.
39. Ibid., 42.
40. Verdelle, Preface to *Imperium in Imperio*, viii.
41. Kathy Russell, Midge Wilson, and Ronald Hall, *The Color Complex* (New York: Anchor Books, 1992), 1.

42. Briggs, "New Negro of the South," 162.
43. Benjamin Franklin, *Pennsylvania Journal*, December 27, 1775.
44. Sandra M. Gilbert and Susan Gubar, *The Madwoman in the Attic* (New Haven, CT: Yale University Press, 1979), 252–53.
45. Gray, *Milton and the Victorians*, 22.
46. Ibid., 46.
47. Cheryl A. Wall, *Worrying the Line: Black Women Writers, Lineage, and Literary Tradition* (Chapel Hill: University of North Carolina Press, 2005), 13.
48. Plutarch, *Roman Lives*, trans. Robin Waterfield (Oxford: Oxford University Press, 1999), 84.
49. Randolph Meade Walker, *Metamorphosis of Sutton*, 38.
50. Bernard figures as a political rebel as well. Later in the novel, he meets his father, who charges him to "break down this prejudice" so that the father can publicly claim his son with the possibility that Bernard's mother will live to "have the veil of slander torn from her pure form [before] she closes her eyes on earth forever." With these instructions, Bernard, like his rival, plunges into a fight for racial freedom and uplift with a militant vengeance (*Imperium* 65, 66).
51. John Shawcross, *John Milton and Influence* (Pittsburgh: Duquesne University Press, 1991), 144.
52. "Rubicon," *Britannica Online Encyclopedia*, britannica.com/EBchecked/topic/511950/Rubicon (accessed September 19, 2013).
53. Ibid.
54. Randolph Meade Walker, *Metamorphosis of Sutton*, 50.
55. Ibid., 50.
56. Briggs, "New Negro of the South," 170.
57. Coleman, *Sutton E. Griggs*, 43.
58. Stephen Knadler, "Sensationalizing Patriotism: Sutton Griggs and the Sentimental Nationalism of Citizen Tom," *American Literature* 79, no. 4 (2007): 684.
59. Randolph Meade Walker, *Metamorphosis of Sutton*, 81, 92.
60. Belton has previously cross-dressed as a female in order to provide for his family. His experience of sexual objectification and harassment by white men invites readers to consider the plight of black women in the unflattering light of Bernard's cross-dressing performance.
61. Gary L. Lemons, "Skinwalking and Color Linecrossing: Teaching Writing against Racism," in *Race in the College Classroom: Pedagogy and Politics*, ed. Bonnie TuSmith and Maureen T. Reddy (New Brunswick, NJ: Rutgers University Press, 2002), 283.
62. Ibid., 283.
63. Joseph Wittreich, *Why Milton Matters* (New York: Palgrave, 2006), 186.
64. Ibid., 186.
65. Tracy Mishkin, "Theorizing Literary Influence and African-American Writers," in *Literary Influence and African-American Writers: Collected Essays*, ed. Tracy Mishkin (New York: Garland 1996), 10.

66. Reggie Young, "On Stepping into Footprints Which Feel Like Your Own: Literacy, Empowerment, and the African-American Literary Tradition," in *Literary Influence and African-American Writers: Collected Essays*, ed. Tracy Mishkin (New York: Garland, 1996), 369.

Notes to Epilogue

1. Dolan Hubbard, *The Sermon and the African American Literary Imagination* (Columbia: University of Missouri Press, 1994), 18.
2. Malcolm X, *The Autobiography of Malcolm X as Told to Alex Haley* (New York: Ballantine, 1992), 202. Subsequent in-text quotations of the *Autobiography* refer to this edition.
3. Malcolm X, *Malcolm X Speaks: Selected Speeches and Statements*, ed. George Breitman (New York: Grove Weidenfeld, 1965), 65.
4. Ibid., 11.
5. Hubbard, *The Sermon*, 5.
6. Ibid., 5–6.
7. Albert J. Raboteau, *A Fire in the Bones: Reflections on African-American Religious History* (Boston: Beacon Press, 1995), 4.
8. *Malcolm X Speaks*, 26, 40.
9. Ibid., 9, 26, 40.
10. Both Ishmael Reed and Jamaica Kincaid have noted Milton's direct influence on their literary imaginations. Commenting on how he came to name the underground literary journal he co-founded in the 1960s, the *East Village Other*, Reed claims, "I named the newspaper...from a book of criticism on 'Paradise Lost' by Jung. He mentioned the 'other' as a devil. It stands for a whole Generation...we're the devils, we're the others, we're the outsiders." See Walt Shepperd, "When State Magicians Fail: An Interview with Ishmael Reed," in *Conversations with Ishmael Reed*, ed. Bruce Dick and Amritjit Singh (Jackson: University Press of Mississippi, 1995), 3–13. Similarly, in a recent National Public Radio interview, Jamaica Kincaid discusses the "perverse effect" Milton's *Paradise Lost* had on her as a child. In Milton's Satan, she found a character with whom she could identify, one whose rebelliousness gave the then rebellious seven-year-old the feeling that "what [she] had done was right" because Satan had also "done something wrong and...gloried in it." See NPR, "Intersections: Jamaica Kincaid and the Literature of Defiance," www.npr.org/templates/story/story.php?storyId=1625888 (accessed November 11, 2004).

Bibliography

Achinstein, Sharon. *Milton and the Revolutionary Reader*. Princeton, NJ: Princeton University Press, 1994.

Alexander, Leslie M. "William T. Hamilton." In *Encyclopedia of African American History*, edited by Leslie M. Alexander and Walter C. Rucker, 144–45. Santa Barbara, CA: ABC-CLIO, 2010.

Andrews, William L. "Frederick Douglass, Preacher." *American Literature* 54 (1982): 592–97.

———. "Narrating Slavery." In *Teaching African American Literature*, edited by Maryemma Graham, Sharon Pineault-Burke, and Marianna White Davis. New York: Routledge, 1998.

———. *To Tell a Free Story: The First Century of Afro-American Autobiography, 1760–1865*. Urbana: University of Illinois Press, 1986.

Aptheker, Herbert. *One Continual Cry: David Walker's "Appeal to the Colored Citizens of the World" (1829–1830)*. New York: Humanities Press, 1965.

Asante, Molefi Kete. *The Afrocentric Idea*. Philadelphia: Temple University Press, 1998.

Baker-Fletcher, Karen. *A Singing Something: Womanist Reflections on Anna Julia Cooper*. New York: Crossroad, 1994.

Barthelemy, Anthony Gerard. *Black Face, Maligned Race: The Representation of Blacks in English Drama from Shakespeare to Southerne*. Baton Rouge: Louisiana State University Press, 1987.

Bennett, Joan S. *Reviving Liberty*. Cambridge, MA: Harvard University Press, 1989.

Bennett, Paula. "Phillis Wheatley's Vocation and the Paradox of the 'Afric Muse.'" *PMLA* 113, no. 1 (1998): 64–76.

Bercovitch, Sacvan. *The American Jeremiad*. Madison: The University of Wisconsin Press, 1978.

Bergner, Gwen. "Myths of the Masculine Subject: The Oedipus Complex and Douglass's 1845 *Narrative*." *Discourse: Berkeley Journal for Theoretical Studies in Media and Culture* 19, no. 2 (1997): 53–71.

Bible. *Thompson Chain-Reference Bible*. Special centennial ed. Compiled and edited by Frank Charles Thompson. Indianapolis: B. B. Kirkbride Bible Co., 2007.

Bingham, Caleb. *The Columbian Orator*. Kila, MT: Kessinger Press, 1811.

Blake, William. *The Marriage of Heaven and Hell*. In *William Blake: Selected Poetry*, edited by W. H. Stevenson, 66–80. London: Penguin Books, 1988.

Bloom, Harold. *A Map for Misreading*. New York: Oxford University Press, 1975.

Bone, Robert. *The Negro Novel in America*. New Haven, CT: Yale University Press, 1968.

Boocker, David. "Garrison, Milton, and the Abolitionist Rhetoric of Demonization." *American Periodicals: A Journal of History, Criticism, and Bibliography* 9 (1999): 15–26.

Boyd, Melba Joyce. *Discarded Legacy*. Detroit: Wayne State University Press, 1994.

Boyle, Marjorie O'Rourke. "Home to Mother: Regaining Milton's Paradise." *Modern Philology* 97, no. 4 (2000): 499–527.

Briggs, Gabriel A. "*Imperium in Imperio*: Sutton E. Griggs and the New Negro of the South." *Southern Quarterly* 45, no. 3 (2008): 153–76.

Brown, Fahamisha Patricia. *Performing the Word*. New Brunswick, NJ: Rutgers University Press, 1999.

Bruce, Dickson D., Jr. *The Origins of African American Literature, 1680–1865*. Charlottesville: University of Virginia Press, 2001.

Byron, George Gordon, Lord. *Childe Harold's Pilgrimage*. In *Lord Byron: The Complete Poetical Works*, vol. 2, edited by Jerome J. McGann, 3–186. Oxford: Oxford University Press, 1980.

Callahan, Allen Dwight. *The Talking Book: African Americans and the Bible*. New Haven, CT: Yale University Press, 2006.

Campbell, Jane. *Mythic Black Fiction*. Knoxville: University of Tennessee Press, 1986.

Carby, Hazel. *Reconstructing Womanhood: The Emergence of the Afro-American Woman Novelist*. New York: Oxford University Press, 1987.

Christian, Barbara. "The Black Woman Artist as Wayward." In *Alice Walker*, Modern Critical Views, edited by Harold Bloom. New York: Chelsea House, 1989.

———. "The Highs and the Lows of Black Feminist Criticism." In *Feminisms: An Anthology of Literary Theory and Criticism*, edited by Robyn R. Warhol and Diane Price Herndl, 51–56. New Brunswick, NJ: Rutgers University Press, 1997.

Coleman, Finnie D. *Sutton E. Griggs and the Struggle against White Supremacy*. Knoxville: University of Tennessee Press, 2007.

Cone, James H. *Black Theology and Black Power*. New York: Seabury Press, 1969.

———. *A Black Theology of Liberation*. Maryknoll: Orbis Books, 1990.

Cooley, Timothy Mather. *Sketches of the Life and Character of the Rev. Lemuel Haynes, A.M., for Many Years Pastor of a Church in Rutland, Vt., and Late in Granville, New-York*. New York: Harper & Brothers, 1837.

Cooper, Anna Julia. "The Answer." Anna Julia Cooper Papers, Box 23-4. Moorland-Spingarn Research Center.

———. "The Intellectual Progress of the Colored Women in the United States since the Emancipation Proclamation: A Response to Fannie Barrier Williams." In *The Voice of Anna Julia Cooper*, edited by Charles Lemert and Esme Bhan, 201–05. Lanham, MD: Rowman and Littlefield, 1998.

———. *A Voice from the South*. 1892. Reprint, New York: Oxford University Press, 1988.

Craciun, Adriana. "Romantic Satanism and the Rise of Nineteenth-Century Women's Poetry." *New Literary History* 34, no. 4 (2003): 699–721.

Crockett, Hasan. "The Incendiary Pamphlet: David Walker's Appeal in Georgia." *Journal of Negro History* 86, no. 3 (2001): 305–18.

Cruse, Harold. *The Crisis of the Negro Intellectual*. New York: William Morrow, 1967.

Davies, Stevie. *Images of Kingship in "Paradise Lost."* Columbia: University of Missouri Press, 1983.

Davis, Gerald L. *I Got the Word in Me and I Can Sing It, You Know*. Philadelphia: University of Pennsylvania Press, 1985.

Deleuze, Gilles, and Félix Guattari. "What Is a Minor Literature?" In *Out There: Marginalization and Contemporary Cultures*, edited by Russell Ferguson, Martha Gever, Trinh T. Minh-ha, and Cornel West, 59–69. Cambridge, MA: MIT Press, 1990.

Douglas, Richard Jordan. *The Quiet Hero: Figures of Temperance in Spenser, Donne, Milton, and Joyce*. Washington, DC: Catholic University of America Press, 1989.

Douglass, Frederick. *Life and Writings of Frederick Douglass*. Vol. 1. Edited by Philip Foner. New York: International Publishers, 1950.

———. *My Bondage and My Freedom*. In *Douglass Autobiographies*, 103–452. New York: Library of America, 1994.

———. *Narrative of the Life of Frederick Douglass, an American Slave, Written by Himself*. Edited by William L. Andrews and William S. McFeely. New York: Norton, 1997.

———. "Self-Made Men." In *The Frederick Douglass Papers*, edited by John W. Blassingame and C. Peter Ripley et al. Series 1, vol. 2: 1847–54. New Haven, CT: Yale University Press, 1982.

———. "Self-Made Men: An Address Delivered in Carlisle, Pennsylvania, in March 1893." In *The Frederick Douglass Papers*, edited by John W. Blassingame and C. Peter Ripley et al. Series 1, vol. 5: 1881–95. New Haven, CT: Yale University Press, 1992.

———. "The Trials and Triumphs of Self-Made Men: An Address Delivered in Halifax, England, on 4 January 1860." In *The Frederick Douglass Papers*, edited by John W. Blassingame and C. Peter Ripley et al. Series 1, vol. 3: 1855–63. New Haven, CT: Yale University Press, 1985.

Dubois, W. E. B. *The Souls of Black Folk*. New York: W. W. Norton, 1999.

Eaton, Clement. "A Dangerous Pamphlet in the Old South." *Journal of Southern History* 2, no. 3 (1936): 323–34.

Empson, William. *Milton's God*. London: Chatto and Windus, 1961.

Equiano, Olaudah. *The Interesting Narrative of the Life of Olaudah Equiano; or, Gustavus Vassa, the African. Written by Himself.* In *The Classic Slave Narratives*, edited by Henry Louis Gates Jr., 10–182. New York: Mentor, 1987.

Finseth, Ian. "David Walker, Nature's Nation, and Early African-American Separatism." *Mississippi Quarterly* 54, no. 3 (2001): 337–62.

Fish, Stanley. *Surprised by Sin*. 2nd ed. Cambridge, MA: Harvard University Press, 1998.

Flannagan, Roy, ed. *The Riverside Milton*. Boston: Houghton Mifflin, 1998.

Flanzbaum, Hilene. "Unprecedented Liberties: Re-Reading Phillis Wheatley." *MELUS* 18, no. 3 (1993): 71–81.

Foner, Philip S., and Robert James Branham, eds. *Lift Every Voice: African American Oratory, 1787–1900*. Tuscaloosa: University of Alabama Press, 1998.

Forbes, Ella. "Every Man Fights for His Freedom: The Rhetoric of African American Resistance in the Mid-Nineteenth Century." In *Understanding African American Rhetoric: Classical Origins to Contemporary Innovations*, edited by Ronald L. Jackson and Elaine B. Richardson, 155–70. New York: Routledge, 2003.

Forsyth, Neil. *The Satanic Epic*. Princeton, NJ: Princeton University Press, 2003.

Foster, Frances Smith. *Written by Herself: Literary Production by African American Women, 1746–1892*. Bloomington: Indiana University Press, 1993.

Foster, Frances Smith, ed. *A Brighter Coming Day: A Frances Ellen Watkins Harper Reader*. New York: The Feminist Press, 1990.

———. Introduction to *Minnie's Sacrifice; Sowing and Reaping; Trial and Triumph: Three Rediscovered Novels by Frances E. W. Harper*. Boston: Beacon Press, 1994.

Foster, Frances Smith, and Valerie L. Ruffin. "Teaching African American Poetry of the Reconstruction Era: Frances E. W. Harper's 'Moses: A Story of the Nile.'" In *Teaching Nineteenth-Century African American Poetry*, edited by Paula Bernet, Karen L. Kilcup, and Philipp Schweighauser, 142–50. New York: Modern Language Association of America, 2007.

Franklin, Benjamin. "An American Guesser." *Pennsylvania Journal*, December 27, 1775.

Franklin, John Hope, and Alfred A. Moss Jr. *From Slavery to Freedom: A History of African Americans*. 7th ed. New York: McGraw-Hill, 1994.

Froula, Christine. "When Eve Reads Milton: Undoing the Canonical Economy." *Critical Inquiry* 10, no. 2 (1983): 321–47.

Frow, John. "Intertexuality and Ontology." In *Intertextuality: Theories and Practices*, edited by Michael Worton and Judith Still. Manchester: Manchester University Press, 1990.

Gage, Frances Dana. *Poems*. Philadelphia: J. B. Lippincott, 1867.

Garrison, Wendell Phillips, and Francis Jackson Garrison. *William Lloyd Garrison, 1805–1879: The Story of His Life Told by His Children*. Boston: Houghton Mifflin, 1889.

Garrison, William Lloyd. *Liberator*, January 8, 1831.

Gates, Henry Louis Jr. "Foreword: In Her Own Write." In *Complete Poems of Frances E. W. Harper*, edited by Maryemma Graham. New York: Oxford University Press, 1988.

———. "Introduction: The Talking Book." In Gates and Andrews, *Pioneers of the Black Atlantic*, 1–29.

———. "James Gronniosaw and the Trope of the Talking Book." In *African American Autobiography*, edited by William L. Andrews, 8–25. Englewood Cliffs, NJ: Prentice Hall, 1993.

———. *Loose Canons: Notes on the Culture Wars*. New York: Oxford University Press, 1992.

———. "Preface to Blackness." In *African American Literary Theory: A Reader*, edited by Winston Napier, 147–64. 1979. Reprint, New York: New York University Press, 2000.

———. *The Signifying Monkey: A Theory of Afro-American Literary Criticism*. New York: Oxford University Press, 1988.

Gates, Henry Louis, Jr., ed. "Criticism in the Jungle." In *Black Literature and Literary Theory*, edited by Henry Louis Gates Jr., 1–24. 1984. Reprint, New York: Routledge, 1990.

Gates, Henry Louis, Jr., and William L. Andrews, eds. *Pioneers of the Black Atlantic*. Washington, DC: Civitas, 1998.

Gayle, Addison, Jr. *The Black Situation*. New York: Horizon Press, 1970.

Gerald, Carolyn F. "The Black Writer and His Role." In *African American Literary Theory: A Reader*, edited by Winston Napier, 81–86. New York: New York University Press, 2000.

Gibson, Donald B. "Literature: Poetry." In *Encyclopedia of Black America*, edited by W. Augustus Low and Virgil A. Clift. New York: McGraw Hill, 1981.

Gilbert, Sandra M., and Susan Gubar. *The Madwoman in the Attic*. New Haven, CT: Yale University Press, 1979.

Gloster, Hugh. "Sutton E. Griggs: Novelist of the New Negro." *Phylon* 4 (1943): 335–45.

Goldner, Ellen J. "Allegories of Exposure." In *Living with the Color of Our Words*, edited by Ellen J. Goldner and Safiya Henderson-Holmes. Syracuse, NY: Syracuse University Press, 2001.

Gordon, Lewis R. *Existentia Africana*. New York: Routledge, 2000.

Graham, Maryemma. "Introduction." In *Complete Poems of Frances E. W. Harper*, edited by Maryemma Graham, xxxiii–lx. New York: Oxford University Press, 1988.

Gray, Erik. *Milton and the Victorians*. Ithaca, NY: Cornell University Press, 2009.

Greenblatt, Stephen. *Shakespearean Negotiations*. Berkeley and Los Angeles: University of California Press, 1988.

Griffin, Dustin. *Regaining Paradise*. Cambridge: Cambridge University Press, 1986.

Griggs, Sutton E. *Imperium in Imperio*. New York: Modern Library, 2003.

Grimké, Charlotte Forten. *The Journals of Charlotte Forten Grimké*. Edited by Brenda Stevenson. New York: Oxford University Press, 1988.

Guillory, John. "Dalila's House: *Samson Agonistes* and the Sexual Division of Labor." In *Rewriting the Renaissance: The Discourses of Sexual Difference in Early Modern Europe*, edited by Margaret W. Ferguson, Maureen Quilligan, and Nancy J. Vickers, 106–22. Chicago: University of Chicago Press, 1986.

Hall, Kim F. *Things of Darkness: Economies of Race and Gender in Early Modern England*. Ithaca, NY: Cornell University Press, 1995.

Hamilton, William. "Mutual Interest, Mutual Benefit, and Mutual Relief." In Foner and Branham, *Lift Every Voice*, 80–85.

———. "O! Africa." In Foner and Branham, *Lift Every Voice*, 91–97.

Harmon, William, and C. Hugh Holman. *A Handbook to Literature*. Saddle Brook, NJ: Prentice Hall, 2008.

Harnsberger, Lindsey C. *Essential Dictionary of Music*. Los Angeles: Alfred Publishing, 1997.

Harper, Frances Ellen Watkins. "Bury Me in a Free Land." In Foster, *A Brighter Coming Day*, 177.

———. "Enlightened Motherhood." In Foster, *A Brighter Coming Day*, 285–92.

———. "Factor in Human Progress." In Foster, *A Brighter Coming Day*, 275–80.

———. "Fancy Etchings [April 24, 1873]." In Foster, *A Brighter Coming Day*, 224–26.

———. "Fancy Etchings [May 1, 1873]." In Foster, *A Brighter Coming Day*, 226–28.

———. *Iola Leroy*. Boston: Beacon Press, 1987.

———. "The Mission of the Flowers." In Foster, *A Brighter Coming Day*, 230–34.

———. *Moses: A Story of the Nile*. In Foster, *A Brighter Coming Day*, 138–65.

———. "Our Greatest Want." In Foster, *A Brighter Coming Day*, 102–04.

———. "Shalmanezer, Prince of Cosman." In Foster, *A Brighter Coming Day*, 295–302.

———. *Sowing and Reaping*. In Foster, *Three Rediscovered Novels*, 93–176.

———. *Trial and Triumph*. In Foster, *Three Rediscovered Novels*, 177–286.

———. "The Woman's Christian Temperance Union and the Colored Woman." In Foster, *A Brighter Coming Day*, 281–84.

———. "Woman's Political Future." In *World's Congress of Representative Women*, edited by May Wright Sewell, 433–37. Chicago: Rand McNally, 1984.

Harris, Leslie M. *In the Shadow of Slavery: African Americans in New York City, 1626–1863*. Chicago: University of Chicago Press, 2003.

Hayes, Diana L. *And Still We Rise: An Introduction to Black Liberation Theology*. New York: Paulist Press, 1996.

Haynes, Lemuel. "Universal Salvation." In Foner and Branham, *Lift Every Voice*, 59–65.

Henderson, Mae G. "Speaking in Tongues: Dialogics, Dialectics, and the Black Woman Writer's Literary Tradition." In *Changing Our Own Words: Essays on Criticism, Theory and Writing by Black Women*, edited by Cheryl A. Wall, 16–37. New Brunswick, NJ: Rutgers University Press, 1989.

Henderson, Stephen. *Understanding the New Black Poetry*. New York: William Morrow, 1973.

Henkel, Michele A. "Forging Identity through Literary Reinterpellation: The Ideological Project of Frederick Douglass's *Narrative*." *Literature and Psychology* 48 (2002): 89–101.

Herman, Peter C. *Destabilizing Milton: "Paradise Lost" and the Poetics of Incertitude*. New York: Palgrave Macmillan, 2005.

Herron, Carolivia. "Milton and Afro-American Literature." In *Re-membering Milton: Essays on the Texts and Traditions*, edited by Mary Nyquist and Margaret W. Ferguson, 278–300. New York: Methuen, 1987.

Herskovits, Melville J. *The Myth of the Negro Past*. Boston: Beacon Press, 1941.

Higgs, Elton D. "The 'Thunder' of God in *Paradise Lost*." *Milton Quarterly* 4, no. 2 (1970): 24–27.

Hill, Christopher. *Milton and the English Revolution*. New York: Viking Press, 1978.

Hill, Patricia Liggins. "Frances Watkins Harper's *Moses: A Story of the Nile:* Apologue of the Emancipation Struggle." *AME Zion Quarterly Review* 95 (January 1984): 11–18.

Hill, Patricia Liggins, ed. *Call and Response: The Riverside Anthology of the African American Literary Tradition*. Boston: Houghton Mifflin, 1998.

Hogan, Patrick Colm. *Cognitive Science, Literature, and the Arts*. New York: Routledge, 2003.

hooks, bell. *Black Looks: Race and Representation*. Boston: South End Press, 1992.

———. *We Real Cool: Black Men and Masculinity*. New York: Routledge, 2004.

Howard-Pitney, David. *The Afro-American Jeremiad*. Philadelphia: Temple University Press, 1990.

Hubbard, Dolan. *The Sermon and the African American Literary Imagination*. Columbia: University of Missouri Press, 1994.

Hughes, Merritt Y. "The Christ of *Paradise Regained* and the Renaissance Heroic Tradition." *Studies in Philology* 35, no. 1 (1938): 254–77.

———. "Satan and the 'Myth' of the Tyrant." In *Essays in English Literature from the Renaissance to the Victorian Age*, edited by Millar Maclure and F. W. Watt. Toronto: University of Toronto Press, 1964.

Hurston, Zora Neale. "Characteristics of Negro Expression." In *Sweat / Zora Neale Hurston*, edited by Cheryl A. Wall, 55–72. New Brunswick, NJ: Rutgers University Press, 1997.

———. *Mules and Men*. Philadelphia: J. B. Lippincott, 1935.

Jablonski, Steven. "Ham's Vicious Race: Slavery and John Milton." *Studies in English Literature 1500–1900* 37, no. 1 (1997): 173–90.

Jackson, Blyden D. *A History of Afro-American Literature*. Vol. 1, *The Long Beginning, 1746–1895*. Baton Rouge: Louisiana State University Press, 1989.

Jacobs, Donald M. "David Walker: Boston Race Leader, 1825–1830." *Essex Institute Historical Collections* (1977): 94–107.

Jefferson, Thomas. *Notes on the State of Virginia*. Edited by William Peden. Chapel Hill: University of North Carolina Press, 1995.

Jenkins, Melissa Shields. "'The Poets Are with Us': Frederick Douglass and John Milton." *Modern Language Studies* 38, no. 2 (2009): 12–27.

Jordan, Richard Douglas. *The Quiet Hero: Figures of Temperance in Spenser, Donne, Milton, and Joyce*. Washington, DC: Catholic University of America Press, 1989.

Juhasz, Suzanne. *Naked and Fiery Forms*. New York: Harper & Row, 1976.

Kelley, Mark R., Michael Lieb, and John T. Shawcross. *Milton and the Grounds of Contention*. Pittsburgh: Duquesne University Press, 2003.

Kendrick, Christopher. *Milton: A Study in Ideology and Form*. New York: Methuen, 1986.

Kendrick, Robert. "Re-membering America: Phillis Wheatley's Intertextual Epic." *African American Review* 30, no. 1 (1996): 71–88.

Knadler, Stephen. "Sensationalizing Patriotism: Sutton Griggs and the Sentimental Nationalism of Citizen Tom." *American Literature* 79, no. 4 (2007): 673–99.

Knowles, Julie Nall. "*The Course of Time:* A Calvinistic *Paradise Lost*." In *Milton Studies*, vol. 18, edited by James D. Simmonds, 173–93. Pittsburgh: University of Pittsburgh Press, 1983.

Kolodny, Annette. "A Map for Rereading: Gender and the Interpretation of Literary Texts." In *The New Feminist Criticism*, edited by Elaine Showalter, 46–62. New York: Pantheon Books, 1985.

Kurth, Burton O. *Milton and Christian Heroism*. Hamden: Archon Books, 1966.

Lares, Jameela. *Milton and the Preaching Arts.* Pittsburgh: Duquesne University Press, 2001.

Lauter, Paul. *Canons and Contexts.* New York: Oxford University Press, 1991.

Lemert, Charles, and Esme Bhan, eds. *The Voice of Anna Julia Cooper.* Lanham, MD: Rowman and Littlefield, 1998.

Lemons, Gary L. "Skinwalking and Color Linecrossing: Teaching Writing against Racism." In *Race in the College Classroom: Pedagogy and Politics,* edited by Bonnie TuSmith and Maureen T. Reddy, 277–85. New Brunswick, NJ: Rutgers University Press, 2002.

Levander, Caroline. "Sutton Griggs and the Borderlands of Empire." *American Literary History* 22, no. 1 (2009): 57–84.

Lewalski, Barbara Kiefer. "Genre." In *A Companion to Milton,* edited by Thomas N. Corns, 3–21. Oxford: Blackwell, 2001.

———. "Milton on Women—Yet Once More." In *Milton Studies,* vol. 6, edited by James D. Simmonds, 3–20. Pittsburgh: University of Pittsburgh Press, 1974.

———. *Milton's Brief Epic: The Genre, Meaning, and Art of "Paradise Regained."* Providence, RI: Brown University Press, 1966.

Lewin, Jennifer. "Milton's Sonnets and the Sonnet Tradition." In *Approaches to Teaching Milton's Shorter Poetry and Prose,* edited by Peter C. Herman, 80–87. New York: Modern Language Association, 2007.

Lewis, C. S. *A Preface to "Paradise Lost."* London: Oxford University Press, 1961.

Logan, Shirley Wilson. *"We Are Coming": The Persuasive Discourse of Nineteenth-Century Black Women.* Carbondale: Southern Illinois University Press, 1999.

Lowenstein, David. *Representing Revolution in Milton and His Contemporaries.* Cambridge: Cambridge University Press, 2001.

Machacek, Gregory. *Milton and Homer: "Written to Aftertimes."* Pittsburgh: Duquesne University Press, 2011.

Malcolm X. *The Autobiography of Malcolm X as Told to Alex Haley.* New York: Ballantine, 1992.

———. *Malcolm X Speaks: Selected Speeches and Statements.* Edited by George Breitman. New York: Grove Weidenfeld, 1965.

Marrant, John. "You Stand with the Greatest Kings on Earth." In Foner and Branham, *Lift Every Voice,* 27–37.

Martin, Waldo E. *The Mind of Frederick Douglass.* Chapel Hill: The University of North Carolina Press, 1984.

Mason, Julian D., Jr. Introduction to *The Poems of Phillis Wheatley*, edited by Julian D. Mason, 1–22. Chapel Hill: The University of North Carolina Press, 1989.

May, Vivian M. *Anna Julia Cooper, Visionary Black Feminist*. New York: Routledge, 2007.

Mayer, Henry. *All on Fire: William Lloyd Garrison and the Abolition of Slavery*. New York: St. Martin's Press, 1998.

McBride, Dwight A. *Impossible Witnesses*. New York: New York University Press, 2001.

McColley, Diane Kelsey. *Milton's Eve*. Urbana: University of Illinois Press, 1983.

McConnell, Frank D. *Byron's Poetry*. New York: W. W. Norton, 1978.

McDowell, Deborah E. "In the First Place: Making Frederick Douglass and the Afro-American Narrative Tradition." In *African American Autobiography*, edited by William L. Andrews, 192–214. Englewood Cliffs, NJ: Prentice Hall, 1993.

McHenry, Elizabeth. *Forgotten Readers*. Durham, NC: Duke University Press, 2002.

McKittrick, Katherine. *Demonic Grounds: Black Women and the Cartographies of Struggle*. Minneapolis: University of Minnesota Press, 2006.

McWilliams, John P., Jr. *The American Epic: Transforming a Genre, 1770–1860*. Cambridge: Cambridge University Press, 1989.

Mieder, Wolfgang. "'Paddle Your Own Canoe': Frederick Douglass's Proverbial Message in His 'Self-Made Men' Speech." *Midwestern Folklore* 27, no. 2 (2001): 21–40.

Mills, Charles. "White Ignorance." In *Race and the Epistemologies of Ignorance*, edited by Shannon Sullivan and Nancy Tuana, 13–38. Albany: State University of New York Press, 2007.

Milton, John. *Areopagitica*. In Flannagan, *The Riverside Milton*, 987–1024.

———. *Of Reformation*. In Flannagan, *The Riverside Milton*, 873–901.

———. *Paradise Lost*. Edited by Scott Elledge. 2nd ed. New York: W. W. Norton, 1993.

———. *The Reason of Church-Government*. In Flannagan, *The Riverside Milton*, 902–25.

———. "Sonnet 16: 'To the Lord Generall Cromwell.'" In Flannagan, *The Riverside Milton*, 290–91.

———. "Sonnet 22: 'Cyriack, This Three Years Day.'" In Flannagan, *The Riverside Milton*, 293.

Mishkin, Tracy. "Theorizing Literary Influence and African-American Writers." In *Literary Influence and African-American Writers: Collected Essays*, edited by Tracy Mishkin, 3–20. New York: Garland, 1996.

Mitchell, Henry H. *Black Preaching: The Recovery of a Powerful Art.* Nashville: Abingdon Press, 1990.

Mitchem, Stephanie Y. *Introducing Womanist Theology.* Maryknoll: Orbis Books, 2002.

Moore, Leslie E. *Beautiful Sublime.* Stanford, CA: Stanford University Press, 1990.

Morrison, Toni. *Playing in the Dark: Whiteness and the Literary Imagination.* New York: Vintage Books, 1993.

———. "Unspeakable Things Unspoken: The Afro-American Presence in American Literature." In *Criticism and the Color Line,* edited by Henry B. Wonham, 16–29. New Brunswick, NJ: Rutgers University Press, 1996.

Moses, Wilson Jeremiah. *Black Messiahs and Uncle Toms: Social and Literary Manipulations of a Religious Myth.* University Park: Pennsylvania State University Press, 1982.

———. *Creative Conflict in African American Thought.* Cambridge: Cambridge University Press, 2004.

———. *The Golden Age of Black Nationalism, 1850–1925.* New York: Oxford University Press, 1978.

National Public Radio. "Intersections: Jamaica Kincaid and the Literature of Defiance." www.npr.org/templates/story/story.php?storyId=1625888; accessed November 11, 2004.

Nell, William C. *Colored Patriots of the American Revolution.* New York: Arno Press and *The New York Times,* 1968.

Nelson, James G. *The Sublime Puritan: Milton and the Victorians.* Madison: University of Wisconsin Press, 1963.

Newlyn, Lucy. *"Paradise Lost" and the Romantic Reader.* Oxford: Clarendon Press, 1993.

Newman, Richard, Patrick Rael, and Phillip Lapsanski, eds. *Pamphlets of Protest: An Anthology of Early African American Protest Literature, 1790–1860.* New York: Routledge, 2001.

Nielsen, Aldon L. *Writing between the Lines: Race and Intertextuality.* Athens: University of Georgia Press, 1994.

Nyquist, Mary. "The Genesis of Gendered Subjectivity in the Divorce Tracts and in *Paradise Lost.* In *Re-membering Milton: Essays on the Text and Traditions,* edited by Mary Nyquist Margaret W. Ferguson, 99–127. New York: Methuen, 1987.

Nyquist, Mary, and Margaret W. Ferguson, eds. Preface to *Re-membering Milton: Essays on the Texts and Traditions*. New York: Methuen, 1987.

O'Connor, Lillian. *Pioneer Women Orators*. New York: Vantage Press, 1952.

O'Meally, Robert G. "Frederick Douglass' 1845 *Narrative:* The Text Was Meant to Be Preached." In *Afro-American Literature: The Reconstruction of Instruction*, edited by Dexter Fisher and Robert B. Stepto, 192–211. New York: Modern Language Association, 1978.

O'Neale, Sondra. "Wheatley's Use of Biblical Myth and Symbol." *Early American Literature* 21 (1996): 144–65.

Othello. "Essay on Negro Slavery, No. I." *American Museum*, May 10, 1788. In Othello, "What the Negro Was Thinking during the Eighteenth Century: Essay on Negro Slavery," *Journal of Negro History*, no. 1 (1916): 49–68.

Oxford English Dictionary. 2nd ed. 1989. OED Online. Oxford University Press. www.dictionary.oed.com.

Padgett, Chris. "Finding His Voice: The Liberations of Frederick Douglass, 1818–1848." *Proteus: A Journal of Ideas* 12, no. 1 (1995): 10–14.

Plutarch. *Roman Lives*. Translated by Robin Waterfield. Oxford: Oxford University Press, 1999.

Quilligan, Maureen. "Freedom, Service, and the Trade in Slaves: The Problems of Labor in *Paradise Lost*." In *Subject and Object in Renaissance Culture*, edited by Margreta de Grazia, Maureen Quilligan, and Peter Stallybrass, 213–34. London: Cambridge University Press, 1996.

Raboteau, Albert J. "African-Americans, Exodus, and the American Israel." In *African-American Christianity: Essays on History*, edited by Paul E. Johnson, 1–17. Berkeley and Los Angeles: University of California Press, 1994.

———. *A Fire in the Bones: Reflections on African-American Religious History*. Boston: Beacon Press, 1995.

Rael, Patrick. *Black Identity and Black Protest in the Antebellum North*. Chapel Hill: The University of North Carolina Press, 2002.

Redding, J. Saunders. *To Make a Poet Black*. Ithaca, NY: Cornell University Press, 1988.

Ricks, Christopher. *Milton's Grand Style*. London: Oxford University Press, 1963.

Riffaterre, Michael. "Compulsory Reader Response: The Intertextual Drive." In *Intertextuality: Theories and Practices*, edited by Michael Worton and Judith Still, 56–78. Manchester: Manchester University Press, 1990.

Robinson, William H., Jr. *Early Black American Poets*. Dubuque, IA: William C. Brown, 1969.

Rose, Gillian. *Feminism and Geography: The Limits of Geographical Knowledge*. Minneapolis: University of Minnesota Press, 1993.

Rose, Mary Beth. "Why Is the Virgin Mary in *Paradise Regained?*" In *Visionary Milton: Essays on Prophecy and Violence*, edited by Peter E. Medine, John T. Shawcross, and David V. Urban, 193–213. Pittsburgh: Duquesne University Press, 2010.

Ross, Marlon B. *The Contours of Masculine Desire*. New York: Oxford University Press, 1989.

Rudoff, Shaindy. "Tarring the Garden: The Bible and the Aesthetics of Slavery in Douglass's *Narrative*." *ESQ: A Journal of the American Renaissance* 46, no. 4 (2000): 213–37.

Rumrich, John P. *Milton Unbound: Controversy and Reinterpretation*. Cambridge: Cambridge University Press, 1996.

Russell, Kathy, Midge Wilson, and Ronald Hall. *The Color Complex*. New York: Anchor Books, 1992.

Rutkowski, Alice. "Leaving the Good Mother: Frances E. W. Harper, Lydia Maria Child, and the Literary Politics of Reconstruction." *Legacy* 25, no. 1 (2008): 83–104.

Sartre, Jean-Paul. *Being and Nothingness*. Trans. Hazel E. Barnes. New York: Washington Square Press, 1956.

———. "Freedom to Have, to Do, to Be: Being and Nothingness." In *Of Human Freedom*, edited by Wade Baskin, 32–98. New York: Philosophical Library, 1966.

Savage, J. B. "Freedom and Necessity in *Paradise Lost*." *ELH* 44, no. 2. (1977): 286–311.

Schulman, Lydia Dittler. *"Paradise Lost" and the Rise of the American Republic*. Boston: Northeastern University Press, 1992.

Scruggs, Charles. "Phillis Wheatley and the Poetical Legacy of Eighteenth-Century England." *Studies in Eighteenth-Century Culture* 10 (1981): 279–95.

Seeyle, Joseph. "The Clay Foot of the Climber: Richard M. Nixon in Perspective." In *Literary Romanticism in America*, edited by William L. Andrews, 109–34. Baton Rouge: Louisiana State University Press, 1981.

Sensabaugh, George. *Milton in Early America*. Princeton, NJ: Princeton University Press, 1964.

Shawcross, John T. Introduction to *Milton: The Critical Heritage*. London: Routledge & Kegan Paul, 1970.

———. *John Milton and Influence*. Pittsburgh: Duquesne University Press, 1991.

———. *With Mortal Voice*. Lexington: University Press of Kentucky, 1982.

Shelley, Percy Bysshe. "A Defence of Poetry" and "Prometheus Unbound." In *Shelley's Poetry and Prose*, edited by Donald H. Reiman and Neil Fraistat, 509–38, 202–85. New York: W. W. Norton, 2002.

Shepperd, Walt. "When State Magicians Fail: An Interview with Ishmael Reed." In *Conversations with Ishmael Reed*, edited by Bruce Dick and Amritjit Singh, 3–13. Jackson: University Press of Mississippi, 1995.

Shields, John C. *Phillis Wheatley's Poetics of Liberation*. Knoxville: University of Tennessee Press, 2008.

———. "Phillis Wheatley's Subversive Pastoral." *Eighteenth-Century Studies* 27, no. 4 (1994): 631–47.

———. "Phillis Wheatley's Use of Classicism." *American Literature* 52, no. 1 (1980): 97–111.

Smith, Ian. *Race and Rhetoric in the Renaissance*. New York: Palgrave Macmillan, 2009.

Smith, Neil. "Afterword to the Second Edition." *Uneven Development: Nature, Capital, and the Production of Space*. 3rd ed. Athens: University of Georgia Press, 1990. 213–38.

Smith, Valerie. *Self-Discovery and Authority in Afro-American Narrative*. Cambridge, MA: Harvard University Press, 1987.

St. Hilaire, Danielle A. *Satan's Poetry: Fallenness and Poetic Tradition in "Paradise Lost."* Pittsburgh: Duquesne University Press, 2012.

Steadman, John M. *Milton and the Renaissance Hero*. Oxford: Clarendon Press, 1967.

———. *Milton's Epic Characters*. Chapel Hill: University of North Carolina Press, 1968.

Stein, Edward. *Wordsworth's Art of Allusion*. University Park: Pennsylvania State University Press, 1988.

Stepto, Robert B. "Teaching Afro-American Literature: Survey of Tradition: The Reconstruction of Instruction." In *Afro-American Literature: The Reconstruction of Instruction*, edited by Dexter Fisher and Robert B. Stepto, 8–24. New York: Modern Language Association, 1979.

Stewart, Maria. "Religion and the Pure Principles of Morality, the Sure Foundation on Which We Must Build." In *Maria Stewart, America's First Black Woman Political Writer*, edited by Marilyn Richardson, 28–42. Bloomington: University of Indiana Press, 1987.

Still, William. *Underground Railroad*. New York: Arno Press and *The New York Times*, 1968.

Stuckey, Sterling. *Slave Culture: Nationalist Theory and the Foundations of Black America*. New York: Oxford University Press, 1987.

Sundquist, Eric J. "Frederick Douglass: Literacy and Paternalism." In *Critical Essays on Frederick Douglass*, edited by William L. Andrews, 120–32. Boston: G. K. Hall, 1991.

———. *To Wake the Nations: Race in the Making of American Literature*. Cambridge, MA: Belknap Press, 1993.

Tanner, John S., and Justin Collings. "How Adams and Jefferson Read Milton and Milton Read Them." *Milton Quarterly* 40, no. 3 (2006): 207–19.

Thompson, E. N. S. "The Rebel Angel in Later Poetry." *Philological Quarterly* 27, no. 1 (1948): 1–16.

Thurman, Garner, and Carolyn Calloway-Thomas. "African-American Orality: Expanding Rhetoric." In *Understanding African American Rhetoric*, edited by Ronald L. Jackson II and Elaine B. Richardson, 43–56. New York: Routledge, 2003.

Thurman, Howard. "Community and the Self." In *Say It Plain*, edited by Catherine Ellis and Stephen Drury Smith. New York: The New Press, 2005.

Tillich, Paul. *The Shaking of the Foundations*. New York: Charles Scribner's Sons, 1946.

Tillyard, E. M. W. *Milton*. New York: Collier Books, 1966.

Van Anglen, K. P. *The New England Milton: Literary Reception and Cultural Authority in the Early Republic*. University Park: Pennsylvania State University Press, 1993.

Verdelle, A. J. Preface to *Imperium in Imperio*. New York: Modern Library, 2003.

Walker, Alice. "In Search of Our Mothers' Gardens." *In Search of Our Mothers' Gardens*, 231–43. San Diego: Harcourt Brace Jovanovich, 1983.

Walker, David. *Appeal in Four Articles; Together with a Preamble, to the Coloured Citizens of the World, but in Particular, and Very Expressly, to Those of the United States of America*. New York: Hill and Wang, 1995.

Walker, Randolph Meade. *The Metamorphosis of Sutton E. Griggs*. Memphis: Walker Publishing, 1991.

Wall, Cheryl A. *Worrying the Line: Black Women Writers, Lineage, and Literary Tradition*. Chapel Hill: University of North Carolina Press, 2005.

Walters, Tracey L. *African American Literature and the Classicist Tradition*. New York: Palgrave MacMillan, 2007.

Washington, Mary Helen. "These Self-Invented Women: A Theoretical Framework for a Literary History of Black Women." In *Politics of Education: Essays from Radical Teacher*, edited by Susan Gushee O'Malley, Robert C. Rosen, and Leonard Vogt, 89–98. Albany: State University of New York Press, 1990.

Waterman, Catherine H. *Flora's Lexicon: An Interpretation of the Language and Sentiment of Flowers with an Outline of Botany, and a Poetical Introduction*. Boston: Crosby and Nichols, 1863.

Webber, Joan. *Milton and His Epic Tradition*. Seattle: University of Washington Press, 1979.

Welter, Barbara. *Dimity Convictions*. Athens: Ohio University Press, 1976.

West, Cornel. Introduction to *Imperium in Imperio*. New York: Modern Library, 2003.

Wheatley, Phillis. *Complete Writings: Phillis Wheatley*. 4th ed. Edited by Vincent Carretta. New York: Penguin Books, 2001.

Whitaker, Juanita. "'The Wars of Truth': Wisdom and Strength in *Areopagitica*." In *Milton Studies*, vol. 9, edited by James D. Simmonds, 185–201. Pittsburgh: University of Pittsburgh Press, 1976.

Whitney, Charles. "Appropriate This." In *Borrowers and Lenders: The Journal of Shakespeare and Appropriation* 3, no. 2 (Spring/Summer 2008). www.borrowers.uga.edu.

Wilburn, Reginald A. "Malcolm X and African-American Literary Appropriations of *Paradise Lost*." In *Milton in Popular Culture*, edited by Laura Lunger Knoppers and Gregory Colón Semenza, 199–210. New York: Palgrave Macmillan, 2006.

———. "When Milton Was in Vogue: Cross-Dressing Miltonic Presence and William Craft's Slave Narrative." In *Milton Now: 25 Years after "Re-membering Milton,"* edited by Catharine Gray and Erin Murphy. New York: Palgrave Macmillan, forthcoming.

Wilentz, Sean. "Introduction: The Mysteries of David Walker." In Walker, *Appeal to the Colored Citizens*, vii–xxiii.

Williams, Patricia Robinson. "Poets of Freedom: The English Romantics and Early Nineteenth-Century Black Poets." PhD diss., University of Illinois at Urbana-Champaign, 1974.

Williams Jr., Peter. "Abolition of the Slave Trade." In Foner and Branham, *Lift Every Voice*, 66–72.

Wittreich, Joseph. *The Romantics on Milton*. Cleveland: The Press of Case Western Reserve University, 1970.

———. *Visionary Poetics: Milton's Tradition and His Legacy.* San Marino, CA: Henry E. Huntington Library and Art Gallery, 1979.

———. *Why Milton Matters: A New Preface to His Writings.* New York: Palgrave Macmillan, 2006.

Wonham, Henry B., ed. Introduction to *Criticism and the Color Line.* New Brunswick, NJ: Rutgers University Press, 1996.

Wortham, Thomas. "William Cullen Bryant and the Fireside Poets." In *Columbia Literary History of the United States,* edited by Emory Elliott. New York: Columbia University Press, 1988.

Wright, Richard. *12 Million Black Voices.* New York: Thunder's Mouth Press, 1941.

Wynter, Sylvia. "Beyond Miranda's Meanings: Un/Silencing the 'Demonic Ground' of Caliban's Woman." In *Out of the Kumbla: Caribbean Women and Literature,* edited by Carole Boyce Davies and Elaine Savory Fido, 355–72. Trenton, NJ: Africa World Press, 1990.

Young, Reggie. "On Stepping into Footprints Which Feel Like Your Own: Literacy, Empowerment, and the African-American Literary Tradition." In *Literary Influence and African-American Writers: Collected Essays,* edited by Tracy Mishkin, 359–89. New York: Garland, 1996.

Zeitz, Lisa. "Biblical Allusion and Imagery in Frederick Douglass' Narrative." *College Language Association Journal* 25, no. 1 (1981): 56–64.

INDEX

Abdiel, 73–74, 146, 173, 329
abolition, 132, 133, 193
abolitionists, 30, 137, 149. *See also* Othello
Abraham, 204, 215
accommodationalism, 279, 281. *See also* Griggs, Sutton E.
Achilles, 248
Adam, 18, 72, 143, 219, 227, 235; Cooper and, 267, 269, 274; Douglass and, 153, 164, 174; Haynes and, 118, 135
Adam and Eve, 89, 90, 118, 135, 174; banished, 153–54; and Satan, 75, 119, 142
Adams, John, 103
Adams, John Quincy, 103
Addison, Joseph, 42, 141, 152, 235, 273
aesthetic: audio-visionary, 134, 144; freedom, 195–96; Harper's wayward, 192, 194–202, 206–07, 225; language, 265; liberating, 198; literary, 280
Africa, 106–07, 126–29, 133–38
African American Interpretive Communities, 40, 51
African American Methodist Episcopal Church Review, 205
African Congo, 316
Africanism, 2, 9, 123, 250, 304
African Methodist Episcopal Zion Church, 125
Alexander, Leslie, 132
Alpha Kappa Alpha, 231
American jeremiad, 132

American Revolution, 101–02, 303, 304
American Universalism, 117
Amorphel, 221, 225, 226
Andrews, William L. 30–31, 151, 157, 174, 184–85, 187–88
antislavery, 28–29, 45, 135, 137, 149; Douglass and, 158, 166, 173, 178, 185; Equiano and, 94, 111; Pollok and, 182–84; rebellion, 105–06, 148, 157; Walker and, 141; Williams and, 129, 131. *See also* Garrison, William Lloyd; *Liberator, The*
Anti-Slavery Office, Boston, 190
Aptheker, Herbert, 148
archangels. *See* Michael, archangel; Raphael, archangel
Arnold, Matthew, 206, 251, 285
audio-visionary, the, 96, 119, 124, 131, 147. *See also* poetics, audio-visionaries and; poetics, audio-visionary
Auld, Hugh, and Mrs., 151, 168, 186
authors, African American: 3; double voiced heritage of, 267, 307; early, 51–52, 235; and lifting of the race, 235–36. *See also* literature, African American; poetics, African American; writers, black female; writers, black male
autobiography, 170, 171, 249. *See also* Douglass, Frederick, works by; Equiano, Olaudah; slave narratives; Turner, Nat

379

Babbit, Elizabeth, 117
Baker-Fletcher, Karen, 62
ballad form, 53–54, 191–92, 194, 196–200
Ballou, Hosea, 117, 119, 121, 124
Baptists, 125
Bascom, John, 246
beautiful science, 341n6
beautiful sublime, 244–45, 269–70, 272, 275
Beelzebub, 135–36, 221, 291, 317
Belial, 146, 220, 221, 317
Benezet, Anthony, 137
Bergner, Gwen, 160
Bible, the, 118, 125, 190, 251, 283–84; Cain, 246–47; earnest faith in, 204; Egypt, 204, 224; Ephesus, 323; as talking book, 18–19, 50. *See also* Harper, Frances Ellen Watkins, *Moses: Story of the Nile*; Israel; Israelites
Bible, books of: Corinthians, 179–80; Exodus, 194; Genesis, 117, 164; Hebrews, 180, 214; Isaiah, 136; Judges, 155; New Testament, 217; Psalms, 130; Revelation, 96, 100
Bingham, Caleb, *The Columbian Orator* (1797), 151–52, 157–59, 166–67, 169, 175
Bishop College, 281
black authors. *See* slave narratives; writers, black female; writers, black male
black codes. *See* slave codes
black liberation theology, 38–39, 113, 152, 323–34; audio-visionaries and, 99–100, 124–25, 148
blackness, 2, 17–30, 81, 99, 108, 330; representability of, 104, 110–11; trope of, 123
Blair, Hugh, 103–04
Blake, William, *The Marriage of Heaven and Hell*, 32–33, 35

blank verse: Harper and, 191, 195–200; Tennyson and, 258, 260, 265; Wheatley and, 60, 62, 65
Blassingame, John W., 154
blind spots, 188, 294
blindness, 40, 328; Douglass and, 154, 155, 156, 168, 170–72; Milton and, 42, 75–76, 238. *See also* color blindness
Bloom, Harold, 41
Blyden, Edward Wilmot, 276
Bone, Robert, 292
Booker, David, 44
Boyd, Melba Joyce, 190, 192, 200, 212
Boyle, Marjorie O'Rourke, 209–10
Bradley, Stephen R., 137
Briggs, Gabriel A., 284, 290, 302, 318
British Romantics, 29–32, 34, 46, 100; and African Americans, 37, 188, 271; and Milton's Satan, 14, 26, 225
Bronze Muse, the, 189, 193, 202, 226. *See also* Harper, Frances Ellen Watkins
Brown, William Wells, 30, 45, 53, 327
Bruce, Dickson D., Jr., 101, 104
Bryant, William Cullen. *See* Fireside Poets, the
Byron, George Gordon, Lord, 30, 33, 246–48, 297

Callahan, Dwight, 18–19
Campbell, Jane, 290
Carby, Hazel, 253
Carey, Matthew, 94
Channing, William Ellery, 155
Charmian, Pharaoh's daughter, 211–13, 222; dialogue of with Moses, 196, 203, 207–08; naming of, 206–07; and origins of Moses, 215–16
Chaucer, Geoffrey, 8–10

Christian, Barbara, 194–95
Christian heroism: Cooper and, 253–54; Griggs and, 292–93, 296, 310, 312–13, 316, 321–22. *See also* heroism
Christianity, 9, 14–16, 245, 271, 283; black, 36, 124–25, 177; Cooper and, 253–54
civilization, 288–89, 291, 317; African, 130, 135, 137; African American race and, 234–36; American, 244–45, 288; the arts of, 286–87; Cooper and, 252–54, 267–68, 272, 276; Egyptian, 135; European, 244–45; modern, 239, 241; Western, 3, 15, 61, 230, 289; women and, 236, 239
civil rights, 292, 317–18
Coffin, William C., 180
Coleman, Finnie D., 280–81, 292, 297–98, 321
Collings, Justin, 103
color blindness, 25
color line, the, 20; Griggs and, 280, 282, 292, 296; in literary studies, 6–8, 29–30
Columbian Centinel (Boston), 138, 144, 147
Columbian Orator (1797), 151–52, 157–59, 166–67, 169, 175
Columbia University, 231
Common Book of Prayer, The, 141
Cone, James H., 39, 99, 108
Congress of Representative Women at the World's Columbian Exposition, 248
Cooper, Anna Julia: biography of, 230–32; and equality for women, 274–75; and feminism, 253; and Islamic religion, 239, 355–56n23; and music, 229–30. *See also* womanism, Cooper and
Cooper, Anna Julia, works by: "The Answer," 243; *L'attitude de la France à l'égard de l'esclavage pendant la Révolution* (France's Attitude toward Slavery during the Revolution), 232; "The Higher Education of Women," 249–50; "One Phase of American Literature," 268; *Le Pèlerinage de Charlemagne*, 231; "Soprano Obligato," 229; "Tutti ad Libitum," 229, 230; "Vital Element in the Regeneration and Progress of a Race," 43; "What Are We Worth," 267; "Womanhood: A Vital Element in the Regeneration and Progress of a Race," 234–44, 252, 297; "'Woman versus the Indian,'" 267
Cooper, George A. C., 230
Craft, William, 45
Cromwell, Richard, 267–68
Crummell, Alexander, 53, 276, 288
Cruse, Harold, 288
cultural paternalism, 287–88, 318

Darwin, Charles, 283
Davis, Ossie, 33–34
Death, 68–69, 77, 78, 86, 113
Declaration of Independence, the, 140, 283–84
deep space, 201, 219, 226
deep time 201, 219, 226
Delaney, Martin, 286
Deleuze, Gilles, 8, 20
demonic grounds: African American writers and, 12, 35, 37; black audio-visionaries and, 95–96, 98, 116; of contention, 3, 6, 12–13, 31, 40, 195; Cooper and, 234, 249, 264; Douglass and, 53, 150, 159–62, 164–65, 168, 173, 182; Equiano and, 111, 115–16; Griggs and, 55, 314–15; Hamilton and, 136; Harper and, 54, 192, 198, 200–01, 207,

225–26; of hell, 28–29, 58, 73; of interpretation, 14, 47, 57, 80; of Miltonic presence, 51–52; Othello and, 105–06, 108; of racial-sexual displacement, 4; Walker and, 138, 141, 147; Wheatley and, 57–59, 64–69, 75–76, 84–88, 91–93; Williams and, 126, 128. *See also* Griggs, Sutton E., and demonic grounds

Dickens, Charles, 251

diction, 131; Cooper and, 246, 252; Douglass, 163, 176, 179, 186; Griggs and, 289, 299; Hamilton and, 135; Harper and, 203, 205; Haynes and, 120; Miltonic, 45, 71, 145–47; Othello's, 107; Walker and, 139–40; and Williams, 127

didactic impulse, 269, 271, 272

divine trickster, the, 25, 26, 28. *See also* Signifying Monkey, the

Dixon, Thomas, 282

domestic sphere, 213, 241–43, 250, 256, 262

double consciousness, 20, 21

double-voiced: companionship, 307; heritage, 61; rhetoric, 250

Douglass, Frederick, 29, 30, 53, 225, 276; biography of, 150, 159–60; and Colonel Lloyd's plantation, 161–65; and Mr. Covey, 169, 171, 174–76, 186; and William Lloyd Garrison, 44, 152, 184–86

Douglass, Frederick, works by: *Frederick Douglass' Papers*, 152, 190; *The Heroic Slave*, 152; *The Life and Times of Frederick Douglass* (1893), 152, 153; *My Bondage and My Freedom* (1855), 31, 150, 152–53, 157, 184–88; *Narrative of the Life of Frederick Douglass, an American Slave, Written by Himself* (1845), 150–53, 157–85; "Trials and Triumphs of Self-Made Men" (1860), 45, 151–60, 167–68, 170–76, 180–82, 184–88; "Trials and Triumphs of Self-Made Men" (1893), 172

Dubois, W. E. B., 20, 21, 23, 281; *Souls of Black Folk* (1903), 20, 328

Durant, Will, 328

East Village Other, 360n10

Eden: and fallenness, 127–28, 134, 239–40, 266; imagery of, 135, 164, 236, 331; and paradise, 35–37, 117, 212, 235, 244

Eden Cemetery, 227–28

education for blacks, 190, 250, 258–59, 288–89, 298, 300, 307 317; establishments, 45, 125, 176, 190, 230–31; Malcolm X's homemade, 328, 329, 333; and miseducation, 142; and students, 144

education for women, 250, 256, 260–62, 266; college catalogues, 264–65

Elaw, Zilpha, 256

elegies, 66–69, 77

emancipation, 81, 179

Emancipation Proclamation, 191, 193, 200, 226

Emerson, Ralph Waldo, 244–45

Emmett, Robert, 304

Empson, William, 46

enslavement imagery, 330; Equiano and, 111, 112–14; Malcolm X and, 328–29; Wheatley and, 78, 80, 81, 84–85, 87, 88, 93

epic muses. *See* Urania

epic tradition, 60, 205; Cooper and, 248–49, 252; Griggs and, 285; Harper and, 192, 198–99, 201; and prophecy, 97, 100–01

Episcopalians, 125, 230
epyllion, 62–65, 88
equality, 110, 318
Equiano, Olaudah, 53, 111, 115, 148; *The Interesting Narrative of the Life of Olaudah Equiano*, 94–95, 109–15
Esu-Elegbara, 25, 26
Ethiopianism, 129–30
European Africanism, 19
Eve, 18, 90, 135, 143, 235, 238, 269; Cooper and, 262–64, 269, 273–75; corrupted, 75, 89, 121; Douglass and, 153, 164, 173–74; Harper and, 219, 227; Haynes and, 117–21; origins of, 273, 275. *See also* Adam and Eve

Fall, the, 18, 31; Satan's, 63, 112, 223
fallen angels, the, 26, 30, 46–47, 86, 222, 238, 291; Abdiel and, 146; Belial, 221; the *Columbian Orator* and, 152; Haynes and, 121–22; Moloch, 287; vanquished, 73, 152, 225; Wheatley and, 73, 75, 78, 84–86, 88, 91. *See also* Satan
fallenness, 104, 256, 261, 267, 284, 320; poetic, 5, 18, 269; trope of, 1, 127–28, 239–40, 295
Fanon, Frantz, 168
feminism, 259, 273; Cooper and, 242, 273; and Douglass, 188; Harper and, 192, 195, 199. *See also* womanism
Fireside Poets, the, 44, 191
First Baptist Church of East Nashville, 282
Fish, Stanley, 27, 46–47, 254
Flanzbaum, Hilene, 70, 78
flight, 73–76
floral language, 353n52, 353n53
Forbes, Ella, 150, 167
forbidden fruit, 89, 164, 262–63, 265

Foreign Tongues by Council of State, 293–94
Forsyth, Neil, 35–36, 47, 115, 149, 166, 186; and Satan, 10, 25, 26–27, 173, 178
Fortune, Timothy Thomas, 276
Foster, Frances Smith, 7, 78, 191, 216
founding fathers, 283, 303, 313
Freedmen's Bureau, 230
Freeland, William, 176
French Revolution, 103, 232
Froula, Christine, 242–43, 273–74
fugitive, 78, 82

Gadsden flag, the, 303
Garnet, Henry Highland, 44, 53
Garrison, William Lloyd, 44, 184–86; and *The Liberator*, 44, 149–50, 179–80, 190
Gates, Henry Louis, Jr., 5, 17, 23, 25, 66. *See also* signifyin(g)
gender, 232, 237, 245, 253, 256, 258
generation, trope of, 235, 237–39, 244. *See also* regeneration
geographical space, 52; audio-visionaries and, 96, 98; Cooper and, 234, 242; Harper and, 192, 195, 219, 224; Wheatley and, 90
geographies, 4, 29, 136, 219; black, 51–52, 98, 243, 255–56; Cooper's, 232–34, 247, 255; demonic, 201, 220, 232; and geographical arrangements, 8, 219, 226; Wheatley's, 70–75, 79–81, 84, 86, 90–91
geography, 8, 72, 179; cultural, 4, 36, 43, 195; of domination, 37, 80, 90, 93, 234; hellish, 57–58, 93, 128, 141–42; imprisoning, 61, 74, 84, 86; and rupture, 54, 150
Gibson, Donald, 60
Gloster, Hugh, 280

Goldsmith, Oliver, 141
Graham, Maryemma, 190
grammar books, 103–04. *See also* Murray's *English Grammar*
Gray, Erik, 50, 202, 258, 260, 285; and perfect passivity, 54, 254, 255; and Victorian culture, 44, 61, 294, 304–05, 348n15
Great Chain of Being, 52, 58, 83, 93
Grégoire, Henri, 104
Griffin, Dustin, 41, 42
Griggs, Sutton E., 54–55, 281–82; and black nationalism, 279–80, 290–93, 314, 318; and black nationalist novel (1899), 29, 54, 279, 286, 29; and demonic grounds of rebellion, 281–82, 308; and the Imperium, 286–87, 290, 292, 295–98, 306, 311–21; and Milton's hell, 279, 284, 293, 314–15, 322–23; pamphlets by, 282–83, 294; and racial discrimination, 283, 299–302, 308, 321–22; and Tiberius Gracchus Leonard, 300–07
Griggs, Sutton E., works by: "The Contribution of the Anglo-Saxon to the Cause of Human Liberty," 306; "The Kingdom of God Is within Us," 310; *The One Great Question* (1907), 282–83; *Pointing the Way* (1908), 283; "Robert Emmett," 306
Grimké, Charlotte Forten, 42
Guattari, Félix, 8, 20

Hall, Kim, 123
Hamilton, William, 49, 95, 132–37; and gospels of black revolt, 116, 124–25; "Mutual Interest, Mutual Benefit, and Mutual Relief" (1809), 133; "O! Africa," 135–37

Harlem, 331, 232
Harper, Frances Ellen Watkins, 29, 36, 44, 189, 275; and ballad form, 53–54, 191–92, 194, 196–200; biography of, 190, 227–28; and wayward aesthetic, 192, 194–202, 206–07, 226
Harper, Frances Ellen Watkins, works by: "Bury Me in a Free Land," 227; "Factor in Human Progress" (speech), 205; *Forest Leaves*, 190; *Iola Leroy*, 354n65; "Miriam's Song," 197, 199; "The Mission of the Flowers," 42, 193; *Moses: Story of the Nile*, 42–43, 189–228; "Our Greatest Want" (1859), 204; "Shalmanezer, Prince of Cosman," 227; *Sketches of Southern Life* (1886), 227; *Sowing and Reaping* (1876–77), 227; *Trial and Triumph* (1888–89), 227; "Women's Political Future," (1893), 227
Harrison, Ralph, 103–04
Harvey, William, 237–38
Hayes, Diana, 108
Haynes, Lemuel, 95, 116, 124; and Ballou, 121–23; "Universal Salvation" (1805), 117–21
Henderson, Mae G., 85
Henderson, Stephen, 50, 232, 330
Henry, Patrick, 304, 308
Heraud, John Abraham, 44
Herman, Peter C., 22, 47
heroic couplets, 60–61
heroism, 168, 260, 276, 316, 318; Belton and, 297, 319; female, 209–13, 245, 246, 251, 269; inward spiritual, 202–06, 208–10, 213–17, 219, 254; Moses and, 208, 216–20; poetics of, 254, 275, 285, 292–95; quiet, 204, 206, 208, 209, 213, 216–20, 255, 273, 297, 319; spiritual,

208–09, 215, 217, 288. *See also* Christian heroism
Herron, Carolivia, 9, 20–21, 60, 155
Herskovits, Melville J., 26
Higgs, Elton D., 112, 223–24
Hill, Patricia Liggins, 200
Hogan, Patrick, 240
Holmes, Oliver Wendell. *See* Fireside Poets, the
Homer, 62, 92, 248, 342n13
horticultural imagery, 244, 353n52, 353n53
Howard-Pitney, David, 38, 115–16
Howe, Julia Ward, 181
Hubbard, Dolan, 330
Hurston, Zora Neale, 26, 27–28, 134
hyperbole, 139–45, 147, 149

infernal council, 29, 104, 114; Griggs and, 55, 287, 315–16; Harper and, 220–21, 354n65. *See also* Griggs, Sutton E., and the Imperium; Pandaemonium
infernal eloquence, 111, 129, 137, 140, 185; Griggs and, 315, 317; Satan and, 115, 139, 152, 178; trope of, 28–29, 32
intellectuals, black, 288, 296, 354n65
intertextuality, 8, 24–25, 48–50, 86, 91, 94
Islamic religion, 239, 355–56n23
Israel: Harper and, 196, 210, 211, 218, 227; Malcolm X and, 331
Israelites, 63–64; Harper and, 198, 200, 205, 208, 222–23, 225–26

Jackson, Blyden D., 59, 109, 140, 164; and Haynes, 117, 122
Jefferson, Thomas, 103, 283–84, 313–14; *Notes on the State of Virginia*, 57, 141; and Wheatley, 4–5, 57, 93
Jenkins, Melissa Shields, 157–58

jeremiad: and black tradition, 36–38, 115–16, 124–25, 129–32; Puritan, 49
Joan of Arc, 251
John Street Methodist Episcopal Zion Church, 125
Jordan, Richard Burton, 204, 206

Kendrick, Robert, 63
Kincaid, Jamaica, 360n10
King, Robert, 109
Knadler, Stephen, 321
Knowles, Julie Nall, 182
Koran, the, 239
Kossuth, Louis, 304
Kurth, Burton O., 204

language: and color, 123; divine, 247; the English, 8; fallen, 266; infernal and supernal, 314; performative, 247; scriptural, 120. *See also* diction
Lee, Jarena, 256
Lemons, Gary L., 234
Levander, Caroline, 286
Lewalski, Barbara, 63, 156, 201, 209
Lewis, C. S., *A Preface to "Paradise Lost"* (1942), 46
Liberator, The, 44, 149–50, 179–80, 190. *See also* Garrison, William Lloyd
liberty, 31–32, 39, 52, 287; audio-visionaries and, 106, 110, 120, 129–32, 137, 147–48; Cooper and, 247, 251, 268, 277; Douglass and, 169, 185–87; Griggs and, 283–84, 291, 322; Griggs's Belton and, 298, 301, 304–08, 313, 317–19; Harper and, 192–95, 197, 200, 217, 226; Jefferson and, 313–14; Milton and, 30–32, 39, 43, 45, 325; republican, 101–02, 283–84, 291; Tennyson and, 259–60;

themes of, 16, 27, 43; Wheatley and, 59, 71, 81; women's 261, 265
Lincoln, Abraham, 54, 189, 191, 200
literacy, 252, 288; for blacks, 5, 143, 169, 176; power of, 16, 17. *See also* education for blacks; education for women
literature, African American: 232, 234, 279, 322; crusaders in, 291–92; and the literary color line, 8–9, 21, 50, 59–60, 234, 322–23; studies of, 2–4, 12, 14; tradition of, 267–69, 272, 276, 281
Logan, Shirley Wilson, 261
Longfellow, Henry Wadsworth. *See* Fireside Poets, the
Lowell, James Russell, 44, 191, 270
Lowth, Robert, 103–04
Lugones, Maria, 233–34
Luther, Martin, 304
lynching, 227, 280, 292, 312

Macaulay, Thomas Babington, 244–45
Machacek, Gregory, 11–15, 24, 103, 172, 266; and Douglass, 150, 157–58, 170; and Williams, 130, 131
Madison, James, 103
Malcolm X: *The Autobiography of Malcolm X*, 55, 329; "The Harlem 'Hate-Gang' Scare" (1964), 329; "Harlemite," 331; "Saved," 328, 329, 330
Mammon, 220, 221, 317
manhood, 159, 177. *See also* Douglass, Frederick, works by, "Trials and Triumphs of Self-Made Men"
Maréchal, Silvain, 251, 257, 261–66; *Shall Woman Learn the Alphabet* (1801), 250, 255–56, 257
Marrant, John, 49

martyrdom, 147, 176–77, 292, 295, 308–09, 319, 321, 323
Marvell, Andrew, 40–41
mascon, 50, 73, 220, 330; black audio-visionaries and, 115, 121–22, 124
maternal influence, 211, 216–17
May, Vivian, 230, 233–34, 242, 253
McBride, Dwight, 79
McConnell, Frank D., 33
McDowell, Deborah, 161, 171
McKittrick, Katherine, 4, 5, 35, 51, 98, 233
McKivigan, John R., 154
Meade, Randolph, 281–83, 307, 316
mental darkness, 169–71
messianism, 138, 181, 187
Methodists, 125
Michael, Archangel, 236, 308–09
Middle Passage, 61, 109, 136
Mieder, Wolfgang, 153, 156
militancy: demonic, 55; Griggs and, 55, 290, 292–95, 298, 315, 320; and perfect passivity, 285, 310–11. *See also* rebellion
Mills, Charles, 21–22
Milton, works by: *An Apology for Smectymnuus*, 313; *Areopagitica*, 254, 329; *Comus*, 45, 311; *Doctrine and Discipline of Divorce*, 329; *Of Reformation* and *Of Prelatical Episcopacy*, 313; *The Reason of Church-Government*, 15, 313, 329; "The Verse," 120, 198, 199. See also *Paradise Lost*; *Paradise Regained*; *Samson Agonistes*
ministry, 1, 87, 180, 190; social and political, 310, 333; and vocation, 98, 243
Mishkin, Tracy, 235
Mitchell, Henry H., 18
modernism, 232
Moloch, 220, 287–88, 315–17, 333
Monroe, James, 103

Montgomery, James, 155
Montgomery, Robert, 44
Montserrat, island of, 111–12
Moore, Leslie E., 41–42, 235, 273
Morrison, Toni: Africanisms, 304; *A Mercy*, 2; *Playing in the Dark*, 123; "Speakable Things Unspoken," 19
Moses. *See* Harper, Frances Ellen Watkins, *Moses: A Story of the Nile*
Moses, Wilson Jeremiah, 37, 130, 138, 177, 181; and Griggs, 288, 291
motherhood, 211–12, 248, 289; enlightened, 354n57; Griggs and, 297, 299–301; Jochabed, mother of Moses, 209, 212, 213; Mary, mother of Jesus, 209. *See also* Charmian
M Street High School (Washington, D.C.), 231
Muhammad, Elijah, 328–39. *See also* Islamic religion
Murray, Anna, 152
Murray's *English Grammar*, 139–42, 144, 147
muses, 202–03
music, 234, 266–67
Muslim teachings, 328

naming, 23, 25, 201, 206–07, 243; Griggs, 306–07; intertextual, 105, 207; and Milton, 91–92, 164, 304
Narcissus, 268, 273, 275
nationalism, black, 279–80, 290–93, 314, 318
Navajo tradition, 234
Nermal, Antoinette, 312
New England Unitarians and Transcendentalists, 43
Newlyn, Lucy, 30, 31–32, 34–35, 246–47
New Negro, the, 321

New York African Church, 125–27
New York African Free School, 125
New York Society for Mutual Relief, 132–33
New York Universalist Church, 133–34
Norfolk Prison Colony, 333
Norse legends, 245
North Star, The, 152
nothingness, 160, 161
Nyquist, Mary, 11, 219

Oberlin College, 230–31
Ockham School, 45
O'Meally, Robert G., 158
O'Neale, Sondra, 81
Ophite beliefs, 35–36
oratory, 96, 99–100, 116, 124–28, 152; Douglass and, 180–81, 184–85, 188; Griggs, 302, 306, 316–17; Harper and, 190–91. *See also* Othello
Othello [pseud.], 94, 104–08; "Essay on Negro Slavery," 105, 108
Other, the, 9, 20–21, 91, 167, 203, 221
otherness, 3, 15, 324; Charmian and, 207, 211; signs of, 19, 207
outsider status, 327–28, 330, 360n10; blacks and, 105
Ovid, 62, 248, 251

Page, Thomas Nelson, 282
pamphleteers, 95
pamphlets, 96, 102, 117; Griggs and, 282–83, 293; by Milton, 15, 31; by Walker, 138–39, 141, 144, 147
Pandaemonium, 55, 144, 147, 241, 328; black, 281; Douglass and, 163; and Griggs's Imperium, 286–87, 290, 294, 313, 316; Walker and, 138–39. *See also* Infernal council
paradise. *See* Eden

Paradise Lost, 5, 10, 44, 137, 170, 260; African Americans and, 49, 101; assessments of, 43–49, 53–54, 254, 360n10; audio-visionaries and, 97–98, 101; and the beautiful, 235; as Christian text, 18–19, 46–47; in the *Columbian Orator*, 151–52; Cooper and, 43, 240–42, 246–47, 258, 263–65, 267, 272; C. S. Lewis's preface to, 46; Douglass and, 151–54, 156–59, 162, 165–66, 173–76, 178, 182–84, 188; as epic, 41–42; Equiano and, 95, 109, 111–14; Forsyth and, 10, 25–28, 35–36, 47, 115; in grammar books and newspapers, 103–04; Griggs and, 55; Hamilton, 133, 135–37; Harper and, 54, 191, 354n65; Harper's *Moses* and, 201, 204, 219–25, 227; Haynes and, 117–21; Hurston and, 134; Othello and, 104–07; satanic receptions of, 25–27, 29–32; and trope of generation, 237–38; "The Verse," 120, 198; Walker and, 53, 139, 141–42, 144, 148–49, 347n104; Wheatley and, 69–70, 72–76, 78, 80, 86, 89; Wheatley's "Goliath" and, 57–58, 61–66; Williams and, 127–29, 131–32, 137. *See also* Adam and Eve; Fallen angels; Pandaemonium; Satan

Paradise Regained, 54, 62–63, 210, 213, 217, 312; Harper and, 43, 54, 193–94, 208–10, 227; Harper's *Moses* and, 191, 201–04, 206, 219

Parkhurst Collection, the, 333

passivity, 202, 318; Griggs and perfect, 55, 287, 310–11, 316, 319–20, 322; perfect, 203, 257, 285, 290

patriarchy, 239, 241–42, 248, 252, 259; Cooper and, 263–64, 273–76, 354; and privilege, 234, 250

peculiar institution, the, 144, 165, 193. *See also* antislavery; slavery

Pennsylvania Journal, 303

Petrarch, 251

Pharaoh, 208, 212–14, 218, 220–23

Philadelphia, 109

Phillips, William, 44

Pitt, William, 152

Plutarch, 141, 306, 307

poetics, 10–11, 34, 83, 105, 194, 238; African Americans and, 31, 268–70, 275; audio-visionaries and, 96, 100, 115–16, 138; audio-visionary, 108, 119, 121–22, 125, 128, 148; Christian, 14–16, 285, 293–95; Cooper and, 233, 237–38, 249, 254–55, 262–63; Douglass and, 150, 164; Equiano and, 111, 115, 148; of Ethiopianism, 129–30; of fallenness, 31, 305; fugitive, 58, 66, 68, 80, 84, 88, 91; Griggs and, 285, 289, 322; Harper and, 54, 200–01; Haynes and, 121–22; of landscape, 233, 255–56; and liberation, 20, 67–68, 275–76; messianic, 35–40, 242; Othello and, 105, 108; subversive, 54, 201, 254, 258, 273; visionary, 96, 100, 116, 118–21, 127–28, 131; Walker and, 138, 148; Wheatley's fugitive, 57–58, 66–68, 80, 83–84, 88, 91; Williams and, 125, 129–30

Pollok, Robert, 182–84

Pope, Alexander, 59–60

preaching, 108, 118, 125, 158, 214, 328

predestinarianism, 117–18

Presbyterians, 125

Quakers, 109

quietude, 255, 273. *See also* heroism, quiet

Raboteau, Albert J., 125, 330
race: discrimination based on, 122–23, 148, 267, 283, 302, 308, 321–22; loyalty to, 314–15
Raphael, Archangel, 72, 128, 130–31, 320
readership, black, 54–55, 327
rebellion, 233, 249, 251, 253, 260; demonic, 35–36; Griggs and, 288, 314–16; and patriotism, 303–04; Wheatley and, 85
Reconstruction, 194, 307
Redding, J. Saunders, 59, 149
Red Sea, the, 198, 224–25
Reed, Ishmael, 360n10
regeneration, 131, 269; Cooper and, 43, 54, 234–40, 244, 246, 276
revolution, 34, 48; and black revolt, 96, 114, 125, 152, 180–81; blacks and, 168, 192, 291, 329; Cooper and, 253, 269; Griggs and, 286, 288, 291, 308, 322–23; Malcolm and, 329, 331. *See also* American Revolution; French Revolution
revolutionary: attitudes, 43; authors, 253, 304; conditions, 8; dissidence, 167; gospel, 16; heroism, 26; Milton's approach, 202; patriots, 53; Satan's creed, 114; spirit, 43, 99
Rhadma, 221, 225, 226
rhetoric, 144, 147, 158, 180, 237; art of, 304; audio-visionary, 139; Cooper and, 256, 276; Douglass and, 165–67, 172, 176, 186–88; fallen, 141; Griggs and, 307; Haynes and, 119–20
Richmond Theological Seminary, 282
Riffaterre, Michael, 24
Roe, E. P., 270
romantics, 46, 188, 246; and early African Americans, 31, 37; and Milton, 29, 31–34. *See also* British Romantics
Rose, Deacon David, 116

Rose, Gillian, 195
Rose, Mary Beth, 210
Ross, Marlon B., 30
Rudoff, Shaindy, 164
Ruffin, Valerie L., 216
Rutkowski, Alice, 194

Sabbath school, 176
Samson Agonistes, 54, 62, 155; Douglass and, 155, 170–73; Griggs and, 311–12; Harper and, 43, 193, 203, 206
Sartre, Jean-Paul, 150, 177
Satan, 10–11, 25–39, 49, 53, 291, 295; Cooper and, 241, 243, 247, 262–65; Douglass and, 53, 158, 163, 165–66, 173–78, 182–84, 186–87; Equiano and, 109–15; founding fathers and, 103–04; Griggs and, 55, 291–92, 303, 322; Griggs's Belton and, 303, 308–10, 312, 317, 319–20; Hamilton and, 133, 135–36; Harper and, 201, 204–06, 220–24, 227; Haynes and, 117–22, 124; infernal eloquence of, 29, 115, 139, 152, 178; literary critics and, 46–48; Malcolm X and, 327–34; Othello and, 104–05, 107–08, 115; Romantics and, 14, 25–26, 29–31, 34, 37, 46; and satanic politics, 322–23; and satanic profiling, 220–21, 223; Victorian audiences and, 45; Walker and, 138–48; Wheatley and, 61, 63–69, 72–76, 79–80, 86, 89; Williams and, 126–29. *See also* satanic poetry
satanic poetry: and African Americans, 10, 28, 47, 334; audio-visionaries and, 96, 105, 128–29; Cooper and, 234, 241, 247, 264–67, 273; Griggs and, 282, 284–85, 323; Wheatley and, 35, 79, 86, 88
Savage, J. B., 16

Scales-Trent, Judy, 234
Schulman, Lydia Dittler, 43, 101
Scripture, 130, 155. *See also* Bible, the
Seeyle, John, 174
self-made man, the, 151–60, 167–68, 170–76, 180–82, 184–88. *See also* Douglass, Frederick
Sensabaugh, George, 61, 103–04
separatism, 6, 318–19
serpent, 37, 105, 303; Charmian and, 207, 212, 222; Christ as, 35, 179; Harper and, 117–18; infernal, 74, 145; Satan as, 86, 178, 241
Shakespeare, William, 8, 105, 124, 154, 206–07, 268, 286
Shawcross, John, 3, 104, 156, 200, 313
Shelley, Percy Bysshe, 33–35, 166
Sheridan, Richard Brinsley, 157, 169
Shields, John C., 4–5; and Wheatley, 65, 66, 67–68, 78
signifyin(g), 22–25, 51, 78, 108; Cooper and, 232, 245, 248, 251, 261–62; Douglass and, 179, 183; Equiano and, 114; as force of thunder, 223–24; Griggs and, 304, 320; Haynes and, 118; Walker and, 140
Signifying Monkey, 25, 26, 27–28, 37
skinwalking, 234
slavery, 48, 116, 151–52, 184; Douglass and, 151, 159, 162–65, 176, 181–83, 187; Equiano and, 112–13; Hamilton and, 135–37; Othello and, 105, 108; and slaveholders, 159, 165, 178, 180; and the slave trade, 124–25, 132, 133–37, 178, 183; Walker and, 142, 148; Wheatley and, 78–79; Williams and, 128–29. *See also* abolitionism; abolitionists; antislavery; peculiar institution, the

slaves: codes of, 123, 151, 176; culture of, 122–23; narratives, 17, 45, 96, 345n66. *See also* Craft, William; Douglass, Frederick: works by; Equiano, Olaudah, *The Interesting Narrative of the Life of Olaudah Equiano*; Turner, Nat, *The Confessions of Nat Turner*
Smith, Ian, 123–24
Smith, Valerie, 160–61
Smitherman, Geneva, 23
snakes, 50, 120, 303, 305, 332. *See also* serpent
Socrates, 152, 241, 251
Son, the, 74, 115; Douglass on, 158, 166, 173–75; perfect passivity of, 203–04, 311; quiet heroism of, 203–04, 206, 208–11, 217; and Satan, 10, 27, 173, 201, 206, 329; war with infernal crew, 73–75, 152, 201
Sorbonne, the, 231
speaking in tongues, 84–86, 88, 91, 111
spurring, 24–25, 34, 50, 73; Douglass and, 172; Equiano and, 110, 112; Wheatley and, 61, 63, 73, 78, 88–89; Williams and, 128, 130
St. Augustine's Normal School and Collegiate Institute, 230, 231
St. Hilaire, Danielle A., 18, 235, 247, 295; on Satan, 28, 32, 265; on satanic poetics, 10–11, 47–48
Steadman, John M., 254
Stein, Edward, 220, 284
Still, William, 190
Stowe, Harriet Beecher, 155, 272, 308; strength of, 257–58. *See also* heroism, female
Stuckey, Sterling, 141
subversion, 35, 79, 86, 88, 273; Cooper and, 233–34, 258
Sundquist, Eric J., 185

Tacitus, 245
talking book, 39, 50, 101, 129, 251, 293; black audio-visionaries and, 129–30, 135–39, 147; of black liberation theology, 113, 115; sacred yet secular, 16, 52, 117–18, 325; trope of, 17–30
Tanner, John S., 103
tautologies, 166–67, 179
Taylor, Edward, 181
Tennyson, Alfred Lord, 40–41, 44, 206, 258–61, 286
Thompson, E. N. S., 148
Tillyard, E. M. W., 293
True Womanhood, discourse of, 250, 253, 256, 267
Turkish Muslims, 240
Turner, Nat, *The Confessions of Nat Turner*, 174, 329, 350n62

Underground Railroad, the, 190, 191
Union Seminary, 190
U.S. Constitution, 140, 184
Universal Salvation, 121
Urania, 70–71, 73, 77

Van Anglen, K. P., 43, 102
Varick, James, 132
Verdelle, A. J., 280, 298
Victorian culture, 44–45, 61, 211, 348n15
Victorian texts, 206, 251, 285, 294, 304–05
Virgil, 62, 63, 342n13
Vocey, Edward, 174–75
voice, 264–65, 267

Walker, Alice, 194
Walker, David, 1, 44, 95, 284, 327; *Appeal in Four Articles*, 53, 138–49, 192, 347n104
Wall, Cheryl A., 232, 267, 305
Washington, Booker T., 282
Washington, Mary Helen, 66, 189, 249

Waterman, Catherine H., *Flora's Lexicon* (1863), 211
Watkins, William, 190
wayward aesthetic: Cooper and, 29, 265; Harper and, 189, 191–92, 194–95, 197–203, 206–07, 224–26
Webster, Noah, 103–04
Welter, Barbara, 242, 250
West, Cornel, 291
Wheatley, Phillis, 36, 89, 92, 110, 198; biography, 59; images of flight in, 58, 66–69, 76–82, 88, 90–91; ministry of consolation, 66, 68, 71–75, 77, 87; and white attesters, 123
Wheatley, Phillis, works by: elegies, 29, 52, 58, 61, 66–71, 76–92; "Goliath of Gath," 62–66, 68, 88, 342n17; "Niobe in Distress," 62, 342n17; "On being brought from Africa to America," 83; "On the Death of the Rev. Dr. Sewell," 68, 80–81; "On the Death of the Rev. Mr. George Whitefield," 68, 78–85, 86; "On the Death of a Young Gentleman," 68, 85–88; "On the Death of a Young Lady of Five Years of Age," 68, 85; "Philis's [sic] Reply to the Answer in our last by the Gentleman in the Navy," 41, 91–93; *Poems on Various Subjects, Religious and Moral*, 4–5, 53, 57; "Thoughts on the Works of Providence," 68; "To a Clergyman on the Death of His Lady," 70–75, 76–77; "To a Lady on the Death of Her Husband," 68, 88–90; "To a Lady on the Death of Three Relations," 69–70; "To Maecenas," 61–62; "To the University of Cambridge," 60–61, 62, 266

Whitaker, Juanita, 254
White, William A., 159
Whitman, Albery A., 275–76
Whittier, John Greenleaf, 270. *See also* Fireside Poets, the
Wilberforce, William, 137
wilderness, 201–02, 217, 331
Williams, Peter, Sr., 125, 132
Williams, Reverend Peter, Jr., 49, 95, 116, 124–25; "Abolition of the Slave Trade," 126–32, 135
William Watkins Academy for Negro Youth, 190
Wittreich, Joseph, 3, 118–19, 173, 249; and blank verse, 60, 258; and Milton, 30, 52, 100–01, 105, 170, 234; and "visionary poetics," 96, 100, 127
womanhood: black, 4, 236–37, 242, 246, 248, 255, 276, 352n22; self-invented, 189, 197–98, 200, 203, 249. *See also* education, for women; womanism; women
womanism, 245; Cooper and, 229–30, 233–36, 241–43, 265–68, 273–77; and Cooper's dissent, 248–54, 258–60, 262, 264; and wayward aesthetic, 194–95. *See also* womanhood; women

womb envy, 237
women, 85, 161, 217, 238, 245; Cooper and equality for, 274–75; heroic, 211–12, 251; and the matrimonial market, 263–64. *See also* womanhood; womanism; writers, black female
Wonham, Henry B., 7, 9
Woodson, Carter G., 281, 328
Wordsworth, William, 33, 40–41, 246, 247–48, 297. *See also* British Romantics
World's Congress of Representative Women, the, 227
worrying the line, 232–34, 241, 244–47, 249–52, 255, 257, 260, 263–68
Wortham, Thomas, 191
Wright, Richard, 13
writers: black female, 66–67, 85, 188–89, 232–34, 249; black male, 275–76

Yerrinton, Y. B., and Sons, 190
Yoruba mythology, 25

Zeitz, Lisa, 176–77

www.ingramcontent.com/pod-product-compliance
Lightning Source LLC
Chambersburg PA
CBHW021929290426
44108CB00012B/776